Capital, Interest, and Rent

Studies in Economic Theory

Laurence S. Moss, Editor

Capital, Interest, and Rent

Essays in the Theory of Distribution

By Frank A. Fetter

Edited with an Introduction by

Murray N. Rothbard

SHEED ANDREWS AND McMEEL, INC.
Subsidiary of Universal Press Syndicate
Kansas City

Library of Congress Cataloging in Publication Data

Fetter, Frank Albert, 1863-1949.
  Capital, interest, and rent.

  (Studies in economic theory)
  "Bibliography of Frank Albert Fetter": p.
  Includes bibliographical references and index.
  1. Distribution (Economic theory)—Addresses, essays, lectures. I. Title. II. Series.
HB771.F47 1976 330.1 76-25587
ISBN 0-8362-0684-3
ISBN 0-8362-0685-1 pbk.

PREFACE

I was first apprised of Frank A. Fetter's contributions to the theory of distribution by the references in Ludwig von Mises's *Human Action* (1st ed., New Haven: Yale University Press, 1949; 3d ed., Chicago: Henry Regnery, 1966). Then, while reading Fetter's *oeuvre* in the course of writing my *Man, Economy, and State* (2 vols., Princeton, N.J.: D. Van Nostrand, 1962, reprint ed., Los Angeles: Nash Publishing Co., 1970), I was struck by the brilliance and consistency of his integrated theory of distribution and by the neglect of Fetter in current histories of economic thought, even by those that are Austrian oriented. For Fetter's systematic theory, while challenging and original (particularly his theories of interest and rent), was emphatically in the Austrian school tradition.

The present volume includes all of the essays in which Fetter developed and presented his theory of distribution; the only important writings excluded are his two treatises: *The Principles of Economics* (New York: The Century Co., 1910) and *Economic Principles* (New York: The Century Co., 1915).

I am indebted to Professor Emeritus Joseph Dorfman of Columbia University for examining my introduction and the collection of essays with his usual thoroughness and for making many valuable suggestions. The editor of this series, Professor Laurence S. Moss of the University of Virginia, also made many helpful suggestions. Neither is responsible for any errors that may remain.

I would like to thank the American Accounting Association, publishers of the *Accounting Review;* the editors of the *Quarterly Journal of Economics;* the Academy of Political Science, publishers of the *Political Science Quarterly;* the University of Chicago Press, publishers of the *Journal of Political Economy;* and Macmillan Publishing Company for permission to reprint the articles in this volume.

Murray N. Rothbard
New York, N.Y.
March, 1976

CONTENTS

Introduction

1.

Frank Albert Fetter (1863-1949) was the leader in the United States of the early Austrian school of economics. Born in rural Indiana, Fetter was graduated from the University of Indiana in 1891. After earning a master's degree at Cornell University, Fetter pursued his studies abroad and received a doctorate in economics in 1894 from the University of Halle in Germany. Fetter then taught successively at Cornell, Indiana, and Stanford universities. He returned to Cornell as professor of political economy and finance (1901-1911) and terminated his academic career at Princeton University (1911-31), where he also served as chairman of the department of economics.

Fetter is largely remembered for his views on business "monopoly" (see his *Masquerade of Monopoly* [New York: Harcourt, Brace and Co., 1931]). But long before he published his work on monopoly in the 1930s, he developed a unified and consistent theory of distribution that explained the relationship among capital, interest, and rent. While Fetter's theoretical work, like much of capital and interest theory in recent decades, has been generally neglected, much of it is still valuable and instructive today. In my opinion, microeconomic analysis has a considerable way to go to catch up to the insight that we find in Fetter's writings in the first decade and a half of this century.

Apart from his two lucidly written treatises *(The Principles of Economics* [New York: The Century Co., 1904]; and *Economic Principles* [New York: The Century Co., 1915]), Fetter's major contributions to distribution theory appeared in the series of journal articles and shorter papers that I have collected to form this volume. It was difficult for me to classify Fetter's work into the categories of "capital," "rent," and "interest," because his was

1

an unusually systematic and integrated theory of distribution, all areas of analysis being interrelated.

Fetter's point of departure was the Austrian insights that (1) prices of consumer goods are determined by their relative marginal utility to consumers; and (2) that factor prices are determined by their marginal productivity in producing these consumer goods. In other words, the market system imputes consumer goods prices (determined by marginal utility) to the factors of production in accordance with their marginal productivities.

While the early Austrian and neoclassical schools of economics adopted these insights to explain prices of consumer goods and wages of labor, they still left a great many lacunae in the theories of capital, interest, and rent. Rent theory was in a particularly inchoate state, with rent being defined either in the old-fashioned sense of income per year accruing to land, or in the wider neo-Ricardian sense of differential income between more and less productive factors. In the latter case, rent theory was an appendage to distribution theory. If one worker earns $10 an hour and another, in the same occupation, earns $6, and we say that the first man's income contains a "differential rent" of $4, rent becomes a mere gloss upon income determined by principles completely different from those used to determine the rent itself.

Frank Fetter's imaginative contribution to rent theory was to seize upon the businessman's commonsense definition of rent as the price per unit service of any factor, that is, as the price of renting out that factor per unit time. But if rent is simply the payment for renting out, every unit of a factor of production earns a rent, and there can be no "no-rent" margin. Whatever any piece of land earns per year or per month is rent; whatever a capital good earns per unit time is *also* a rent. Indeed, while Fetter did not develop his thesis so far as to consider the wage of labor per hour or per month as a "rent," it is, as becomes clear if we consider the economics of slavery. Under slavery, slaves are either sold as a whole, as "capital," or are rented out to other masters. In short, slave labor has a unit, or rental, price as well as a capital value. Rent then becomes synonymous with the unit price of *any* factor; accordingly, a factor's rent is, or rather tends to be, its marginal productivity. For Fetter the marginal productivity theory of distribution becomes the marginal productivity theory of rent determination for every factor of production. In this way, Fetter generalized the narrow classical analysis of land rent into a broader theory of factor pricing.

But if every factor earns a rent in accordance with its marginal product, where is the interest return to capital? Where does interest fit in? Here Fetter made his second vital and still unappreciated contribution to the theory of distribution. He saw that the Austrian Eugen von Böhm-Bawerk, in the second volume of his notable *Capital and Interest*, inconsistently returned to the productivity theory of interest after he had demolished that theory in the first volume. After coming to the brink of replacing the productivity theory by a time-preference theory of interest, Böhm-Bawerk withdrew from that path and tried to combine the two explanations—an eclecticism that capital and interest theory (in its "real" form) has followed ever since.

Fetter approached the problem this way: If every factor earns a rent, and if therefore every capital good earns a rent, what is the source of the *extra* return for interest (or "long-run normal profit," as it is sometimes called)? In short, if a machine is expected to earn an income, a rent, of $10,000 a year for the next ten years, why does not the market bid up the selling price of the machine to $100,000? Why is the current market price considerably less than $100,000, so that in fact a firm that invests in the machine earns an interest return over the ten-year period? The various proponents of productivity theory answer that the machine is "productive" and therefore should be expected to earn a return for its owner. But Fetter replied that this is really beside the point. The undoubted productivity of the machine is precisely the reason it will earn its $10,000 annual rent; however, there is still no answer to the question why the market price of the machine at present is not bid high enough to equal the sum of expected future rents. Why is there a net return to the investor?

Fetter demonstrated that the explanation can only be found

by separating the concept of marginal productivity from that of interest. Marginal productivity explains the height of a factor's rental price, but another principle is needed to explain why and on what basis these rents are *discounted* to get the present capitalized value of the factor: whether that factor be land, or a capital good, or the price of a slave. That principle is "time preference": the social rate at which people prefer present goods to future goods in the vast interconnected time market (present/future goods market) that pervades the entire economy.

Each individual has a personal time-preference schedule, a schedule relating his choice of present and future goods to his stock of available present goods. As his stock of present goods increases, the marginal value of future goods rises, and his rate of time preference tends to fall. These individual schedules interact on the time market to set, at any given time, a social rate of time preference. This rate, in turn, constitutes the interest rate on the market, and it is this interest rate that is used to convert (or "discount") all future values into present values, whether the future good happens to be a bond (a claim to future money) or more specifically the expected future rentals from land or capital.

Thus, Fetter was the first economist to explain interest rates solely by time preference. Every factor of production earns its rent in accordance with its marginal product, and every *future* rental return is discounted, or "capitalized," to get its present value in accordance with the overall social rate of time preference. This means that a firm that buys a machine will only pay the *present* value of expected future rental incomes, discounted by the social rate of time preference; and that when a capitalist hires a worker or rents land, he will pay now, not the factor's full marginal product, but the expected future marginal product discounted by the social rate of time preference.

A glance at any prominent current textbook will show how far economics still is from incorporating Fetter's insights. The textbook discussion typically begins with an exposition of the marginal productivity theory applied to wage determination. Then, as the author shifts to a discussion of capital, "interest" suddenly replaces "factor price" on the y-axis of the graph, and the conclusion is swiftly reached that the marginal productivity theory explains the interest rate in the same way that it explains the wage rate. Yet the correct analog on the y-axis is not the interest rate but the rental price, or income, of capital goods. The interest rate only enters the picture when the market price of the capital good as a whole is formed out of its expected annual future incomes. As Fetter pointed out, interest is not, like rent or wages, an annual or monthly income, an income per unit time earned by a factor of production. Interest, on the contrary, is a rate, or ratio, between present and future, between future earnings and present price or payment.

Fetter's theory makes it impossible to say that capital "earns," or generates an interest return. On the contrary, the very concept of capital value implies a *preceding* process of *capitalization*, a summing up of expected future rental incomes from a good, discounted by a rate of interest. Rent, or productivity, and interest, or time preference, are logically prerequisite to the determination of capital value.

2.

Frank A. Fetter's earliest article in this collection, a review of Frank W. Taussig's *Wages and Capital: An Examination of the Wages Fund Doctrine* (New York: D. Appleton, 1896), was written in 1897 and sets the pace for the articles in the first part of this book. Here Fetter criticized Taussig's attempt to revive the classical notion of the "wage fund." Rather than attempting to explain aggregate wage payments, Fetter recommended explaining individual wage rates.

Fetter's first full-length article on capital was his "Recent Discussion of the Capital Concept" (1900). In it he compared the theories of capital offered by Böhm-Bawerk, John Bates Clark, and Irving Fisher. Fetter did less than full justice to Böhm-Bawerk's subtle insistence on the defects of the idea of capital as merely a fund, especially in comparing or measuring concrete capital goods that differ from each other. Above all, Fetter, in properly concentrating on a fund of capital value as an attribute of all durable productive goods, never fully realized the importance between land (the original producer's good) and capital goods (created or produced producer's goods). In fact, Fetter's idea of capital as a fund of value and the Austrian view of capital as concrete capital goods are not inconsistent; they play roles in different areas of capital theory.

Of special interest is Fetter's charge that Böhm-Bawerk's intention was to establish a labor theory of *property* in capital goods. Furthermore, when Fetter declared that Böhm-Bawerk was inconsistent in classifying man-made improvements permanently incorporated into the land as "land" itself, he apparently did not realize that for Austrian economists the crucial criterion for classifying a good as "land" is not its original nature-given state but its *permanence* as a resource (or, more precisely, its nonreproducibility). Goods that are permanent, or nonreproducible, earn a net rent, whereas capital goods, which have to be produced and maintained, only earn a gross rent, absorbed by costs of production and maintenance. Here is a vital distinction between land and capital goods that Fetter completely misunderstood (see my *Man, Economy, and State*, 2 vols. [New York: D. Van Nostrand, 1962], 2:502-4).

Fetter, however, took his stand squarely with Böhm-Bawerk and against Clark when he denied that capital is a permanent fund and that production ever becomes "synchronous," thereby eliminating the time dimension between input and output. This same controversy was to reappear dramatically in the 1930s in publications of Frank H. Knight (advancing the Clark position) and those of Friedrich A. Hayek and Fritz Machlup (representing the Austrian view).

On the other hand, Fetter praised Irving Fisher's theory of capital (*The Rate of Interest: Its Nature, Determination, and Relation to Economic Phenomena* [New York: Macmillan Co., 1907]) in places where it deviated from the Austrian view and criticized it where it conformed to the Austrian position. Thus, Fisher's distinction between capital and income (based on the differences between stock and flow measurements) is commended because it eliminates the need for distinguishing between land and capital goods. On the other hand, Fetter objected to Fisher's highly sensible insistence that the concept of concrete physical capital goods is logically prerequisite to the concept of abstract capital as a fund of value. Furthermore, Fetter objected to the Austrian view, also in Fisher, that capital goods are way stations on the path to producing more consumer goods, and that they are therefore "used up" in production. Fetter cited machines and land ("natural agents") as goods that do not advance toward the status of consumer goods. But machines advance toward consumer goods precisely by being *impermanent,* that is, by being used up in the march of production toward the goal of consumption; and the fact that land is not used up in this way is precisely the reason for distinguishing it from capital goods.

In his 1902 review of Böhm Bawerk's *Einige strittige Fragen der Capitalstheorie* Fetter quite properly pointed to the major textual contradiction in Böhm-Bawerk's theory of interest: Böhm-Bawerk's initial finding that interest stems from time preference for present over future goods is contradicted by his later claim that the greater productivity of roundabout production processes is what accounts for interest. However, when criticizing Böhm-Bawerk's productivity theory of interest, it was not necessary for Fetter to dismiss Böhm-Bawerk's important conception of roundaboutness or the period of production. Roundaboutness *is* an important aspect of the productivity of capital goods. However, while this productivity may increase the *rents* to be derived from capital goods, it cannot account for an increase in the rate of interest return, that is, the ratio between the annual rents derived from these capital goods and their present price. That ratio is strictly determined by time preference.

"The Nature of Capital and Income" (1907) offered a review of Irving Fisher's book of the same title. Fetter hailed Fisher's use of the capitalization concept of capital as well as Fisher's abandonment of his previous view that the stock/flow concept of capital and income applied to the same concrete goods. Here,

Fisher shifted to an abstract and generalized conception of stocks and flows. But, as Fetter noted, this very abstraction rendered the whole stock/flow dichotomy untenable. Fisher's treatment of income as strictly *psychic* income, to the virtual exclusion of money income, is properly criticized, as is the corollary that only consumption is income, and therefore capital gains are not income and should not be subject to an income tax. Finally, Fetter, who had himself been working on an integrated theory of income distribution, found that Fisher's theory of capital and income had an *ad hoc* flavor because it had been developed separately from the remainder of Fisher's distribution theory.

In "Are Savings Income—Discussion?" (1908), Fetter elaborated on his criticism of Fisher's view that savings, or rather additions to capital, are not income, and that the term *income* should be limited to consumption expenditure only. Fetter correctly pointed out that Fisher confused the concept of ultimate *psychic* income, which indeed consists only of consumption, with the concept of monetary incomes acquired in the market, which are partially saved and partially consumed.

Two decades later (1927) Fetter returned to the theory of capital in his contribution to the *Festschrift* honoring John Bates Clark. In the course of reviewing Clark's contributions to the theory of capital, Fetter praised Clark for treating capital as a fund rather than as an array of heterogeneous capital goods and for offering a general definition of rent as the income from all capital goods and not just the income from land. Böhm-Bawerk is criticized once again for clinging to the identification of capital and interest (instead of realizing how interest permeates the entire time-value market), but this cogent criticism is again misleadingly linked to an attack on Böhm-Bawerk for maintaining a distinction between land and capital goods. In this article, F. W. Taussig is criticized for allegedly maintaining that only land, and not capital, is productive. But here Taussig was not simply in the throes of the labor theory of value; rather, he was adopting the subtle Böhm-Bawerkian insight that, while capital goods are evidently productive, they are not *ultimately* productive, for they have to be produced and reproduced by labor, land, and time, so that capital goods earn gross rent, but not net rents, which go only to labor and land factors. Hence again we encounter the importance of the land-capital goods distinction. As for interest, it is entirely the result of time preference; in the case of a capital good, interest depends on first producing the capital good by combining labor and land and then on reaping the fruits of this combination at a later time. The very distinction between land and capital goods so resisted by Fetter was thus used by Böhm-Bawerk to pave the way for Fetter's own theory of interest!

Of particular importance in this 1927 essay is Fetter's critique of Alfred Marshall's capital theory. Always an unsparing logician, Fetter relentlessly criticized the myriad of inconsistencies, confusions, and contradictions in Marshall's discussion. Fetter also added to his previous criticisms of Fisher's capital theory a review of the inconsistency in adopting a wealth-at-one-time/services-at-one-time distinction between capital and income on top of his previous stock/flow dichotomy.

Fetter's contribution entitled "Capital," which appeared in the *Encyclopedia of the Social Sciences* (1930-35), is a convenient summation of his views on capital as well as his criticisms of alternative theories. It is clear that his exclusive concern with capital as a fund, or as "the market value [of] the present worths of . . . individual claims to incomes," is a consequence of his dissatisfaction with the productivity theories of interest and his desire to establish "capital value" as simply the capitalized sum of expected future rental incomes.

3.

Frank A. Fetter's pioneering development of the pure time-preference theory of interest began with his article "The 'Roundabout Process' in the Interest Theory" (1902). Here Fetter hailed Böhm-Bawerk as the first to state properly the central problem of interest theory: To explain why present goods are valued more highly than future goods. But after starting out with time preference as the proper explanation, Böhm-Bawerk introduced his "third ground" for interest—the greater productivity of roundabout processes of production—and argued that it was the most important reason present goods had higher values than future goods.

When offering his detailed critique of Böhm-Bawerk's "third ground," Fetter explained how Böhm-Bawerk had failed to separate the undoubted increase in *physical* productivity, resulting from an increase in capital, from a claimed increase in the "value" productivity of capital. Fetter noted that an increase in the *value* of capital (as distinct from its physical amount) will increase the value productivity of capital if and only if the interest rate remains constant. In other words, Böhm-Bawerk's productivity explanation of interest makes use of the concept of the present value of capital and therefore assumes that the interest rate is already given, since it is needed to determine the present value of capital. Thus, Böhm-Bawerk's productivity explanation of interest involved circular reasoning. Similarly, Fetter noted that one determinant of the degree of capitalization, or the degree of roundaboutness of production processes in the economy, is precisely the interest rate—the rate of present capitalization of future rents. Here is still another example of circular reasoning.

For the remainder of his 1902 article, Fetter elaborated on his critique (outlined above) of the Austrian separation of land and capital goods, and the idea of the period of production. Here it might be noted that Fetter's perfectly valid point about land capitalization in the market by way of the interest rate does not negate the Austrian distinction between land and capital goods. According to the Austrian school "capital" and "capital goods" are separate and distinct concepts. Furthermore, Fetter's repeated attempts to attribute a labor theory of capital value to Böhm-Bawerk are contradicted by his own admission that both land and time enter into the Austrian view of the production of capital. Fetter, however, made an important point in criticizing Böhm-Bawerk's formulation of the "average period of production," especially the idea of *ex post* averaging of the various periods of production throughout the economy. Fetter also cogently attacked Böhm-Bawerk's attempt to leap from the increased physical productivity of roundabout processes to value productivity by the use of purely arithmetical tables. Here Fetter levelled a (characteristically Austrian) critique of the use of mathematics in economics against an economist who was himself a leading critic of the mathematical method.

In his 1902 article, Fetter offered another brilliant criticism of Böhm-Bawerk's "third ground." Böhm-Bawerk tried to use the greater productivity of capital to explain why these "present goods" are worth more than "future goods" when the capital comes to fruition as consumer goods. But, as Fetter pointed out, since capital instruments only mature into consumer goods at various times in the future, capital goods are really *future* goods, not present goods. If, then, we concentrate on utility to consumers, capital goods are seen to be *future* goods, and the "third ground" for an extra return to these (future) capital goods as being more productive "present goods" becomes totally invalid.

We may apply Fetter's insight to the current textbook explanations of interest rate determination in the market for productive loans. The supply curve of loanable funds is conventionally explained by time preference, while the demand curve for loans by business firms is explained by reference to the "marginal productivity of capital"—in short, by the "natural" rate of interest embodied in the long-term normal rate of profit. But the firm that borrows money in order to hire workers or to buy capital goods is really buying *future* goods in exchange for a present good, money. In short, the business borrower, like the saver-creditor who lends him money, is buying a future good whenever he makes an investment. If we assume, for example, that there are no business loans but only stock investment, this point is easier to understand. When a man saves and invests in a productive process, he pays workers and other factors *now* in exchange for services that will yield a product, and therefore an income, at some *future* time. In short, the capitalist-entrepreneur hires or invests in factors now and pays out money (a present good) in exchange for productive services that are future goods. It is for his service in paying factors *now*, in advance of the fruits of production, that the capitalist normally earns an interest return, a return for time preference. In sum, every factor of production (whether labor, land, or capital goods) earns, not its marginal value productivity, according to the current conventional explanation, but its marginal productivity *discounted* by the interest rate or time preference; and the capitalist earns the discount.

Fetter also cogently argued that Böhm-Bawerk in effect used one explanation (the "third ground") for interest on producer goods and another (the notion of time preference) for interest on consumer loans. Since interest must have a unitary explanation, Böhm-Bawerk's analysis is something of a retrogression.

Fetter stressed the basic weakness of all productivity explanations of interest. It is not enough, he pointed out, to show that more capital is productive in physical or even value terms; the problem is to explain why the value of capital on the market today is low enough to generate a surplus value return tomorrow. The productivity of capital has nothing to do with the solution to this problem. As Fetter wrote:

The essence of the interest problem is to explain a surplus of value over the value of capital employed. It is not enough to show that more capital (or a more roundabout process) will produce more products, or to show that the aggregate of products has a greater value than those secured before. The value of capital being derived from the value of the products, the more the products (in value), the more the capital (value), *unless* the interest rate (the thing to be explained) keeps the capital from increasing proportionately.

Fetter pointed out ironically that Böhm-Bawerk himself, in criticizing earlier productivity theories of interest, had raised precisely the same point. Even conceding that very long roundabout processes may be physically highly productive, Fetter pointed out that the question remained unresolved in Böhm-Bawerk why these processes are not then always preferred to less productive, but more immediately fruitful, processes.

Fetter concluded by reiterating his unique position on the relationship between interest and rent. Rent reflects the (marginal) productivity of scarce factors of production, and interest reflects the present valuation of future services and therefore depends, not at all on roundaboutness, but on the postponement of use. The theory of interest, Fetter concluded, "must set in their true relation the theory of rent as the income from the use of goods in any given period, and interest as the agio or discount on goods of whatever sort, when compared throughout successive periods."

In the presentation of his theory before the American Economic Association, "The Relations between Rent and Interest " (1904), Fetter pointed out the confusions and inconsistencies of previous writers on the theory of rent and interest. In place of the classical distinction between rent as income from land and interest as income from capital goods, Fetter proposed that *all* factors of production, whether land or capital goods, be considered either "as yielding uses, . . . as [a] bearer of rent," *or* as "salable at their present worth, . . . as [a] discounted sum of rents," as "wealth" or "capital." As a corollary, rent must be conceived of as an absolute amount (per unit time), whereas interest is a ratio (or percentage) of a principal sum called capital value. Rent becomes the usufruct from any material agent or factor—the use of the agent considered apart from using it up. But then there is no place for the idea of interest as the yield of capital goods. Rents from any durable good accrue at different points in time, at different dates in the future. The capital value of any good then becomes the sum of its expected future rents, discounted by the rate of time preference for present over future goods, which is the rate of interest. In short, the capital value of a good is the "capitalization" of its future rents in accordance with the rate of time preference or interest. Therefore, marginal utility accounts for the valuations and prices of consumer goods; the rent of each factor of production is determined by its productivity in eventually producing consumer goods; and interest arises in the capitalization, in accordance with time preference, of the present worth of the expected future rents of durable goods. Such is Fetter's lucid, systematic, and unique vision of the relative place of rent, interest, and capital value in the theory of distribution.

Fetter's paper was considered so important that nine economists were assigned to discuss it. As Fetter indicated in his reply, few of his commentators demonstrated that they understood his positive theory, and many were only interested in defending the classical school against Fetter's criticisms. To Thomas Nixon Carver's major point that since land, in contrast to other factor services, need not be supplied, land rent does not enter into cost, Fetter replied: (1) that the same sort of surplus, or no-cost, elements may be said to permeate all factors of production, and (2) that land, like other factors, must also be served, maintained, and allocated efficiently. Furthermore, several of the commentators, as Fetter pointed out, mistakenly identified Fetter's theory with that of John Bates Clark and proceeded to criticize Clark's assimilation of rent and interest, despite the fact that Fetter held an almost diametrically opposed view.

A decade later Fetter returned to the theory of interest, in "Interest Theories, Old and New" (1914), as part of a critique of Irving Fisher's recantation from his previous adherence to pure time-preference theory, a position he had approached in his *The Rate of Interest* (1907), and one that influenced Fetter in developing his own theory. But now Fisher was taking the path of Böhm-Bawerk and returning to a partial productivity explanation. Moreover, Fetter discovered that the seeds of error were in Fisher's publication of 1907. Fisher had stated that valuations of present and future goods imply a preexisting money rate of interest, thereby suggesting that a pure time-preference explanation of interest involves circular reasoning. By way of contrast, and in the course of explaining his own pure time-preference, or "capitalization," theory of interest, Fetter showed that time valuation is prerequisite to the determination of the market rate of interest. The market rate of interest on loans is, for Fetter, a reflection of a general rate of time preference in the economy, a capitalization process that discounts, in the present prices of durable goods and factors of production, the future uses of these goods. Consumers evaluate directly enjoyable consumer goods, then evaluate durable factors according to their productivity in making these goods, and then discount these future uses to the present in accordance with their time preferences. The first step yields the prices of consumer goods; the second, the incomes or rents of producer goods; the last, the "underestimation" of, or the rate of interest yielded by, the producer goods.

Again restating his case, this time in criticizing the views of Henry R. Seager, Fetter pointed to the crucial problem: why does entrepreneurial purchase of factors seem to contain within itself a net surplus, an interest return? The productivity of capital goods does not explain why the value of this expected productivity is discounted in their present price, which in turn permits the entrepreneurs to pay interest on loans with which to buy or hire these factors of production. As Fetter stated: "The amount of interest which 'enterprisers estimate' they can afford to pay . . . is the difference between the discounted, or present, worth of products imputable to these agents and their worth at the time they are expected to mature." Fetter added that there of course must be productivity to account for the expected future income, just as there must be people and markets; but there would be no rate of interest if the future value of the products were not *discounted*. Market interest can be paid out of a value surplus that emerges from an antecedent time discount of the "value-productivity" of the factors of production. Or, putting it another way, Fetter readily admitted that productivity of capital goods brings greater value to the final product. "But the value-productivity which furnishes the motive to the enterpriser to borrow and gives him the power, regularly, to pay contract interest, is due, not to the fact that these products will have value when they come into existence, but to the fact that their expected value is discounted in the price of the agents bought at an earlier point of time."

Fetter also sharpened the contrast between his own theory and the productivity theory of interest in another way. The productivity theorists assert that as capital grows the economy becomes more productive, and that the interest rate increases owing to the greater productivity of capital. But Fetter countered with the insight that, as the economy advances and more present goods are produced, the preference for present goods is lowered, and the interest rate therefore may be expected to fall. Or, as it might be put more elaborately, everyone has a time-preference schedule relating his supply of present goods with his preference for the present over the future. A greater supply of present goods would move to the right and down along a given time-preference schedule, so that the marginal utility of present goods would fall in relation to future goods. As a result, on the given schedules, the rate of time preference, of degree of choice of present over future, would tend to fall and so therefore would the interest rate.

Fetter also anticipated Frank Knight's classic distinction, in *Risk, Uncertainty, and Profit* (1921), between interest, or long-run normal profits, on the one hand and short-run profits and losses earned by superior, or suffered by inferior, entrepreneurs on the other—superiority or inferiority defined in terms of the ability to forecast the uncertain future. Why does an entrepreneur borrow at all if in so doing he will bid up the loan rate of interest to the rate of time preference as reflected in his long-run normal rate of profit (or his "natural rate of interest," to use Austrian terminology)? The reason is that superior forecasters envision making short-run profits whenever the general loan rate is lower than the return they expect to obtain. This is precisely the competitive process, which tends, in the long run, to equalize all natural and loan rates in the time market. Those entrepreneurs "with superior knowledge and superior foresight," wrote Fetter, "are merchants, buying when they can in a cheaper and selling in a dearer capitalization market, acting as the equalizers of rates and prices."

Fetter also pointed out, quite correctly, that the process of capitalization and time discount applies as fully and equally to land as it does to capital goods. From the point of view of capitalization, there is no fundamental distinction between land and produced means of production. In fact, Fetter might have pointed out that under slavery, where laborers are owned, they, too, become capitalized, and the present price of slaves becomes the capitalized value of expected future earnings (or "rents") of slaves, discounted by the social rate of time preference. But the fact that slaves, too, can be capitalized does not justify obliterating for other purposes any and all distinctions between slaves and capital goods.

Not only is Fetter's pure time-preference, or capitalization, theory the only one that offers an integrated explanation of interest on slaves, land, and capital goods, but it is also, as he pointed out, the only one that provides an integrated explanation of interest on consumption loans and on productive loans. For even the productivity theorists had to concede that at least in the case of consumer loans interest was occasioned by time preference.

In Fetter's final and extensive treatment of interest, "Interest Theory and Price Movements" (1927), pessimism has replaced his optimism of earlier years; for after an illuminating discussion of early interest theories (in which he rescued Turgot from the deprecation of Böhm-Bawerk), Fetter sadly noted that his insight into interest theory had been ignored. The old productivity theory of interest, having at last conquered Böhm-Bawerk and Irving Fisher, survived as the dominant explanation of interest in the eclectic theory of Alfred Marshall. Among English and American economists, productivity remained the major explanation of interest on productive capital, and time preference was relegated to an explanation of consumer lending.

Fetter proceeded to a particularly extended discussion of the nature of time preference and the time market. Time preference enters into primitive, Crusoe-type valuations, which predate the development of barter as well as the emergence of money loans and a money economy. The rates of time preference reflect all the conditions, the interactions, and the choices of human beings. In almost all cases, present goods are preferred to future goods, and this preference is most marked in primitive man. But, Fetter added, with the development of civilization, the advent of thrift generally means a lowering of the premiums placed on present goods and hence of the rate of time preference.

In the money economy, just as the utility scales of individuals interact to bring about uniform prices on the market, individual time-preference schedules through exchange bring all time preferences into conformity. The consequence is a social rate of time preference, a "general, average rate of premium of present dollars over future dollars which has resulted from leveling out ... a great part of the individual differences." Through arbitrage time-preference rates tend to be equalized throughout the time market. The price of a durable factor of production is derived from the expected price of its products, being the present discount, or capitalized sum, of all of its future products. This capitalization process precedes, rather than follows, the existence of an interest rate on money loans. The time-preference rate that capitalizes future incomes emerges as the long-run normal, or natural, rate of profit of business firms. Short-run deviations from this norm are caused by special circumstances and by entrepreneurial skills. Profit rates tend to be equalized throughout the market through a continuing reevaluation of the prices of durable agents—those capital goods providing a profit being recapitalized upward and those suffering losses being recapitalized downward. This process of recapitalization and reevaluation tends to bring about uniform profit rates, Fetter noted, rather than according to the conventional theory, uniform costs of producing new durable agents. For Fetter, the interest rate on productive money loans and the normal rate of profit tend to equality because they have a common cause: capitalization of time preferences throughout the time market. As Fetter stated:

The normal profit-making "productivity of capital" (where goods containing future uses rise toward parity with present uses) is thus nothing but the reversal of the former discount-valuation applied to distant incomes. It is a psychological, valuation process, not a physical, technological process. Thus profits no more explain interest than interest explains profits. They offer alternative investment opportunities but neither is the cause of the other. Both opportunities result from discounts and premiums permeating the existing system of prices, and these are traceable to the fundamental factor of time-preference exercised by men individually and collectively.

Having thus elaborated his concept of time preference and the time market, Fetter applied his pure theory to the complexities of determining interest in the real world. In the first place, interest rates, in addition to being determined by time pref erence, vary in accordance with different degrees of risk, entrepreneurial skill, the cost of making loans, different habits, and legal restrictions. Furthermore, as Fetter pointed out, changes in the price level slow up the market process of equilibrating interest rates and lead to widespread errors of overcapitalization and undercapitalization.

In a discussion of money and price levels in relation to the interest rate, Fetter incorporated into his analysis Fisher's insight, now being rediscovered, that interest rates tend to rise during a boom and fall during a recession in response to expected changes in price levels. Rising price levels lower the purchasing power of the creditor's return, and interest rates tend to rise during inflations to compensate for this loss. Conversely, interest rates tend to fall below time-preference rates during a recession to offset the increased real rate of return.

But Fetter was not content to stop there. Noting that empirically interest rates do not rise continually during booms, Fetter developed a monetary theory of the business cycle, one that came close to the Mises-Hayek "monetary malinvestment" theory that was being developed in Austria at about the same time (see my *America's Great Depression* [Kansas City: Sheed & Ward, 1975]).

Fetter explained that a currency inflation from increased government spending raises the price level, which in the long run is determined by movements in the supply of money. But increasing the money supply via bank credit expansion has far more complex consequences. Continuing bank credit expansion not only will bring about a boom and higher prices but also will increase the money supply via a massive increase in the supply of loanable funds emitted by the banks. The increased money supply will keep the rate of interest *below* the free-market rate, at least until later stages in the boom, and will bring about an overcapitalization of durable and producers' goods. Owing to the increase in product prices combined with the artificially low rates of interest, businessmen are led into numerous unsound investments. When the banks are finally forced to stop their credit expansion, the overestimation of capital values is suddenly reversed, and the boom is quickly succeeded by a recession. Business failures, monetary losses, and lowering of capital values bring the various parts of the system of prices and values on the market once more into harmony. In particular, that part of the market not influenced by bank credit is brought into harmony with the remainder of the economy. Such is the function of the recession in response to the distortions generated by the bank credit expansion of the preceding boom.

Criticizing the theory that bank credit should simply be responsive to the "needs of business," Fetter properly pointed out that during a boom business overestimates its "needs" in response to rising prices and the seemingly greater opportunities for profit. In this way, bank credit expansion stimulates those very business "needs" that are supposed to furnish a rigorous criterion for bank credit policy.

Fetter also provided a useful critique of the Swedish economist Knut Wicksell's theory that if banks should continue to hold the interest rate below the natural, or free-market, rate, the price level would rise indefinitely. Fetter pointed out that this could only be true if the lowering of the discount rate was accompanied by a continuous expansion of bank credit.

Fetter concluded this discussion of interest theory by applying it to the economics of war. During wartime there is a sharp increase in rates of time preference, in the demand for present goods immediately usable for war purposes. Consequently, there is a substantial rise in wartime of free-market interest rates. Fetter was therefore highly critical of the common attempts by governments to keep interest rates low during wartime, thus creating economic distortions and preventing high interest rates from smoothly shifting resources from civilian industries to war industries, which have a higher immediate demand for funds.

4.

Fetter's major article on the theory of rent, "The Passing of the Old Rent Concept" (1901), was one of his most notable essays. It is a detailed critique of the several mutually contradictory rent theories found in Alfred Marshall's *Principles of Economics*. First is the Ricardian notion that rent is the return to land. The problem of "explaining" rent becomes equivalent to defining what land is and why it is different from capital. Fetter attacked the distinction made between land and capital by criticizing the idea that land can be distinguished from capital in terms of its alleged inelasticity of supply. Fetter argued that both land and capital can be increased in the long run, while in the short run the supply of capital goods can be as inelastic as the supply of land.

Fetter next turned his attention to the influential doctrine of quasi-rents. According to Marshall, land (as well as other nonreproducible goods, such as paintings and rare jewelry) is permanently fixed in supply and therefore earns a true rent. Capital goods, however, are fixed in supply only in the short run, and therefore their income, while similar to land rent, is only temporary, hence the term "quasi-rent." Fetter uncovered the crucial error in Marshall's claim that quasi-rents are not part of the cost of production. In making this claim, Marshall had quietly shifted his discussion from the entrepreneur to the owner of the capital good who "earns an income" rather than "pays a cost." Thus instead of being a costless surplus to the entrepreneur, rent "is essentially that payment which, as a part of [money] costs, prevents the [entrepreneur] from getting any surplus which can be attributed to the rented agents."

At the base of the Marshallian error in the quasi-rent doctrine, stated Fetter, is a confusion between money costs and the rather mystical concept of "real costs." Money costs of production do not consist of "real" costs; they are simply the market value of the factors of production that the business firm contracts to put to use. To make rent a "surplus" over real cost is tantamount to abandoning the basic notion of rent as a regularly accruing income produced by way of market exchange.

Fetter criticized Marshall's adherence to the classical notion that rent is the one income payment that does not enter into the money cost of production, or into the supply price of factors of production. Fetter noted that the rent of land enters into money costs as does any other contractual payment, as any land-renting farmer or businessman can attest. The Marshallian reply that land is employed up until the no-rent margin and therefore has no effect on decisions to produce a little more or less of the product is dismissed by Fetter's demonstration that the same could be said about any factor payment whatsoever by way of generalizing the law of diminishing returns into the law of variable proportions. There is simply nothing special about land rent in this regard. Furthermore, Fetter pointed out that no producer ever pushes a factor as far as the "no-rent" margin; here economic reality contradicts the infinitesimally small units of mathematical economics. For so long as a factor remains productive *at all*, it will pay a rent in accordance with that productivity, no matter how small. And, furthermore, the supply of any good is determined fully as much by rent-bearing as by marginal units. In sum, land is priced in the same way as labor or capital in terms of the value of its marginal product.

In his "Comment on Rent under Increasing Returns" (1930), Fetter demolished the idea of increasing returns and called for an extension of the concept that rent accrues to land to the notion that rent accrues to the separable uses of any kind of durable good whatsoever. Finally in his article on "Rent" in the *Encyclopedia of Social Sciences*, Fetter traced the history of the notion of rent and defined rent in the common-sense meaning of "renting-out": the amount paid for the separable uses of a durable agent "entrusted by the owner to a borrower, to be returned in equally good condition."

5.

It may be that the hallmark of Frank A. Fetter's approach to economic theory was his "radicalism"—his willingness to discard the entire baggage of lingering Ricardianism. In distribution theory his most important contributions are still too radical to be accepted into the *corpus* of economic analysis. These are: (1) his eradication of all productivity elements from the theory of interest and his development of a pure time-preference, or capitalization, theory and (2) his eradication of everything pertaining to land, whether it be scarcity or some sort of margin over cost, in the theory of rent, in favor of rent as the "renting out" of a durable good to earn an income per unit time. Guided by Alfred Marshall and by eventual retreats toward the older view by Böhm-Bawerk and Fisher, microeconomic theory has chosen a more conservative route.

Despite the attention and the enthusiasm accorded to his writings at the time, Fetter's contributions to distribution theory have fallen into neglect and disuse. It is to be hoped that this collection of essays will bring Fetter's contributions and his lucid and systematic economic vision to the attention of contemporary economists.

BIBLIOGRAPHICAL NOTE

For a recent appreciation of Fetter's contributions to economic thought, see John Appleby Coughlan, "The Contributions of Frank Albert Fetter (1863-1949) to the Development of Economic Theory" (Ph.D. diss., Catholic University of America, 1965). For an early summary of his theoretical system that apparently received Fetter's approval, see Robert F. Hoxie, "Fetter's Theory of Value," *Quarterly Journal of Economics* 19 (February 1905): 210-30. Hoxie concluded that Fetter (in his *Principles of Economics: With Applications to Practical Problems* [New York: Century Co., 1904]) had created a "system which, for logical consistency, is without precedent; a system through which with clearness there runs one essential chain of thought . . . and as successive links of which the problems of the value of consumption goods, rents, wages, and profits, the value of productive agents, and interest are successively solved" (ibid., p. 230). General discussions of Fetter's contribution may be found in Joseph Dorfman, *The Economic Mind in American Civilization,* 5 vols. (New York: Viking Press, 1959), 3:360-65, 385-86; 5:464-79; and Wesley C. Mitchell, *Types of Economic Theory: From Mercantilism to Institutionalism,* 2 vols. (New York: Augustus M. Kelley, 1969) 2:251-300. I have included a bibliography of Fetter's works at the end of this volume.

Part 1
The Theory of Capital

Review of F. W. Taussig, *Wages and Capital:* An Examination of the Wages Fund Doctrine

This book consists of two main parts—a historical resumé of the wages-fund controversy, and a presentation of the author's own conclusions on the subject. The historical portion is by no means unimportant: in fact, it cannot fail to receive commendation from all quarters for impartiality of treatment, acuteness of criticism, fullness of knowledge and clearness of style. This review, however, must be confined to the author's "positive theory" as contained in the first 125 pages of the volume.

Among the limitations which Professor Taussig places on the problem he is investigating is one that deserves a special word of comment. He limits the problem to the determination of "the total that goes to laborers as a whole." "It is only with the total," he says, "that the wages fund, or the discussion of wages and capital, has to do" (p. 109). "The causes which determine the share which a particular set of laborers shall have are different," and present a different set of questions. This distinction, to be sure, is made with practical unanimity by the adherents of the wages-fund doctrine in any of its forms: it may almost be considered their shibboleth. The author accepts it without question. May we venture to suggest that it is the fundamental source of what seems to be the error in the view he presents? "Total wages"

Reprinted from *Political Science Quarterly* 12 (March 1897). The book under review is Frank W. Taussig's restatement of the classical theory of the wage fund, *Wages and Capital: An Examination of the Wages Fund Doctrine* (New York: D. Appleton, 1896).

is an abstraction—and, moreover, a useless and misleading abstraction. To suppose that one set of forces determines the total going to laborers and that another set of forces then distributes this among the different classes and individuals, is to reverse the true order of fact and of thought. Total wages are merely the arithmetical sum of individual wages. The latter are in a sense the dynamic element; the total is a passive result. To view the matter otherwise is to go astray at the earliest stage, and to set one's self seeking for a shadowy and uncertain explanation of a vague and shadowy thing.

Professor Taussig's first chapter, entitled "Present Work and Present Wages," is devoted to a very lucid description of the leading features of the modern industrial process. In the case of the great multitude of products, as he shows, a long series of acts extending over a considerable period is necessary before the finishing touches are put upon them. The conclusion is clearly drawn that "present labor produces chiefly unfinished things, but the reward of present labor is finished things." In the sense that "the current yield of industry" (p. 22) is always having put to it the finishing touches, wages may, indeed, be said to be paid from current product; but in a truer sense "real wages are virtually to their full extent the product of past labor" (p. 17).

The main conclusion of chapter two, entitled "Capital and Wages," is as follows: Taking wages to "mean all the income of all laborers" (p. 43), and capital to mean "that supply of inchoate goods, in all stages toward completion, from which the steady flow of real income is derived" (p. 44), "we may lay it down broadly," says Professor Taussig, "that wages are derived from capital" (p. 43). This proposition "has nothing to do with money or money wages" (p. 45). "The relation of wages to capital," here expressed, "would be the same under any social organization" (p. 45). Real capital, under any rational conception, consists of "things tangible and usable"; real wages, of "the enjoyable commodities which the laborer gets" (p. 46).

The author perceives, however, that this proposition is entirely too general to be used to support a doctrine of a wages fund. He admits that this reasoning, while directed to wages, applies equally to every other form of income. . . . [What] is true of wages is true of interest and rent and business profits. All are derived from capital in the same sense. . . . If any law of wages has been reached . . . it is but a statement of the fact that all the enjoyment of to-day comes from commodities which are the product of past labor [p. 48].

The result thus reached would appear very neatly and conclusively to dispose of the concept and phrase "wages fund," except as a literary curio. In the same sense and with equal scientific significance can it be said that there is a profit fund, an interest fund, a rent fund—a possibility which earlier in the book (p. 16) does not escape the author's notice. Yet he would not have the reader draw a conclusion which his own conservatism hesitates to accept. The reader's judgment is therefore suspended by various expressions: "if any law of wages has been reached" (p. 48); "and yet there is something more to be said of wages and capital than this general proposition;" "the unmistakable differences in the mode in which the various members of the social body get their share of the general income bring some important consequences, both as to distribution at large and as to wages and the *wages fund*." These expressions indicate that the author intends to retain the expression "wages fund," and to show that there are good reasons for looking upon such a fund as differing in some points worth the noting from the part of the social income going for rent, for profits and for interest.

In carrying out this purpose the author may fairly be expected to conform to certain minimum requirements. First, we are justified in expecting that real wages, and not mere money wages, shall be the subject of his discussion. Professor Taussig keenly appreciates the proneness of other writers to err at this point. "The obvious distinction between real wages and money wages," says he, "makes its appearance in every book on the elements of economics, but it is too often forgotten when the causes determining wages come to be examined" (p. 15). As he elsewhere expresses it (p. 231), this is a convenient short cut which breeds confusion in the mind of the reader while veiling the real question. (See also pp. 17, 19, 45, 46, 47, 231, 245, 247, 297 *et passim*.)

Secondly, we may expect that he will avoid the error, to which he so frequently refers, of considering that the "capital"—the "fund," whatever it be called, that constitutes real wages—is "necessarily owned by the individual who pays wages." "Such reasoning," as he says, "does not touch real capital or real wages" (p. 46).

The capitalists who directly employ laborers have usually no ownership of the commodities which make real wages. If these real wages come from capital, the capital is certainly not in the hands of the employers [p. 20. See also p. 258 among others].

Thirdly, we may justly require of the author a comprehensible explanation of the way in which the "wages fund" is marked off from, or carved out of, the total income of the community; and we may expect that in some important respects this shall be shown to differ from the process which apportions the shares of the other factors in distribution. This "total income," elucidated by the author in the first two chapters, is essentially the "subsistence fund" of Böhm-Bawerk. Yet the author says: "There is an obvious difficulty in the fact that the general subsistence contains the income not only of laborers, but of the whole community" (p. 316). Indeed, he thinks the Austrian writer has gone "but a very little way toward explaining just how the total subsistence fund and its ripening installments are diverted to one and another class in the community" (p. 317). When Professor Taussig further adds that "an investigation of the machinery of distribution . . . is the essential part of the wages-fund problem" (p. 317), he seems to imply a promise to make an examination of these "essential" questions before quitting the subject. Moreover, the promise is made distinctly (p. 16) where the author says that the question "whether there can be any possibility of separation of this net income into parts destined for any one set of persons, or appropriated to them," will engage his attention "at a later stage."

Every one of these minimum requirements the author fails to

meet. First, instead of striking straight at the fundamentals and refusing to consider the mere "machinery by which laborers are enabled to get their real wages" (p. 15), he makes this machinery, that is, money wages, a central object of his attention. Having devoted some discussion to "real income and real wages," he begins a fresh chapter with the announcement: "In the present chapter money and money income play a vital part" (p. 51). The suddenness of this change of face comes as a surprise and a disappointment to the reader. Moreover, throughout the chapter the discussion blooms with that perennial error, emphasis of the superficial monetary aspects of the problem. Money income and money payments, flowing first into the hands of the immediate employers, absorb all the author's attention. Further, repeated use is made of "funds" in the sense of money funds in the hands of the employers. Among numerous instances one of the most noteworthy is the following:

The hired laborer gets his wages from capital in a sense in which the independent workman does not. His money income . . . is turned over to him by capitalists. It comes from *funds* in the possession of a body of which his immediate employer is a member. . . . In this sense his earnings depend on a wages fund—on the sums which the employers judge it expedient to turn to the hire of labor [p. 75]. . . . [With the same connotation he says:] In an important sense hired laborers are primarily dependent for their wages on the *funds* which the whole body of active capitalists can and will turn over to them [p. 78].

It is unnecessary and, indeed, impossible here to follow out all the details of the reasoning on these points. The author himself in his criticism of others has most satisfactorily shown that such a treatment but skims over the surface of the question. It ends in what seems little more than a mere verbal quibble.

The second requirement is met no more satisfactorily. The capital or funds that are discussed are throughout looked upon as in the hands of the employing class, except where the conception is widened to include the great body of money-lenders "whose business it is to make advances to the more immediate directors of business affairs" (p. 63). Throughout the chapter the concept of capital, or funds, fails to include all the sources of the real income that the laborers enjoy—for example, stores of goods in the hands of independent producers, and even a portion of labor itself, so far as personal services make up that real income. There is no hint that such elements may play a part in determining the remuneration of labor.

Nor is the third requirement fulfilled in the author's discussion. He practically brushes aside, when he reaches it, the problem of the fixing of the shares in distribution. Nowhere does he show that there is anything peculiar about the part going to labor that can entitle it, in distinction from the other parts, to be called a fund. He summarizes his own results in these words:

In fact the wages-fund doctrine, or what there is of truth in it, . . . can tell us little . . . as to the fundamental causes which . . . determine the share of that real income which in the long run shall go to wages or interest or rent (p. 322).

Moreover, Professor Taussig does not show what the fundamental causes are which determine the different shares at any given time. Once he confesses that his examination of "the immediate source of the money wages of hired laborers is at best incomplete; the inquiry as to the source of real wages remains the important one in the background" (p. 64). But with the remark that "the questions as to the machinery of immediate money wages are important enough" (p. 65), he returns to their consideration. The reader looks in vain for any further light upon this question in the remaining chapters.

The "main conclusions" reached by the author appear to be that there is more than one tenable sense in which a wages fund may be spoken of—that, indeed, there are *two* wages-fund doctrines. Neither is quite like the doctrine as held by the older economists. The one is broader than theirs—so broad, in fact, that it seems to the reviewer nothing more than a statement that what the laborers enjoy is a part of the total income of society. In this it is hard to recognize more than a bald truism. The second doctrine which the author presents is the one wherein the superficial monetary aspects alone are kept in view. This is impressed upon the reader with much emphasis; yet, as my italics show, the author's faith fails him when he comes to state it for the last time:

Hired laborers are dependent on a wages fund (*if one chooses so to call it*), which is in the hands of the capitalist class. Their money income is derived from what the capitalists find it profitable to turn over to them [p. 321].

No further citation is needed to indicate that the author has, without intending it, given the *coup de grâce* to what was left of the old wages-fund doctrine. He intends to be conservative, and he shrinks from the logical conclusions of his own reasoning; yet no one, so effectively as he, has shown that the wages-fund doctrine, in any tenable form, is *nominis magni umbra*.

Recent Discussion of the Capital Concept

To most readers the reopening of the question as to the concept of capital will seem to call for an apology. If after so much discussion the fundamental definitions have not been generally agreed upon, some will say that further argument on terms and concepts is a waste of time. While practical questions of great importance await profounder study, impatience of metaphysical quibbling is pardonable; but in recent years many students have felt that there was need of earnest effort to make clearer and more consistent the fundamental concepts. These are the tools which aid men to think on economic subjects. A flaw in these concepts, an unsuspected ambiguity in a word or phrase, not only mars the conclusions of the student, but affects the popular judgment on the most practical questions. The circumstances and special problems of former generations have caused the grouping of unharmonized ideas under one term; and it is the business of the economist to measure, mark, and correct the concepts, to make the parts consistent with each other and the whole fitted to the needs of social discussion. The writer believes that there is no economic term to which this statement applies more fully than to capital, and this belief is the apology for the present paper. The concept of capital holds a central place in every economic system, and on its treatment have always depended the leading categories in the theory of economics. All agree, whatever definition may be held, that this is increasingly "a capitalistic age." The place, therefore, of the concept in all practical problems is growing more and more dominant; and a better definition of it is the most urgent need of the abstracter branch of economic science.

Reprinted from *Quarterly Journal of Economics* 15 (November 1900).

1. BÖHM-BAWERK

A point of departure admirably fitted for our purpose is
found in the *Positive Theory of Capital* of Böhm-Bawerk, which
was given to the English reading public in 1891, and at once
gained a large following. There are several advantages in beginning here. As the author's purpose was to present not only a
theory of interest, but, as the title indicates, a Positive Theory "of
Capital," we get the most typical cross-section of the study. We
start with the known; and we direct our criticisms not against
abandoned errors, but against views widely accepted.

Böhm-Bawerk undertook in his two large volumes to deal
thoroughly with the theories of interest, and, to do so, was led to
deal with the concepts of capital; for, thought he, it is capital for
which interest is paid. However much he disputed the relation of
production and interest, he had no doubt, in undertaking his
study,[1] as to the relation of capital and interest. Interest is the
yield of capital in the broader sense, and capital the source of
interest. They are correlative terms. To clear the field for his
own concept of capital, Böhm-Bawerk, therefore, passes in review the various conceptions of capital that have been employed.
He begins by following the historical order,[2] and later groups the
concepts in logical order.[3] In the chapter on historical development he begins with a mention of the mediaeval view of
capital as "an interest-bearing sum of money," gives a few words
to Turgot's "saved goods" (a very inadequate, not to say mistaken, interpretation of Turgot's view), and passes on to Adam
Smith's division of these into consumption goods and capital that
brings an income. In Smith's treatment the author thinks he
finds the germ of the productivity theory of interest, which he
considers false. Smith, in giving two varieties of the concept,—
capital as a means of acquisition to the individual, and capital as a
means of social production,—has in reality given, says Böhm-
Bawerk, "two entirely independent conceptions, resting substantially on quite different foundations, and only connected
externally by a very loose bond."[4] After devoting several pages to
discussing this difficulty, the author abandons the historical

order, and enumerates eight other variations of the concept: Hermann's "every durable foundation of a utility which has exchange value"; Menger's "groups of economic goods of higher rank [productive goods] now available to us for future periods," Kleinwächter's "tools of production"; Jevons's "sustenance of the laborer"; Marx's "instruments for the exploitation of the laborer"; Knies's goods available to satisfy wants in the future; Walras's goods which can be used more than once; MacLeod's "value of the productive power contained in material goods."[5] These are discussed more at length in Chapter V., the most important contentions being that the distinction between consumption goods and what he calls "the true instrument of production" is essential; that labor must not be confused with capital; that land must for many important reasons also be kept distinct; and that capital should be looked upon not as a "sum of value" hovering over goods, but as the "complex of goods" itself.[6]

Among these many variations the author gives his approval to that of Adam Smith, giving it "a more distinct formulation,"[7] however, and distinguishing between the wider and narrower conceptions, acquisitive (private) and productive (social) capital.

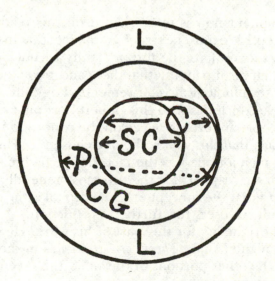

Of the former he says: "Capital in general we shall call a group of Products which serve as means to the Acquisition of Goods. Under this general conception we shall put that of Social Capital as narrower conception."[8] The problem of interest, he thinks, is connected with private or acquisitive capital, not necessarily with social or productive capital.

We may represent in the above diagram the results of the author's long inquiry. The large circle represents the entire material wealth of society. The outer band marked L is land, or all natural agents. The entire circle P contained within that band consists of "products." The next band, C G, is consumption goods. The concentric circle S C, within, is social capital, and the oval C is "capital in general," or private capital, embracing all social capital and, in addition, such consumption goods as are let for hire. Representing this in another way, we have the following classification:—

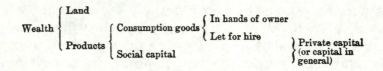

What judgment now is to be passed on this reading of the capital concept? We must be struck by the fact that in the matter of simplicity the results of the author's study are not ideal. But he asserts with a tone of triumph that the "conception meets all our logical and terminological requirements. Logically, it is unassailable."[9] He concludes with this hopeful prophecy: "If, then, unbiased people are ever to agree on the conception of capital, we may expect that this will be the one chosen."[10] His strongest ground for such a hope was the fact that he had made a place under the name "capital" for the two most generally employed concepts, and that the concept of social capital is the one widely held,—"products used for further production." He did not claim much originality for this part of his work. He says: "The heavy part of the *Positive Theory of Capital* lies in the theory of interest. In the other portions of the subject [he seems to mean the concept of capital] I was able, at least on the whole, to follow in the footsteps of previous theorists."[11]

The immediate reception of this portion of the author's work largely justified his hopes. His careful restatement of the concept and the authority of his name undoubtedly added to the prestige it already enjoyed. The more usual point of attack on the author has been his interest theory, not his capital concept, which has been far less questioned,[12]—in fact, has usually been accepted as flawless. Some protests, however, have already been raised against it; and, although it is still the dominant concept, discontent with this and other features of the older economic thought has been spreading. The earnest teacher, using the available text-books, and attempting to correct their treatment in accord with recent criticisms, is in despair. To one who has watched the course of the discussion it might seem that the service of Böhm-Bawerk's work, so far as it touches the capital concept, lay not in settling, but in reopening the whole question. Remembering, however, that most students still accept Böhm-Bawerk's statement of the concept, we turn to a group of thinkers who would give other readings to it; and we shall confine our study to the leading representatives of two differing views on the question.

2. *J. B. CLARK*

This part of the Austrian writer's work, especially, was attacked by Professor John B. Clark,[13] who defends the productivity theory of interest, though that point we need not raise in this paper. His own views had been published[14] at the same time as the German edition of the *Positive Theory of Capital;* but more attention was attracted to them, it is probable, as a result of this controversy than at their first publication. I shall not enter into the merits of the discussion as a whole. It was carried on with great skill, with some later confessed misunderstandings, and at times, perhaps, with an over-subtlety which makes it exceedingly difficult to follow. I shall simply try to state the issue involved as to the capital concept.

In every-day speech and in the writings of economists there have been, since before the time of Adam Smith, two broadly marked ways of thinking of capital: one views it as concrete goods, such as tools and machines; the other, as the money expression, or market value, of the goods. It is probable that no writer has long kept from the use of the term in both these ways, no matter what his formal definition. Frequently both uses will be found on the same page. A few writers only have chosen to frame their capital concept in accord with the second of these ways of thinking.[15] Böhm-Bawerk has taken the former way, defining capital as the concrete goods; and in the interest problem he insists on the need of comparing goods of like kind and quantity. Clark declares this to be an error, and defines capital in harmony with the second way of thinking of it. He says, "There is in existence a permanent fund of productive wealth, expressible in money, but not embodied in money; and it is this that business men designate by the term capital."[16] The concrete things which make up this fund he calls "capital goods." In contrast with this list of goods he often speaks of his kind of capital as "true capital," or "pure capital," which, as he says elsewhere, "resides in many unlike things, but consists of a single entity that is common to them all. That entity is 'effective social utility.' "[17] Again, he says: "Capital goods are . . . vanishing elements. True capital . . . is abiding."[18] Elsewhere he clothes his definition, which he calls "the common and practical sense of the term," in these words: "Capital is an abiding fund of wealth employed in production."[19]

Needless to say, Böhm-Bawerk defends himself vigorously against the charge of "side-tracking" the theory of capital in defining the concept as he had done. The controversy turned about the phrase "goods of like kind and quantity," and the question as to the real nature of the comparison of present and future goods. Clark holds that it is two sums of "quite different goods" that are compared. Böhm-Bawerk saves his phrase by the expedient of making the "goods of like kind and quantity" mean "dollars," "exactly as does Professor Clark."[20] This is not a novelty with him; for, as he points out,[21] he had "in many, and in some of the most important, passages of the *Positive Theory of Capital* . . . used money as an illustration of the proposition that present are worth more than future goods." Without quite indorsing Clark's comment on this point, we may agree with him that this appears to surrender the entire question concerning the formula "of like kind and quantity."[22] What meaning is in the phrase "the technical superiority of present goods over future goods," when those goods are made to mean dollars? What becomes of the elaborate analysis of the roundabout method of production?[23] Certainly, it means something very different, when the present goods employed are taken merely as circulating medium which is not in the normal case retained by the individual producers nor used up by society. The truth is, Böhm-Bawerk had fallen into the common error of using two different conceptions of capital, and at the first attack was found in an untenable position. This phase of the controversy seems to end by showing that the conception of capital made use of by Böhm-Bawerk himself, when he discusses business problems, takes the money expression, and differs in important ways from that of concrete goods expressed in his elaborately framed definition. A word as to the relation of these two views. It is to be noted that both parties agree that economists must study wealth under both these aspects. Böhm-Bawerk admits that he does so. The point against him is that, while framing his concept and basing his argument as to interest on the first, he introduces the second view, in some ways inconsistent, without recognizing the shift of concept. And Clark says that "the issue is not whether concrete capital goods are or are not to be studied at all. For certain purposes they have to be studied."[24] But he would confine the term "capital" to the sum of wealth or "permanent fund" constituted of the perishable goods.

The conception championed by Clark is of great significance; and, before going further, it is important to consider some peculiarities and difficulties in Clark's way of setting it forth.

(1) The discussion is confined by Clark at the outset to social capital.[25] He uses this term in a wider sense than Böhm-Bawerk does (as is explained in the next paragraph), but not differently

as to the exclusion of consumption goods. Social capital is that kind which Böhm-Bawerk himself considers to be productive. Clark gains thus a distinct tactical advantage over his opponent in upholding the productivity theory of interest, though that is not of immediate importance to us here. The fact, however, that Böhm-Bawerk does not note this limitation, but fights the issue on the ground chosen by his adversary, shows that he himself is caught in the confusion of the two concepts, and is the strongest evidence of the inexpediency of the division of capital into social and private.[26] On the other hand, the fact is of immediate interest to us that Clark gives this narrower content to the term "capital," confining capital to "material forms of wealth that do not directly minister to consumers' wants,"[27] and does not make a place for acquisitive consumption goods, nor explain the interest from them, as is done by Böhm-Bawerk in his concept of private capital. In this respect the concept evidently needs addition or correction.

(2) In the second place, Clark's explanation of the genesis of capital is inconsistent with his own concept. Land used productively—for example, a farm, a waterfall, a mine, any rare and useful natural agent—is capital according to his definition. In his earlier utterances, such things are in plain words included.[28] In the later articles this is still the inevitable implication of the definition,—"a fund of productive wealth expressible in money"; but a reader new to the author's doctrine would find no specific statement to this effect, and there would be small chance that the meaning in question would be gathered. The whole logic of the argument is against it. "The genesis of capital," we are told, "takes place by a process for which the good old term 'abstinence' is, as I venture to maintain, the best designation."[29] This does not seem to give a place in capital to natural agents. There are, we are told, two classes of accumulators: the typical capitalists, who save to make permanent additions to their capital; and the quasi-capitalists, who "save sums now, intending to spend them later."[30] There is no place here for the unearned increment of a newly discovered mine, which to-day forms for many men the chief productive wealth expressible in money. If

this is saving, it is a sense so unusual as to require a special explanation by the author; and it is difficult to see how it can consistently be given. There certainly would be no attempt to evade the real question by assuming that the dollars that bought the mine had been saved; for the mine may not have been sold, and, if so, it is irrelevant to the issue. If the definition adopted by Clark is consistently applied, there are necessarily many things forming a part of capital which never have been saved, and which never have called for abstinence, as Clark employs that term.[31] In fact, Clark seems to show here, as did Böhm-Bawerk, some traces of the error of the labor theory of value, so difficult to throw off.[32]

(3) Again, Clark would seem to err by extreme statement in making it in the nature of capital to be a "permanent fund." "In creating capital, we put the personal good away from us forever. . . . An addition to the social fund of perpetual capital is brought into existence." "Nothing generates capital that does not add to the permanent fund of invested wealth."[33] "True capital . . . is, in the absence of untoward accidents, perpetual, and yields perpetual fruits."[34] Many other expressions emphasize the same thought. Now this evidently does not apply at all to the author's quasi-capitalist, who saves to spend later. That, of course, is why he uses the term "quasi," which evades the issue. Either such savings are capital (in which case why quasi?) or they are not capital, and may be omitted from the concept. The author, after stating that a part of the accumulation of capital is due to these quasi-capitalists, proceeds as if there were none such. If better or more tools and larger stocks were accumulated, and were then allowed to deteriorate while in use without being replaced, our author must certainly call them capital while they lasted; and, if so, the element of permanency is no essential part of the capital concept. Indeed, if a fund of productive wealth must be permanent to be capital, we cannot be sure that there is any such a thing; for we have not the gift of prophecy, and all human interests are fleeting.[35] Clark himself says, "Capital . . . normally will never perish"; but "this is not saying that no capital ever perishes in fact."[36] This says clearly enough that permanency is

not an essential mark of the concept, and makes meaningless both the word itself in that connection and a number of sentences, besides those quoted, in which this feature is emphasized as a vital mark of the concept. There is a valid thought in his contention, but it is not that capital is in its nature perpetual. There is ambiguity in the phrases "increase of capital" and "decrease of capital," because they may mean either some of the parts or the whole. A part of capital may perish while the total amount of capital is preserved or even increased. Clark would confine the expression to the whole of capital, and objects to the form of statement "capital is destroyed" when the value of the concrete goods is passed on to other goods. But what of the cases where the total value is not preserved? The zeal of his attack carries him to an extreme and untenable expression, and makes him insist upon an unessential.[37]

(4) Less successful than his contention against Böhm-Bawerk about "goods of like kind and quantity" is Clark's claim that capital "synchronizes all industry and its fruition," that because of capital "industry and its fruition are simultaneous." There are several objections to such an expression.

(a) I am not quite in sympathy with the point of view of either of the parties to the discussion, but between them it is a question not as to what happens,—not of fact,—but of expression; and Böhm-Bawerk's opinion commends itself when he says[38] it is a "figure of speech" that is "misleading" to say that the real wages, consisting of "consumption goods" received to-day for work done on goods not be completed for years, are the "true and immediate fruit" of, *e.g.,* the tanner's labor.[39] To the tanner, of course, they are the "immediate" and only fruits, since they are all he gets for his labor. The question is, does it seem logical and expedient from the general standpoint in economic discussion to consider and speak of them as the "true fruits" of that day's labor? The expression chosen appears to say merely that these things express the present market value of the laborer's services; that is, it is a roundabout and somewhat whimisical way of stating the truism that they are the man's wages.

(b) Further, it may be urged that the inaptness of this expression is more apparent when something other than subsistence goods is considered. In the example chosen of the tanner, it is at least debatable whether it is best to call the shoes he gets to-day the "true fruit" of his labor. But in the case of the laborer receiving food and clothing for digging a canal or working on a marble palace, it is straining the point further to use the expression. If here, too, his wages are called the "true fruit" of his labor, it still appears that the peculiar power ascribed to capital is due only to one part of capital, the finished consumption goods. No matter how large a stock of capital in the form of machines, buildings, and raw materials may be on hand, if there be no stock of finished goods, labor and its results are not synchronized.[40]

(c) A further objection to this way of conceiving of the nature of capital's work is that it would, if true, be applicable only to "produced" forms of capital. As indicated by the phrases "industry and its fruition," "labor and its fruits," it implies vaguely the labor theory of value as to the origin of capital. The picture of labor continuously flowing into the reservoir of capital and consumption goods at the same time flowing out[41] is not satisfactory as applied to products; for it implies that the inflow of a quantity of labor forces out consumption goods whose quantity is determined or measured by the quantity of inflowing labor. The value of consumption goods flowing out, however, is greater in varying degrees than the value of labor flowing in; and it is only through their values that we can compare at all the quantities of the two streams. Further, it is not a happy figure; for it suggests that all the goods that are a part of capital will eventually become consumption goods, whereas in many cases this is not expected nor desired. It is significant that Clark in describing the process speaks only of "the materials, raw and partly wrought," of which an article for consumption is made. He ignores machines and durable goods. It is only in the gradual passing on of their value, as they are used up, to the things that are made by them, that machines and more durable agents can be said to ripen at all.[42] Even Clark's value conception of capital, however, though it explains this point better than does the concrete concept of capital, does not avoid the difficulty. The point may be most clearly seen in the case of natural agents, which, as we have noted, are in Clark's treatment included in the "fund" of capital. If we consider not merely capital in the form of products more or less fitted for consumption, but, as his concept requires, durable natural agents also, the phrases we are criticizing appear hardly short of absurd. Clark forgets this kind when he says: "The capital goods that are set working are not permanent. They pass away, and are replaced."[43] Natural agents, the field, the waterfall, insofar as they are thought of apart from betterments upon them, have not been originated by labor; and they are not in a state of transformation that will eventually ripen them into consumption goods. They stand there to be used by man, if he wishes, as an aid in securing future harvests or products; but neither the things themselves nor their value or money expression is "synchronizing" labor and its fruits. If there is any synchronizing, it is done not by this, but by some other part of capital, and is, therefore, not an essential mark of the capital concept.

(5) It is likely that to some points in what has been thus far said the answer will be made that they are due to misunderstanding of the author's meaning. No doubt the author attaches great weight to the constrast he draws between true capital and capital goods, which it might seem I had neglected. The reply is a criticism stronger, perhaps, than any of the foregoing against Clark's capital concept. There is in his mode of thinking of this contrast an over-abstraction that is neither expedient nor logical; and there results in his presentation some inconsistency of thought and statement. In some passages, capital is said to be as concrete a thing as can be. It "consists in goods. It is not an abstraction, and it is not a force independently of matter. It has substance. If at any instant we could collect in one place all the material forms of wealth that do not directly minister to consumers' wants, we should have the fund for the moment before our eyes in substantial embodiment."[44] Capital is thus "productive wealth, expressible in money, but not embodied in money."[45] That is plain enough, and we are still on solid ground: we are not puzzled here by the "entity, effective social utility," of

the earlier statement,[46] where capital does not consist of the concrete things, but is the "fund that resides in many unlike things," and is "embodied in instruments of production." This has the unpleasant flavor of Marx's labor jelly, though it need not be taken as more than a loose, convenient way of expressing the market value of the concrete things. But the development that follows of the paradoxical contrasts between capital goods and true capital appears to be mischievous subtlety. The very adjectives "true" and "pure" applied to capital are suspicious. Why not plain "capital"? We are told that "the genesis of capital goods is unlike that of capital."[47] It would seem that, if capital consists of concrete goods, then making concrete goods is making capital. But the author says not, unless those goods are net additions to the stock; that is, more than replace the capital destroyed in the same time. "Build an altogether new engine. That is creating capital. Renewing an old one is only preserving capital."[48] The simple mode of expression that some capital has been created, while an equal amount has been destroyed, is thus not to be permitted. Surely, since capital has substance and consists in goods, there is only one way in which its amount can be preserved while some of it is being destroyed; and that is, by "creating" more capital to replace that destroyed. And what would be the circle within which the balance must be struck? Would it be the individual, the national, or the world economy? If John builds a machine while his neighbor lets one decay, then has John created no capital? It is true that care is often needed, in speaking of any increase, to indicate whether it is a net increase or not, but no more needed in the case of a "fund of capital" than in that of a herd of cattle. The striking antithesis of the goods that make up capital with the capital itself appears thus to be over-abstraction and unreality.

To sum up the objections to Clark's conception of capital:[49]

(1) It includes only goods used in "production," and does not recognize nor prepare to explain the interest-bearing qualities of consumption goods.

(2) It is confused in attributing the genesis of capital to abstinence (as he uses that word) while including in capital natural

agents for whose origin no abstinence was required.

(3) It errs in making permanency, or perpetuity, an essential mark of capital.

(4) The statement that an important, if not the chief, function of capital is to "synchronize industry and its fruition" is a misleading figure of speech. It can be affirmed, even figuratively, only of the part of produced goods that is to be at once consumed, and is quite meaningless as applied to the durable natural agents which are a part of his capital concept.

(5) The conception, starting from concrete goods, is developed away from them into a more abstract, dematerialized "pure" or "true" capital, which is put into contrast with real things.

3. Irving Fisher.

We now turn to the notable contribution of Professor Irving Fisher.[50] He lays a basis for his own treatment with sound statements as to the requisites of a good definition, and careful studies of the definitions and usage of the leading authorities. He believes that a mistake has been made as to the real character of the problem, that it is not one of the classification of wealth, and that unavoidable difficulties "attend every effort to delimit capital from 'other wealth.' "[51] His own conclusion, then, is that capital should be taken to mean simply all wealth at a point of time.[52] It is contrasted not with other wealth,—for that category is exhausted,—but with the same wealth as a flow during a given period, and at a rate. The contrast, then, is between a stock and a flow, and still more important "between stock and *rate* of flow."[53] This conception is ingeniously developed, use being made of mathematical terminology, and is applied in criticism of rival definitions. Finally, the attempt is made to show how it could be employed in the discussion of various economic questions.

To grasp more fully the import of this radical proposal in economic terminology, let us note in what regards it differs from the conceptions we have been considering.

(1) Its content is wider than that of any foregoing concept. Böhm-Bawerk excludes all natural agents and most consumption goods from his wider concept, private capital, and excludes the other consumption goods used in acquisition from the narrower concept of social capital. Clark appears at first to include all natural agents, though excluding all consumption goods, then treats capital as if it originated only in labor, and did not include natural agents, and finally mystifies us by his contrast of capital goods and pure capital, leaving us in doubt whether he would include any concrete things as such. Fisher's concept takes them all in, sweeps down the wall between the old concept of capital and consumption goods on the one hand and natural agents on the other. To my mind this suggestion is the most fertile part of Fisher's discussion.

(2) It agrees with Böhm-Bawerk's and differs from Clark's conception in considering that the concrete things should be estimated by physical measurements, and not in their money expression. The objection to Clark's view in this regard, he says, "is not that this summation of value is inadmissible, but that it is a secondary operation. Objects of capital are antecedent to the value of those objects. . . . Wheat must be measured in bushels before it is measured in dollars."[54] He, therefore, finds it a "serious objection to Clark's definition" that he endeavors "to include different sorts of capital in the same fund, reduced to a common equivalent in terms of value." Here, in my opinion, is a radical defect in Fisher's view. (a) It is true that wheat must "be measured in bushels before it can be measured in dollars," but it must also be tested for quality. One will not value as highly a small apple as a large one, a sour as a sweet one, a rotten as a sound one. We could thus say that apples must be measured in sweetness before being measured in value. But an inventory of all possible measurable qualities, while helpful in estimating, would not itself express the amount of capital, for the things might after all have no value at all. (b) Though an intelligible description of the quantity of any single kind of goods could be made in such terms, yet the total quantity of many different kinds of goods cannot be expressed for economic purposes in a

single sum excepting in terms of value. A capital account in which five pounds of feathers were added to a bushel of wheat and a yard of cloth would give a curious total. *(c)* Fisher is inevitably betrayed into inconsistency when he comes to estimate the quantities of wealth, and express in percentages the relation between the stock and rate of flow; for this can be done only by comparison of values.[55]

(3) This conception shares what I believe to be an error, common with it to both of the others,[56] in that it makes the income of a community consist of "streams . . . of the very same commodities"[57] that compose the total capital. This, again, implies that all things of value originate in labor, and are on their way towards the goal of consumption goods: whereas many things, standing where they are, may be made to push other things towards that goal, though never getting nearer to it themselves; *e.g.,* machines and natural agents. Fisher means by income a "flow of things" (material things), and rejects Mr. Edwin Cannan's conception "of income as a flow of pleasure," or satisfactions.[58] The book-keeping of society will be thrown badly out of balance if services be not counted as a part of income; but, even if services be included as a part both of income and of capital at a point of time, there are still many things, as above indicated, that are a part of Fisher's capital only, and never are a part of the flow of income. They never have been made for consumption, and never will be fitted for consumption.

(4) A final objection is that the term "capital" is made synonymous with wealth, and two good words are employed in the same sense. Fisher anticipates this objection, and recognizing its validity, if the fact be true, defends by saying that wealth presents the two aspects of income and stock (capital),— differences important enough to merit separate terms. This defence fails, if the point made in the preceding paragraph is sound. By wealth, Fisher must mean here "all wealth." As I have shown, all capital must be considered wealth, and all wealth capital by Fisher's definition, though all wealth has not been nor will all wealth become income. Wealth and capital thus are synonymous, while income differs from them not merely as an

aspect, but in the group of goods which composes it.

The concept under discussion is credited in part to Professor Simon Newcomb, is indorsed in the main by Mr. Edwin Cannan, and has received the approval of Professor Hadley in his *Economics.* Its merits and the ability of its presentation by Fisher have surely attracted other followers to one or another feature of it. It has therefore a worthy standing among the competing conceptions. Some portions of the presentation are most illuminating, and must be looked upon as distinct contributions to economic theory. Careful distinction between a stock of capital regularly employed, the turn-over in a business, and the income from a business have not always been made; and confusion has resulted. But this difficulty is not such as to call for the construction of the capital concept with that distinction as the central thought. On the whole, there is little probability that this conception will triumph, its defects both as to consistency and expediency being of an essential nature, its points of merit being capable of adaptation to another and better central thought.

We now have finished our review of the more notable recent conceptions, rivals to that put forward by Böhm-Bawerk. Though confined to a few names, it has necessarily taken a somewhat wide range in the points considered. It is hoped to use the fruits of this study in the next two divisions in which the analysis of Böhm-Bawerk's conception is resumed. I shall then go on to formulate more positively a capital concept which will be free, I trust, from the many objections that have been considered.

4. PRIVATE AND SOCIAL CAPITAL: AN ILLOGICAL DISTINCTION

I have sought in the foregoing to give a clear statement to the capital concept of Böhm-Bawerk and its recent rivals, those of Professors Clark and Fisher, to show the main points of difference, and finally to criticize in some detail the conceptions of these later writers. We are now prepared to return to the criti-

cism of Böhm-Bawerk's views which were the starting-point of
our study, and, taking up more thoroughly than before some of
the issues involved in his definition, to work towards a positive
conclusion.

The distinction between private and social capital is considered by Böhm-Bawerk to be of the very greatest importance,
and he deems his clear distinguishing of them to be one of his
highest services to economic theory. The failure to distinguish
them, he thinks, is the chief reason for the "false" productivity
theory of interest. If the difference is not seen between capital,
the source of interest, and capital, the tool in production, interest, he argues, is naturally thought to be due to productivity.
But, if it is clearly seen that a part of interest-bearing capital is not
a tool in production, then productivity cannot be the one essential explanation of interest. This point was evaded by Clark, as I
have shown;[59] for he simply considers social or productive
capital, and omits mention of acquisitive consumption goods. It
was not raised in his discussion with Clark by Böhm-Bawerk
himself, for his attention was fixed on other points; but in his
reply to Walker it is put very clearly. "There is interest without
any production whatever. . . . I refer, for example, to interest on
consumption loans and to the return on durable consumption
goods, such as rented houses, pianos, and the like."[60] Private
capital is, by his view, social or productive capital plus some other
things, enjoyable and more or less durable products let for hire
to the user. Of what importance is this class of goods that makes
all the difference between the two concepts? He has here
mentioned rented houses and pianos: the stock illustration is the
masquerade suit let by the costumer. A complete list of these
articles would include a very small amount of wealth compared
with that in social capital, and, doubtless, very much less than
that in the rest of consumption goods. Yet it would be wrong to
claim on this account that it is not worth while to make a difference in the concept. Logical differences of any importance
call for distinctions in concepts, no matter how slight be the
quantitative differences. I pass, therefore, to a criticism of the
logical grounds for such a distinction.

(1) There is no need to make an independent conception on account of this group of income-bearing things, if an explanation can be given that will dispose of them in a simpler way. Here are two houses lived in by the owners in two neighboring towns. They are called consumption goods, bearing no income. Owner A moves into another house, paying $300 rent, letting his own for an equal sum. His house then becomes acquisitive capital. Owner B does the same, and his house becomes capital. Chance or choice leads each to occupy the other's house. Each, through a broker and without knowing who his tenant is, pays the other $300 yearly, and both houses are capital. Shortly, they move back into their own houses, which at once cease to be capital; and the "income" of each man is reduced $300.

The puzzle is an old one. It compels us to say that a thing becomes capital or ceases to be capital not because of any change in its physical or economic nature, not because it is more or less serviceable to the community, not because the use to which it is put is altered, but simply because the man who owns it does or does not happen to be the one who enjoys that use. Now Böhm-Bawerk himself, in his interest theory, has given us a hint of the way such an absurdity can be avoided without the use of a separate concept,[61] though he does not see the application possible here. The person who rents a house buys the "material services" of the thing during a definite period. The whole value of the house is simply the sum of a long series of uses. To the logical eye, though not to the technical eye of the law, the tenant or user is the owner of the thing during the time, with only such conditions as will insure its safe keeping and return at the close of the period. It may be looked upon as a sale to the tenant of a use or a group of uses defined by a period of time, and with the agreement to return the use-bearer when a group that has not been purchased begins to mature. The value of the unpurchased uses does not appear in the transaction, but they are bound up with the use-bearer that is given and returned. The dancer is often compelled to deposit the price of the masquerade suit when he takes it out. After the ball is over, his subjective valuation having fallen, he is the gainer by returning it at an agreed price which to the costumer represents its worth as stock to him. The latter keeps such things in stock because there are, on an average, enough such sales to pay his trouble, expenses, and a return on that amount of stock. Such rented consumption goods, being owned for the time by the user, form, then, no exception to the general class of consumption goods The income of the dealer or the house owner is explained as a profit gained in exchange, like that of any other retail merchant, and includes a payment for services, risk, and income from stock employed. To explain such transactions as the sale of a group of uses (which is actually the temporary sale of the use-bearer) is entirely consistent with Böhm-Bawerk's treatment of interest, and makes needless the elaborate distinction between private and social capital.

(2) The foregoing would seem to be a valid reply, at all events as an *argumentum ad hominem,* to Böhm-Bawerk; but it may appear to some to be too elaborate and artificial. The distinction in question may then be attacked on the still stronger ground that it confuses things economic and legal. It is based on an unclear view of the relations of economic and contract interest. Let us look at this distinction. Contract interest is the interest actually paid by one person to another as the result of an agreement. Economic interest is the advantage attributable to the possession and use of a thing during a given period, regardless of its ownership. There is economic interest when a man uses his own plough to raise a crop or his own storeroom as a place of business.[62] Now, in the case of all the things included under social (productive) capital, contract is based on and tends to conform to economic interest. In all such cases it is economic interest that we seek to explain logically through the economic nature of the goods. Contract interest is a secondary problem,—a business and legal problem,—as to who shall have the benefit of the income arising with the possession of the goods. It is closely connected with the question of ownership. Only by accident, mistaken judgment, or old agreements, can the contract interest connected with social capital continue when

economic interest does not. The two are related as cause and effect. Yet in the case of the relatively small group of consumption goods let for hire there is in the current view here represented by Böhm-Bawerk only contract interest, there being supposed to be no economic interest on which it is based. The economist's problem in distribution is essentially an impersonal one, to determine the economic contribution regardless of the question of legal ownership. Here, if it be held that there is no economic interest or contribution, we have an anomalous case where the final answer to the interest problem must contain a mixture of economic and legal elements. No solution of this contradiction will, I believe, be found short of the view that contract and economic interest are normally inseparable. By "normally" I mean that no man contracts to pay interest, or, being free to choose, actually does pay it, unless he has reason to believe that he thereby will gain the benefit of what must be called economic interest of a somewhat greater amount.

(3) This brings us to another objection to the distinction between social and private capital; namely, that it involves a wrong conception of the nature of income. I shall maintain that income must be looked upon as a series or group of satisfactions, not as a series or group of material things. Though scattered authority may be found for this view, it is at variance with the views alike of Böhm-Bawerk, of Clark, and of Fisher, as well as those of the great majority of economists, and requires explanation and defense. The thesis is that the economic goods which are "produced" either by human effort or by the material services of goods must, in their last analysis, be looked upon as satisfactions. Böhm-Bawerk notices this view as expressed by Roscher, and rejects it;[63] yet the view is one peculiarly in harmony with the psychological treatment of value which Böhm-Bawerk favors. Indeed, it seems to me the view to which that value theory logically and inevitably leads. Roscher fails to apply this thought consistently, as Böhm-Bawerk rightly shows;[64] and with that we will not concern ourselves. The view suggested looks upon all material goods as means of production or capital, their

value being derived from the states of satisfaction to which they minister or which they enhance. Böhm-Bawerk's objection to this lacks validity. He says: "Any unbiased person can see how unfortunate this is. Without due cause it obliterates the very important distinction between the production of goods which satisfy want and their consumption. It christens, for example, the idler as a zealous producer, always thinking how he may produce the personal goods of satiety, of ease, of contentment, and so on." It needs only to be replied to this that the idler in such case would be wrongly christened. The term "means of production" must be confined to objective means of producing a subjective state, not to subjective states, to Buddhistic dreams that unite the dreamer with Nirvana. The pleasure of basking in the sun is a fact of which economic theorists must take note; but that pleasure can be secured usually by the use of free goods, and thus is not an economic satisfaction. It becomes an economic satisfaction when it is conditioned on the control of some scarce material agent or can be secured only by effort. The test, then, of economic personal goods or satisfactions is dependence on either objective things or persons, or on reaction against the outer world by the man seeking the satisfaction. If the objection of Böhm-Bawerk is urged beyond the extreme and inapplicable example he has given, and is applied to the personal services of one man for another, it leads to the old and abandoned distinction between productive and unproductive labor. We do christen many men "as zealous producers because they are producing the personal goods of satiety,"—in other men. Such services must be counted as ephemeral forms of wealth, enjoyed or consumed at the moment of their production. This is no more obliterating the distinction between production and consumption than eating a hot cake fresh from the griddle obliterates that distinction. The two things are as logically separable in thought when they occur simultaneously as when a second or a decade intervenes. We have ceased to consider it essential to "productive" labor that it should be first embodied in material form, however fleeting. The same untenable distinction is adhered to almost universally in the case of the services of material goods.

Their productive contributions must be put on the same basis as those of labor, to be measured by the intensity of the wants they aid in satisfying and the psychic states they help to produce. The house of the mill-owner is, logcially considered, producing directly, his mill is producing indirectly; for only after a devious journey will the contribution of the mill reach its goal in the satisfaction of wants. Our economic book-keeping can be made to balance only when *real* income be looked upon as a flow of pleasure in all cases, not as a flow of goods in some and a flow of pleasures in others, as is done generally now.

(4) This view makes possible the correction in the concepts of private and social capital of another fault which calls for our fourth and last objection to this part of the almost universally accepted treatment. The fault is this. Interest is looked upon as connected with a special class of goods: it must be recognized to be connected with everything of value.[65] The value of anything is built up on its uses or services to men. Wherever there is a postponed use, that use is subject to a discount. Its present worth is less than its worth will be at maturity. Consider the case of consumption goods. In the orthodox view a bushel of apples, kept by the grocer from fall till spring, is capital, and normally shows economic interest in enhanced value. Bought in the fall and stored in the cellar by the housewife, it is a consumption good; and economic interest is absent. But that early purchase can only be rationally explained as we take account of the increment of value on the apples thus stored, and this is economic interest. Larger purchases in advance effect, of course, economy of labor, and bring an additional motive to make them; but this is not saying that the whole saving is wages, and that no interest is gained.

The radical consequences of this view are evident. It erases all distinction between the essential economic character of so-called productive and consumption goods. The term "consumption goods" may still be conveniently retained to mean, as at present, the material good in its final form in the hands of the one intending to use it; but it ceases to be an essential economic category. Every material good and every human service has value only as it is a condition to the satisfying of a present or prospective want. The abiding value of the diamond is built on no more substantial foundation than its flash and sparkle. Market values are the capitalized economic contribution of objective agents to psychic states; and these states are the final, highest, only essential economic products.

To sum up the objections to the concepts of private and social capital:

(1) The distinction between them rests on a supposed difference in the interest-bearing character of different groups of consumption goods. This difference can be explained in a simple way that makes needless an additional concept.

(2) The distinction between them rests on legal, not on economic grounds, and involves a confusion of economic and contract interest.

(3) The distinction rests on an incomplete and illogical view of the nature of income and the services of goods. The income that needs to be explained by economic theory is the flow of objectively created pleasures coming to the individual and the community.

(4) In these concepts the interest-bearing quality is confined to the conventional production goods and such consumption goods as yield contract interest. Many actions connected with "consumption goods" are left unexplained. The interest phenomenon is found wherever there is abiding value.

Our conclusion, then, is that the distinction between social (or productive) and private (or acquisitive) capital rests on illogical grounds. Böhm-Bawerk thinks it a great advantage that "not withstanding the material difference there is between capital, the factor of production, and capital, the source of interest, it is not necessary in [his] reading to make two conceptions of capital that are entirely foreign to one another."[66] We must assert on the other hand that the two conceptions he has given us are so largely foreign to one another[67] that, instead of an advantage, it is a source of much confusion that they are called by the same name, as every careful reader of Böhm-Bawerk's work must have noted. For example, he defines capital at the beginning of his discussion[68] as "nothing but the complex of intermediate products which appear on the several stages of the roundabout journey." By this he evidently means his social capital; and he then proceeds to show that "capital in general"—that is, private capital—is something more than such a complex. The reader is frequently in doubt which one of these different concepts is designated when the word "capital" is used. A great advantage will be gained when, dropping unessential distinctions, we are able to save the term from double meanings.

5. *CAPITAL AS PRODUCT: THE LABOR-VALUE FALLACY*

Thus far we have considered only the question of the uses to which goods are put as determining whether they are capital. Böhm-Bawerk's definition, however, in common with nearly all usage, limits the conception of capital in another way; namely, with regard to its origin. As well private as social capital consists of a "group of products." In the foregoing, I have widened the term productive as applied to consumption goods; but the products there mentioned (feelings, satisfactions), being ephemeral, do not increase the capital stock existing at a given moment. And, being final products, these states of feeling cannot be used in further economic processes, and do not, therefore, widen the definition Böhm-Bawerk has given us. The test so far applied to these concepts has been alone that of economic function. Confining capital to material "products," as does Böhm-Bawerk, applies an additional and distinct test,—that of economic origin,—and must be separately examined.

The purpose of the adjective "produced" in the phrase "produced means of production" is to exclude land. While conceding that there are some good reasons for including land under capital, Böhm-Bawerk declines to do so for the reasons which we may enumerate, as follows:—

1. Land is immovable. Capital is, for the most part, movable.

2. Land is a gift of nature. Capital is a result of labor.

3. Land cannot be increased, capital can be.

4. The social and economical position of the landlord is essentially different from that of the capitalist.

5. Property in land and property in movables are justified on essentially different grounds, and they are commonly attacked by quite distinct people.

6. Land is the special agent in a kind of production [agriculture?] that is economically distinguished by many important peculiarities.

7. The income from land differs in many ways from income from capital.

8. Using capital for all material means of acquisition leaves us no name for produced acquisitive instruments.

9. Popular usage does not put land under capital, but opposes the two.

10. Usage does not apply the term "interest" to the income from land.[69]

He concludes that "it is most convenient to keep land quite distinct from other kinds of productive wealth," and that "there is a considerable balance in favor of defining capital as the 'produced means of acquisition,' and against the inclusion of land."[70]

Of this formidable list it must be said that not a reason given, considered singly, is free from flaw, some are quite mistaken, and collectively they are not conclusive. The worth of 1 is destroyed for purposes of definition by the limitation "for the most part." It is not that a definition may not be based on a difference in degree, where qualities grade off from one extreme to another; and, if something of importance depends on the degree, it may often be expedient to draw a line of division more or less arbitrarily somewhere. Here, however, it is not so. Things, like houses, ditches, trees, that are as firmly fixed as the soil itself and whose value would be quite lost if they were moved, are, without a question, included in capital. Turning to the other part of the statement, that land is immovable, it is found quite as untrue. Parts of land are shifting from day to day. It is usual for those who follow this definition to consider that a thing ceases to be land and becomes capital the instant it is moved by man's agency or effort; but to appeal to this to prove the point is to confound "unmoved" with "immovable." No matter is immovable. To say that "land" means something that has not been moved by man begs the question, and this is evidently an untenable definition of nature or material agents. Some writers who have followed out such reasoning have been led to narrow the essential concept of land down to mere situation,[71] or, differently expressed, to the "geometric relations in which any part of it stands to other parts.[72] This is a very different idea from the one here defended by Böhm-Bawerk, and would not be consistent with some of the other reasons of this list. Reason 1 in the list appears to be an illogical use of reason 2, it being falsely assumed that results of labor are necessarily movable in the relative sense in which we can use that term of material things, and that gifts of nature are immovable. No such parallelism exists, and the two reasons are often in conflict.

Passing 2 and 3 for later and fuller consideration, we take up 4 and 5, which appeal to social and personal grounds of distinction, not to economic and impersonal ones. Here is again a confusion of the political or legal question of ownership with the real economic question, the function performed or contribution made by material agents. This difference, moreover, in the social position of landlord and capitalist, so emphasized, can be shown to rest on accidental historical grounds which we cannot now discuss. Again, the emphasis of this difference is largely due to the misleading terminology which is under discussion. And, finally, I would contest the statement that property in land and "movables" is justified on essentially different grounds. They must be, and are by most political theorists of to-day, justified on exactly the same ground.

In 6 and 7 appeal is made to differences in economic nature. In reason 6 there is again the fallacy of thinking of land as a field used for agriculture. It must be said, first, that land, in the sense of the word under discussion,—*i.e.*, natural agents—is an indispensable agent of the milling industry, carpentry, and every other art, as well as of agriculture. To call land the "special" agent of agriculture because that part of land which consists of fertile soil is necessary for plant life is to make a very crude distinction, based on no logical principle. At most a difference of degree only is involved, in that a larger area is usually needed to produce a given value of food than is needed to produce that value of other things; but the reverse is frequently true. Secondly, it may be said that "the important peculiarities" (the chief of which no doubt is thought of as the law of diminishing returns) here attributed to agriculture are in no way peculiar to it. The belief that they are rests largely on the basis of a false terminology. As to 7, likewise, we have a begging of the question; for the differences in our ways of regarding interest and rent are primarily due to the terminology whose correctness is under discussion. Finally, it must be noted that, when Böhm-Bawerk comes to explain interest from durable goods,[73] he refutes the statement that income from land differs in many ways from income from capital, and, "obeys many distinct laws of its own."[74] He then finds that the two incomes "have one common final cause."[75] "Land rent is nothing but a special case of interest obtained from durable goods."[76]

In 8, 9, and 10 the appeal is to usage which is shifting, and by no means uniform in the direction Böhm-Bawerk assumes. As to 8, the reply is that it will be an advantage not to designate by special names the group mentioned if it is shown, as will be done later, that such a group should not, either for logical or practical purposes, be marked off from the other parts of capital. Indeed, it is one of the most important advantages of a different terminology that it gets rid of the figment in question. Reasons 9 and 10 contain doubtful statements. Popular usage and economists, even those who favor Böhm-Bawerk's terminology, in many cases class land under capital, speaking of the investment of capital in land, and reckoning the land with the man's capital thereafter. So, when a loan is made in money, we are always told that the thing really borrowed is what the money buys: if machines, then it is really these for which interest is paid;

if a farm, then it is this for which interest is paid. The moment you give the money aspect to the loan, no attempt is made to distinguish between the income from land and the income from other material agents.

I have left to the last reasons 2 and 3, which, stated together, read that land is a gift of nature and cannot be increased, while capital is a result of labor and can be increased. This thought is the central one in the distinction: it is the parent of all the other reasons; and we here trace to their source the errors just considered. The trail of the serpent, the mark of the labor theory of value, is over the whole treatment of capital as the product of former labor. Böhm-Bawerk does not escape it. He has indeed given a most able refutation of that theory,[77] and takes frequent opportunities to stamp it with his disapproval. In his later volume he says that the phrase "stock of accumulated labor" is a metaphor,[78] and, again, that it is employing a mere "figure of speech" to speak of capital as "previous labor" or "stored-up labor."[79] In refuting socialist views, he has shown that capital "is not exclusively 'previous labor' "[80]; but he is not free from his own criticism when he adds: "but it is partly and, indeed, as a rule, it is principally, 'previous labor'; for the rest, it is valuable natural power stored up for human purposes."[81] Later he again makes greater limitations on the proposition, and says: "The asserted 'law,' that the value of goods is regulated by the amount of the labor incorporated in them, does not hold at all in the case of a very considerable proportion of goods; in the case of the others, does not hold always, and never holds exactly. These are the facts of experience with which the value theorists have to reckon."[82] In these statements we have the view that the value of capital is not in proportion to previous labor, and that capital owes its value partly to scarce and valuable natural powers. The same idea appears elsewhere. "Capital—to keep the same form of expression—is 'stored-up labor,' but it is something more: it is also stored-up valuable natural power."[83] The part attributed to natural powers reaches at times the vanishing-point as Böhm-Bawerk shows;[84] but he does not draw the obvious inference that the part of labor reaches at times the vanishing-point, and that many products, many things classed by him as capital, are exclusively "stored-up" natural powers. Why continue to apply the phrase "products of labor" more than "products of nature" to those things which owe to labor proportions of their value varying from all to nothing? Where there is no labor, would Böhm-Bawerk cease to call the thing capital? Certainly not, must be the answer, if that is the only difference. To take his own illustration, used against Rodbertus for another purpose: "If a lump of solid gold in the shape of a meteoric stone falls on a man's field,"[85] will it not be capital as much as any other piece of gold? According to proposition 2, which we are criticizing, it would not be capital, but land, being a "gift of nature."

In truth, Böhm-Bawerk does not concern himself about any such difficulties, but speaks literally of capital in the very phrase he has called a metaphor. He says, "The next stage of the controversy brings us to the question whether we are to give the name of capital only to the *products of labor* that serve for acquisition, the 'previous stored-up labor,' or are to include land."[86] Again, he approves the same usage when he says, "Mill has so far yielded to the pressure of facts as to admit that capital is itself the product of labor, and that its instrumentality in production is, therefore, in reality, that of labor in an indirect shape."[87] It seems to Böhm-Bawerk self-evident that capital is produced. "Every child knows that a piece of capital, say a hammer, must be produced if it is to come into existence."[88] Now there might be some uncertainty, taking the sentence alone, as to just what is meant here by "produced"; but the context shows that this means just what the last-quoted sentence does, that capital is produced by labor. In the discussion of the roundabout method of production he consciously omits[89] from the productive powers the uses of land "for the sake of simplification," and assumes that the annual endowment of powers consists only of "labor years." There is the danger in this omission that it may accustom the author and his readers to the thought that capital indeed consists of stored-up labor alone. In fact, most products are due to the use of both sources of production; but supposing he had omitted "for the sake of simplification" the labor years, and had assumed that the productive powers of land alone produced all goods. Such cases, in fact, occur where a fixed flow of goods from natural agents has an annual value without the aid of man. Yet it probably never would have occurred to Böhm-Bawerk to speak of such goods as products if, as is usually the case, they were not fully fitted for consumption, hence were intermediate goods. I have looked in vain not only in his writings, but through economic literature, for an admission that capital may be a "product" of unassisted nature as fully as it can be the product of labor. Yet there seems no valid reason why that view should not be held, the only reason why it is not being that the labor theory of value still influences the thoughts and utterances of men.

Our immediate study, let us recall, is the validity of a distinction between capital and land, on the ground that the one is and the other is not the product of labor. We have just seen the difficulty of applying it in the case of capital. We must now note that Böhm-Bawerk gives up the attempt to apply it strictly to land. He says that improvements on land, so far as they are completely incorporated with it, "are to be kept separate from capital *for the same reasons*[90] which made us keep land itself separate from capital."[91] Evidently, the author deceives himself. He has forgotten one of the most important reasons for the distinction, the one we are discussing; namely, that capital is the result of labor, and land is not. In this case he is classing the improvements with land, not because, but in spite of the fact that they are the results of labor. He sees the difficulty, and in a note says: "I may be accused of want of logic here on the ground that such improvements are always products which serve towards further production, and therefore come under our definition of capital."[92] But he argues, "The criticism is correct as to the letter, but wrong as to the spirit." What can the spirit of the distinction be that is so opposed to the words of the definition? We get this answer: "A stay propped up against a tree is certainly not the tree itself, but an outside body. But who would still call it an outside body if after some years it had grown inseparable from the tree?"[93] So far as this has any application at all, it disproves what the author wishes to support; for we should not call a stick around which the tree had grown a part of the tree. The tree has the unity of life and organization, and the stay is no part of it. The essential thing for us, however, is that here also is a set of cases in which Böhm-Bawerk finds it practically impossible to make the distinction between capital and land depend on whether their source is in labor. Though the source of their value is in labor, some things are to be classed with natural agents because they are physically inseparable from natural agents. May we not ask why, if the labor is incorporated in the land, does not the land become capital? In some cases a touch of labor is all that is needed to "produce" goods of large value from natural materials, which are then called capital. Why call a combination of natural agents and labor land at one time and capital at another? A satisfactory reason, if there be one, has never yet been given.

To sum up the objections to the attempt to make the distinction between land and capital rest on the absence or presence of labor:—

1. Some capital, things treated as such by Böhm-Bawerk and others, is not the result of labor at all,—for example, the meteoric lump of gold, the annual crop of fruits on an untilled field, the yield of a mineral spring.

2. It is not logical to call capital a result or product of labor, any more than to call it a result or product of land. Nearly all capital owes in part its economic existence to labor; but its value is not measured by the "amount of labor," whatever that may mean, any more than it is measured by the amount of uses of land. In fact, we have no way of expressing the amount of labor or of uses of land, except through their value.

3. If the mere presence of labor in producing the present values is what is meant by "production," then, practically, all land must be classed as capital; for there is little of it that has not had its value enhanced by labor applied to it.

4. The attempt to distinguish between the part of the value of a material thing that is due to labor and the part that is due to nature, keeping thus nature (or land) and capital distinct, is vain

when once the labor has been spent. This is recognized by Böhm-Bawerk in certain cases, like permanent improvements on agricultural fields; but this case differs in no essential from every other case where scarce natural materials are united with labor. It is purely arbitrary to call some such combinations land, and others capital.

5. Finally, it is not true that land, as understood by the business man or the economist when he really comes to his problem, consists only of the gifts of nature. Large areas are made and reclaimed, and then are treated precisely the same way as the land that exists little changed since coming from nature's hand.

The reasons are so many and conclusive against this distinction that only the influence of the labor theory of value over those who think themselves emancipated from it can explain the persistence of the error. Yet this distinction is of the essence of Böhm-Bawerk's concept of capital. A consistent capital concept never can be based upon it.

6. *A RESTATEMENT OF THE CAPITAL CONCEPT.*

We have seen[94] that Böhm-Bawerk holds the view that capital should be taken to consist of concrete goods, and that he opposes strongly any attempt to make "some kind of abstraction the essence of capital."[95] He does not think that capital should be spoken of as a "sum of value" or as "circulating power" or as "purchasing power."[96] He believes that capital consists of "the common material goods called mills, looms, ploughs, locomotives." It is these, and not "an immaterial sum of value," which "can grind corn, or spin yarn, or plough up land, or carry a load."[97] We have seen that the attack of Clark on the work of Böhm-Bawerk assumes that the concrete conception is the one that Böhm-Bawerk makes use of, and that it is a false one. Our criticism of Böhm-Bawerk's treatment is on a different line; namely, that he has not one, but two concepts of capital,[98] and that, while defining capital as if it could be spoken of without reference to value or the use of value expressions, he employs a value concept almost entirely in his reasoning on the interest problem. He makes a shift without being conscious of it, and makes use of the concept which Clark criticizes him for ignoring.

In the concept of capital must be united both the thought of concrete things and that of their value, for their quantity is only measurable in a way that permits of comparison in terms of value. There is nothing metaphysical or abstract about this: it is what business men are doing constantly. They do not attempt to compare amounts of capital by physical standards of measurement. Things which lose their value are no longer counted as capital, no matter how large their amount. A change in the quality involving a change in value or in value of a given quality is at once counted as a change in the quantity of capital. And the idea of capital is carried over to all things of value, regardless of the question of the origin of the good. Böhm-Bawerk illustrates this usage frequently, for example, when he speaks of the "capital value of land,"[99] and, again, in making use of the word "capitalization" in explaining the value of land and interest arising from it.[100]

The business man, followed by the economist when he comes to discuss practical problems, starts with the thought of a man with a sum of money to spend for buying goods; and this buying is called "investing" his capital, or, as the word originally meant "clothing," the money in the form of other material things. When the money is thus "invested," it may be in the form of machines, buildings, lands, products on which labor has been employed. If the investment has been fortunate, we say, comparing the values with the value of the money expended, that the capital has increased. Now there is of course some danger of confusing capital with money, but no more than in every case where money is used to express the value of other goods. What is the capital? Either the money or the thing whose value is expressed in money. Money is itself a concrete thing, one in which the value of other things is expressed. It is this expression and measurement of market value which is the essence of the capital concept in much business usage, as well as in most economic discussion, no matter what may be the formal definition. This must be recognized in our definition.

Capital, in our conception, is an aspect of material things, or, better, it consists of material things considered in one aspect,—their market value. It is under this aspect that men have come more and more to look at wealth. The growth of a money-economy has made it more and more convenient to compare and measure the value of dissimilar things in terms of dollars. Things are thus capitalized. A writer, tracing the development of the wealth concept, has well pointed out that at one time wealth was looked upon as consisting of things of use to the owner, lands, flocks, herds,—use-values, to use the old phrase,—but that now it is looked upon as made up of things having exchange value, estimated in terms of the general standard of value in the community.[101] He would confine the term "wealth" to this latter concept, leaving the former without any special name; while the proposal here is to confine the term "wealth" to the former concept, and apply to the latter the term "capital." We thus adhere as closely as possible to popular usage. We should thus speak of a man's wealth as consisting of a number of acres of land, a herd of horses or cattle, a number of machines or ships; but we should say that his capital consisted of so many thousand dollars' worth of land, cattle, and the like. We say that a company has a capital of so many thousand dollars, and it is invested in buildings and machinery. The distinction between nominal capital and paid-up capital, and that between the capital stock consisting of paper certificates or shares and the capital of valuable material things, present no serious difficulties. Wealth and capital consist of precisely the same things. Wealth is the popular expression for goods the exact valuation of which is not stated. Capital is merely the ordinary market value expression of wealth. As we cannot give to the value of anything an arithmetical expression except in terms of some other concrete thing, we find it most convenient to express it in terms of money. The increase or decrease of capital is not measured by any ultimate standard. The changes in its money expression do not necessarily reflect changes in the welfare of the community or of the individual. Over periods of time, changes in the quantity of capital can only be determined in a conventional way, by men's agreeing to accept one commodity or group of commodities as a standard. But at any moment the different portions of capital are homogeneous, and can be compared, added, or subtracted as we see men doing every day in business.

The term "property," again, is loosely used in place of wealth or capital, but can be clearly distinguished from them as the legal, not the economic, aspect of valuable material things. In short, "property" has as its essence the idea of legal right; and in connection with material things the important right is that of control. Ownership is simply a greater or less degree of control. The term "property," meaning legal rights of control, is broader; that is, extends to more things than the terms "wealth" or "capital," for it includes patent rights, legal monopolies, valuable agreements from men to do or not to do certain things, all having the common feature that the value is not attached to or connected with or attributed to a material thing, but is due to the legal right to control or limit some person's action. It seems inadvisable to try to make the content of wealth as large as that of property by considering that men become wealthy to the degree that their rights are limited in the interest of others.[102] To illustrate the use of the terms "wealth," "capital," and "property," we would say that a stock of goods is wealth, it is (or it represents) a capital of $10,000, and it is the property of Jones, and the property is worth $10,000. If Brown holds a mortgage of $5,000 on the property, however the lawyers may look at it, we must consider that Jones's property (or right) is only of the value of $5,000. The property of Brown and that of Jones are both found within the capital of $10,000, and in total value cannot exceed it. The value of the property owned never can exceed the capital that is the object of the legal right. Many absurdities in our laws of taxation have resulted from confusing the economic view of wealth with the legal question of ownership, and of confusing, still less excusably the mere paper evidences of legal rights with the wealth to which those rights apply.

To restate the definition that has been arrived at: *Capital is economic wealth whose quantity is expressed in a general value unit.* It is used as applying to a single thing or to a group of things. There is no place in it for the distinction, the inconsistencies of which have been discussed, between individual and social capital. We do not call the services of things that minister directly to satisfaction unproductive while calling the personal services of men productive, even where nothing material results. We do not retain the distinction between consumption and production goods as essential in economic discussion. All valuable things of more than momentary duration are "intermediate goods," are capital, in that they are valuable because designed to satisfy future wants. While the definition thus sweeps away any limitation on the content of capital because of a difference in future use, it likewise sweeps away any limitation because of a difference in the origin or source of its value. Capital is not thought of as made up only of goods whose value is the result of labor. It has been shown that the prevailing distinction between "natural agents" and "produced agents" of production involves radical defects of logic and is practically not maintained. This definition is emancipated from the false labor theory of value. In regard to the contending views—first, that capital consists of concrete goods, and, second, that it is the value of goods,—the definition harmonizes them by defining capital as consisting of the concrete things, but only when considered as homogeneous and comparable units of value.

I would not exaggerate the significance of the change here proposed in the capital concept, yet it would be folly to ignore the consequences its acceptance would involve for economic theory. Text-books must be rewritten, and many questions must be re-examined. This is not because the concept is unused by the older writers, but because they have used it without recognizing how different it was from their formal definitions and the concept employed in other parts of their work. Many students of recent years have felt the need of a readjustment of the leading economic concepts. This concept requires and makes possible such a readjustment. The current theories of land value, of rent, of interest, to a greater or less extent rest on the unsound ideas which have been criticized throughout this paper. On another occasion the writer will attempt to state the outlines of an economic system of thought in harmony with the capital concept here presented.

NOTES

1. We will note later his abandonment of this idea, calling the rent of land "interest" (*Positive Theory*, 355) and ascribing interest to all consumption goods, even those not included in capital. Ibid., 350.

2. *Positive Theory*, p. 24, ff.

3. Ibid., p. 42, ff.

4. Ibid., p. 27.

5. Ibid., p. 31, ff.

6. *Positive Theory*, pp. 43-59.

7. Ibid., p. 31.

8. Ibid., p. 38.

9. *Positive Theory*, p. 59.

10. Ibid., p. 60.

11. Ibid., Preface, p. xxiii.

12. E.g., Horace White on "Böhm-Bawerk on Capital," *Political Science Quarterly*, vii. 133-148; General Walker, "Böhm-Bawerk's Theory of Interest," in *Quarterly Journal of Economics*, vi. 399-416.

13. "The Genesis of Capital," *Yale Review*, ii. 302-315; "The Origin of Interest," *Quarterly Journal of Economics*, ix. 257.

14. *Publications of American Economic Association*, iii. (1888).

15. *Positive Theory*, pp. 33, 34.

16. *Yale Review*, ix. 307.

17. *Publications of American Economic Association*, iii. 91.

18. *Yale Review*, ii. 308.

19. *Quarterly Journal of Economics*, ix. 257.

20. *Quarterly Journal of Economics*, ix. 116.

21. Ibid., 380.

22. Ibid., 263.

23. *Positive Theory*, pp. 17-23.

24. *Quarterly Journal of Economics*, ix. 258.

25. *Yale Review*, ii. 304.

26. A fuller discussion of this point is given later, p. 49.

27. *Yale Review*, ii. 307.

28. *Publications of American Economic Association*, iii. 95, 112.

29. *Yale Review*, ii. 309.

30. Ibid., 303, 304.

31. *Yale Review,* ii. 309. I must dissent from Clark's opinion that the term "abstinence" is, in the discussion of value theories, to be applied only to the first act of saving. See this view in *Quarterly Journal,* ix. 260, 261. In a more useful sense it is a power of choice that is continuously present during the foregoing of the right to consume wealth, at every moment during which a man could convert the principal of interest-bearing capital into a source of present enjoyment.

32. This point is treated more fully later, p. 57.

33. *Yale Review,* ii. 309.

34. Ibid., 312.

35. This has already been observed by Fisher, *Economic Journal,* vi. 530.

36. *Yale Review,* ii. 309.

37. See further on this, *infra,* pp. 44-45.

38. *Quarterly Journal of Economics,* ix. 124, 125.

39. *Yale Review,* ii. 312.

40. This is a somewhat different presentation of Böhm-Bawerk's argument in *Quarterly Journal of Economics,* ix. 125-128.

41. *Yale Review,* ii. 310, 311.

42. Böhm-Bawerk appears to have very much the same conception of products ripening into consumption goods, in his circles of production periods. See *Positive Theory,* 93, 106-108.

43. *Yale Review,* ix. 312.

44. *Yale Review,* ii. 307.

45. Ibid.

46. *Publications of American Economic Association,* iii. 11.

47. *Yale Review,* ii. 308.

48. *Quarterly Journal of Economics,* ix. 275.

49. This article was in the editor's hands before the appearance of Professor Clark's latest work, *The Distribution of Wealth.* The views of the author on the capital concept there expressed show no essential change from those here examined, and the criticism stands as first written.

50. In three articles, *Economic Journal,* vi. 509; vii. 199, 511 (1896-97.)

51. Ibid., vi. 513.

52. Ibid., p. 514.

53. *Economic Journal,* vi. 515.

54. Ibid., p. 530.

55. *E.g.,* at the very outset, *Economic Journal,* vi. 515.

56. See as to Clark, *supra,* p. 43.

57. *Economic Journal,* vi. 514, ff.

58. *Economic Journal,* vi. 534.

59. *Supra,* p. 39.

60. *Quarterly Journal of Economics,* ix. 253.

61. Especially in *Positive Theory,* 339-349.

62. I should add, if the income is estimated as a percentage of the capital value.

63. *Positive Theory,* p. 44.

64. Ibid., p. 45.

65. Here we develop some of the thoughtful suggestions of Fisher, though differing with his view in ways already suggested. See *Economic Journal,* vii. 525.

66. *Positive Theory,* p. 40.

67. Ibid., p. 61. He says here, flatly contradicting his own words just quoted: "Substantially, [the conception of social capital] is a quite independent conception. In every essential respect (in definition, in scientific employment, and in scope) it stands on entirely independent principles."

68. Ibid., p. 22.

69. *Positive Theory,* pp. 55, 56.

70. Ibid., p. 56.

71. Commons, *Distribution of Wealth,* p. 29.

72. Marshall, 2d ed., p. 198.

73. *Positive Theory,* pp. 339-357.

74. Ibid., p. 55.

75. Ibid., p. 357.

76. Ibid., p. 355. The explanation given by Böhm-Bawerk is open to serious criticism.

77. *Capital and Interest, passim,* but particularly pp. 237-387.

78. *Positive Theory,* p. 33.

79. *Positive Theory,* p. 53.

80. *Capital and Interest,* p. 341.

81. Ibid., p. 341.

82. Ibid., p. 387.

83. *Positive Theory,* p. 99.

84. *Capital and Interest,* p. 341.

85. *Capital and Interest,* p. 338.

86. *Positive Theory,* p. 55.

87. Ibid., p. 98.

88. Ibid., p. 117.

89. *E.g.,* ibid., pp. 89 and 106.

90. The italics are my own.

91. *Positive Theory,* p. 65.

92. Ibid., p. 65.

93. *Positive Theory,* p. 65.

94. See *supra.,* p. 37.

95. *Positive Theory,* pp. 33, 34.

96. Ibid., pp. 58, 59.

97. See other definitions of capital as concrete in *Positive Theory,* pp. 22, 65, and *passim.*

98. One of which differs both from the social and the private capital; three, therefore, including both of them.

99. *Positive Theory,* p. 344.

100. Ibid., p. 348.

101. Charles A. Tuttle, in *Annals of the American Academy of Political and Social Science,* i. 615, ff.

102. Such a view is taken by Irving Fisher, *Economic Journal,* vii. 206.

The Next Decade of
Economic Theory

To forecast from present tendencies and current theories the direction of further development in the abstracter economics is, as I fully realize, an undertaking venturesome and liable to error. Even when years have passed, it is not always possible to characterize a decade or a generation of growth in any science, to say that just this or that tendency was the dominant one during the period in question. There are so many lines of thought, so many practical problems to influence, so many varieties of thinkers, that there has not been a year since Adam Smith published his work in which almost every leading aspect of economics has not been to some degree under discussion. There has been continuity in the growth of economic thought, yet certain periods are marked by the peculiar development of some leading economic doctrine. As the thoughts of men have been ripe for a new study of a special group of industrial phenomena, and for a new statement of their relations, and as the practical needs of the day have prompted to new attempts at economic theories, that subject or group of subjects has taken the center of the field of attention. On this basis we may distinguish various epochs in economic theory.

Reprinted from American Economic Association, *Papers and Proceedings of the Thirtieth Annual Meeting* 2 (February 1901). A lively discussion followed this paper in which E. R. A. Seligman, C. A. Tuttle, F. M. Taylor, and E. A. Ross took part. Their discussion of whether Fetter had not exaggerated the break between marginal economics and the classical school is not reprinted here but may be found in the published proceedings, pp. 247-53.

EPOCH OF THE UTILITY VALUE DISCUSSION.

Certainly the years from 1885 on belong to the utility value theorists. The Austrian writers, read at once in the original by English and American students, and quickly introduced to the broader English speaking public through excellent translations, hold the center of the stage. The work of Jevons, in date of publication so much earlier, must be credited to this later period if the decision is made with reference to the interest attracted and the discussion aroused. American economics may almost be said to have won its spurs in the independent development of some essential parts of the doctrine and in the opening up of new fields of psychological analysis which have yielded some of the most valuable fruits of the discussion. This sudden revival of abstracter or deductive economics, just as such studies seemed to be growing into discredit, is one of the most remarkable chapters in economic theory. Without question the period has been one in which economic analysis has grown keener and economic thought has taken a broader view.

SOME RESULTS OF THE VALUE DISCUSSION.

The President of this Association not long ago published a survey of the last "Decade of Economic Theory" in the United States. Some may dissent from portions of it (for when did one economist ever agree entirely with another?), but as a whole it is, though condensed, so comprehensive and satisfactory that it would be idle to attempt to cover that ground again. Let us then merely put in relief some results of the value discussion, the principal feature of this period, so far as it concerns abstracter economic analysis. Certain of its results which must be recognized are the following:

The old cost-of-production theory of value is discredited as anything more than an immediate and superficially practical explanation of prices.

The utility principle is no longer a supernumerary member, but is the strongest limb of our value theory.

The importance of wants, motives and consumption in the discussion has been greatly and permanently enlarged.

The marginal principle as a device of explanation and as a mode of thought, has become indispensable, and is finding new applications constantly.

A satisfactory statement of the relations of supply and utility in the determination of value, though attempted by many, does not seem to have yet been attained, though the essential nature of this relation is certainly perceived by a large number of students.

That a universal law of value is possible, which will explain in a broad way the value importance assigned to every economic agent, has become almost unconsciously, within the last few years, the firm conviction of students.

The old artificially cumbersome system of separate "laws" and explanations for each of the leading factors of production, has become an anachronism in our text books.

These ideas, so startling a short time ago, have become a part of the accepted stock of economic doctrines to the great body of oncoming students. Those of us who got our first bent in economic theory more than ten years ago, before this notable development, must beware of the personal equation in judging of the progress of such doctrines. The younger generation is adjusting itself to these new modes of thought; to it they are no longer in controversy. The significance of these developments in economic theory we cannot yet fully realize. They are changing our methods of approach to every practical problem in economics. They are having further results in economic theory.

THE CHANGING VIEW OF THE FACTOR CAPITAL.

Let us turn now from these attained results of the value discussion, to some of the yet immature though ripening fruits. A central doctrine like that of value cannot undergo such great changes as these without compelling soon a readjustment of all the doctrines with which it is intertwined. One of the most important to note is the change in the whole conception of the factors of production and of the relation of the conventional shares to each other. First to mention is the concept of capital. There has been a marked lull for several years past in the discussion of this branch of economic theory, which might give the impression that the discussion was generally considered closed and that interest in it had ceased. Such is far from the case. The seeds of doubt sown by the able series of articles on the nature of capital that appeared from 1890 to 1896 have been ripening in many minds. The main connection of this with the value discussion is found in the idea of the origin of capital. The conventional capital concept is a cost-of-production concept. The value of capital is traced to former labor which has been needed to produce it. Such a concept involves many internal inconsistencies, manifest on any close study, and many external inconsistencies manifest on its every application to practical affairs. So dominant, however, has been the cost-of-production theory of value in the thoughts of men, that these essential objections have been waved aside as only petty and apparent exceptions which must be found in any application of general formula to actual affairs. Capital has been treated as the product of labor, though there were thousands of things included in capital which, as monopolized fruits of natural resources, had cost no labor or but an insignificant show of it. We have been told at one moment that rent was not measured by labor or due to it, but was a surplus gained without labor, and in the next we have seen the wealth that was paid over to the landlord as rent used by him as capital and defined as the product of labor. We are told in all the text books that capital is "stored up labor," that "its value is due to labor," that "it is labor in another form," both the ideas and the antique phrases reflecting the labor theory of value. We have continued to use these phrases after we have made laughing stock of that theory, and after we have recognized utility, regardless of the origin of the good, as the measure of value. Writers who use in a masterly way the utility and marginal concepts, nevertheless accept as an ultimate standard of value a rejuvenated Ricardian or Marxian labor unit. Nothing could more emphasize the hold of the old thought modes and the vigorous effort that must be made to be rid of them.

The old capital concept is in unstable equilibrium. The difficulties are too apparent and too many minds are seeking a way to avoid them, for this situation long to continue. Thousands of students are treading the paths of doubt and inquiry. Logical consistency demands that the capital concept be framed without reference to labor as its source or origin, and without limits as to its use. When the utility theory displaced the cost-of-production theory of value, this change of the capital concept became a logical necessity.

With this, of course, must go a change in the whole conception of interest, which likewise is connected in the still current treatment with a factor that has been produced by labor. The multitudinous and naïve inconsistencies of the older treatment became apparent when viewed in the light of the later value theory.

THE CHANGING CONCEPT OF RENT.

While this change is going on in the capital concept the rent concept is changing also, and from the same logical causes. The old rent concept, long supposed to be the surest attainment of economic theory, depended in a negative way on the labor theory of value. While capital was supposed to be the product of human effort, and interest in an indirect way a payment for it, rent on the contrary was a surplus coming without human effort. It was the one great exception to the cost-of-production theory, an exception, however, which was supposed not to weaken but to strengthen the theory, by giving it a paradoxical, carefully guarded and completed air. A favorite test of economic acumen for generations has been a comprehension of the phrase, "Rent does not enter into the cost-of-production." Though this may be true (it is the central thesis of a recent and valuable book on economic theory), many students are coming to believe that it is merely an illogical trick in the explanation of values. The difficulties of the rent theory as confined to natural resources began early to manifest themselves, as a study of the older authors shows. Long before the utility theory brought such doubt into the economic world, the theory of rent, the "*pons asinorum*" of political economy, as Mill called it, was becoming a very difficult bridge for even the most orthodox thinkers to cross, without cutting some very asinine capers, judged by Mill's maxim. A study of our contemporary writers shows the concept in ruins. Marshall, who has connected "quasi rents" with every agent of production, and made land rent only a species of a large genus, has gone further from the old system of distribution than he appears to have dreamed of in starting. Macfarlane has made an interesting and able attempt to give to the rent concept some excuse for being, but in widening it to the "price determined" factor, he has wrecked it beyond recognition. Hobson has retained the conventional division of the two material factors with no hint of doubt of their consistency, but has extended the concept of rent until it enwraps the economic world. Clark started twelve years ago, it would seem, from the idea of Bastiat, that the rent of land can be reduced to a payment for labor, and applied this in criticism of the single tax doctrine. As he has developed this independently he has met the other converging lines of thought on rent, and in his last work gives the most satisfactory statement yet made of an emancipated rent concept. The situation is not final, and at no time since Adam Smith has greater confusion of terminology existed, or have opinions upon important questions of economic theory been more unsettled. The logical development of the theory of value must bring us soon to more general agreement as to a theory of monopoly, scarcity, or differential gains, which was the starting point of the development of the theory of rent. Whether the rent concept is to be broadened to cover all such cases, or is to be defined as something still different, is one of the important questions of economic theory to be settled in the next decade.

THE PRACTICAL NEED OF NEW CONCEPTS.

What has been said must not be taken to imply a belief in the growth of theory from internal logical necessity, independent of, and uninfluenced by, the practical needs of the times. Few cherish now such an idea of theory. The conventional concepts of capital and interest, land and rent, were largely determined, as is now generally recognized, by the conditions of the times in which they were developed. The living questions and practical interests of to-day are having no less influence in determining the lines of economic speculation and the form it shall take. And it is likely that when the future chapter shall be written on the economic theory of this day, it will be said that industrial needs were stimulating to a development of the leading economic concepts in the same direction along which theoretical consistency was urging. This thought may be stated more specifically.

STAGES OF INDUSTRIAL DEVELOPMENT AND CORRESPONDING CAPITAL CONCEPTS.

A century ago, when economic concepts were taking the form they have in the main retained, even then they were an illogical compromise between two sets of ideas belonging to two different economic epochs. The mediaeval agricultural and natural economy had rent payments and physical measurements as its typical and general form of contract and payment. The new industrial, capitalistic, and money economy was developing rapidly, but had not become dominant as it is to-day. Even such city men as Ricardo were so under the influence of the old ways of thought that the real difference between these two kinds of economic conceptions could not be clearly seen by them. Rent as a return to natural resources seemed a different kind of return, with a different source, from interest as a return to city wealth, so evidently the work of man's hands, whose value was so easily transferable, and whose return always took the money expression. They never doubted that they were taking the same point of view as they looked at the two factors, two shares, two economic laws, that seemed so essentially different. In fact they were taking two different points of view, one of the 16th and one of the 19th century, and were thus finding contrasts and distinctions which corresponded, not with reality, but with their own shifting modes of thought. The enormous development recently of capitalistic enterprise, the marketing of every form of natural resource by means of shares and bonds, the expression in money form of the value of nearly every kind of wealth and the decline of the agricultural and extractive industries in relative social and economic importance, have made this unconscious confusion of mediaeval and modern viewpoints in economic theory an increasing hindrance to clear and practical thinking. In order to be suited to the discussions of an age that is increasingly industrial, the capital concept must be unified and cleared of its feudal elements.

THE SCARCITY FACTOR THEN AND NOW.

The old rent concept also is found to be inadequate in this age of rapid growth of industrial corporations which enjoy some public franchise or peculiar economic situation, of large industry exercising a power on prices over areas and periods more or less extended, and of multiplying trusts and monopolies. The theorists of a century ago, looking on value from the cost-of-production standpoint, thought of monopoly as a rare thing, due generally to political favor, and almost negligible in ordinary economic discussion. The contribution and value of land, the only exception to the law of labor value that was quite obvious to them, was accounted for by "the law of rent." Now when our economic growth is bringing to our attention every day new instances of the influence of scarcity on value, often by social changes outside the control of the one who gains by them, often by the capitalists' own manipulations, it can no longer be ignored that the coat of economic theory is a bad misfit. It is in Hibernian phrase, too long at one end and too short at the other. The rent theory explains so much that it is not true in one direction, and in the other it does not explain at all. This difficulty worried even Ricardo, it caused Mill a deal of anxiety, and industrial developments have made it greater every year. There is no solution short of a new terminology. The Ricardian law of rent is being relegated by industrial development to the curiosity shop of outgrown economic theories.

SOME PROPOSITIONS.

These are some of the difficulties. In order that the suggestions as to the kind of work to be done in the next decade may be specific, and may serve as a basis for thought and discussion, some propositions expressed or implied in the foregoing paragraphs may be recapitulated.

1. The concept of capital must be given an importance in economic theory corresponding to the dominant place of capitalistic enterprise in present industrial affairs.

2. The concept must be re-defined so as to correspond more closely with commercial usage and the needs of practical discussion.

3. The conventional division of the factors of production is illogical, and must be abandoned. This involves a re-study of many problems and a re-writing of large portions of economic literature.

4. The old idea of rent as a payment for a gift of nature must be rejected; it is questionable whether the later tendency to extend the term rent to every differential gain will prove to be a fortunate development.

5. The labor theory of value and the notion of labor units as in some way usable for a standard of value, are persistent errors which vitiate a large part of current economic discussion, and must be completely thrown aside.

6. The doctrines of rent and interest as currently taught are hopelessly entangled in these old and illogical distinctions. The two forms of return for material goods must be considered as

differing in modes of calculation, not as to kinds of agents and as kinds of return.

RESTATEMENT OF THE OBJECTS OF THIS PAPER.

The object of this paper may now be restated as follows:

1. To account rationally for the conviction that has been growing among economists that economic terminology is in an unsatisfactory state.

2. To show the necessity of rewriting the theory of distribution along radically new lines.

3. To reduce the mental friction and waste of social energy that must accompany the acceptance of doctrines, a readjustment of which is shown to be inevitable.

4. To indicate specifically the direction which the new doctrines must take, the points at which energy of thought may most effectively be applied.

Review of Böhm-Bawerk,
Capital und Capitalzins

It is over sixteen years since the first edition of this work was published, and nearly eleven since the English translation appeared. The great activity in economic and social studies which has marked the intervening period has been due in large measure to the rapid industrial changes that have been in progress; but if one book is to be named more than any other as influencing and stimulating to the abstracter studies, as furthering the philosophic analysis of economic questions during this period, it is this book to which the honor must be given. Its importance lay not so much in the conclusions it reached, for it was almost entirely historical and critical, as in its method of acute analysis, its example of tireless research and scholarship, and its awakening of thought. Even the remarkable second and companion volume, *The Positive Theory of Capital*, does not surpass it in these regards. The later volume, though much more widely read and discussed, and arousing a keener interest in the student, owes to the earlier critical volume much of the air of authority and scholarship which are its strength and its charm.

In the case of a work that is so well known it is unnecessary to dwell on the parts that remain unchanged. Interest will center

Reprinted from *Journal of Political Economy* 9 (March 1901). This review is of the second German edition of *Capital und Capitalzins,* which was published in 1900. The English title of the book under review is *History and Critique of Interest Theories,* and it is now customary to use the title *Capital and Interest* (or the German equivalent) to refer to the entire three-volume set, of which the book under review is volume 1. See Eugen von Böhm-Bawerk, *Capital and Interest,* trans. George D. Huncke and Hans F. Sennholz (South Holland, Ill.: Libertarian Press, 1959).

around the alterations and additions. The author says of these in the new preface: "The changes are not important. They are limited to a few improvements in the composition and the correction of a few errors that had been overlooked. On the other hand I have had occasion to make copious additions, increasing by more than a third the size of the book." On every essential question the author's views remain unchanged. The additions count up 192 pages, of which 23 are in the new preface, 54 are in the added section on John Rae, 25 are in the discussion of Marx's third volume and the controversy connected with it, and 90 are in the new concluding chapter entitled "Contemporary Literature on Interest." Some clew to the activity of economic discussion in the various countries may be found in the *Autoren-Register*. There are 88 names that did not appear in the first edition, distributed by nationalities as follows: Germans, 25; Americans, 16; Italians, 14; English, 12; Austrians, 4; Norwegians, 4; Swedes, 3; Dutch, 3; Danes, 2; Swiss, 2; French, 2; Russian, 1. Grouping these by languages it is seen that 35 per cent. write in German, 32 per cent. in English, 6 per cent. in Italian, 10 per cent. in Scandinavian, 3.5 per cent. in Dutch, 2 per cent. in French, and 1 per cent. in Russian. But this alone is not a fair test of the relative attention given to them by Böhm-Bawerk. Many of the authors are merely mentioned, or are cited in a footnote, as is the case with all but those writing in English or German. As to the text additions it is not easy to determine what justly should be credited to each group. Rae is spoken of by the author as a Canadian, but John Stuart Mill refers to him as "a Scotchman settled in the United States." His book was published in Boston in 1834, and its recent prominence is due to Mr. Mixter's essay in the *Quarterly Journal of Economics* on "A forerunner of Böhm-Bawerk." It would seem that America might claim him. Macvane receives a page, Walker two, and Carver nine, a total of 66 pages to America. The English writer singled out for attention is Marshall, to whom in preface and text 29 pages are given. The German writers receive 67 pages, nearly half turning immediately about the belated volume of Marx, and much of the rest connected with the old discussion of surplus

value. Omitting thirty other pages, not assignable to special
writers or countries, it appears that 42 per cent. of the additions
are devoted to German writers and 58 per cent. to writers of
English, of which America has 41 per cent. and England 17 per
cent. This is a showing that may well justify a little harmless pride
if it represents at all fairly the relative activity of economic studies
in the different lands. The exceptional length of the section
given to Rae, a forgotten author of earlier date, it may well be
said, invalidates any such claim for America; but, on the other
hand, it may be said that the German additions are in large
measure given to Marx's posthumous book, that there is a strong
tendency for an author to exaggerate the importance of the
writers in his own language, and finally that the most important
of American contributions, probably the most important of all
recent contributions, to the interest problem, those of Fisher and
Clark, not to mention several others, are barely referred to. It is
hard to reconcile oneself that so much energy has been wasted in
refuting trite eclecticism, when original and farreaching contributions by these Americans are all but passed in silence.

Amends may be made for this, however, in the revision of *The
Positive Theory of Capital*, which is promised at an early date. This
will be looked forward to with interest none the less keen because
of the difficulties in which the author is sure to find himself. The
movement of economic thought is rapidly leaving behind it the
concept of capital with which Böhm-Bawerk works. It is not to be
expected that the able author will change his point of view, but to
the task of meeting objections and eluding the charges of inconsistency he will bring that remarkable acuteness and ability
which he has shown himself in these volumes to possess.

Review of Böhm-Bawerk, *Einige strittige Fragen der Capitalstheorie*

This little group of essays, dedicated to the "true friends of theory," is a reprint of three articles which appeared during 1899 in the *Zeitschrift für Volkswirtschaft, Socialpolitik und Verwaltung*. The author's object, as he explains, is not to present any new theory of capital or interest or to make any changes in the one which he had before presented, but rather to examine more carefully some questions of detail in the doctrine of capital that are essential for the solution of the main question. Of the five distinguishable subjects discussed, the four less important ones comprise the last third of the pamphlet and may be first mentioned.

The author maintains that the confusing of interest, the return of capital, with the earnings of the entrepreneur, as is done by Philippovich, is a step backward away from clear thinking and a clear economic terminology. He refutes Dietzel's idea that there must be, not one, but several theories of interest—that in turn, or according to the particular problem, the abstinence, the productivity, the exploitation, the time-value theory or others, must be employed. The author makes a telling criticism of this eclectic method of avoiding the real problem involved. He then replies to the objection made to his own theory by Philippovich, to the effect that it explains only a part of the cases of interest. And, finally, he criticizes the loose acceptance by Lexis of the

Reprinted from *Political Science Quarterly* 17 (March 1902). Böhm-Bawerk's *Einige strittige Fragen der Capitalstheorie* was published in Vienna and Leipzig by Wilhelm Braumuller in 1900.

socialistic exploitation theory of interest, sharply and powerfully arraigning that sentimentality which has led many thinkers, especially in Germany, to concede validity to the socialistic theory of interest, while rejecting the reasoning on which alone rational validity can be demonstrated.

Let us turn now to the major theme of the essay—the nature of the roundabout process. Böhm-Bawerk's conception of the "average production period" as that period which elapses between the application of productive agents and their reward in the form of satisfaction, and his proposition that by roundabout methods a greater product can, as a rule, be attained, have been variously criticized and attacked. Especially the assaults of Lexis called for a reply. In defense of his ideas, the author retraces much of the argument of his earlier works, developing and illustrating the thought in many details. He first clears away some misunderstandings, by defining the production period not as the absolute time that elapses from the first application of labor and capital until the securing of the enjoyment, but as the *average* length of the interval. As the main objection turns on the effect of inventions which shorten the various industrial processes, while giving a larger product, he considers at length the effect of inventions and improved processes. He concludes that they are dynamic factors that check, but do not reverse, the movement of the rate of interest, and maintains the truth of the general rule set forth in his theory. He returns to the same argument in the next division, maintaining that the greater productivity of the longer period can be shown both by observation and experience (pp. 43-52).

He then turns to a different but related question, as to whether (pp. 51-63) the rate of interest is fixed in the whole range of industry or, as Lexis has maintained, in a particular branch of it. The same question appears under a slightly different aspect in this form: whether the different branches of trade have an essential effect on each other in the matter of the rate of interest. Böhm-Bawerk analyzes the methods by which the rate of interest and the successive uses of capital are equalized in the various lines of industry. From the standpoint of the author and that of

Lexis, who apparently approaches the subject from the same side, this is a subtle and convincing piece of analysis. Its defects, viewed from a different standpoint, will be suggested below.

Finally, in this division Böhm-Bawerk vigorously resents the view that his notion of the production period and the length of the roundabout process is unsound, in that it deals with magnitudes practically not determinable. Admitting that it is impossible to measure the productive period, he says that this is equally true of many causes which must be recognized and reasoned about in the various sciences. He says it would be very pleasant and interesting to know all these facts, but that a lack of knowledge does not invalidate his theory. The details of the arguments presented cannot be discussed here, but it must be confessed that, despite the great ingenuity displayed, they leave the vague impression that somehow the real question has been evaded. Not a single concrete example has been given where an individual producer practically measures this period, whereas in the cases of cost of production and of the marginal buyer in market value, which Böhm-Bawerk adduces as strict analogies, there are clearly evident some points at which the magnitudes of satisfaction or cost, usually unmeasured, appear for a moment in concrete and measurable forms.

Considering as a whole the author's argument on the central theme, it can be called successful only in a negative way, as a refutation of various objections that have been made against it. The author has not advanced the solution of the problem, positively, a single step. Critics of the *Positive Theory* have frequently declared in effect that, while its author had ejected the productivity of capital from the front yard of his theory, he had opened to it the side door and had given it the freedom of the house. For what place are we to assign in the broad theory of interest to the "productiveness of the roundabout process"? Is it the main and fundamental, or is it only a supplementary and partial, explanation of the cause of interest? The essay under review certainly puts it in the central and leading place: it is the greater productiveness of labor when applied in a long and roundabout way which is the great and efficient cause of interest on capital. If that is not the impression left on the reader of this essay, and the one the author intends to leave, then we have missed its purpose. And yet this is out of harmony, first, with the author's own strong negative criticisms of productivity theories as affording only incomplete answers to the interest problem and, secondly, with his formal statement of the theory of interest as due to the difference between the value of present and that of future goods.

Let us venture to suggest very briefly an explanation of this appearance of wavering in the author's conclusion. Starting with a narrow concept of capital as composed of things produced by labor, he has not succeeded in escaping various of the old errors of the labor-value theory which he himself has elsewhere so successfully discredited. That concept suggests the thought that labor is put into the material form of capital to appear later as enjoyment. Some cases may be found in seeming support of this view, but others that clearly forbid it. When or in what way will the labor expended in digging the Isthmian canal become enjoyment? There will be an annual yield of enjoyment, but the "principle," or result of the labor, is, as John B. Clark has strongly emphasized, an abiding thing, never to be used up. Again, Böhm-Bawerk recognized before he concluded his *Positive Theory* that the capitalization of land is only another aspect of the interest problem, yet his productive period or roundabout process has no validity there. Indeed, his capital concept is a cost-of-production concept and does not make possible a consistent explanation of the theory of interest or the capitalization of scarce agents—"natural" means of production. The period of production seems plausible when illustrated by examples of capital thought of as "previous labor" (see *Strittige Fragen*, pp. 11, 12, 17, *et passim*). An "average waiting time," however abstract and unrelated to any practical calculation which business men make in determining investments, appears to be a possible thing, if capital can be reduced to applications of labor at various times, destined all to appear at a later moment in the form of consumable goods. But when the problem of comparing present and future goods is thought of in the form of a balancing of present and future rentals, as is done in the case of capitalizing scarce natural agents, the fallacy is evident. Then there is no "roundaboutness" in the application of labor. There is neither a series of technical processes nor an application of labor which will mature as enjoyment at a later period. The rate of interest falls gradually, as future rents increase in value relative to present rents, and accordingly are discounted at a lower rate of interest. Great as have been the services of our author in stimulating to clearer and deeper thinking in economic theory, his presentation of a *Capitalstheorie* evidently is not destined to be a finality. Some development it is sure to undergo, and is undergoing. And that development clearly lies along the lines of a value concept, as opposed to a cost-of-production concept of capital.

Review of Böhm-Bawerk, *Positive Theorie des Capitals*

This second edition, long awaited with lively expectation by students of economic theory, proves to be an unchanged reprint of the first edition published some fourteen years ago. The author has found it impossible in the midst of his duties, recently undertaken as finance minister of Austria, to carry out his revision of this part as he had already done with the first part of *Capital und Capitalzins*. The author still adheres to his purpose of revising the *Positive Theory*, but is unable to do so until a more favorable time arrives. The student acquainted with recent magazine articles by the author, in which he has replied to his various critics, is aware, however, that no appreciable change has taken place in Böhm-Bawerk's views on the interest theory. His writings on the problem in the past fifteen years have been taken up, not with the revision and amendment of his interest theory, but merely with a restatement and defense of his well-known views against the critics who have assailed it from many directions. Each year is making the revision of the *Positive Theory* a more difficult task. The work of Böhm-Bawerk has been the most stimulating influence that has come into economic theory in the last half century, and yet his *Positive Theory* seems fated to go the way of its many predecessors. Its acceptance by students is each year becoming less and less possible.

Reprinted from *Journal of Political Economy* 11 (December 1902). The second edition of Böhm-Bawerk's *Positive Theorie* was published in Innsbruck by Verlag der Wagner'schen Universitäts-Buchhandlung in 1902. The English title of this work is *Positive Theory of Capital*, and it is volume 2 of Eugen von Böhm-Bawerk, *Capital and Interest*, trans. George H. Huncke and Hans F. Sennholz (South Holland, Ill.: Libertarian Press, 1959).

The Nature of Capital
and Income

The work before us[1] notably strengthens the forces making for the new conception of capital. Professor Fisher here renders a threefold service. He demonstrates mathematically the inconsistency of the old classification and conception of factors and incomes; he shows the mathematical consistency of the value concept of capital and of the capitalization theory of interest; and he illustrates by actuarial methods the application of the new conceptions to business problems. All three of these proofs have been offered before in verbal form, and the results are already accepted by a number of American economists. But it is always possible to miss the point more easily in a verbal argument, especially when it involves the rejection of familiar conceptions. The argument at a number of points is here restated fully, clearly, and conclusively. The peculiar endowment and training of Professor Fisher as both mathematician and economist made him uniquely capable of this notable performance in economic exposition.

The chief topics and the order in which they are treated are as follows: The introduction treats of the nature of wealth, of property, and of utility. Part one deals with the nature of capital, of capital accounts in private and corporate business, and of various correct and incorrect methods of summing up capital, as revealed in a study of the principles of accountancy. Part two deals with income in the usual concrete form of commodities and money, applies the methods of accountancy to the estimation

Reprinted from *Journal of Political Economy* 15 (March 1907). This is a review of Irving Fisher, *The Nature of Capital and Income* (New York: Macmillan Co., 1906).

and summation of incomes, and concludes with the discussion of psychic income as the final or true form of which all others are but reflections. Part three approaches the central theme of the book, the ratios between capital and income: here are treated the interest rate, capitalization, and various accountancy questions involving the distinction between capital and income. Summaries of the last part and of the whole work conclude the text which is followed by appendices, aggregating seventy pages, mostly on the mathematical formulae and methods of expressing capital and income. Many parts of the text also are illustrated with diagrams and mathematical examples. Such a brief list of topics gives no adequate idea of the methods and style of treatment. For these, as well as for substance of doctrine, many of the chapters merit and must receive careful reading by economic students.

Agreeing so fully with the general doctrines defended by Professor Fisher in opposition to the conventional conceptions, the reviewer deems it unneedful to attempt here a mere epitome of the various arguments. Nor would it be profitable to dissipate the discussion over a score or more of minor questions where the author may be in error. It seems best in the cause of economic science, however, to call attention to some doubtful conclusions, and, as a help to the interpretation of this work, to indicate how Professor Fisher's views have developed since his first essays in this subject ten years ago. These comments conveniently group themselves about the three parts of the text: (1) the nature of capital, (2) the nature of income, (3) the relation of capital and income, with a conclusion (4) on the relation of Fisher's doctrines to contemporary speculation.

The nature of capital.–Professor Fisher sees the essence of his contribution to the theory of capital in the distinction between a fund and a flow, "the most important application" of which "is to differentiate between capital and income."[2] He gives this definition:

Capital is a fund and income a flow. This difference between capital and income, is, however, not the only one. There is another important difference, namely, that capital is *wealth*, and income is the *service* of wealth. We have therefore the following definitions: A *stock of wealth* existing at an *instant* of time is called *capital*. A *flow of services* through a *period* of time is called *income*.[3]

Thereafter he refers not to one but to two fundamental distinctions between capital and income, those "between fund and flow, and between wealth and services."[4] Here without comment or footnote, is introduced into the definitions of capital and income which he had presented ten years before a radically new element, and one denoting the abandonment of the former thought. His original view is indicated in the following quotations:

All wealth presents a double aspect in reference to *time*. It forms a *stock* of wealth, and it forms a *flow* of wealth. The former is, I venture to maintain, capital, the latter, income and outgo, production and consumption.[5]

The total capital in a community at any particular instant consists of all commodities of whatever sort and condition in existence in that community at that instant, and is antithetical to the streams of production, consumption and exchange of *these very same commodities*.[6]

These [older] definitions .... assume that capital is one sort of wealth and income another. .... Economists have thought of capital and income as different kinds of commodities instead of different aspects of commodity in time.[7]

Endeavoring to account for the fact that Marshall did not apply this antithesis of fund and flow to capital and income, Fisher says:

Possibly the reason why this step was not taken lies in the fact that Marshall conceives of income as a flow of pleasure rather than of goods. He conceives of capital as antithetical to the enjoyable income which it brings in. But the simpler antithesis is not between a stock of goods and the particular flow which it may earn or purchase, but between the stock and the flow of goods of the *same* kind.[8]

Marshall .... allowed the notion to survive that capital is one species of wealth and income another.[9]

In criticizing an expression of Edwin Cannan's Fisher expresses what in his view is the error in it:

the omission of the explicit statement that income and capital consist of the self-same goods.[10]

Speaking of the distinction between capital and income, Fisher rejects again

the old and harmful notion . . . . that this distinction implies some difference in the kind of goods concerned.[11]

At the beginning of the second article he reiterates the view that the sole distinction between capital and income is that between fund and flow.

A full view of capital would be afforded by an instantaneous photograph of wealth.[12]

The reviewer pointed out some years ago[13] the impossibility of this view, saying:

this conception shares what I believe to be an error common with it to both of the others [Clark's and Böhm-Bawerk's] in that it makes the income of a community consist of "streams . . . . of the very same commodities that compose the original capital." There are many things that are a part of Fisher's capital only and never are a part of the flow of income. Income differs from wealth not merely as an aspect but in the group of goods which compose it.

In the book one may search in vain for the idea that wealth and income consist of goods of the same kind. It has been without comment abandoned and therewith has been taken away the very *raison d'être* of the contrast between fund and flow. The original concept was unsound, the new idea is the all important one.

Let us look more closely at the origin and defects of the original concept. The only applicable definitions of stock that are found in the two authorities at hand are as follows: *The Standard Dictionary* definition (6): "any accumulated store or reserved supply that may be drawn on at will;" (7) "material accumulated or ready for employment." *The Century Dictionary,* definition (18) reads: "hoard or accumulation; store; supply; fund which may be drawn upon as occasion demands." These meanings accord fairly well with the thought of fund and flow of the same things, but accord ill with a stock of wealth and a flow of services. The stock of wealth of concrete goods is not an accumulation of services nor of incomes to be drawn upon as occasion demands, or a supply that may be drawn on at will.

Is it not possible for the reader to make a shrewd guess as to one or two of the causes leading to the error in Fisher's original definition? The first is, that he apparently identifies two very different propositions. He is contending for a conception of capital that includes all existing wealth and not merely produced productive agents. The proposition that "capital is not any particular kind of wealth, but a stock of wealth of any kind existing at an instant of time," he deems equivalent to the proposition that capital is a fund and income a flow. So long as he held the idea that income consisted of the same things as capital, it was easy to identify the two thoughts. When later the idea of sameness of substance was given up, the definition was retained.

Another contributory cause of this error may be better understood after the discussion of income and of ratios, but may be referred to now. Fisher began his study of capital[14] with his attention fixed upon the relations between the inflow and outflow of concrete goods. Not until the third article[15] do other relations take a prominent part. All his illustrations in the first two articles apply to the conception of stocks and flows of the same goods (not incomes at all, as he later comes to see). Some examples will make this clear:

Stock relates to a *point* of time, flow to a *stretch* of time. Food in the pantry at any instant is capital, the monthly flow of food through the pantry is income.[16]
Commodities of which a large stock exists are usually commodities whose flow is not conspicuous, while in those where the flow is large,

the stock in turn is insignificant. Factories, ships and railways illustrate the first class; food, drink, fuel, illuminants, the second. The former are therefore set down as capital and the latter as income.[17]

The stock of carpets in a store is not so closely associated with the flow of interest paid by the merchants in maintaining this stock, or of the profits earned by its use, as it is with the flow of *carpets* into and out of the store. The distinction between a stock and a flow of the same kind of goods is prior to that between a stock of one kind and a flow of another.[18]

Other examples implying the same view are found in the contrast of rivers and lakes where in fact the water is the same, and of which Fisher says that behind the "arbitrary classification lies the real scientific distinction between 'gallons' and 'gallons per second.' "[19] In another illustration of the case of money loans, the language used is: "the sum lent being a stock and the succession of interest payments constituting a flow," Speaking of the wage fund, he says that it should have been looked upon as a flow dependent

not upon the magnitude of the fund, but upon the rate at which it is replenished. This rate is not a fund at all, but a flow; it bears the same relation to a fund that a flow of so many gallons per hour does to a reservoir holding so many gallons of water.[20]

At a later point, Fisher seems unconsciously criticizing his own doctrine when he says:

in [most theories of income] the annual supply or consumption of food and clothing, not their use, is regarded as income. That is, income is conceived as a flow of the first of three kinds distinguished in this article instead of one of the third.[21]

This is in the last article in which he has come to look upon services as the only thing deserving the name of income.

Thus in the first article Fisher forms his peculiar concept of capital and frames a definition to fit a case which later analysis compels him to relegate to a non-fundamental place in his theory. Beginning by emphasizing as essential the sameness, he ends by emphasizing the contrast, of the things composing capital and income.

   The instant we include any such concrete wealth under the head of income, that instant we begin to confuse capital and income.[22]

The misleading phrase "fund and flow" must be looked upon as a historical accident and one unsuited to the better capital concept which Professor Fisher has now adopted.

   Another difficulty that will be more clearly seen later in this review is that the earlier concept applied to stocks or sums not expressed in terms of value. The reviewer has, on a previous occasion, directed a criticism to this point.[23] In the first of the earlier articles, Fisher objected to Clark's definition of value on the ground that he tried to include different sorts of capital under the same fund, reduced to a common equivalent in terms of value. He added: "the objection is not that the summation of value is inadmissible, but that it is a secondary operation."[24] The whole implication is not clear but this much is, that in Fisher's opinion the value summation is no essential part of the capital concept, and that a summation of concrete objects by inventory or by description of physical qualities, not only is a capital sum, but that it is the primary and essential capital sum. In the second article,[25] value of wealth and value of property are admitted as two of the senses of capital, but stocks of wealth and of property as quantities (inventory and description without valuation) are given the titles of capital-wealth and capital-property. In the book these terms are retained but as hardly more than formalities, for nearly the whole attention is given to the value concept of capital. Fisher's own treatment becomes subject to his own former criticism directed against another, for he includes "different sorts of capital in the same fund, reduced to a common equivalent in terms of value." Capital is still thought of as the "flash-light picture" of incomes,[26] but it is said to be

heterogeneous; it cannot be expressed in a single sum. We can inventory the separate columns, but we cannot add them together. They may, however, be reduced to a homogeneous mass by considering not their kinds and quantities, but their values. And this value of any stock of wealth is also called capital. . . . . Unless it is otherwise specified, the term capital will be understood in this sense.

This brings the treatment pretty nearly in harmony with the criticism to the effect that "the total quantity of many different kinds of goods cannot be expressed for economic purposes in a single sum, except in terms of value."[27] That this is a good and necessary change is unquestioned, but that it shifts Fisher's concept from its original basis is no less certain.

The nature of income.—Fisher's income concept has undergone a change no less radical and beneficial than has his capital concept. Three stages can be pretty clearly distinguished. First, income is conceived of as the flow of the same concrete commodities which make up the fund of wealth, as seen in the examples given above. "The monthly flow of food through the pantry is income."[28] It is because he thus thinks of wealth as "used for both capital and income"[29] that Fisher framed his concept as he did. He criticized Marshall for conceiving of "income as a flow of pleasure rather than of goods." Quite as strongly he criticized Cannan:

> Like Marshall, Cannan seems to conceive of income as a flow of *pleasure,* but capital as a stock of *things;* and thus, in spite of the clear statement of the time distinction between them, this distinction is not regarded as fully adequate, and there persists a trace of some additional distinction between the substances of which capital and income are composed.[30]

No hint of any other view appears in the first article.

In the second article in distinguishing between wealth and property, a different thought is suggested of the services of wealth, i. e., the desirable events it occasions. A footnote refers to several writers who have discussed this subject. The thought lies near that these services are the income of the wealth; but no statement to that effect is made. Near the end of the third article, these services suddenly are presented, not only as income, but as the only income. The last problem treated in the article, that "of income and its distribution,"[31] begins:

In some respects, the third group of relations, those between stocks of wealth and the flow of services they render is the most important and fundamental of all. . . . . The value of the services we shall call the income from the wealth. . . . . Textbooks now usually point out that a "part" of income consists of services of man and uses of durable wealth. I propose to go a step further and show that *all* income consists of services.[32]

The services cease in this view to be tangible things of the nature of wealth.

Every article of wealth is to be pictured as simply the tangible and visible handle to hold fast invisible streamers or filaments of services reaching into the future.[33]

In the book this is in the main the notion of income presented:

The only true method, in our view, is to regard uniformly as income the service of a dwelling to its owner (shelter, money or rental).[34]

The belief is implied that this sum of money-rentals and enjoyable services is a homogeneous income because it all consists of services to the owner.[35] This is a complex of contractual money incomes and economic services of goods to men. This summation of heterogeneous elements, direct services from goods and money payments by men in exchange for services of goods, is not a satisfactory solution of the problem, but it is "the solution offered in the present book" as a homogeneous expression of the real income concept.[36]

Fisher is not satisfied with this himself, and in the third stage of his concept he is led to the "psychic stream of events as final income."[37] The income of enjoyable objective services leads up to subjective satisfactions. He says: "it is usually recognized by economists that we must not stop at the stage of this objective income. There is one more step before the process is complete." He then defines subjective income "as the stream of consciousness of any human being,"[38] or "simply one's whole conscious life."[39] Does this not go a bit too far in the widening of the concept, and ought it not to be limited to certain of the states

of consciousness, making the definition run somewhat as follows: "the pleasurable psychic impressions which objective goods
aid to produce"?[40] Fisher implies this limitation in saying later
that to evaluate this income "it is only necessary for the individual to answer the question what money is he willing to pay for
any enjoyment brought about by means of external wealth."[41]
The chapter has many just observations on the subjective items
which "are by no means to be despised by the economist, who has
far too long busied himself with a study of the superficial objective phenomena."[42] The thought, however, is far removed from
that of an income of concrete wealth, indeed the original idea has
quite disappeared.

Fisher ends his formal analysis by enumerating three kinds of
income, subjective, objective services, and money.[43] It is true, as
Fisher says, that "we are at liberty to consider any one of them as
income in its proper place," but there is still danger of confusion,
and he does not escape it. The argument that the process of
exchange cannot contribute anything to the total income of
society becomes involved in ambiguities. The sale of a book
occasions "an element of income to the seller and an element of
outgo to the purchaser."[44] And it is said that the book yields no
income until the reader peruses it. This evidently confuses mere
accounting in terms of money with psychic income. In the same
vein it is said that "book selling adds nothing to the income of
society, but the reading of the book does." The error of this
appears when we consider that, using words in the same sense,
labor however productive, wealth however well directed toward
increasing the fitness of goods to gratify wants, would add
nothing to income; the final act of consumption alone would add
to the income of society!

A number of other passages present difficulties of the same
kind. It is especially hard to tell what is the real or the "realized
income" under discussion. At times it is purely "psychic satisfactions";[45] again it seems to mean money income actually
secured;[46] again money expenditure, even when largely made
by using up invested capital.[47]

This same shifting meaning of income possibly accounts for

the origin of Fisher's doctrine that increase of capital value is not income.[48] The doctrine in brief is that the increase of capital as it grows in value, as for example between two interest payments, is not income when both capital and increase are reckoned in terms of money. If a forest, worth $20,000 ten years ago, is now worth $32,000, the increment of $12,000 may be counted as capital but not as income during that period.[49] Fisher would not speak of income until the wood is cut and sold, and insists upon the distinction "between income that is realized by the investor and income which is earned by the capital."[50] This implies some idea of a kind of income that does not come to any person. He goes on:

Realized income is the value of the actual services secured from the capital; earned income is found by adding to realized income the increase of capital value, or deducting from it the decrease.[51] Expressed in a single sentence, the general principle connecting realized and earned income is that they differ by the appreciation or depreciation of capital.[52]

It is venturesome to question mathematical examples when presented by Professor Fisher, but these seem quite misleading. He says the truth of the doctrine "is evident from the fact that this item is never discounted in making up capital value."[53] This example follows:

Suppose, for instance, with interest at 4 per cent., that a man buys an annuity of $4 a year, which does not begin at once but is deferred one year. Since this annuity will be worth $100 one year hence, its present value will be about $96, which, during the ensuing year, will gradually increase to $100. If this increase of value of (about) $4 is itself to be called income, it should be discounted. But this is absurd. The discounted value of $4 would be $3.85, which, if added to the $96, would require $99.85, or practically the same as a year later instead of $4 less as is actually the case. In other words, the hypothesis which counts an increase of value as income is self-destructive; for if the increment *is* income, it must be discounted, but, if discounted, it is practically abolished.

It would indeed be absurd to discount the income a second

time and add it to the capital value, for it has already been discounted and added to the capital sum. If it had not been, the capital sum would be the discounted value of an annuity to begin two years hence, which would be about $3.85 less than $96. And so every successive annuity has been included to arrive at the capital sum. Of course it would be an error to count it first as increase of capital and then as an additional sum of income the moment it becomes payable. But take away this increase of the capital value during the year and you take away the income, which is nothing but the increment in capital value detached at certain conventional points and put at the disposal of the owner.

Does not the thought shift in this example from the stage of money income to the stage of enjoyable income? Yet Fisher is discussing money income and deems the income to be realized whenever the money is paid to the owner of the capital. In the merely monetary aspect of the question, there is as yet no enjoyment, but in a developed money market the capital value of the annuity would be salable any day for a sum including the accrued income. On the other hand, the annuity at the expiration of the year may be money income not expended for gratifications, but reinvested in other future incomes. The increment of money income in any elapsed year is therefore the primary fact, and increase of capital occurs only on condition that the accrued money income is not withdrawn but is added by reinvestment, or is saved.

The same difficult doctrine is set forth in an elaborate illustration in which three brothers are supposed to be subjected to an income tax. Each supposedly inheriting $10,000, the first invests the sum in a perpetual annuity of $500; the second puts his in trust to be invested in an annuity of $1,000 after fourteen years when the capital has doubled; the third, a spendthrift, buys an annuity of nearly $2,000 for six years.[54] In Fisher's view, the $500, the $1,000 and the $2,000 are the true realized incomes, which alone should be taxed under income taxation. The second brother should be taxed on nothing until after fourteen years, as until then he would be spending nothing, and the third brother would be taxed during his brief spendthrift career on an income of $2,000, the amount he is spending. The argument is substantially that a tax on expenditures is more equitable and expedient than either a tax on the annual net increase of capital in the owner's hands (the usual ideal of an income tax), or a tax on capital value (the general property tax). The general argument as to the virtues of consumption taxes is frequently made, but if true it hardly supports the proposition Fisher is advancing. There is no pretense that the ordinary income tax is a consumption tax; it is frankly, however crudely, a tax on net earnings which are at the disposition of the taxpayer either to save or to spend without encroaching upon his other capital. Where, therefore, is the fallacy to which reference is made?[55] There is no pretense that the general property tax is a consumption tax; its ideal is frankly the taxation of all property rights in proportion to their present capitalized value. The double taxation and injustice too frequently found in its practice is caused by bad administration and by bad reasoning of quite a different nature.

In this illustration "true realized income" is used in the sense of the amount of money expended for enjoyment, whether it is taken from the current earnings of capital or from the original capital sum invested. According to this usage income is never money coming in but always money going out. Income is not an addition but always a subtraction. The confusion between money income and subjective income could not be more evident.

No more convincing are the other illustrations. In the case of the vacant land rising in value,[56] it is not necessary to wait until the land is built on and enjoyed, for it is money income that is to be calculated and that is realized in every resale of the land. Is this not a "proper place" at which money income can logically be estimated? According to the view taken[57] the exemption from taxation of forests in Europe, cited as a "more rational system" due to longer experience and to a recognition that the growing forest should not be treated as income, is not, it is safe to say, based upon the reason assigned by Fisher. It is simply a social expedient, a conscious subsidizing of forestry, because forests more than most other wealth in the hands of individuals confer broad social benefits upon others than the owner.

Another minor point in this connection. The treatment of money income is out of harmony with the conception and definition of income as a flow. Capital is repeatedly spoken of as "for the present yielding no income;"[58] there are long periods "during which no income is realized;"[59] in annual contractual payments of interest or annuities, it is said that "during the entire year up to the very end there is no income at all."[60] Income thus is treated not as a flow but as a number of sums of money due at definite though perhaps very irregularly distributed points of time.

The relations between capital and income.—Coming to the examination in detail of the relations between capital and income, Fisher presents "the four income-capital ratios," capital being called a stock of wealth or of property and being expressed either in physical terms or in value.[61] These four "ratios" are: (1) physical productivity, (2) value productivity, (3) physical return, (4) value return. "The ratio of the quantity of services per unit of time to the quantity of capital which yields those services may be called physical productivity." These quantities are expressed physically as acres, as bushels, not as values. The first difficulty here is that a large part of the services yielded by goods is not physical, and in such cases and in so far there is not physical productivity. The examples chance to be chosen where there is some (wheat from acres, cloth from looms). But the second difficulty is that it is not possible to ascribe to a particular piece of "capital" in a physical sense the whole product which is at the same time and in the same sense the product of labor and of other pieces of "capital," such as the building, the land, etc. This physical productivity is not a measurable thing which can be compared with the physical pieces of "capital."[62] Not until value has been imputed to it can it be so compared, and that is the fourth ratio.

These objections do not apply to the third ratio called "physical return" (bushels per $100 of capital applied), for here it is not the whole product but the part imputed by marginal measurement that seems to be considered. The second ratio is the "value productivity" (dollars rent per acre or per dwelling, and wages per laborer). The fatal objection lies to all three of these so-called ratios that they are not ratios. With some diffidence the point must be raised that *ratio* in mathematics implies the relation between two numbers or magnitudes of the same kind. There may be a "rate" described as dollars per acre per year, but not a "ratio," for that must be a numerical relation between two quantities of similar dimensions. No wonder that after only three pages of formal definitions this statement is made: "in this book we are concerned chiefly with the fourth relation, value return, or the ratio of the value of income to the value of capital."[63] Most of what has preceded and all of what follows pertains to this value ratio, which is the essential feature of the capital concept, though a different idea is embodied in Fisher's definition, as has been indicated above. The author as he proceeds comes to recognize that no other subject is engaging his attention. At the conclusion of the part on the relations between capital and income, he says: "we have finished our study of the relations between capital-value and income-value."[64] "Our special theme has been the value return—the relations between income-value and capital-value."[65] Still more significant is the last page but one of the text.

It is to the relation between capital and income in the value sense that our attention throughout this book has been chiefly devoted. It has been noted that the relation between capital and income, taken in the value sense, is profoundly different from the relation between capital and income when either or both are measured in their various individual units. When capital and value are measured as "quantities," capital may be said to produce income; but when they are measured in "values," we find that it is necessary to reverse this statement, and to say that income produces capital.[66]

In this it appears that the rejected stone has become the headstone of the corner. This *profound difference* between capital and wealth comes very near being recognized as the essence of the capital concept. But the thought halts short of the inevitable conclusion that the wealth aspect of value is to be found in the production of incomes, whereas the essential capital aspect is the evaluation of incomes and the expression of their present worth. Fisher early committed himself to a conception of capital that has dimmed this distinction, from which conception criticism has as yet only partially freed him.

Relation to contemporary speculation.—With these exceptions this work presents the modern capitalization theory with an invigorating air of practicality. There is no worship of the old fetiches, such as artificially produced or as hypothetically unimproved agents. There is no illusion that the income of land bears a peculiar relation to price, or that the influence of time upon value is limited to some classes of produced agents. Capital is treated as the present worth of expected incomes, and the essence of the capital problem is found in the value relations between incomes and capital sums. Professor Fisher here shows that this problem has now, by the aid of the new value concept of capital, been brought within the range of logical and mathematical treatment and of the usages of business. As Professor Fisher's suggestive articles ten years ago helped to attract attention to this subject and to present the issues involved, so this riper and weightier contribution will help to tip finally the scales of judgment. A book not appealing directly to a large audience, it will be carefully read by the critical few, and its influence will spread with the new conception of distribution to ever-widening circles of thought.

Every author draws his inspiration from sources of which he is rarely quite conscious. Fisher's mathematical interest led him to ascribe to the mathematician Simon Newcomb the paternity of his original conception of capital and income as fund and flow of the same goods, although his account of the influence shows that it was only a phrase caught from a quite different connection, and that it was not intended by Newcomb to have attached to it the thought that Fisher gave it.

Newcomb applied his distinction only to problems of monetary circulation. . . . . Intent on elucidating questions of monetary circulation, Newcomb failed to see that the same conception would clear up questions of capital. . . . . The fact that the author of the distinction between stock and flow did not apply it to capital, and the fact that also Professor Marshall, who was quick to see the importance of Newcomb's distinction, did not so apply it, have often caused serious doubts in my own mind as to the propriety of that application.[67]

There was indeed occasion for serious doubt. Fisher did not note that because Newcomb's use of it was confined to monetary problems the funds and flows were expressible in homogeneous units of value, whereas Fisher extended the thought to heterogeneous masses of agents and their incomes, even when not expressible in value units, and insisted that the concept of capital be not limited to funds expressed or measured in terms of value. All the development of the concept since has been away from Fisher's original idea toward a conception derived from other sources.

So quickly have the sounder and tested fruits of the studies of Patten and Clark been appropriated, so thoroughly have they become a part of our thought, that they now seem simple truths. Many remember the stimulus they found in Patten's analysis of the ideals, tastes, and economic nature of man. How revolutionary was the thought that life, aspirations, and effort were the center of economic study rather than acres, clay, and iron. Under the influence of a theory of consumption, economics has changed from a study of the physical sources of wealth to a psychological science. The novel of yesterday has become the commonplace of today.

A score of years ago Clark reopened the question of the capital concept by challenging the usual classification of capital and land, of rent and interest. His thought so traversed the conventional definitions and conceptions that for years it found few disciples, yet its fault was rather that it changed the old view too little than too much. Slowly the new thought became familiar as it was presented in its different aspects; the difficulties of the older view became more evident; while here and there the new idea bore fruit in comment or critical essay that clarified details or showed new applications to practical problems.

Among such essays showing the awakened interest in the concept of capital must be classed the articles from Professor Fisher's hands ten years ago. The present work is an evidence of the growing part now played in economic theory by the psychological analysis and of the development that the capital concept has undergone of late. Fisher's present views are in some regards the logical outcome of the recent psychological studies in economics, and in other regards, of the Clarkian protest against the old classification of economic factors. The relation to the latter is probably more close and direct than Fisher has recognized.

However it may be as to the particular influences, Fisher in his later thinking has probably been more affected by the spirit of his times than his citation of authorities would indicate. Outlining his conceptions of capital and income with little conscious reliance upon contemporary speculation, and guided largely by a mathematical analogy, he has been forced as he developed the thought to take account more and more of the conclusions reached by others. His first articles had, as he later found, been to a considerable extent anticipated.[68] The capital concept of a fund of concrete wealth changes beyond recognition into a valuation or present worth of rights to future incomes. The income concept of a flow of the same goods that compose the flow of wealth is transformed into the at-first-rejected thought of psychic gratifications. The four capital-income ratios shrink in the course of the treatment to one, and that the very one whose character as capital he at first most doubted. Yet he still believes that the whole book is "only the elaboration of the ideas outlined some years ago in the *Economic Journal.*"[69] His treatment continues to labor under the incubus of the original erroneous definitions and of the original impossible fourfold hyphenated terminology, compelling us to talk of wealth-capital, property-capital, etc.

These are perhaps but the inevitable penalties of a certain isolation in Fisher's capital theory. He began the analysis and reconstruction of the capital concept as if it were a task apart from the theory of distribution as a whole. Beginning with the *a priori* mathematical concept of stock and flow, he tried to embrace under it all the forms and the whole problem of wealth. A large part of this is prior to, and a necessary condition of, a theory of capital, which is peculiarly the time aspect of value. His study as it has advanced has led to the incidental consideration of difficulties which demanded systematic and fundamental treatment. The capital theory presented has therefore a certain character of intellectual aloofness that leaves it out of touch with the larger theory of distribution of which it should be but one part. Much of what is best in the present work is thus somewhat belated, keeping the plane of the discussions of a decade ago and lacking that sense of unity and co-ordination in the theory of distribution which of late has been increasingly felt and expressed.

These criticisms are offered to center attention upon the points most controverted, and to give the perspective in which the work should be viewed. The work as a whole has a marked significance. It puts into convincing form some important disputed conceptions, and it must rank among the memorable contributions made by Americans to economic study.

NOTES

1. *The Nature of Capital and Income*, by Irving Fisher, Ph.D., Professor of Political Economy, Yale University. Pp. xxi+427. New York: The Macmillan Co., 1906.

2. *The Nature of Capital and Income*, p. 52.

3. *Op. cit.*, p. 52. The italics in all the quotations in this review follow exactly the original texts.

4. *Op. cit.*, pp. 58, 324, *et passim.*

5. "What is Capital?" *Economic Journal*, Vol. VI (1896), p. 514.

6. *Ibid.*, p. 514.

7. *Ibid.*, p. 516.

8. *Ibid.*, p. 527.

9. *Loc. cit.*, p. 528.

10. *Ibid.*, p. 533.

11. *Ibid.*, p. 534.

12. *Ibid.*, Vol. VII, p. 199. So desirous was the author to emphasize

the idea of stock as the essence of the capital concept, that he framed a definition doubly tautological: "stock of wealth existing at an instant of time." In any applicable sense of the word stock, the stock of wealth must be both existing and at an instant of time. "Stock of wealth" tells it all.

13. *Quarterly Journal of Economics*, Vol. XV (1900), p. 19.

14. Three articles in *Economic Journal*, Vols. VI and VII (1896 and 1897).

15. *Ibid.*, Vol. VII, p. 511.

16. *Op. cit.*, Vol. VI, p. 514.

17. *Ibid.*, p. 516.

18. *Ibid.*, Vol. VI, p. 527.

19. *Ibid.*, p. 516.

20. *Ibid.*, p. 526.

21. *Ibid.*, Vol. VII, p. 530.

22. *The Nature of Capital and Income*, p. 106.

23. See *Quarterly Journal of Economics*, Vol. XV, p. 19. Further comment on Fisher's present use of the value relation is found above, p. 106.

24. *Economic Journal*, Vol. VI, p. 530.

25. *Ibid.*, Vol. VII, p. 199.

26. *Nature of Capital and Income*, p. 66.

27. "Recent Discussion of the Capital Concept," *Quarterly Journal of Economics*, Vol. XV, p.19.

28. *Economic Journal*, Vol. VI, p. 514.

29. *Ibid.*, p. 532.

30. *Ibid.*, p. 534.

31. *Ibid.*, Vol. VII, pp. 512, 522.

32. *Ibid.*, p. 526.

33. *Ibid.*, p. 526.

34. *Nature of Capital and Income*, p. 106.

35. *Ibid.*, pp. 105, 106, 112.

36. *Ibid.*, pp. 105, 112. In a later summary of enjoyable objective services the money income is not named (p. 165), and it is recognized as a different method of reckoning, apparently in conflict with the former view (p. 107).

37. *Op. cit.*, p. 177. This is the view that was rejected by Fisher in the articles; see above, p. 99.

38. *Ibid.*, p. 168.

39. It is very questionable whether this is "usually" recognized. Only one reference in support of the statement is given in the footnote p. 165, and that one is to the reviewer's text which cites few precedents for the view.

40. Fetter, *The Principles of Economics*, p. 43 (1904).
41. *Nature of Capital and Income*, p. 177.
42. *Ibid.*, p. 176.
43. *Ibid.*, p. 177.
44. *Ibid.*, p. 149.
45. *Ibid.*, p. 326.
46. *Ibid.*, p. 232.
47. Chap. xiv, *passim*, especially p. 250.
48. It first appeared in criticizing Edwin Cannan, *Economic Journal*, Vol. VII, p. 532.
49. *Op. cit.*, p. 232.
50. *Ibid.*, p. 234.
51. *Op. cit.*, p. 234.
52. *Ibid.*, p. 238.
53. *Ibid.*, p. 248.
54. *Ibid.*, p. 249.
55. *Ibid.*, p. 253.
56. *Op. cit.*, p. 230.
57. *Ibid.*, p. 177.
58. *Ibid.*, p. 230.
59. *Ibid.*, p. 232.
60. *Ibid.*, p. 235.
61. *Ibid.*, p. 184.
62. In these cases the word "wealth" would be more fitting than the word "capital."
63. *Op. cit.*, p. 188.
64. *Ibid.*, p. 303.
65. *Ibid.*
66. *Ibid.*, p. 327. See also above, p. 99, where is shown Fisher's change from this earlier thought to the value concept.
67. *Economic Journal*, Vol. VI, p. 526.
68. *Economic Journal*, Vol. VII, p. 511, note.
69. *Nature of Capital and Income*, Preface, p. viii.

Are Savings Income?
—Discussion

We are discussing a question of terminology but not a question "merely" of terminology. In "the bright lexicon" of the newer economic criticism there is no such word as "merely" in application to questions of terminology. Against such a word the literature of economic thought gives many warnings in the fallacies resulting from ambiguity of terms. "Merely" terminological differences soon appear in the form of real and practical differences when ambiguous terms are applied in the discussion of practical questions. Even in this case Professor Fisher has promptly deduced from his peculiar concept of income some peculiar conclusions as to the justice of certain forms of taxation; and at a time when economic theory and financial practice alike are leading to the taxation of the unearned increment on land held for speculation, Professor Fisher is led to condemn both this theory and this practice.

Professor Fisher confesses that his conception is opposed to the usual view of economists, of business men, and of accountants, and that therefore the burden of proof rests upon him. More than that, his denial that additions to capital are money income is a paradox of the sort that economics is now generally rejecting. It is just such a paradox as that "rent does not enter

Reprinted from American Economic Association, *Papers and Discussions of the Twentieth Annual Meeting* 9 (April 1908). These remarks refer to and follow an article by Irving Fisher entitled "Are Savings Income?" (ibid., pp. 21-47). In his discussion Fetter criticizes Fisher's figure 2 (see ibid., pp. 40-41) for confusing pyschic and nominal income by measuring them on the same axis. Other discussants were Winthrop M. Daniels (ibid., pp. 48-51), A. W. Flux (ibid., pp. 55-56), John Franklin Crowell (ibid., p. 57) and Maurice H. Robinson (ibid., p. 57-58).

into price," or that "savings are at once consumed," or that "demand for commodities is not demand for labor"—such paradoxes, once considered to be the quintessence of economic wisdom, are now, by economic criticism, being relegated to the lumber room.

The very title of Professor Fisher's paper presents a terminological question, and is misleading. The subject is not so much "Are savings income?" as, Is an increment in the value of capital in a given period to be considered money income? Whether or not that increment of capital, when it is at the disposal of the owner, will be saved or spent is a later question and not involved in our present inquiry. Our question and our attention may be confined to the period within which the income accrues and matures. Professor Fisher's critics contend for the almost universal business usage of the term income as an increment of business power expressed in money value. What is the kind of income here under discussion? The term "income," rightly or wrongly, is applied to two (indeed, several) different things. We contend that the question here is of money income, whereas Professor Fisher has his attention fixed upon a different kind, namely, psychic income. He apparently agrees that capital as a business concept is the anticipated value or present worth of future psychic incomes. And he therefore concludes that in the period of its acquisition this capital is not money income to its owner. This is a *non-sequitur*.

In Professor Fisher's paper is meant by income evidently psychic income or value of the gratification. He presents us with a diagram which depicts the larger part of the argument in his paper. But what do those lines mean? In themselves they are but chalk marks. The lines *a, b, c, d,* and *e* in his diagram represent the income when it is detached and converted into enjoyment, when, in so far, the capital ceases to be capital, and is converted into a present realized psychic result. At that moment the line does not represent a monetary income, but a monetary outgo. He is looking at the end and ultimate goal of the valuation process, whereas the business man is estimating the objective income, the money value accruing in the period, regardless of whether that money will in the next period be saved or consumptively spent.

The chief reliance of Professor Fisher in his rejection of common practice and common judgment is undoubtedly his belief that the increments of capital value of future periods are not discounted from the present moment as is the psychic income. It may be said that the question is not as to the discounting of future incomes, but as to the view to be taken and the term to be used in reference to past and present increments of value. He says that the increment of value up to date is not income. We say that it is, and, of course, if it is saved, not spent, and is added to capital, it will continue to contribute its portion to the subsequent increments of capital. It is this estimate *up to date* in any accumulative period that is in question here. Treating the past increments of capital as income simply recognizes the increments that have accrued to the moment.

But the capital sums of an accumulating capital, taken at different points of time, are the actuarial equivalent one of another, when viewed from the present moment. The money income at the moment it occurs is the actuarial equivalent of a later larger money income that will result from the saving of the present monetary income. With this thought in mind it is evident that the incomes a, b, c, d, e of the diagram can be treated as Prof. Fisher treats them only on condition that they be consumptively used; in other words, that they be converted at that moment into psychic income. If they are kept by the owner and used normally and rationally, they accumulate in the hands of the owner. If Professor Fisher transfers them to another capital account at that moment, it is simply concealing beneath a new bookkeeping entry a source of additional income for the future. If, therefore, incomes e, d, etc., are not detached from the owner's capital, but merely given another entry in the accounts, the curve $N\,n$ would be extended toward the right and upward. The money income of the earlier periods, being saved and added to the capital sum, become themselves the source of new increments of value in the succeeding period. And this shows again that the detached incomes of which Professor Fisher speaks, must be not money incomes, but money outgoes, consumptive expenditure of a part of the capital value.

Indeed, there is here seen a difference between Professor Fisher's mode of conceiving of the problem of income and the mode in business calculations. Professor Fisher is thinking of the income as subjective; business deals with income as objective or as objectively expressed. Professor Fisher thinks of the income as occurring only when it is detached from the capital, a conception true at the moment of monetary expenditure and psychic income. Business thinks of the income for the most part as occurring when it is attached to the owner's capital, a conception true of the monetary income. These two conceptions have perhaps the relation that Professor Fisher elsewhere calls an interaction. Business practice, the logic of which we are defending, treats the income as occurring within the given period in which it either attaches or is enjoyed as usufruct. When a portion of the capital is spent for gratification, that much money value is detached and becomes psychic income.

It must be recognized that the capitalistic estimate and expression of incomes is not an ultimate psychological analysis of the problem of value. It is an estimate of income in objective terms, but an estimate at once logical in its place and indispensable in practice,—a statement probably true of the whole "cost of production" conception when rightly limited and understood. Professor Fisher's use of terms flies in the face of usage. While thinking of the income as detached value, he ignores the significance of the present and past attached value. Once a disbeliever in psychic income, he now, with the zeal of an apostate, becomes intolerant of any other conception even when monetary income is the subject under discussion. Is a thousand dollars in money received as a gift not an income when it is received? Is a ten-thousand-dollar estate received by legacy not an income to the beneficiary? Is a hundred dollars earned within this month by personal service not income because it is not yet enjoyment? Is the hundred dollars interest received from a mortgage or the hundred dollars rental received from a farm not income? To all these receipts Professor Fisher must deny the name of income for the same reason he has denied it in his discussion and in his book. He does so deny, defending a conclusion out of harmony with common usage and theoretical expediency, a conclusion only to be accounted for by his ambiguous use of the word income as both monetary and psychic.

Clark's Reformulation of the Capital Concept

1. STATEMENT OF CLARK'S DOCTRINE

The eightieth anniversary of the birth of John Bates Clark, our honored master in social philosophy, calls renewed attention to those economic issues in the discussion of which he has had a most vital part.

As a humble contribution to the volume which his fellow economists here bring as token of their regard, I would essay to review Clark's reformulation of the capital concept, and to trace its continuing influence upon economic opinion. No one can say what its total effect ultimately will be, but we may now form some judgment of its logic and of its aptness in practical discussion, and of the measure of acceptance which it has up to the present attained in America and England.

It is almost forty years since the publication of Clark's monograph entitled *Capital and Its Earnings*.[1] Hardly larger than a magazine article (merely 61 pages of text) it is yet one of the important milestones in the history of American economic theory, and likewise marks significantly new interests and a new stage of development in Clark's own thought. He was then in his forty-second year and had, since the age of thirty, been contributing toward "the reformulating of certain leading principles of economic science," through occasional magazine articles. These were "republished with varying amounts of revision and the discussion extended" in his first book, *The Philosophy of*

Reprinted from Jacob H. Hollander, ed., *Economic Essays Contributed in Honor of John Bates Clark* (New York: Macmillan Co., 1927).

Wealth, in 1885. While the work of that decade shows Clark to be, in his own words, "in revolt against the spirit of the old political economy," unsatisfied with its "defective" premises and its "degraded conception" of human nature (mere selfishness), and discontented with the actual relation of "capital" (the employing class) with "labor" (the wage earning class), it gives no hint or warning of the author's purpose to replace with a new conception the conventional notion of capital as an economic factor of production. That came in 1888 seemingly out of a clear sky.

Let us first restate, as briefly as we can, just what the thought was, and then seek to account for its appearance at that time. The more essential points in which Clark departed from the then prevalent views of capital may be reduced to five. He said:

(a) The conventional capital concept is ambiguous, meaning both "pure" capital and concrete "capital goods."
(b) "Pure capital" is a fund of value.
(c) Land in all its forms is a part of concrete capital.
(d) All concrete goods yield rents.
(e) All pure capital yields interest.

(a) Clark declared that economic science had and was using two unlike conceptions of capital, while believing that it had but one. Hence ambiguity, confusion, "logomachies." Clark would frankly accept both concepts, clarify them, and distinguish them by somewhat different names. One is the abstract, the other is the concrete concept. The abstract conception, paradoxically, is the one "employed in business a hundred times where the concrete conception is employed once";[2] whereas "the actual practice of economic science has been to first define capital in the concrete, and then, in the problems connected with it, to tacitly substitute again and again the abstract conception."

(b) Clark calls capital in the abstract sense "pure capital," which is a "fund," a "single entity" common to all the concrete forms of capital. This fund or entity is expressly declared to be "effective social utility," but this mysterious notion is repeatedly spoken of more simply though somewhat puzzlingly as "the value that a business man invests" in the various instruments and materials he uses. This is the value conception of capital in contrast with the concrete goods conception as defined by the conventional definition of the older political economy.

(c) Clark classed as concrete capital not merely the artificial, humanly "produced means of production," but all instruments and materials, including land and all other natural agents.

(d) Clark correspondingly widened the meaning and application of the term rent beyond that of the orthodox English economics, making it apply to the "sums earned by outward and material instruments of production" of any and every kind, *i.e.*, the earnings of concrete capital. The rent law is universal.

(e) Clark called the earnings of "pure capital" interest, and he conceived of this as rent (value) expressed as a percentage of the value of the abstract capital. Thus interest, as Clark wished to express it, did not consist of uses, yields, earnings, or incomes other than those composing rents, but simply was rent, expressed as a price in relation to the price of the instruments that embody the fund.

That these ideas appeared at that time to be radical novelties in American and English economic theory, is evident. The vigor and incisiveness of their statement helped them to command immediate attention even from those who were not ready to accept them as true. It must have been obvious that their acceptance would involve sweeping changes in the structure of the then accepted theory of distribution, with its sharp division between (natural) land and (artificial) capital as factors of production, and between rent (of land) and interest (on capital) as forms of "earnings" or incomes. Clark himself began at once to shape and build a structure of distributive theory but faintly forecast in his earlier essays, and increasingly to this day these ideas have exercised an influence upon theoretical opinion.

2. POSSIBLE SOURCES; THE AMERICAN TRADITION

Ideas departing so far from prevalent opinion rarely if ever spring as pure inventions of the moment from one mind. Nor does a change in the content and direction of an individual's thought, as marked as that of Clark at that time, occur without some influence from other thinkers or from environing conditions. But to trace such influences to their sources seems, in the case of Clark, at first unusually difficult. His literary style is didactic rather than polemical, and his thought seems to move along positive lines hardly at all conscious either of his forerunners or of hostile opinions, once he has formulated his own views. His writings give slight internal evidence of the sources of his thought. In the monograph in question the only references to the opinions of others are in minor matters, in three cases dissenting (from Ricardo, J. S. Mill and Sydney Webb) and in three approving (A. Smith, S. N. Patten, and Clark's co-worker, Giddings). The sources or the starting points of Clark's own thought must be sought more widely in the circumstances of his life and of his surroundings.

The first possibility might seem to be close at hand in the fact that Clark was an American. A scholarly study has recently shown[3] that with few exceptions writers on economics in the United States from Raymond in 1820 to Perry in 1877 (including Phillips, Wayland, Vethake, M. Wilson, Cardoza, Tucker, Carey, and Amasa Walker) defined capital as privately owned means of production, emphasized its valuation or price aspect, and included land among the concrete goods in which this value was embodied. Some of the exceptions serve to prove the rule, for these exceptions were men of English training or faithful disciples drawing their ideas directly from Ricardian text books. Such unorthodox views arose naturally in America where were lacking the artificial feudal limitations upon the sale of land, and where landholders were not marked off socially from capitalist merchants as a separate class. Here land was readily bought and sold and was from the earliest settlement the chief object of investment with a view to speculative profit. This environment had prompted one American writer after another (apparently without mutual influence) to develop conceptions radically different from those of the English school. It might have likewise prompted Clark quite independently to his very similar thought.

And there were particular circumstances at the time Clark was writing, namely, the active discussion of Henry George's single tax proposal, which undoubtedly had directed Clark's attention strongly to this problem of the capital concept. Of this, more later.

But if Clark got this thought either directly or indirectly from American economists, it is not evident in his writings. The generation of young economists who in the seventies and early eighties brought a new spirit into American economic studies, did not develop the indigenous traditions, but unfortunately neglected them and turned to Germany for the new sources of their inspiration. At the same time there was in some quarters (*e.g.*, Dunbar, Macvane, Laughlin, Sumner) a reactionary movement toward a new affirmation of Ricardian "orthodoxy" as reformulated in the work of J. S. Mill. Even Francis A. Walker did not develop his father Amasa's more original American treatment, but built his scheme of distributive theory on the older foundations of "land, labor and capital." There was thus, in the thinking of both the rival schools of thought of that time, a lack of reality and of rootage in the solid earth of our own economic conditions. American economic theorizing suffered then and still suffers from this defect. Clark's reformation of the capital concept, though couched in excessively abstract phrases, was the most vital attempt made in that period to find that reality. It was a new and distinct declaration of independence for American economic thinking.

3. TRACES OF GERMAN ECONOMIC PHILOSOPHY

Almost equally lacking in Clark's writings are any suggestions that the ideas now under discussion were derived from German sources; but that such is the case can hardly be doubted in view of all the circumstances. Clark was a student in Germany in 1876-1877 and was for a considerable period at Heidelberg under Karl Knies. Clark's writings in the first ten years after his return, mostly embodied in his *Philosophy of Wealth*, evidence the deep influence of the ideas of the historical school and of the economic-ethical doctrines then current in Germany. Knies himself had published in 1873 *Das Geld* subtitled also "a discussion of capital"; a second, enlarged edition of this was dated 1885. In this work appears a conception of capital strikingly like the one of Clark which we are examining. This conception had become traditional in German economics after the original work of Professor F. B. W. Hermann[4] first began to exercise an influence upon German thought. Hermann based his capital concept on property,—though it cannot be said that he succeeded in clearly distinguishing the thought of the value of property from the thought of the concrete goods. He included not only land within the concept of capital, but also immaterial goods or legal rights to income, even though the claims were upon persons and to services, and not to material goods. Probably the greatest change made by Hermann was to extend the definition of capital beyond artificial, produced, goods and to include as capital anything (or at least its value) that is the durable foundation of a use that has value.

Very similar ideas were developed by Carl Rodbertus in the thirties and forties, most significant because of the great influence they exercised upon later thinkers in the period of developing German state socialism after 1870. Especially Adolf Wagner acknowledged his profound indebtedness to Rodbertus.[5] To Wagner is due the much wider circulation and influence in the last quarter of a century of these ideas which he restated and endorsed.[6] Wagner credits Rodbertus with "the essential distinction between capital in the purely economic sense as any stock of material agents and means of production, and capital in the historico-legal sense as capital-possessions." He cites the statement of Knies that political economy uses capital in two senses, as concrete means of production, and as a stock of goods acquired by an owner. Both Wagner and Knies recognize the double meaning of capital as a tool in economic processes (technological sense) and as a source of private income (acquisitive sense), the distinction on which so much of the thought of Thorstein Veblen as well as of Karl Marx, seems to have been based. When Knies says approvingly that what has been called capital is "fundamentally nothing but a mere abstraction,"[7] the expression might be the original of Clark's "entity," "this abstract conception of capital."[8]

Clark, in common with all other Americans pursuing graduate economic studies in Germany, must have become familiar with these ideas. Yet why did no trace of them ever appear in the writings of other students returning from Germany, or even in Clark's writings, until 1888? Is not the explanation to be found in the fact that Americans went abroad with minds already cast in the mold of the Ricardian-Mill "orthodox" scheme of distributive theory, and these concepts persisted. It was possible for these students to acquire a zeal for displacing (or for supplementing) deductive methods with historical studies, and in favor of state activity vs. laissez-faire, without any essential change in the old conceptions of the economic factors and shares in distribution. This is well illustrated by H. C. Adams, R. T. Ely, and many others besides Clark. The more difficult question to answer is: Why did Clark ever, and why did he alone, break through this crust of conventional ideas, and in 1888 advance the views, received as complete novelties, with which his name has ever since been linked.

The important eras of human thought, we are assured by philosophers, rarely, if ever, are initiated by entirely new ideas, but by the rediscovery and restatement of old ones. Therein consists the more effective originality. It has been said, perhaps extremely, that the first time a new thought is expressed or an invention is made, the world simply pays no attention to it. Not until it is repeated independently and rediscovered a hundred times, and then only under peculiarly favoring conditions, does the world look up and say: yes, there is something in it, but nothing original—indeed it is very old. Until the world has received an idea in this way, its rediscovery for the hundredth time is as original as its discovery the first time, and its mere restatement by one aware of its earlier origin and rejection, calls, for that very reason, for as great vigor of thought, and for faith and conviction.

4. EFFECTS OF THE SINGLE TAX AGITATION

The probable source from which immediate stimulation came
to Clark was the contemporary single tax discussion. Started in
1879 by the publication of Henry George's book on *Progress and
Poverty,* it gained within a few years the most remarkable vogue
in popular interest. It attracted at once the attention of leading
economists. Professor W. G. Sumner attacked it in 1881 in
magazine articles.[9] Professor Francis A. Walker, who seems to
have been stirred to indignant protest particularly by George's
proposal to confiscate land values, made it the subject of a series
of lectures at Harvard in 1883, published under the title of *Land
and Its Rent.* But Clark, until after the publication of his first book
The Philosophy of Wealth,[10] and apparently until 1888, gave it no
mention in his published writings. The chief theoretical pillar of
George's doctrine was the Ricardian rent theory, and Walker,
even while assailing George, had avowed himself to be "a
Ricardian of the Ricardians," declaring that "Ricardo's rent
doctrine can no more be impugned than the sun in heaven."[11]
He would have none of Bastiat and Carey, who had sought to
reduce the origin of all land values to labor. Yet Walker somewhat unconventionally treated capital in the aspect of value as "a
capital sum" to be invested[12] as well in land, "in the soil," as in
agricultural improvements, and not as any particular group or
kind of economic agents. No formal definition of capital in the
old terms of "produced" means of production appears, yet
Walker is not conscious of any departure from "the general body
of orthodox economic doctrines," the "validity" of which he
thinks he is merely confirming.[13]

Events were just at that time crowding each other fast in the
single tax propaganda. *Progress and Poverty* was translated into
many languages and was said to have had a larger sale than any
other book ever written by an American. In 1886 George was
nominated and ran for the mayoralty of New York City, and of
the three candidates he polled the second-highest number of
votes. In 1887 George was a candidate for the Secretaryship of
New York State but was defeated. No other economic subject at

the time was comparable in importance in the public eye with the doctrine of *Progress and Poverty.*

At this moment Clark stepped into the arena of discussion armed with a new weapon, a valuation, or investment, concept of capital. His little monograph wears the mien of pure theory, and lingers for a time as its author himself says "in a region of abstract thought." But having in mind the circumstances just described, one can hardly fail to see on almost every page reflections of the contemporary single-tax discussion. In the brief preface is expressed the hope that "it may be found that these principles settle questions of agrarian socialism." Repeatedly the discussion turns to "the capital that vests itself in land," declared to be "a form of investment neither more nor less lucrative than others." On the ethics of confiscation Clark concludes that morally as well as legally "pure capital when invested in land, has the same rights that elsewhere belong to it." And as to confiscating all land values by the single tax, he exclaims: "would it be robbery? No; it would be the quintessence of robbery."

Two years later at the "Single Tax debate" at Saratoga, Clark developed in a very interesting way his ideas of pure capital as seeking investment in whatever form the State has said it may take. He sees it as a policy of expediency for the public welfare in the long run. The State "has said that it [capital] may go into land. For ends of its own it has so decided; and the ends are good."

But Clark felt that he had got hold of a deeper truth, more than a mere argument on a current issue. This monograph represents in most respects a completely new start toward a systematic theory of distribution which has little in common with his views in *The Philosophy of Wealth,* excepting "effective utility" (the marginal principle). It is needless to restate the argument of this well-nigh classical essay. Though brief, it is rich in ideas, and any one who has not read it will be well repaid by its careful study.

But read to-day, even by the most friendly critic, the argument reveals certain defects, partly arising out of its original polemical impulse, and partly due to the influence of the older conceptions upon Clark's thought. As to the latter, traces of the labor theory of value remain in the confusion between the process of evaluating "concrete instruments," including natural land, and the "personal sacrifices incurred in the service of society" in bringing concrete instruments into existence. When "the fruit of twenty years of labor" is exchanged for a piece of unimproved land, the value in the land is declared to embody "the fruit of personal sacrifice" of the buyer.[14] But whence came the value of the land before it was sold? Again, though including the most imperishable land among the things which embody pure capital, Clark sees the "concrete forms of capital" as constantly vanishing. "The bodily tissue of capital lives by destruction and replacement." In truth, Clark had not developed a consistent capitalization concept, or made a clear distinction between, on the one hand, technical production as the source and origin of what he called "capital goods," and, on the other hand, financial valuation of rights, incomes, claims (to land and also to personal services, good will, privileges, etc., as well as to "artificial" concrete goods) as a source of his "pure capital."

Nevertheless, his great achievements in this matter were that he brought out into the open the old ambiguity between "capital value" and certain concrete things called capital, and that he presented "capital" as essentially an investment concept; and that he gave a broader reading to the idea of rent. These notions have been apples of discord, and even yet professional opinions have not attained to unity upon them. It is of interest to observe the position taken toward the value concept of capital by some representative economists.

5. THE MORE CONSERVATIVE VIEWS

Böhm-Bawerk's conclusions on the capital concept were surprisingly old-fashioned. Beginning with a new conception of the so-called "interest problem" as that of differences of the value of goods because of time, he wrecked his attempt at the very first by his conception of capital (goods) as limited to produced means of production. For if, as he believed, "capital" and interest are coextensive facts, he cannot explain with such a capital concept the manifold time differences that appear everywhere, in land uses, legal rights, financial incomes, human services, etc. On no other point did Böhm-Bawerk differ with Clark so categorically as on this; he would have none of the valuation concept of capital.[15] Not even the most conservative of his contemporary neo-Ricardians were so uncompromising on this point. Yet not for a single page does he succeed in avoiding the valuation concept of capital when once he begins to use one. His capital is always an investment sum, expressed as so many kronen, pounds sterling, or dollars.

Professor Taussig devoted large space in his text to the discussion of the capital concept, returning to it again and again, evidently troubled and more or less impressed by nearly every count in the newer criticism on this subject. It seems a just characterization to say that Taussig's general conclusions and position resemble somewhat those of Marshall, outlined below, but show certain significant differences. First, he is somewhat more definitely conscious that the adoption of the valuation concept involves a radical break with the older doctrines. Secondly, he therefore more explicitly (though with various concessions and doubts) adheres to the older formal definition of capital in terms of concrete goods, and to the older idea of the two-fold division of the "instruments of production and the different sorts of return to their owners" (*i.e.*, land and capital, rent and interest, respectively).[16] Third, he, much more explicitly than Marshall, reaffirms a pretty bald labor-theory-of-value to account for the origin and distinctiveness of capital (concrete),[17] conceived of as "artificial" in contrast with land as "natural." In accord with this thought, he (probably unique in this regard) denies "productivity" alike to capital and to land, and thinks labor alone can properly be said to be productive, more so to be sure if applied "through the use of tools" than without them, more applied "on some land . . . than on other land," but in any case it is always labor alone that has "productivity."[18] Fourth, far more than Marshall, he struggles to escape from the meshes of the inevitable valuation concept. He sees, as Marshall did not, that he is being trapped into a repudiation of the older views. He was forced to recognize that "the ordinary business method of measurement" of capital is "in terms of value." He confesses that the old distinctions between rent and interest "find no response in the world of affairs."[19] Earlier[20] he had recognized that it was "often convenient to measure and record capital in terms of value and price,—as so much money," and he had even issued fair warning that he would "sometimes" so far conform "to everyday terminology" as to speak of capital in terms of its "value or price." (Of course, he always does express capital in those terms whenever he discusses investment of capital and interest as a rate per cent of return—no one can do otherwise.) Yet he explicitly rejects the "valuation principle"[21] and indicates what he thinks are its absurdities.[22]

Professor Seager, a colleague of Clark's at Columbia, acknowledges in the preface of his text his indebtedness to writers so far apart as Böhm-Bawerk, J. B. Clark and Alfred Marshall, and his treatment of this particular question betrays some of the discordant results. He seems to accept both the old view and in part that of Clark. He defines capital as "the product of past industry used as aids to further production."[23] Yet he cites, apparently with approval, the business man's use of capital as "the complex of capital goods, used in connection with each branch of production, measured in terms of money,"[24] a valuation investment concept. But he does not, as did Clark, include land among "capital goods"; these are purely artificial things, "products of past industry,"[25] thus plainly differing with the business usage cited. Seager was insistent on keeping sharply distinct the two classes of concrete goods (land and capital goods) which represent "man's part in production and nature's part."[26] Soon, however, Seager is found talking about buying land, quite in the sense in which the business man speaks of the purchase of other goods, as an "investment" involving the "capitalization of rents."[27]

6. MARSHALL'S ECLECTIC CAPITAL CONCEPT

In the first edition of his *Principles* (1890), Alfred Marshall was well aware of the issue before us, and gave it a good deal of attention. He showed acquaintance with J. B. Clark's work of two years earlier,[28] with Böhm-Bawerk, Newcomb,[29] and the several German economists above named, who contrasted capital as ownership and as means of production.[30] Marshall listed with approval a veritable catalog of definitions mutually inconsistent, but admitted that the divergent usage "has been a great stumbling block to many readers" and "appears to land the science in confusion." He comforts himself, however, with the thought that "the difficulty is much less serious than it seems at first sight."[31] The plan by which he hopes to minimize the confusion, if not avoid it, is to adopt *two* standard definitions, one each for individual and social capital respectively (apparently following Böhm-Bawerk), and then (apparently forgetting that he himself has two) "to supplement his standard definition by an explanation of the bearing of each of several elements of capital on the point at issue." His definition of individual capital is "that portion of a person's external goods by which he obtains his livelihood"; and of social capital is "those things made by man, by which the society in question obtains its livelihood." The latter consists, first, of goods in a form to satisfy wants directly ("consumption capital") and, secondly, of production goods ("auxiliary capital.") He recognizes that individual capital "is most commonly taken to include land and other free gifts of nature," but this is to be left "to be decided by an interpretation clause in the context wherever there is room for misunderstanding on the point." He evidently here thinks of "capital" (either individual or social) as consisting of concrete goods rather than of their value or the purchasing power they embody; and both his "standard definitions" make capital consist of the external goods themselves. Later, in a chapter headed "The growth of wealth,"[32] he discusses it as if it were identical with "the accumulation of capital" and to "the annual investment of wealth." It is almost needless to say that when he comes to discuss capital in business, it is in terms of investment and its monetary expression, while interest or earnings are percentages of a principal sum.[33]

In the successive revisions of his text, terminating with the 8th (1920) Marshall's discussion of this subject steadily increased in length and elaboration without gaining in clarity and consistency. On the whole, though, the change is in the direction of a greater preference for, and emphasis upon the individual concept (and its valuation expression) as compared with the social concept. The individual concept is now cited in the index as the "standard use" of the term,[39] and appears with this comment: "This definition of capital from the individual or business point of view is firmly established in ordinary usage; and it will be assumed throughout the present treatise whenever we are discussing problems relating to business in general." He concludes this chapter with admonitions to economists to "forego the aid of a complete set of technical terms," and not to assign "a rigid exact use to a word" as this "confuses business men"—astonishing counsel to budding would-be scientists.

Marshall's view as to the relation of land to capital is not easy to fix, but on the whole it seems to be that land is among the (concrete) things comprising *individual* but not social capital. *E.g.,* he says: "This illustrates the fact that land from the point of view of the individual cultivator is simply one form of capital."[35] Speaking more generally of manufacturers and traders as well as of farmers he says: "It is to be remembered that land is but a particular form of capital from the point of view of the individual producer."[36] Though Marshall here distinctly excluded land from capital from the social point of view;[37] nevertheless, only three pages later, still speaking of the social point of view, he says: "In purely abstract, and especially in mathematical, reasoning the terms Capital and Wealth are used as synonymous almost perforce, except that 'land' proper may for some purposes be omitted from capital." Are we to understand then, that for *most* purposes, land is by Marshall included in capital, at least land "proper," whatever that may mean, which here seems to mean "in the scientific sense," if it means anything?

The reader must take his choice among these contradictions, for his bewilderment will only be enhanced by further search amid the mazes of Marshall's tome. But, though Marshall's formal definitions of capital run in terms of concrete agents, there is no doubt that whenever he comes to discuss individual capital in problems relating to business in general he resorts to a valuation concept. The resources of an individual "are in the form of general purchasing power."[38] He declares that the idea of interest is strictly applicable only to fluid capital, evidently meaning readily available purchasing power. "The rate of interest is a ratio and the two things which it connects are both sums of money."[39] Thus it appears that after many contradictory assertions and formal definitions that reaffirm the older Ricardian scheme, Marshall really uses capital in nearly all his discussions of price and of business problems in his later editions as an individual (acquisitive) concept, expressed in (market) valuation terms. Yet unsuspecting students still are led to seek in Marshall a source of theoretical illumination instead of a smoke cloud.

7. THE YALE ECONOMISTS

The influence of Clark's views of capital showed itself at Yale within the following decade in the writings of A. T. Hadley and of his younger colleague, Irving Fisher. Hadley published in 1895[40] a noteworthy article marked by an insight and a clarity in nearly every feature in advance of its date, and by a realism in advance of Clark's abstraction of an entity of pure capital. Hadley recognized both the broad social and the narrow individual conception of wealth, and the broad and the narrow conception of capital. "Individual wealth is more accurately designated as property." "The capital of an individual is more accurately designated as an investment." "A title to property is not necessarily productive as held by Clark." Here Hadley briefly, but in essence, anticipated what Veblen (and in part Davenport) developed many years later regarding the contrast between acquisition and production, while avoiding Veblen's exaggeration of the contrast and his caricature of the profit motive. Hadley's text *Economics* published the next year, reproduced in its first chapter (on Public and Private Wealth) the substance of this article, but with certain additions (unfortunate, in our view) involving, as Hadley says,[41] "a combination of the ideas of Knies and Newcomb," but for which he acknowledges his chief indebtedness to be due to his colleague, Dr. Irving Fisher.

The essential addition due to Fisher was a distinction between capital and income as "modes of measuring" which Hadley had come to believe "is almost as important as the distinction between public and private wealth"[42] which he had presented in his essay of the year before. This new distinction is, however, certainly more than a mere detail; it introduces into Hadley's earlier clear and simple thought of capital as the value of rights of individual ownership, a different idea of a *stock* of wealth[43] as contrasted with a *flow* of wealth. The latter was pretty clearly Fisher's own idea at that time, as appeared in his contemporary articles.[44] In these Fisher presented this distinction between a "stock," or a "fund," and a "flow," or a "stream," as the *one* essential test of capital, as he conceived it. He is intent (not as was Hadley) on distinguishing capital as valuation from wealth as objects (for he thinks of both simply as material) but in distinguishing income as a *flow of things* from wealth as a fund, reservoir or *stock of things*. There is not a hint in Fisher's definitions that capital consists of "rights" expressed in terms of monetary valuation, or financially, or of its being a sum of purchasing power, a business investment concept. Fisher specifically objects to Clark's expression of the amount of true capital in terms of price, instead of by physical measurements. However, as soon as he attempts to discuss the percentage rate of flow, he assumes the measurement of both stocks and streams in monetary terms, for in no other way could a percentage appear. Fisher's contrast was that between a stock and a stream of the "very same commodities."[45] The present writer soon afterward[46] sought to show that this view was untenable in that it overlooked the durative nature of many of the objects comprised in Fisher's material "capital," and involved the erroneous assumption that all indirect agents eventually appear in substance as direct (enjoyable) goods. However, when Fisher next expounded his definition, though he referred in no way to this criticism, he introduced alongside of the old distinction a new one designed to obviate the difficulty with the unfortunate result that his unified conception is converted into the dualistic conception already foreshadowed by Hadley. This is the passage:[47]

> Capital is a fund and income a flow. This difference between capital and income is, however, not the only one. There is another important difference, namely, that capital is *wealth,* and income is the *service* of wealth. We have, therefore, the following definitions: A *stock of wealth* existing at an *instant* of time is called *capital.* A *flow of services* through a *period* of time is called *income.*

Now it must be said of these dualistic definitions that they are quite useless for the purpose in view. Fisher's own work on capital and income deals mainly with financial conceptions untouched in these definitions, incomes as price-quanta, discounted and summed up in capital (also a price quantum) conceived of as the present worth of claims to future monetary incomes, no matter whence or how derived (even from intangible rights). And the definitions are at least in part tautological, for while it would be logically possible (even though theoretically useless) to have a fund of wealth (material goods) and to contrast it with a flow of the same goods, it is not possible to conceive of a literal stock of services at an instant of time; it is possible only to conceive of their present worth as a financial fund at an instant of time. Services (taken in the sense of *uses* either of wealth or of human beings) may conceivably be delayed or hastened, but they are in their very nature a *flow;* they cannot be heaped up and constitute a *stock* of services. They can at most, as they occur, be "incorporated" in durable forms of wealth. If this is so, then why this elaborate contrast between a *flow* of services and a *fund* of something quite different? It is the vestigial remains of the older conception that Fisher has been obliged to discard.

The idea of a "fund" as a financial sum, estimate, or valuation, at an instant of time, has become confused with the idea of a "fund" as a heap or store of physical goods existing at an instant of time. The phrases of Fisher's definitions form a superficial, verbal bond of connection between the old conception and the new one, while in fact the essential distinction has become that not between income as a flow and capital as a fund (of the "very same" material things) but that between a valuation of services (incomes) when accruing separately throughout time and the valuation of those same services when discounted and summed up at an instant of time. Capitalization thus does involve a comparison of a financial fund (the single present worth) and a flow (a series of future worths) of the very same things, namely, valuations of services. Only through the common element, valuation, do capital as a valuation fund and income as a valuation flow become comparable.[48]

The text of Fairchild, Furniss and Buck, emanating from Yale, starts in the old paths, formally defining capital as a third factor of production, produced instruments of production. The tool, the indirect agent, seems to be the typical capital in mind in the historical survey, and the older definitions are repeated.[49] "Land, labor and capital" are presented in the familiar roles of the three factors of production.[50] But the first time that there is any real occasion to use the capital concept, a simple footnote makes kindling wood of these museum pieces and the reader is informed that "In the present discussion we shall use the term capital including land as well as man-made instruments. The term is generally so used in discussions of investments."[51] Thereafter capital appears as a fund of value, an investment fund, expressed in terms of dollars. Yet from time to time the discarded notion of the difference between land and man-made capital instruments is weakly reëchoed.[52] The treatment of interest and capital seems pretty nearly in accord with that of Fisher.

8. OTHER REPRESENTATIVE OPINIONS

Professor Seligman, a colleague of Clark's at Columbia, took an advanced position on the concept of value, as well as on the various related questions of rent, capitalization, etc. He declares repeatedly: "capital is capitalized income," and makes use almost exclusively of a valuation concept in that sense. Professor J. R. Turner too makes use[54] consistently of an advanced valuation concept of capital. These views and those of the writer[55] are in large measure in accord.

Ely as early as 1893[56] began with a dual capital concept as "every product which is used or held for the purpose of *producing* or *acquiring* wealth," but almost immediately speaks of capital from the individual standpoint as "any economic good" (not merely products) held "for the purpose of gaining wealth." Later editions, though repeating old definitions, give increasing emphasis to the individual, valuation conception, which finally becomes the only one actually used. "The business world . . . speaks of the total investment—the amount of money 'tied up' in a business unit—as its capital. This is the better and more common usage."[57]

Professor Fred M. Taylor[58] speaks approvingly of "one new way of conceiving of capital" as a "fund of value . . . rather than things themselves"; and adds: "Even those who doubt the soundness of this distinction are almost compelled to use it more or less on account of the ambiguities in which current controversies have involved the word capital."

Professor Bye[59] in his formal definition follows Fisher: "a stock of wealth in existence at a given time," including land as "natural capital," and "intangible property rights or titles to wealth as a part" of an individual's capital. He thus glides insensibly into the value conception of "net property rights," "net worths," etc.[60] Still the ghosts of the older conceptions of "natural" land and "produced" capital haunt almost every paragraph of the later chapter entitled "Income from artificial capital."

Professor O. F. Boucke[61] endeavors to give impartial recognition to the two different main concepts (besides several minor variations), capital "as technical aids used in production, or as any source whatsoever of incomes."[62] The latter idea is later expressed as "a sum of money or its equivalent," a "capital value" concept which includes such things as the "value of patents or copyrights, or of personal reputations," etc.[63] Thereafter, whenever capital is referred to in connection with credit, interest, or any sort of business problems, this value concept seems to be the one preferred.

Professor L. D. Edie[64] likewise starts by repeating the older definitions and distinctions based on the concrete goods notion, noticing, only to chide, the business man's thought of his business capital as money, or as "borrowed money on credit."[65] But he cannot long escape recognizing "capital values," and "capital is, from this viewpoint, not merely a mass of physical goods, but this plus a mass of property rights, good will, and other intangible assets." He adds: "To be realistic, our use of the term capital must harmonize with prevailing business facts" and declares that, "This modern view is amplified later in the present chapter."[66] A peculiarity of this author's view is that he seems to admit the valuation concept of capital only under the corporate form of organization.

9. *CLARK'S MESSAGE STILL VITAL*

It would be too great a task to pursue our inquiries further into the mass of recent business texts that touch upon this subject. It is a paradox that the more emphatically an author professes to have written for students of business, the more remote from actual business usage his conception of capital is likely to be. How long must it continue to be a sort of ritual for the writer of economic text books to at first repeat piously old definitions from which all vital meaning has departed (if they ever had any) only to throw them aside later when the time comes to use them. Must every year the minds of thousands of beginning students of economics be crammed with this useless intellectual lumber? In what other field of study could such a practice continue? The way to consistency and clearness has been clearly shown by the labors of the past generation. Ambiguity must be banished from economic terminology. Wealth and capital are not the same or even related as genus and species. Capital is essentially an individual acquisitive, financial, investment ownership concept. It is not coextensive with wealth as physical objects, but rather with legal rights as claims to uses and incomes. It is or should be a concept relating unequivocably to private property and to the existing price system. Social capital is but a mischievous name for national wealth. The so-called, misnamed, "interest problem" is not to be conceived of as correlated with a narrow class of artificial goods but rather as the time-value element permeating all cases of valuation of groups of uses differing in time. The admission of these and a number of logically related truths is partially, haltingly, inconsistently implied in much of the current treatment of the fundamentals. When will it be made frankly and clearly? When will the dead hand of Ricardianism be lifted from our economic texts?

John Bates Clark in his young manhood struck straight and telling blows for a newer, truer and more realistic conception of distributive theory. He did not attain an ultimate goal, but he advanced in the right direction, showing the way to us. The sincerest tribute that we, and that men of younger generations, can render to him is to seek and to find the truths implicit in the work of the notable era of which he was so large a part.

NOTES

1. May, 1883, in *Publications of the Amer. Econ. Asso.*, Vol. III, No. 2.
2. *Op. cit.*, pp. 11-12.
3. J. R. Turner, *The Ricardian Rent Theory in Early American Economics,* 1921.
4. Staatswirtschaftliche Untersuchungen, etc., Munich, 1832.
5. The ideas of Rodbertus on capital are scattered throughout his writings, but perhaps more systematically presented in his work *Das Kapital,* written 1850-51 but published first in 1885 by A. Wagner and

T. Kozak. (Known to the writer only in the French translation, Paris, 1904.)

6. See Wagner's *Grundlegung*, 3rd. ed., 1892, p. 307 ff.

7. Knies, *op. cit.*, p. 43.

8. Clark, *op. cit.*, p. 11.

9. See Dr. A. N. Young, *The Single Tax Movement in the United States* (1916), *passim*. Prof. R. T. Ely noticed it in his *Recent American Socialism* in 1885.

10. Largely a republication of a series of articles the publication of which was begun ten years earlier. See preface to first edition.

11. *Op. cit.*, p. 86.

12. *E.g.*, *op. cit.*, pp. 33, 34.

13. *Op. cit.*, p. 86.

14. *Op. cit.*, pp. 55, 66.

15. See the discussion, *Quarterly Journal of Economics* (1895-1896), Vol. 9 (Clark), p. 238; (Böhm-Bawerk), pp. 113, 235, 380; Vol. 10 (Clark), p. 98, (Böhm-Bawerk), p. 121.

16. *Principles of Economics*, 1st ed., 1911, Vol. 2, p. 115.

17. *E.g.*, Vol. 1, pp. 72, 75; Vol. 2, p. 119ff.

18. *Ibid.*, Vol. 2, pp. 5-8, 58.

19. *Ibid.*, Vol. 2, p. 118.

20. Vol. 1, pp. 84, 85.

21. *Ibid.*, pp. 121-123.

22. In part his objections result from his not seeing the full import of the principle; however, his objection to Professor Irving Fisher's view of capitalizing human beings is in my judgment well taken. The reference to my text at this point in the 3rd edition (1921) is misleading. (Vol. 2, p. 126)

23. *Introduction to Economics* (1904), p. 108.

24. *Ibid.*, p. 126, and, in revised form, *Principles of Economics* (1913), p. 14.

25. *Principles*, p. 148.

26. *Ibid.*, p. 149.

27. *Ibid.*, p. 239.

28. *E.g.*, note p. 615; and specific reference to Capital and its Earnings in note, p. 492.

29. *Ibid.*, p. 137.

30. *Ibid.*, pp. 135-136.

31. *Ibid.*, p. 133.

32. *Ibid.*, p. 284.

33. *Ibid.*, pp. 513, 620 ff., 635, 648, etc.

34. 8th ed., p. 72. But still, in his last word on the subject (p. 790), Marshall justifies his own adoption of "the two-fold definition of capital."

35. *Ibid.*, p. 170.

36. *Ibid.*, pp. 430-431. Also p. 535 *et passim*.

37. *Ibid.*, p. 78.

38. *E.g., ibid.*, p. 411.

39. *Ibid.*, p. 412.

40. *Yale Review*, Vol. 4, pp. 156-170, "Misunderstandings about economic terms."

41. In a footnote, p. 5.

42. It would be a more accurate description of this distinction to say, using Hadley's own phrases: between public wealth as the sum of the "means of enjoyment" or "means of happiness," in existence, and private capital as the value of individual property rights.

43. Material objects by Fisher's definition, *Nature of Capital and Income*, p. 3.

44. *Economic Journal*, Vols. 6 and 7, 1896, 1897. A number of references to J. B. Clark's ideas occur in the three articles.

45. *Op. cit.*, Vol. 6 (1896), p. 514.

46. See *Quarterly Journal of Economics*, Vol. 15 (1900), p. 19.

47. *The Nature of Capital and Income* (1906), p. 52. Italics in the original.

48. The thought is hardly to be avoided that some of the peculiar ideas regarding savings and income to which Fisher has adhered so uniquely despite criticism are traceable to this confusion of definitions. We refer especially to his reiterated proposition that "savings are not income." As a financial fact, there can be no saving and addition to capital value until there is first a property right to an income calculable in monetary terms (a financial present worth) to be saved. Hence to deny that monetary savings are monetary income is in simple common sense to deny a *fait accompli;* it is to assume the existence of the effect before its cause.

49. *Elementary Economics* (1926), Vol. 1, p. 32 ff.

50. *Ibid.*, p. 40.

51. *Ibid.*, Vol. 1, p. 355.

52. *E.g.*, Vol. 2, pp. 163 and 189.

53. *Principles of Economics* (1905), see pp. 17, and ch. xiv, p. 204, on "The Capitalization of Value."

54. *Introduction to Economics*, 1919.

55. As developed in various places; see, among other, *Quarterly Journal of Economics*, Vol. 15 (1900), pp. 1-45, "Recent Discussion of the Capital Concept"; "The Relations between Rent and Interest," paper read at the New Orleans meeting, with discussion, *Publications of the American Economic Association*, 3rd series (1904), Vol. 5, pp. 176-240; *The Principles of Economics* (1904); *American Economic Review*, Vol. 4 (1914), pp. 68-92; *Economic Principles* (1915), p. 267: "Capital is a

person's investment power as expressed in terms of money, being a person's property rights to income, estimated, as to amount, with reference to market conditions." The definitions given in the references dating 1900 to 1904 followed in part Clark's and Fisher's leads in conceiving of capital more nearly as the valuation expression merely of (material) wealth. In developing after 1904 a more adequate capitalization and "interest" theory, the writer returned with clearer convictions to the conception of capital that he had glimpsed before 1900.

56. *Outlines of Economics.*

57. *Outlines of Economics,* 4th revised edition (1923), p. 206; see also p. 103 *et passim.*

58. *Principles* (1913), p. 69.

59. R. T. Bye, *Principles of Economics,* 1924.

60. *Op. cit.,* p. 24.

61. *Principles of Economics,* 2 Vols., 1925. Ref. to Vol I.

62. *Op. cit.,* p. 95. These ideas are more elaborately set forth, pp. 370-376.

63. *Ibid.,* p. 381.

64. *Economics,* 1926.

65. *Op. cit.,* p. 247 ff.; also p. 254.

66. *Ibid.,* p. 255.

Capital

Capital is a word derived from the adjective form *capitalis* (Latin root *caput*, head), meaning principal, chief. Its various meanings as a substantive are explained as the "several elliptical uses of the adjective" (*Oxford Dictionary*). As first used in commerce capital meant an interest bearing sum of money. The manifold derivative meanings are all of two types, the one implying ownership of a valuable source of income, the other the stock of physical goods constituting the income source. The one idea was from the first characteristically individual, acquisitive and commercial, that of any financial fund having a monetary expression; the other idea was characteristically impersonal and technological, that of the physical goods used to extract, transport, create or alter goods: ships, stores of merchandise, money, tools, machines, houses and, usually but not always, lands.

By a simple association of ideas the original thought of capital as a "fund" for investment was generally connected with lending by the class of passive capitalists, but capital as a "stock" of instruments was connected with borrowing by active enterprisers for the purpose of buying the physical instruments of trade and manufacture. This contrast disappeared, however, when the active enterpriser was pictured as neither borrower nor lender but one who "invests" (clothes) his purchasing fund in the physical equipment in his own possession. Thus the business as a whole might be thought of either as the sum or fund of purchasing power invested, or as the mass of goods which, although not bought with borrowed funds, embodied the owner's business fund.

These two types of capital concepts are so distinctive in es-

Reprinted from *Encyclopedia of the Social Sciences*, s.v., "Capital."

sential thought and practical application that confusion inevitably resulted from the use of one word to designate both. This confusion occurred not later than the early years of the seventeenth century, when capital was defined by Cotgrave in 1611 as "wealth, worth; a stocke, a man's principall, or chiefe, substance." Here the idea of "worth," implying a valuation, is thoroughly mixed with that of substance, no doubt in the sense of material things in possession. "Capital" thus used is a superfluous and confusing synonym of wealth, goods and stock.

This transition and duplication of terms was confirmed by association of the words capital and stock. The latter, an old Germanic root word, developed in English manifold meanings. The term stock was used in business in the sixteenth century as "a collective term for the implements and the animals employed in the working of a farm, an industrial establishment, etc."; and at the same time as "a capital sum to trade with or to invest." Even earlier, in the fifteenth century, stock meant "a sum of money set aside to provide for certain expenses; a fund," but this became obsolete.

As English trading companies developed after the fifteenth century, the terms joint stock, capital stock, stock and capital were used with little clear distinction. Adam Smith (*Wealth of Nations*, bk. v, ch. i, pt. iii, art. i) says of the East India Company, chartered in 1600 by Queen Elizabeth: "In the first twelve voyages which they fitted out for India, they appear to have traded as a regulated company, with separate stocks, though only in the general ships of the company. In 1612, they united into a joint-stock." This and other similar examples indicate that at first the "stocks" meant the physical merchandise composing the cargo, and a joint stock company was one in which these stocks were held jointly instead of severally. But Smith refers at once to the "capital" of the joint stock company as so many thousand pounds sterling. His treatment of capital as a whole manifests all the errors that have accompanied the use of this elusive term ever since: the employment of the term as meaning both investment fund and goods bought with it or sometimes "talents" or "skill" acquired by means of it, and as denoting both value and a stock of physical agents, etc. Incidentally Smith suggests a thought that was destined to grow until a certain kind of "circulating" capital, subsistence for laborers, came to be looked upon by J. S. Mill and others as the very essence of the capital concept.

In the three quarters of a century after 1776 the changes in machine production and transportation and in financial and commercial organization were epoch making. Not only did factories owned by individuals and by partnerships increase greatly in size and resources, but great corporations building and operating factories, canals, railroads, steamships, commercial enterprises and banks were chartered and their shares widely distributed to subscribers. At the same time the functions of banks and the agencies for investment of capital funds grew apace. These changes put into the foreground of attention the thought of capital as investment, both active and passive. Whether as cause or as effect this change was accompanied by the ever increasing attention given to commercial profits as contrasted with national welfare (or rather profit was assumed, in the doctrine of laissez faire, to be identical with welfare). It was during this period too that the word stock was increasingly displaced by "capital." In Ricardo's work (*Principles of Political Economy*, 1817) this transition is perhaps half completed. His "profits" is still from the first word "the profits of stock," and the phrase recurs occasionally, but his training and interests account for his few references to "stock" as physical agents used in technical processes, and for his many references to employers' investment expressed with the pounds sterling symbol. The emphasis is different from that of Smith, but the confusion of two meanings remains.

J. S. Mill, however (*Principles of Political Economy*, 1848), scarcely uses the word stock after the definition of capital as "this accumulated stock of the produce of labor." But the "function of capital is production," the goods mentioned are all physical and usually their function is described as technological. He is soon, however, hopelessly confused in attempts to distinguish between capital to the individual and capital to the nation. The "capital" employed in production is "worth ten thousand pounds." The chapter on "increase of capital" is mostly concerned with "the produce of past labor"—physical objects; but that on "the profits of capital or stock" treats mainly a "rate" of profits on a valued investment. Mill stumbles at length into the notion that all advances "have consisted of nothing but wages," a large portion as direct payment and the rest as "previous advances" which "consist wholly of wages." Nothing could be more explicit—or more erroneous as an explanation of the origin of capital values—ignoring as it does every influence from scarcity of natural materials, from monopoly, from previous profits, from manifold speculative influences and from recapitalization (the revaluation of agents). Mill's capital concept at this point is the fruit of his labor theory of value—herein, however, he has substituted wages for Ricardo's quantity of labor, thereby better concealing the difficulty due to various qualities and values of labor.

The capital concept remained in the circle of English "liberal" price economists as Mill had left it until the late eighties. Among them Marx's conception of capital as an agency of exploitation found no echoes. Yet unquestionably there was here an aspect of truth, one which at that time and since then has been given wide recognition in Germany. Capital both with Marx and with Mill involved the confusion of acquisition and "production," Marx seeing chiefly the acquisitive and Mill the technical aspect. Classification of capital as one of the three factors of production implies its physical nature and its technological function. Its yield (profit, or interest, as by preference it began to be called) was assumed to be coordinate in nature with rent (of land) and wage (of laborer); yet profits (or interest) as a rate percent of an investment manifestly does not fit into this scheme, and there is a consequent confusion in the theory of incomes.

The psychological school after 1870 made earnest attempts to revise the prevailing capital concept. Jevons, in his incomplete studies of capital (e.g. *The Theory of Political Economy*, 1871, ch. vii; also appendices i-ii in 4th ed. London 1911), offered some original suggestions, but in the end adopted Mill's subsistence (food for laborers) concept. Böhm-Bawerk (*Kapital und*

Kapitatzins, 2 vols., 1884-89) as a disciple of Menger sought to make the theory of capital his peculiar domain, but after beginnings which pointed toward a value investment concept and after painstaking studies of earlier views he adopted the conventional confused concept of "capital in general" as "a group of [physical] products which serve as means to the acquisition of goods." This foredoomed him to a productivity theory of interest—the very thing he had attempted to avoid. He also developed a sort of subsistence theory of capital investment in connection with his periods of production in "the roundabout process." J. B. Clark, while engaged in controversy over the single tax, detected the duality of the "orthodox" Mill-Ricardian capital concept and proposed (*Capital and Its Earnings,* 1888; also *The Distribution of Wealth*, 1899) to match it with twin terms, "capital-goods" or physical agents including land, and "pure capital" as the (supposedly) permanent fund of value resident in them. Yet in accounting for "the genesis of capital" (physical) and for the capital value Clark too lapsed inconsistently into the old labor theory of value.

Clark's eclectic terminology of "capital goods" and "pure capital," although an unfortunate compromise, has had wide vogue. His reformulation served to stimulate much further discussion, some futile and some fruitful. Partly no doubt this discussion, partly the rapid changes in business organization, notably incorporation, banking, financial investment and more refined accounting, have caused the trend in recent economic texts toward the more general usage of capital in the valuation, property, investment sense of the terms.

The history of the capital concept helps to explain the early and still persistent confusion of money (a part) with capital (as the whole, of a person's fund of purchasing power) and this, in mercantilist doctrine, with wealth in general. The discussion of the ethical justification of interest (first in the original sense of a premium for a money loan, then in the widened sense of any income from private property) easily became confused because of the ambiguity of "capital." The conservative justified acquisition through capital ownership by pointing to the value of the technological uses of physical wealth; the communist denied to wealth any valuable technological uses, attributing all value to labor and depicting private property as merely a tool of exploitation used by employers to rob the workers of the "surplus value" they had created.

Economic as well as ethical interest theory has suffered from this ambiguity. All use and productivity theories are attempts to explain the rate of premium (or yield) from a financial fund (capital value) by reference to the rent or usance value of a stock of indirect technical agents, without a theory of capitalization to explain first the value of the capital sum or principal.

The terms fixed and circulating capital are distorted expressions of the truth that various kinds and various portions of investments are more or less readily saleable, confused with the technological truth that various physical agents are more or less durable in nature.

The definition of capital determines in turn the meaning more or less vaguely attached to such phrases as capitalistic system, the growth of capitalism and the capitalistic age. Some see in capitalism essentially the use of labor saving machines (perhaps also power driven); this is a technological conception of capitalism. Others, more eclectic, see in capitalism essentially the wage system where the employer owns all the physical agents. But consistently with the value concept capitalism is merely the price system, the commercial exchanging organization of industry, where valuations, incomes and property take on the financial expression.

It is necessary to distinguish certain popular uses of the term capital, notably "nominal capital" of a corporation as the total face value of shares of stock outstanding, taken at par (or sometimes the total authorized); this, however, can mean only number of shares in the now frequent cases of shares with no par value. Sometimes nominal capital is used to mean the total denomination value of all securities, even bonds, and "capital of a corporation" as denoting these taken at their market value. None of these is properly called "capital" but rather "nominal value [or market value respectively] of corporation shares or securities." Capital as applied to corporations is rather a figure of speech than a consistent scientific term, inasmuch as a corporation (a person only by legal fiction) has revenues and receipts rather than "incomes," and assets (physical or intangible sources of revenues) rather than capital.

While recognizing divergent usage, we may define capital as the market value expression of individual claims to incomes, whether they have their sources in the technical uses of wealth or elsewhere. This is essentially an individual acquisitive, financial, investment, ownership concept. It is a "fund" only in the financial sense, not a stock of wealth. It is the sum, in terms of dollars, of the present worths of various legal claims. It therefore includes the worth of all available and marketable intangibles, such as credits, promises, good will, franchises, patents, etc. as well as the worth of claims to the uses of physical forms of wealth. Their summation as a financial fund is the resultant of a capitalization process. Physical objects of value are not capital, being sufficiently designated as goods, wealth or agents.

Capital as here defined is a conception of individual riches having real meaning only within the price system and in the market place where it originated, and developing with the spread of the financial calculus in business practise.

Consult: Cannan, Edwin, "Early History of the Term Capital" in *Quarterly Journal of Economics*, vol. xxxv (1920-21) 469-81, and comments on it by R. D. Richards and H. R. Hatfield in *Quarterly Journal of Economics*, vol. xl (1925-26) 329-38 and 547-48; Cannan, Edwin, *A History of the Theories of Production and Distribution* (3rd ed. London 1924); Böhm-Bawerk, Eugen von, *Kapital und Kapitalzins*, 2 vols. (4th ed. Jena 1921), tr. by W. Smart as *Capital and Interest* (London 1890), and *The Positive Theory of Capital* (London 1891); Davenport, H. J., *Value and Distribution* (Chicago 1908); Spiethoff, A., "Die Lehre vom Kapital" in *Die Entwicklung der deutschen Volkswirtschaftslehre im neunzehnten Jahrhundert*, 2 vols. (Leipsic 1908) vol. i, no. iv; Passow, Richard, *Kapitalismus* (2nd ed. Jena 1927); Oppenheimer, Franz, *Theorie der reinen und politischen Oekonomie*, 2 pts. (5th ed. Jena 1923-24) pt. ii, p. 565-606; Fisher, Irving, *The Nature of Capital and Income* (New York 1906); Fetter, F. A., "Recent Discussion of the Capital Concept" in *Quarterly Journal of Economics,* vol. xv (1900-01) 1-45, and *Economic Principles* (New York 1915) pt. iv, and "Clark's Reformulation of the Capital Concept" in *Economic Essays Contributed in Honor of John Bates Clark* (New York 1927) p. 136-56; Veblen, T. B., "On the Nature of Capital" reprinted in *The Place of Science in Modern Civilization* (New York 1919) p. 324-86.

Reformulation of the Concepts of Capital and Income in Economics and Accounting

1.

Examination of a considerable sample of current accounting literature discloses a much divided opinion as to the relationship between economic and accountancy concepts and theory. Occasionally some accountant deplores the fact that "accountants have seldom had much training in economics" and expresses the hope that in the future public accountants may be more thoroughly educated in that subject.[1] The more frequently recurring emphasis, however, is that "the point of view of the accountant differs sharply from that of the economist, and that consequently, the terms, concepts, and principles of economics cannot reasonably be transferred, unmodified, to the field of accounting."[2]

The general attitude of accountants seems to be that the economic concepts may be valid in their own field, but that they cannot be adopted and applied to accounting purposes.[3] I maintain, on the contrary, that there is no necessary conflict between the conceptions and terms in economics and accountancy. It is true that economics ought to deal with some aspects of public, or social, policy which lie outside the field of accountancy, but economics also has to do, as has accountancy, with the price system and the problems of capital, profits, and income in connection with private individual and corporate enterprises, and much of the current economics does this ex-

Reprinted from *Accounting Review* 12 (March 1937).

clusively to the neglect of the social aspects.[4] Our first thesis, then, is this: *If and when accountants and economists are talking about the same things, namely problems of private enterprise, investment, prices, capital, and income, they should talk the same language among themselves, with each other, and with the public.* Words are the symbols of thought, the circulating medium of ideas, and the penalty for confusion in our language must be confusion in our own thinking, magnified further in the minds of the public.

For my part, I concede that economics is primarily to blame for the confusion existing today in both fields of study. The principal economic terms now in use were taken uncritically from popular speech by the earlier writers with little regard either to etymology or to logical consistency. These terms have long been used in special restricted senses in the discussion of contemporary issues without recognition of other misleading associations of ideas. Often in the same paragraph or chapter where the terms are formally defined in one sense, they are used by the author himself in a different sense. In many modern economic texts definitions of this sort still linger as the sacred "idols of the forum" and "of the theater," as Sir Francis Bacon called the errors arising from human language and from traditional doctrines and methods. It is to this arsenal of rusty weapons that the accountants have mostly continued to resort in search of much needed arms of economic theory, whose defectiveness is quickly revealed under hard usage in their hands. Economists often with impunity may be arm-chair theorists; accountants are on the firing line of business, and their weapons of theory feel the full shock of the battle. Their efforts to find consistent and useful terms and concepts have in some respects been hindered rather than helped by their reliance upon the older economic authority. Not until economists of the Marshallian, Neo-Ricardian, school have more fully recognized their errors and reformed their terminology, can the accountants hope to derive much help from many of the current economic texts.

It should be observed also that the close contact of accountants with the hard realities of business has made more difficult for them the task of formulating logical and consistent concepts for their own use. Consider particularly the necessity they are under of protecting their clients by conforming with the requirements laid down in legislative statutes regarding the maintenance of "legal capital" (or "stated capital") and regarding the permissible distribution of dividends. Such statutes, often varying and conflicting in different jurisdictions, carelessly and inconsistently drafted or later so interpreted by the courts, frequently force the accountants to bend logical terminology to legal and practical requirements. As Hatfield says:[5] "The accountant can not disregard the decisions of the courts, or he may find that he has led his clients into an action for which they may be held liable." But surely it is the highest duty of both accountants and economists, while meeting the legal and practical demands of the moment, to point the way towards truer economic conceptions in the law instead of merely passively submitting to its sometimes blundering dictation. That, indeed, is the ideal of this session.

2.

Regarding the important place of the concepts of capital and income both in economics and in accountancy there is no dispute. Not long ago an accountant in a thoughtful article[6] on "The maintenance of capital" declared: "The fundamental purpose of accounting consists of an attempt to distinguish clearly between capital and income." Another accountant has recently said:[7] "The primary and central problem of business and hence of accounting and finance, will always be income." Here the emphasis is on income but the context rightly implies that the conceptions of capital and income are so interwoven that the determination of one is impossible without that of the other. This is implied also in the generally accepted view that the fundamental divisions, or classifications, of accounting are the balance sheet and the income sheet.

It is remarkable, therefore, that clear and tenable definitions of these fundamental terms are almost impossible to find either in economic or in accountancy texts. The authors seem to shrink from defining what is not really clear in their own minds. There is much talk of specific forms or phases of "capital" but rarely any generic use of the term capital. Thus free and almost reckless use is made of the terms "stated capital," "legal capital," "capital of the enterprise," "owners' capital," "capital stock," "capital charges," (or "charges to capital") "capital accounts," "capital assets," "capital owned," "physical capital," "fixed capital," "circulating capital" and (repeatedly, but without definition) "true capital," and "true economic capital,"—whatever that may mean to the writers—, but never a clean-cut essential definition of "capital" itself. The occasional, partial, or most nearly explicit definitions are mutually conflicting, some identifying capital with what most writers call the "assets" as a whole,[8] and what Paton would prefer to call "properties";[9] while others identify capital with what usually seems to be called "net worth" or "proprietorship."[10]

3.

It is rash to hope that order can be brought at once into this chaos of terminology; but let us at least try to make a beginning. There is no obscurity about the origin of the term "capital." It made its appearance first in medieval Latin as an adjective *capitalis* (from *caput*, head) modifying the word *pars*, to designate the principal sum of a money loan. The principal part of a loan was contrasted with the "usury"—later called interest—the payment made to the lender in addition to the return of the sum lent. This usage, unknown to classical Latin, had become common by the thirteenth century and possibly had begun as early as 1100 A.D., in the first chartered towns in Europe. The use of money was long confined almost entirely to the towns, and the lending of money occurred mostly between merchants, and only rarely between merchants and others. The chartered towns with their merchant guilds and markets and fairs were at first merely little islands of money economy, commerce, and contractual prices, dotting the wide sea of feudalism where prevailed conditions of status with customary dues and services, and where the use of money and the monetary expression either of wealth or of incomes, were scarcely known. Both the use of money and its lending by merchants to each other and to the feudal nobles became much more common during the Crusades which recurred at intervals for nearly two centuries (from 1096 to 1270). For centuries the rural-feudal and the urban-commercial conceptions of wealth and income continued to grow apart. The more static feudal conceptions of landed property and customary dues began to come into violent conflict with the more dynamic ideology of contractual prices and capital values in the world of commerce, with the gravest consequences in politics, religion, and social relations.

Sometime in this period the adjective *capitalis*, by an easy transition, came to be used elliptically in common speech as a substantive, dropping the words *pars*. At the same time, doubtless very gradually, the meaning of "capital" was widened in the marketplace to include besides actual money loaned, the monetary value of wares sold on credit, and still more generally the worth of any other credit (receivable) expressed in terms of money.

The next inevitable expansion of the meaning of capital made it include the estimated value of merchant's stock of goods and of agents (such as tools, shops, ships, lands, etc.) employed in his business by himself as well as when loaned to another for an agreed interest or rental. Included with these as "capital" was the monetary valuation of debts and bills receivable and of valuable rights of all kinds pertaining to the business. All these were resources, or assets (to use a later term) which might be sold for money and which were thus alternative forms of business investment, the equivalents in their money's worth of a principal sum loaned at interest. Each such asset item was at first a separate "capital," invested in a specific way, or form, and collectively they were long spoken of in the plural as "the capitals"; but gradually the net sum of all the separate items after deducting debts, or liabilities, came to be called a person's capital (in the singular number). The first authentic example of this usage (which had doubtless become common) is a somewhat confused definition of date 1611: "Capital: wealth, worth; a stocke, a man's principall or cheif substance."[11] Here the notion of capital as the physical store of goods, called also "wealth," "stocks," or "substance," is mingled with that of capital as a valuation (worth), constituting a man's principal in a financial sense.

The use of the word "capital" in this definition as a synonym both for "worth" or "principal" and for "stock" or "substance" is evidence that already a confusion was present which was destined to plague economics, the law, and accountancy from that day till this. "Capital" in the original sense of the principal of a money loan, later expanded to include the worth of any kind of business asset or investment, is a purely financial conception; but "capital" in the sense of a man's "stock" or "substance" is essentially a physical-goods conception. Still other confusions were foreshadowed. The use of the Anglo-Saxon word "stock," in the definition just quoted, made easy the transition from the term "capital" as a sum of values to the hybrid and ambiguous term "capital stock" as a mass of physical goods,[12] the value of which was the financial investment in the enterprise. Within the next century other confusions appeared as the terms capital and income were extended to relate to corporations, not merely to individuals.

These changes occurred not suddenly but during the seventeenth century. In the definition of date 1611, capital was still something thought of as belonging to "a man," a natural person, and not to a corporation. This individualistic conception of capital had been unquestioned for centuries and still survived at the end of Queen Elizabeth's reign. The complicating notion of corporation capital came within the next hundred years. The English trading companies numerously organized as Merchant Adventurers in the fifteenth century for trading on the Continent had retained this distinctly individualistic conception of capital as the sum invested by a natural person in the hope of profit. The company as such had no permanent investment, and each trading trip was a separate "adventure" for which a stock of goods was provided by subscribers in various proportions each of whom recovered his "capital" and shared in the profits (if any) after each adventure in proportion to his investment.

Temporary shifting investment is not suited to undertakings that must be carried on continuously for long periods to show results. Further, the interests of the public and of creditors require that when the liability of the shareholders is limited the amount of capital subscribed should be a stated amount. In a continuing enterprise this is necessary also, in order to determine the amount to be retained as capital or distributed as profits, and for other purposes, such as taxation, etc. These principles which seem so obvious now were only gropingly arrived at between 1600 and 1657 by the experience of the great companies chartered in England for overseas trade and colonization. The London East India Company, chartered the last day of the year 1600, obtained large powers and privileges. The first voyages, or "adventures," as they were called, were separate enterprises, each new group of adventurers taking over from the last group the assets such as ships, warehouses, etc., at an agreed valuation. Beginning in 1612 several voyages (e.g., those for the years 1613-1616) were treated as a single joint stock, and not until 1657 was this procedure extended by a new charter under which was created "The New General Stock" as a permanent investment.[13]

The experience of the East India Company is fairly illustrative of the changes under way at that time. Toward the end of the seventeenth century occurred the incorporation of the Bank of England and other financial companies with permanently subscribed "capital stock." Business corporations were not only legal entities having an artificial existence apart from that of the natural persons who united to form them, but they now had funds permanently committed to them by the subscribers. The concept of capital thereupon entered upon a new stage of ambiguity. Is "capital" the collective name for the financial amount of ownership by the subscribers (natural persons), in other words, the net worth, or proprietorship; or is it a name for the assets owned by the corporation as such; or is it the amount of "capital stock" in the sense of the "legal" or "the stated capital," a nominal sum not corresponding with either of the other conceptions? Or is it some confused mixture of all three? From that day to this, conflicting usage has left the answer in doubt.

The confusion of terms that thus came to prevail in the seventeenth and eighteenth centuries may be inferred from Adam Smith's usage in 1776, which greatly influenced his successors. He used the terms "stock," "capital stock," and "capital" for the most part indiscriminately, but in some cases with evident purpose to distinguish them. "Stock," the term he uses most frequently, is the more general, usually seems to include "capital" and "capital stock" as the things in which the capital "worth" is contained; indeed, stock is usually synonymous with them and sometimes with "wealth." Occasionally, however, the generic term "stock" is broader than "capital stock," including things reserved for consumption. Smith sometimes, too, suggested the distinction that "stock" consists of physical goods, while "capital" is the investment value of goods used to obtain a profit.[14] It appears therefore that (so far as Smith is fairly representative) the conceptions of capital as a stock of physical objects or as monetary investment and as something owned either individually or collectively were pretty thoroughly confused in the seventeenth and eighteenth centuries.

Further, Adam Smith introduced the terms fixed and circulating capital, distinguishing them by the criterion of change of ownership; and forty years later the Ricardians, without realizing the difference, distinguished these terms by the criterion of durability versus physical destruction by a single use. These confused terms are still retained in most of the economic texts, and are given too respectful attention by the accountants, who, however, find them troublesome and unworkable.[15]

In the period from Smith to John Stuart Mill (1776-1848) other confusions appeared. The then current labor-theory of value was grafted upon the physical-goods concept of capital and for the first time capital was defined as "produced means of production used for further production." This still remains the standard definition of capital in most of the economic texts. By "produced" was meant "produced by labor," but what, in turn, that meant was never clearly defined. Misled by an abnormal and temporary situation in England at that time, the Ricardians magnified to supreme theoretical importance a fallacious distinction between land (in the sense of natural, that is "unproduced," agents) and "capital" (as consisting of "artificial" or labor-produced agents) used for further production. "Land" (in that broad sense) even when used in business for profit was by definition excluded from the concept of capital, as also was the money valuation of natural agents. This conception of capital, apparently unknown before the so-called classical economics, was deemed by the Ricardians to be one of their most important contributions to theory. I need not argue in this presence, however, that it is of no possible use to accountants, and they have wisely discarded it, still mistakenly believing, however, that it is the best that recent economics has to offer. Although the Ricardian and neo-Ricardian definition of capital as "produced means of production" is framed explicitly in terms of physical goods, it was always in practice almost immediately abandoned (as is done by the Marshallians today) for a valuation, investment conception, including the value of national agents. The discussion of capital in all the conventional economic texts is permeated with this ambiguity.

While the corporation was swiftly becoming the dominant type of manufacturing and commercial organization after 1870, the new subjective, or psychological, schools of value theory appeared nearly simultaneously in several lands and began a needed revision of some of the fundamentals in economic theory. For a time thought was stimulated in right directions in regard to value and price, but quickly became entangled in the phrases of utilitarian psychology, already discredited in philosophic circles. Jevons in England and the Austrian school stopped short of any lasting contribution to better concepts of capital and income. The Austrian Böhm-Bawerk—in some respects one of the greatest of economic dialecticians— undertook to make himself master in that particular domain; yet he finally reverted to the most sterile version of the Ricardian definition of capital as "produced goods" which we have just described. He thus doomed to failure his own hopeful effort to construct a new "positive theory" of capital and interest, and ended in an anti-climax of a productivity theory of interest. In contrast, the American John Bates Clark recognized the ambiguity in the old concept of capital in which stocks of physical goods are confused with their monetary valuation, but, he left his task far from completed. He stopped half way with a confusing terminology of "capital goods" and "true" capital, and he, as well as Böhm-Bawerk, retained a false labor-theory and cost theory of the genesis of capital. However, by his valuation concept of capital Clark notably advanced the truth, and some traces of his influence appear in every American economic text of the last quarter century, as I have elsewhere sought to show.[16] Nevertheless, the Ricardian definition of capital—reinforced rather than weakened by Böhm-Bawerk's great influence—has continued to hold the field with the powerful support of the Marshallians, still so largely dominating the economic theory of price throughout the British Commonwealth and in the United States.

A few of those who had been influenced by the earlier psychological thought were not content with the opportunism and illogical compromises which were the most evident results of the Austrian and Clarkian labors on the capital concept. These students of theory—chiefly American, but including notably Edwin Cannan of England—have persisted in their endeavors to develop a logical value concept of capital, usable alike by economists and by accountants. The story in detail of their various discussions, contributions and not yet completely harmonized results is far too long to be told here. I must therefore limit myself to a brief summary of what I deem to be the valid conclusions.

The concept of capital is coextensive with exchange and the price system and is not to be confused with wealth. "Capital" should be defined to mean the monetary summation and expression of enterpriser's purchasing power. It is essentially a financial concept, relating to business investment, and includes the present market valuation of all legal rights to income possessed by natural persons. The business entity as such, whether incorporated or not, has assets, but no capital, the net worth of which (i.e., assets minus other liabilities) is the capital of the collective investors. The so-called "capital" of a corporation is at most a quasi, fictitious, or pseudo capital, created by and corresponding to the legal fiction of the separate corporate entity. The corporation owns the assets but the shareholders own the capital. The same thing cannot be owned at the same time and in the same sense by two different owners. A corporation is not a capitalist. A sufficient proof of this to accountants should be the simple fact that "capital" always appears on the liability side of the balance sheet. The corporation *owes* the capital, it does not *own* it. The shareholders own it.

The cost-of-production theory, still lingering in most of the textbooks, looks to the past to account for present valuations; it must be replaced by a consistent theory of the capitalization process.[17]

4.

The terminology of income is no more satisfactory than is that of capital. Economists and accountants, at least by implication, seem initially to agree that income is something related to capital so closely that the determination of one involves that of the other. This thought is reflected in the title of this session. Yet surprisingly little use is made of the term income in accounting texts, and that is often in strange new meanings, loosely related to the concept of capital, and income is not defined beyond the generous suggestion of other ambiguous terms as synonyms. A few examples are given in the note.[18]

The word "income" is broadly self-defining, as anything that comes in, and at one time or another it has been used in many senses that are now obsolete or archaic, including such an unfamiliar idea as that of calling a person an income when he entered a room (that is, a new comer). The earliest recorded use of the word income (in an Anglo-Saxon version of the Bible in 1000 A.D.) was as a verb, meaning to enter. The meaning of the noun income that is now deeply rooted in popular speech and is most usual in its application to business and economic purposes appears to be that of *any sort of goods (or valuable rights) coming into the possession of a person,* with the further implication that this is something *additional and available for consumers' use without depletion of a formerly existing physical stock, or of a financial capital fund, as the case may be.* This is now the generic meaning in current economics where, however, various specific terms such as "real income," "income in goods," "income in kind," "labor income," "funded income," and "psychic income" have indispensable uses in connection with, and often in contrast with, "pecuniary income." However, there has recently been a tendency in business and popular speech toward narrowing this concept to include only incomes expressed in terms of money.[19] At the same time "income" has largely displaced the term profits in the accountants' treatment of the business entity, and particularly of the business corporation.

The result of these several shifts of meaning, so unequally and variously accepted in different circles and applications, has been to create a greater confusion in the term income than ever has reigned before, with practical consequences of importance both to economics and to accountancy. Few appreciate how completely until of late the term income had been limited in its application to individuals nor how recently it has been applied to business corporations. In the numerous quoted examples collected in *The Oxford Dictionary*, none until late in the nineteenth century clearly implies that an income could accrue to anybody but a natural person. The shift in usage has come only since the recent great increase of business corporations. The Accountants' Committee on Terminology (p. 68) speaking of the usage of terms that "it is believed are now well established" makes the following just observation: "Income, while sometimes used by corporations, frequently as applied to net earnings, applies more particularly to the compensation or profits received by a person." This idea, however, is immediately contradicted in definitions of more specific forms of income, as gross, net, from investments, miscellaneous, operating, non-operating, etc., all of which are evidently treated as applying in accounting to corporations as well as to any other impersonal business entity.

In economic usage the term income is still, in greater part, applied broadly to things accruing to individuals and available for consumption; whereas profits are peculiarly the impersonal yield of any business no matter what the type of ownership. In conformity with earlier and long established usage it would not be permissible to speak of the "income" of a corporation. A corporation if successful has profits which when distributed are incomes to the receivers; but a corporation is a creature of the law once vividly described as having "neither a body to be kicked nor a soul to be damned." As such it has no capacity to enjoy and can have no "income" except in a recently distorted sense of the word. It can hardly be doubted that in most cases where accountants now use the term "income" to designate the surplus accruing to the impersonal business entity or to some special branch of its operation, the term profits would be more proper; and usually in the other cases neither income nor profits is a fitting term.

It may be ungracious to suggest that accountants and business men have largely themselves to blame if now they are unable to find any tenable difference in the meanings of income, earnings, profits, revenues, etc. They have made their task more difficult by the careless use of terms. With a wealth of words from which to choose to fashion a logical system of terminology, each term with a clear distinctive meaning, accountants have lost themselves in a maze of terms: income, gain, profits, earnings, revenue, receipts, increase in equities, increase in wealth, accrual of wealth, periodic return, benefit or advantage, surplus from the earnings, dividends, rents and interest payments, etc. Confusion is then multiplied by limiting adjectives such as gross, net, pure, economic, from operation, sales, investments, other incomes, etc. Every canon of sound terminology is violated; each term is applied to two or more ideas, and each idea is expressed by several different terms. The client, the reader, and the public never can know just what any of these terms means in a particular corporation report and must seek, often vainly, to discover from the context whether the term income means before this, or after that, or what not. Even the most enlightened of accountants is driven to exclaim in despair: "the average income sheet is a hodge-podge of illogical, non-illuminating classifications."[20] Is this not a truly intolerable situation?

The conception of income as a surplus has likewise taken on a new complexity with the advent of the corporation as the dominant form of business organization with which the accountant has to deal and to which the economist must adjust his thinking. Let us test our previous definition in the simplest conditions of which anthropology gives any account, namely, the ceaseless search for food by the primitive man always on the verge of starvation. Then anything that he finds that is fit to eat, wear or enjoy in any way is essentially income, that is, newly acquired goods available for use. If it is not eaten or otherwise used but is laid aside ("saved") for use in a later period, it becomes part of a store (or stock). This is wealth but not capital. Income (in goods) in succeeding periods is to be reckoned as a current surplus over and above the stock, that is, an addition to the amount in store. The simplest conception of *accumulative saving* makes it follow income; that is, saving is the act of refraining from the present use of an income of goods in the period when it occurs. Then *conservative saving* sets in, to maintain the existing stock by continually refraining from its consumption. Both types of saving of physical goods imply comparisons of current incomes with stocks in successive periods, and the factor of time-preference is introduced into the individual's whole system of valuations. In simple self-sufficing economies the comparisons of incomes and of stocks of goods in successive periods are all in physical terms, and their relative valuations are expressed "in kind," that is, by a sort of barter relationship. As soon, however, as money trade begins and the valuations of goods begin to be expressed in terms of prices, there enters the capital value concept. The comparison of current incomes with the value of existing stocks is expressed in terms of price. The value of the present income is compared with the capital sum, or present worth, of the anticipated incomes which the stock or fund contains or represents. Accounting may be defined as the capitalistic calculus in modern business, in other words, the calculus of capital and income. This complex calculation may be the bane of the accountant's existence—but, happy thought—it is what makes necessary his services and generous fees. No capital, no accountants!

5.

It is indeed rash for a layman in accounting to offer even a suggestion to the accountants, but in the light of the foregoing it would seem that they should begin by making far more generous use of the simpler, descriptive categories of receipts and disbursements classifying them and balancing them for different purposes before beginning to use any such terms as revenues, earnings, profits, or income. The term revenues might, perhaps, in accord with the usage in public finance, be reserved for those receipts, such as rents, royalties, interest, dividends from outside investments, etc., that do not strictly result from the operations of the enterprise itself, but are derived from sources outside. Then, and not till then, should come the more detailed study of receipts and disbursements in various departments of the business provisionally treated as minor separate entities, such as transportation operation, manufacturing, merchandising, etc. The several "balances," "results" or "earnings" (if that term be preferred, despite its original root meaning which was limited to incomes from human labor) would then be ready to be summated algebraically with revenues, taxes, capital changes, etc., to arrive at a figure for current "profits" of the enterprise as a whole. Current profits added to previous profits and capital values would yield the figure for the accumulated net worth, or proprietorship, of the collective enterprisers. Then, and not till then, would appear the term income as the amount accruing or distributed to the several investors, the return to each on his capital in the enterprise.

We cannot enter here into the difficult question of costs and overhead costs, or into that of adjusting capital values to the purchasing power of the dollar unit in periods of rapid changes in the general price level, although these, too, are problems of capital theory.

The accountant has the hard task of analyzing and recording true market valuations, expressed in terms of prices and the monetary standard. He cannot escape the difficulties by tying capital value to original cost. That "cost" is at best simply evidence of what the directors of the enterprise *thought* the things were worth when bought at some time in the past—either as a whole plant or as successive items. Original cost did not infallibly reflect either good sense or good morals in the past; still less does it accurately tell what things are worth now. The other horn of the dilemma is to reevaluate the assets, with all of the chances of human error, exaggerated hopes, or intentional misstatement that such a process affords. The same chances were present, however, in original cost, as sad experience often shows. Moreover, where could there be a greater range for error in individual judgment, or for intentionally conservative misstatement, or for downright deception, than in present estimates of depreciation, depletion, and obsolescence? We cannot get far in sound accountancy unless we postulate that the accountant, like Quintilian's ideal orator, is "an honest man." And this, we are assured, is the noblest work of God.

NOTES

1. Prof. A. C. Littleton in the *Accounting Review*, September, 1935, p. 270.

2. Prof. W. A. Paton, *Accounting* (1924), p. 22. It is to be remarked that the author bases this statement on his belief that "the economist in general deals with the general or social point of view," whereas "the accountant takes the point of view of the individual enterprise." The fact is, however, that the greater part of the discussions of capital and income in the current economic texts is as completely concerned with the individual enterprise and as fully overlooks "the social point of

view" as is done by the accountants. Much current economics is pervaded by a confusion of individual and social conceptions. See note 4 below, and related text.

3. A recent text, Porter and Fiske, *Accounting*, 1935, pp. 15-16, contrasts the economists' concept of capital which, it says, is "ordinarily" limited to "material wealth" with that of the accountants which includes property rights and claims. Let it be noted, however, that the authors somewhat vaguely imply in the adverb "ordinarily" their awareness that this concept is not universally or consistently employed in economics; and they incidentally recognize the growing influence of the unorthodox school to which I belong when they say: "The sharp distinction drawn by older economists between land and capital has tended to break down and to result in grouping the two as a single factor."

Another leading accountancy text (Hatfield, *Accounting*, p. 173 n) repeatedly refers to some unquestionable contrast between the economic and the accounting definition of capital without, however, anywhere defining capital either in the economic or in the accounting sense. The author does, however, imply his meaning; for example, when referring to one definition of "capital stock" frequently used in statutes, he quotes an explanation of it as meaning "not the shares of which the nominal capital is composed but the actual capital, that is, the assets with which the corporation carries on its corporate business." Whereupon the author comments: "This corresponds to the economic, not to the accounting definition of capital." I take this to mean that the author believes the economist's definition of capital to be "the assets" of the corporation, and the accountant's definition as "the capital account of a corporation"—explained in his text as "a nominal sum, the par value of the capital stock." In another passage—the phrase: "using capital in the economic, but not in the accounting, sense" [p. 375] carries the same implication, that "invested capital" in the economic sense includes all assets of the corporation whether financed by stocks or by bonds, whereas capital in the accounting sense means only the amount represented by shares of stock, the "capital stock," or perhaps "the stated capital." See below, notes 8 and 10, two other conceptions of "capital" that are held by accountants.

4. The writer has discussed this contrast in two articles in the *American Economic Review*, Vol. x, pp. 467 and 719: "Price economics versus welfare economics."

5. *Accounting*, 1927, p. 294.

6. H. W. Sweeney, in the *Accounting Review*, December, 1930, p. 277.

7. A. C. Littleton, "Contrasting Theories of Profit," *Accounting Review*, March, 1936, p. 15.

8. *E.g.*, Porter and Fiske, *Accounting*, 1935, p. 16: "Business capital and business assets are synonymous. Business assets consist of the material goods, claims and property rights applied to the business project.... Assets are capital." And again, p. 544: "The term capital ... refers to the assets employed in the business and not to that portion of the claim against the assets vested in the stockholders." See also quotation from Hatfield in note 3 above, where he calls this the "economic" definition, in contrast to that of the accountants, which, he says, is merely the stated capital, "a nominal sum."

9. Paton, *Accounting Theory*, 1922, p. 37.

10. *E.g.*, Kester, *Accounting Theory and Practice*, 3d. ed., 1930, Vol. I, p. 290. "From an accounting viewpoint, the capital of any business enterprise is the excess of its assets over its liabilities." The same view is expressed in these words by a legal student of accounting and disciple of Hatfield: "Capital should be defined as the difference in value between the total assets and the total liabilities of a business at a given moment of time." (Prosper Reiter, *Profits, Dividends and the Law*, 1926, p. 5.)

11. Quoted in *The Oxford Dictionary*.

12. The Germanic word "stock" had the root meaning of "stick" and hence main stem (as of a tree), hence, figuratively, a collection of physical things viewed as a fund of goods and resources constantly renewed—all of which meanings still persist in good use in various contexts. Evidently the "capital" of individual subscribers meant something quite different from "capital" in the sense of the "capital stock" of the whole enterprise, the latter corresponding rather to the physical aspect of what today are generally called assets.

13. The writer is indebted to Prof. Stanley E. Howard for the opportunity to consult an unpublished manuscript further developing this subject.

14. Thus he says: "The stock which is lent at interest is always considered as a capital by the lender.... The borrower may use it either as a capital or a stock reserved for immediate consumption." *Wealth of Nations*, Book II, Ch. 4. Cannan ed., p. 332. The word "stock" as used by Smith suggests a collection of useful things, and "capital" seems only meant to suggest that these things are used in business as a source of income, either to individuals or to the whole nation. In the latter case the thought of their money valuation is lacking. Such phrases occur as "the capital stock of the society," "the stock of the country," "the wealth of the society," "the capital of a great nation" and "the capital stock of Great Britain" (*Ibid.*, Book I, Ch. 9, pp. 94, 95) with no hint of distinction; but also occurs the phrase, "the capital of a private man" *Ibid.*, p. 93).

15. The preliminary report (1931) on Accounting Terminology says

(p. 31) of "circulating capital": "This expression appertains to economics rather than to accounting"; and of "fixed capital": "A rather vague term, used in economics more than in accounting." In further comment the Committee uncritically accepts both mutually inconsistent criteria of the distinction between fixed and circulating capital, saying of fixed capital: "It has been defined as wealth used in the production of commodities, the efficacy of which is exhausted by a single use," and in the next line: "The term 'circulating' is derived from the circumstance that this portion of capital requires to be constantly renewed by the sale of the finished articles and repurchase of raw materials, etc." The former makes the criterion a physical quality (durability), the latter makes it a financial quality (continuous and ready saleability, i.e., liquidity).

It is to be observed, however, that the older economic distinction between fixed and circulating capital survives in slightly altered, and perhaps equally troublesome, form in the accountants' attempt to divide assets into fixed and current. For example, the *Accountants' Handbook* (14th printing, 1934, p. 151) calls this "the most satisfactory basis of asset classification," adding: "This is founded on the economists' distribution of all capital goods into fixed and circulating capital, and has genuine economic and operating significance." The confusion of technical and financial criteria is plainly evident in the context.

16. In my essay on "Clark's Reformulation of the Capital Concept," in *Essays in Honor of John Bates Clark* [see above].

17. A capitalization theory is completely wanting in Clark's treatment, and was lost sight of by the Austrians after a promising beginning in its recognition. By this is meant the process of estimating capital as the present worth of the proprietorship of sources to future incomes, which is not to be confused with the very different process of issuing various kinds of shares in nominal amounts, as the term capitalization is often used in statute law and elsewhere

18. A recent text (Porter and Fiske, 1935, p. 327) declares in the chapter on "Income—its nature and determination," that "it is impossible to find a universal definition of income" and then proceeds at once to discuss profits as synonymous with it, as if that solved the problem. (*E.g.*, 327, 338.) A veteran in academic accounting having, as he says, "vainly tried to find any accepted differentiation between" the terms income and profits and finding no aid in the preliminary report of the accountants' Committee on Terminology (1931) explains that in his "treatise, therefore, the words are used indiscriminately." (Hatfield, *Accounting*, 1927, pp. 214-242.) A writer in the June, 1936, *Accounting Review*, (G. A. D. Prienreich, p. 130), still further complicates the problem by announcing that "the terms 'income' and 'profits' are

synonymous with 'earnings' for all purposes germane to the present discussion," and a moment later discouragingly adds: "Apparently discussion will be facilitated by avoiding the use of the term 'income.'" Thus he disposes of half the subject matter of this paper, and we may feel tempted to emulate his discretion by pitching the other half out of the window. But what then becomes of "the fundamental purpose of accounting"—"to distinguish clearly between capital and income?"

19. See *Oxford Dictionary* to this effect.
20. Paton, *Accounting Theory*, p. 53.

PART 2:
THE THEORY OF
INTEREST

The "Roundabout Process" in the Interest Theory

1. THE NATURE OF THE INTEREST PROBLEM.

Professor Eugen von Böhm-Bawerk's critique[1] of the older interest theories marks a new era in economic thought. The highest point attained in his more positive discussion is his statement of the real nature of the interest problem, as that of the exchange of present goods against future goods. This thought was an inspirational break with the past, and was charged with possibilities for the future of economic theory.

Nevertheless, Böhm-Bawerk has failed to formulate a consistent and satisfactory theory of interest. A statement of the nature of the problem and a solution of it are not the same. The English translater implies his belief that they are when he calls this statement "the essence" of "Böhm-Bawerk's theory of interest"[2]; the author likewise appears to identify the two when, in his *Positive Theory*,[3] he says: "Present goods are, as a rule, worth more than future goods of like kind and number.[4] . . This proposition is the kernel and centre of the interest theory which I have to present." This, however, is but the fact which the interest theory is to explain logically. The proposition is not open to question: it is a novel, but unquestionably better, way of stating the nature of the problem. Explanations may differ after the nature of the problem is well agreed upon. Böhm-Bawerk shows not only in manifold expressions, but by devoting several hundred pages to setting forth his theory of interest, that he does not consider his work done when the proposition above quoted is stated. He adds immediately: "The first part of our explanation

---

Reprinted from *Quarterly Journal of Economics* 17 (November 1902).

(Book V.) will try to prove the truth of the proposition."[5] What he does, however, is to give his peculiar explanation of the causes for this fact. The truth of the original proposition cannot be invoked as a proof of any one theory to explain it. The conception of the interest problem as one aspect of exchange value must be considered merely as preliminary to the formulation of an interest theory, not as the theory itself.

2. THE ROUNDABOUT PROCESS AND THE PRODUCTIVITY OF CAPITAL.

It is our purpose here to consider only one of the three principal features of Böhm-Bawerk's explanation "why present goods are, as a rule, worth more than future goods"; but that one is the most important. It is the technical superiority of present goods as instruments of production when used in "roundabout" processes.[6] He repeatedly refers to this as "the most fundamental conception in the theory of capital,"[7] as "the chief pillar,"[8] and as "the empirical corner-stone" of his theory. He has recently offered an elaborate defense and restatement of it.[9]

Again, we shall narrow our discussion to one only of the three supports[10] offered for the proposition that roundabout processes are more productive than direct ones; that is, its agreement with the old proposition that "capital is productive." This proposition is so generally accepted that, if the two propositions can be shown to be identical in thought, differing merely in expression, his thesis, so Böhm-Bawerk declares, is established. The main purpose of the author is to prove that a more roundabout process means identically the same as production with "more capital." If he can show that the two propositions are interchangeable, he will gain for the one all of the authority and belief that attaches to the other among economic students.

It may enable the reader to see a unity in the various criticisms that are to follow: it may serve to show that the negative views expressed proceed not from a spirit of captiousness but from a somewhat positive conception of the nature of the solution, if at this point is indicated the standpoint from which our discussion proceeds. We must demand of the theorist dealing with capital and interest (1) that the term "capital" be used consistently in the various stages of his argument, and (2) that the fundamental explanation apply to interest wherever it is manifest and in all its forms. On another occasion I have given reasons for the belief that in these respects Böhm-Bawerk is at fault.[11] In the following discussion these tests are applied to the particular question in hand.

If it be allowable to epitomize many pages of the author's argument into a single syllogism, it would run thus:—

First premise: The proposition that capital is productive (which means that, the more capitalistic agents[12] labor has, the more productive it is) is unquestionable.

Second premise, first link: More capital means identically the same as a longer production period; second link: A longer production period means the same as a more roundabout process.

Conclusion: Therefore the statement that the roundabout process is more productive is unquestionable.

Böhm-Bawerk does not deem it necessary to labor long to prove the general proposition that capital is productive. He first states the proposition in this form:[13] "Labor is more productive according as it is equipped with more capitalistic agents." This may suggest the idea of a greater number or quantity of agents, physically considered; but he immediately uses in his illustration the value expression of capital in these words: "National labor yields more when supported by a capital of five hundred florins per head than without any capital at all, and yields still more when the capital is five thousand florins or ten thousand florins per head." The implication, here as elsewhere, is that, while this increase may not be in exact proportion to, it is some function of, the increase of capital. So much depends on the sense in which the word "capital" is used that we must examine its meaning in this connection.

"More capitalistic agents" evidently tend to more technical production. Two spades, two fields, two ploughs, in place of one, and perfect tools in place of crude ones, mean a more bountifully endowed world to work in; and, while an increase of one particular kind of agent may sometimes burden rather than aid industry, the possibility of adjusting and interchanging the supply of different agents makes the proposition a valid one in general. But, when one passes over to the value expression of capital, the nature of the statement as an abstract theoretical proposition changes; for, unless we are assured that the greater value expression at the later period stands for a greater number or better quality of physical agents, the technical productivity may vary in any conceivable degree or direction, becoming even absolutely less with the greater amount of capital. The two concepts, it is true, would be the same in practice if we were speaking of the increase of capital applied to a particular industry at a given moment in which there was no change in the supply of capital in the community. But Böhm-Bawerk has chosen to discuss, not the greater roundaboutness of production in a particular industry to which more capital is applied, but the greater roundaboutness in industry as a whole where the value expression of capital has increased. That is, he discusses not the case of a static supply of capital as a whole, but that of a changing supply of capital, the change being measured by the value expression. The conclusion he draws, therefore, is not theoretically sound; for there is no certainty or even probability that the two features of effectiveness and value will vary at the same rate, or, in the extreme case, that more "capital," containing a larger element of various scarcity values, will represent productive agents even as great or (technically) as effective as those of smaller value did in the preceding period.

Regarding the second premise, first link, Böhm-Bawerk must show that the longer production period is identical with the use of "more capital." Let us examine his concept of capital in this immediate connection.[14]

Böhm-Bawerk answers the question "What is capital?" not by using either of the definitions referred to in the last paragraph, but by a figure of speech intended to direct attention to what it has been and to the source of its value. "Previous labor," he says, "is a rough but essentially true definition." But he adds in a note, "It is more exact to say, stored-up, previously applied productive force, which can be not only labor, but also valuable natural forces or uses of land."[15] Then, returning to the text: "a small capital evidently represents little previous labor, a large capital much. A capital of fifty florins can represent, in the extremest case, one-sixth of a labor year when the common wage is three hundred florins a year," etc. This comes near to the discredited labor value theory; and the author, seeing the difficulty, adds in a note: "Probably considerably less, because on the one hand comes into play a higher paid quality of labor, and on the other the value of the stock of capital goods cannot by any means be resolved into labor or wages respectively, but contains for a considerable part accumulated interest, profits, monopoly gains, and the like."[16] Despite these important alterations in the meaning of the term "capital" the author has gone on to use it in the simpler, unmodified form, drawing, as to the nature and effect of capital as a whole, conclusions which at the most can be true of that part of capital reducible to terms of previous labor. This conception of capital is confusing by reason of its attempt at a simplicity that is untrue to the facts. It must be noted, however, that it is a value concept of capital. The capital embodies a value which it derives from the value of the labor that has produced it (sometimes thought of together with the value of all the other factors admitted in the note above quoted). It is a value concept despite the use of the terms "labor-month" and "labor-year"; for the labor can be spoken of as representing a certain fraction of the value of the capital only after the amount of the labor itself has been expressed in terms of value, not of time.

In attempting to show the identity of the thoughts of a longer period of production and a more roundabout process (second link of second premise), he says that the ripe consumption goods needed within the year will be secured by a union of new labor with the old labor in the form of capital. It is evident to him that, when little old labor is present, the new labor must be in large proportion, and the average production period[17] must be short, and *vice versa*. "The mass of existing capital shows how many labor-months are on their way at any one time, have been performed as labor, and have not yet arrived at the goal of ripened enjoyment. If now, with a capital of fifty florins per head, no more than two labor-months are on their way at one time, it indicates, in an unmistakable way, a shorter average duration of the roundabout method adopted than when, with a mass of capital ten or a hundred fold greater, twenty or two hundred labor-months at once are in the transition stage of unripe intermediate product." This being to Böhm-Bawerk quite "evident," he believes that production with the aid of more capital is identical with the lengthening of the average production period, and hence with the adoption of a more roundabout method of production.[18]

3. FAILURE OF THE ARGUMENT TO IDENTIFY INCREASE OF CAPITAL AND ROUNDABOUTNESS.

We must, for several reasons, question the argument by which are thus identified the thoughts of a larger capital, a longer production period, a more roundabout process, and a greater productiveness. First, in Böhm-Bawerk's concept the natural agents are not a part of capital; and, unless the natural agents, the fertile soil and natural forces, are as great per capita, the technical productiveness of the larger capital may be less than before. His conclusion, therefore, would hold good at most with the added proviso: the amount and effectiveness of natural agents increasing proportionally. In an extreme case conceivable the greater supply of capital (however measured) might be more than offset in its technical effect by a smaller per capita equipment of natural agents.

Secondly, the argument contains the fallacy of the vicious circle by implying the rate of interest. With a value concept the "amount of capital" corresponding to a given product each year varies with the rate of discount in capitalization.[19] If the prevailing interest is at 20 per cent., an annual product valued at 10 supports a capitalization of fifty; but, if the interest falls to 1 per cent., the same product supports five hundred. Of the two parts of the proposition that more capital means a greater productivity and a more roundabout process, the first portion, therefore, is unsound unless it be qualified by the phrase: provided that the rate of interest has remained the same. But it is the change of the rate of interest which he is attempting to explain through a change in the technical productiveness.

Thirdly, the argument is unsound in the degree to which the capital contains accumulated interest or monopoly gains. It sounds plausible to say that, if the capital per head represents a value one-sixth the average value of a year's labor, the process is one-sixth as roundabout, and the production period is one-sixth as long, as if the capital were just equal in value to a year's labor. But this is an entirely hypothetical proposition, whose truth depends on the fact assumed in the "if"; and the author himself has hastened to add that a considerable part of the value of the capital is due to other elements, among them accumulated interest.[20] If the value of the capital always can be traced back to labor, and two amounts of capital are proportionate to the labor that has been put into them, then, on an average, the length of the production period would be the quotient of the value of the capital divided by the value of a year's labor. But every unit of capital that represents the other sources of capital disturbs and falsifies that relation. If one hundred and fifty of the three hundred florins capital consists of accumulated interest, the capital represents a production period of only one-half of a year: if two hundred and fifty florins so consists, the production period would be only one-sixth of a year, the same as if capital were only fifty florins, all due to labor.[21] The proposition in question will be true, therefore, only with a third proviso reading thus: an increase of capital is identical with a more roundabout process, provided that the increase represents labor only, and not accumulated interest or monopoly gains.

A fourth objection to the argument is that, in admitting the value of the uses of land into the value of the stock of capital, Böhm-Bawerk has given a blow that wrecks the capital concept that he employs. What is it that goes roundabout in production when capital is used? According to Böhm-Bawerk's idea it is not the capital itself, but something that passes through and abides for a time in the capital. The capital, he says, is previous labor; or, correcting himself,[22] it is, more exactly, "stored up previously applied productive force, which can be not only labor, but also valuable natural forces or uses of land." Their value is thought of as originating or given off at a certain moment; and, evidently, it is this value, rather than the physical things, which goes a roundabout journey, and at length arrives at the goal of finished, enjoyable goods. The average production period must be the average time that elapses, throughout the industrial system, between the moment that a use of land originates and the moment it reaches its goal. Any valuable use of land that is not yet matured or available for present wants is a postponed or future value. Anything, such as a table or a house, that contains a number of these uses owes a part of its present value, therefore, to the capitalization or discounting of these future uses at a prevailing rate of discount. In this way the uses of land are made a part of the capital value of all things. Farms or mines have values due to the capitalization of the value of their uses; and this, by Böhm-Bawerk's admission, is just what constitutes any capital value. There is left no logical or consistent test to divide capital, as formally defined by Böhm-Bawerk, from those things which he would exclude from that concept.

If we put together these objections to the argument, we have it in this form: if it were true in any case, it would be true (1) only when the diminishing returns of natural agents did not offset it; (2) when the change in the amount of capital is not merely the expression of a change in the rate of interest; (3) when the increase does not represent accumulated interest or monopoly gains embodied in capital; and (4) when the increase is not the capitalization of the uses of natural agents. There is involved in Böhm-Bawerk's argument, therefore, the fallacy of an unsound premise. If all capital does not consist of, or owe its value to, previous labor, a false conclusion is drawn when the length of the production period is assumed to be fixed by the relation between the stock of capital, counted as previous labor, and the annual amount of labor. Arithmetical examples of the kind given by him[23] prove nothing as to the proposition advanced unless it can be shown that the increase in the capital represents labor only.

If the concepts of the roundabout process and of the average production period are so defective, and yet have obtained wide currency, it must be because they contain a partial truth. In fact, the author at the outset transfers the reader's thought to the point from which the conceptions appear simple and reasonable. This may be better understood if we state the proposition as a hypothetical truth. If the value of capital consisted entirely of the value of labor, if the amount of capital varied directly with the "amount of labor" and with nothing else, if capital were distributed to the industries of longer and shorter processes in a fixed proportion, then every increase in the ratio of existing capital to current labor would represent an increase of the average period of labor between the application of labor and its fruition. But every one of the "ifs" is contrary to reality. The author states the proposition with all these conditions implied, makes, in a note, passing comment on its inexactness, fails to see how his general proposition is affected, and goes on to draw a conclusion.

Hasty and rough observation seems to support the proposition; for, taking the extreme cases, evidently a larger proportion of the efforts of men is applied to current wants in primitive society, while in a more advanced and richer society a larger proportion is embodied in durable agents. But, labor being only one of the factors entering into the amount of capital, the ratio of capital to current labor does not express at all exactly the length of "the roundabout process." The amount of capital varies as a function of several factors, of which labor is only one. Most important of the neglected factors is the rate of interest,—that is, the rate at which all of the existing rentals, no matter what their nature, shall be capitalized, and shall enter into the value expression of the stock of capital.

4. FUTILITY OF THE CONCEPT OF AN "AVERAGE PRODUCTION PERIOD."

Were all the foregoing objections beside the mark, there still would remain a fundamental weakness in the conception of the average production period, unfitting it to bear any part in the solution of the theoretical interest problem. It involves the fallacy of averages. The production period, with Böhm-Bawerk, is not an average time in one industry, but an average period during which the value of the total productive force of the community is supposed to be embodied in the total existing body of capital.[24] Such an average of widely divergent facts is not the significant thing in the explanation of interest. The average production period, whose length is assumed to express the degree of roundaboutness of the productive process, is an average of a multitude of different productive processes of every conceivable length. In a great many industries the labor is said to mature almost immediately; in others, only after a long period. If at one time one-half of a given capital, and at a later time one-tenth, is employed in industries with a short-time period, the average productive period would be lengthened without any change in the amount of capital.

```
50 units in industries with 1 mo. period=    50 units for one month
 50    "      "        "       "      2 yrs.  "   = 1,200 "     "     "     "
100    " average              12½ mos. production period.
```

In the second case we might have the following: —

```
10 units in industries with 1 mo. period=    10 units for one month
 90    "      "        "       "      2 yrs.  "    = 2,160 "     "     "   "
100    " average              21.7 mos. production period.
```

The average production period for industry as a whole (even if it were correct to conceive of it as Böhm-Bawerk does) would have no logical relation to the productiveness of capital or to the rate of interest. What is significant is not the average period, but the marginal application. One cannot explain market price by an average of the subjective estimates of all the buyers and sellers. In any particular industry at any moment the use of more capital (value) may, perhaps, yield a larger product, either technical or economic; but this may even accompany a decrease of the average production period for industry as a whole, if the capital has been transferred from an industry with a longer production period to one with a shorter. Along the margin of possible uses the existing stock of capital is applied, equalizing thus the rate of interest in the different uses, and altering likewise the ratio of labor and capital invested. In determining this distribution, however, the average production period, as Böhm-Bawerk conceives of it, has no causal influence whatever. It is itself nothing but an arithmetical resultant of all the changes that have taken place. It is a figment of the same kind as the wage fund. A lengthening of the average productive period could therefore accompany as well a fall as a rise of the productiveness of capital.

It remains to mention the mathematical support for his proposition by which the author is himself misled. Taking up his final discussion of the roundabout process, he says:[25] "I venture to think we may now assume it as proved," and then he frames some arbitrary arithmetical tables "to represent the product which may be turned out by increasingly lengthy processes under the picture of a series increasing in a certain ratio, regular or irregular." In the first one he represents a month of labor in 1888, for that year producing 100 units; for 1890, producing 200; for 1892, producing 400, etc. Plainly, these figures add no proof whatever to the proposition, which, therefore, is in no way strengthened by the statement that, "whatever period of time we take as our standpoint of comparison, the earlier (present) amount of productive instruments is seen to be superior, technically, to the equally great later (future) amount."[26] When the author goes on to the further proposition, that technical superiority is accompanied by a superiority of value, he declares that it "may be made absolutely convincing by mathematical evidence."[27] The "evidence," however, is merely another set of illustrative tables, arbitrarily constructed on the assumption of the truth of the proposition in question. Introduced with the statements quoted in the third line of this paragraph, they are dismissed with the remark: "on the single assumption that longer methods of production lead generally to a greater product, it is a necessary result."[28]

5. THE CAPITAL CONCEPT AS THE SOURCE OF ERROR.

The validity of the assumption being the question under consideration, we return from the mathematical evidence to the question of the greater productiveness of the roundabout process. Glancing back over the many difficulties in the author's argument, it appears that they may all be traced more or less clearly to the defects of his capital concept. In advance of his time, and presenting a twentieth-century theory of value, he has been content to use the clumsy eighteenth-century capital concept. This involves him in inconsistencies at every step. An advocate of the theory of marginal utility, he yet employs what is essentially a cost-of-production concept of capital, and, despite his various statements to the contrary, he is looking to the past rather than to the future of goods for an explanation of their value. It is "previous labor" and not future utility, regardless of the quantity, time, or value (however it may be measured), that distracts his attention, and fixes it on the figment of the average production period of industry as a whole. A value concept of capital, wherein capital is thought of as merely the present worth or capitalized value of the future uses of existing agents, makes the conception of the roundabout process appear fragmentary, inadequate, and false because only a half-truth. Almost immediately he is compelled to go over to the value concept of capital, for that is the only one that permits of the discussion of interest as a percentage of the principal. Thus at every step the two ideas conflict, a greater capital at one moment meaning more physical instruments, at another meaning durable instruments of greater value expressed in terms of present goods. Before beginning his task, Böhm-Bawerk has expressed the hope that he might give a solution of the problem of interest that "invents nothing and assumes nothing."[29] The conceptions of the average period of production and of the roundabout process appear to err both in inventing and assuming.

6. RELATION OF ROUNDABOUTNESS TO THE OTHER GROUNDS FOR THE HIGHER VALUATION OF PRESENT GOODS.

Our author says he considers that the "statement of how the productivity of capital works into and together with the other two grounds[30] of the higher valuation of present goods, is one of the most difficult points in the theory of interest and, at the same time, the one which must decide the fate of that theory."[31] There is a flaw in the argument at this crucial point. Foregoing a detailed criticism here, let us observe that the technical productiveness is not co-ordinate with the other causes assigned, and that the words "present wants" and "future wants" are used in the propositions in different senses. In the statement that present goods are worth more than future goods because of differences in wants and provision for wants, the present goods are objects which confer enjoyments or satisfactions at the present moment: the future goods are the same goods thought of as secured at a future moment. But, in the statement that present goods are technically more productive than future goods, the "present goods" are not "present enjoyments," but "intermediate goods," or "productive agents," to use the phrases elsewhere employed by Böhm-Bawerk. Whether they will mature physically and become enjoyable goods in the future, or whether they will merely permit the securing of future goods, in either case they may be said to represent rather future goods (enjoyments) than present goods in the sense of the other proposition. To identify the two things as present goods is entirely misleading. It would be a far more consistent use of language to call intermediate, or productive, agents "future goods" than present goods.

To Böhm-Bawerk these three reasons together seem to make a complete explanation. The first two reasons account for the agio on present over future consumption goods, the third accounts for the agio of present production over future production goods,—*i.e.*, those available at a later period. But there is only a mechanical or arithmetical completeness: there is no logical unity in the explanation.[32] A satisfactory theory of interest is not attained until time differences in all kinds of goods are traced back to a single principle. That principle is the greater want-satisfying power of present as compared with future consumption goods. The essence of the explanation must be found not in technical production, but in the subjective comparision of goods.

7. THE WEAKNESS OF PRODUCTIVITY THEORIES.

It has been a surprise to many students of Böhm-Bawerk to find that he has presented a theory, the most prominent feature of which is the technical productiveness of roundabout processes. His criticism of the productivity theories of interest has been of such a nature as to lead to the belief that he utterly rejected them.[33] But evidently such is not the case. Critics have pretty generally agreed that the theory of the roundabout process is a productivity theory of interest; and it appears from Böhm-Bawerk's later statement that he does not object to the productivity theory as a partial, but as an exclusive, explanation of interest. He believes particularly that interest on consumption goods cannot be explained in that way. But he says repeatedly that the idea of the roundabout process contains the essential truth in the productivity theory, and he uses it to explain that part of interest yielded by produced goods employed in lengthened productive processes. Böhm-Bawerk's theory, therefore, so far as it rests upon the productiveness of roundabout processes, is a productivity theory; and as such it is to be judged by the tests which he has set up, and rightly, in criticizing such an argument. The essence of the interest problem is to explain a surplus of value over the value of the capital employed.[34] It is not enough to show that more capital (or a more roundabout process) will produce more products, or to show that the aggregate of products has a greater value than those secured before. The value of the capital being derived from the value of the products, the more the products (in value), the more the capital (value), unless the interest rate (the thing to be explained) keeps the capital from increasing proportionately.

In criticizing others, Böhm-Bawerk has said:[35] "I grant that capital actually possesses the physical productivity ascribed to it .... But there is not one single feature in the whole circumstance to indicate that this greater amount of goods must be worth more than the capital consumed in its production; and it is this phenomenon of surplus value we have to explain." Now, coming to this explanation in his own positive argument,[36] he asks regarding the earlier productive instrument which he has shown to be technically superior: "But is it superior also in the height of its marginal utility and value? Certainly it is. For, if in every conceivable department of wants for the supply of which we may or shall employ it, it puts more means of satisfaction at our disposal, it must have a greater importance for our well-being." This argument curiously has involved in it the whole question; for, if the importance of the future use were, at the present moment, always greater than the present use, everything would be kept for the future. The reason why this is not done is that the future uses are discounted at the prevailing rate of interest. What we must demand at this point from the author, according to his own canons of criticism, is some proof that the greater technical product of the future has a greater value at this moment than the value of the capital consumed in it. This he quite fails to give. Instead, he says, after confessing that sometimes the opposite is the case: "For one and the same person at one and the same point of time the greater amount has always the greater value."[37] But the crucial question why the greater amount may have a less value at the present moment, when the two products are at two points of time, is not touched. The problem of interest is one that involves a ratio between the value of the capital and the value of the interest. The fact that the value of a given number of productive agents may be the same in any one of a dozen possible uses, though in some of them very long "roundabout processes" would give enormous sums of products and in others smaller amounts are at once secured, shows that the amount of technical product may diverge indefinitely from the value. Böhm-Bawerk has not bridged the gulf between the technical productivity and the surplus of value over the capital investment any better than those whom he has criticized.

8. RELATION OF TECHNICAL PRODUCTIVITY TO THEORIES OF INTEREST.

If the foregoing is true, most of what is characteristic or significant in Böhm-Bawerk's *Positive Theory* must be rejected.[38] It must be said that he starts with brilliant intuitions into the true character of the interest problem, only to go astray on the road of the old productivity theory. Let us venture an opinion as to the nature of the difficulty and the direction that must be taken to reach a correct conclusion.

The initial error in the older theories of interest was mistaking the nature of the problem. Interest and rent were believed to be co-ordinate and essentially similar aspects of value, the difference lying in the kind of agents with which they were connected. Rent was thought to be due to the surplus value of the products of the soil, and interest in general to the surplus value of the products from capital. Böhm-Bawerk seems at many points of his earlier criticism ready to break away from this; but, in adopting the concept of capital that he employs, he made a correct solution of the problem impossible. He looks upon capital as consisting of certain *kinds* of agents, and of interest as the surplus value or product peculiar to those agents. Glimpses of a different view appear, but one which certainly falls far short of a correct one.[39]

Let us suggest the view that rent and interest are very dissimilar aspects of the value of goods. Rent has to do with "production" or scarce and desirable uses of things. To the interest theorist this is in the nature, one might almost say, of an ultimate fact. The interest theory begins with the valuation of these different rents or incomes, distributed through different periods of time. The "productiveness" of a material agent is merely its quality of giving a scarce and desirable service to men. To explain this service of goods is the essence of the theory of rent. Given this and a prospective series of future services, however, the problem of interest arises, which is essentially that of explaining the valuation set on the future uses contained in goods. Interest thus expressing the exchange ratio of present and future services or uses is not and cannot be confined to any class of goods: it exists wherever there is a future service. It is not dependent on the roundaboutness of the process; for it exists where there is no process whatever, if there be merely a postponement of the use for the briefest period. A good interest theory must develop the fertile suggestion of Böhm-Bawerk that the interest problem is not one of product, but of the exchange of product,—a suggestion he has not himself heeded. It must give a simple and unified explanation of time value wherever it is manifest. It must set in their true relation the theory of rent as the income from the use of goods in any given period, and interest as the agio or discount on goods of whatever sort, when compared throughout successive periods. For such a theory the critical work of Böhm-Bawerk was an indispensable condition; but, the more his positive theory is studied, the more evident it is that it has missed the goal.

NOTES

1. *Capital und Capitalzins,* Innsbruck, 1884. The second edition, Innsbruck, 1900, is reviewed by F. A. F. in the *Journal of Political Economy,* January, 1902. The English translation of the first edition, cited in this article, bears the title *Capital and Interest.*

2. *Capital and Interest*, preface, p. xix, referring to text pp. 257-259.

3. *Positive Theory of Capital*, p. 237.

4. The last five words, if taken in a literal and objective sense, are open to criticism. See my discussion in the *Quarterly Journal of Economics*, vol. xv. p. 8 [see above, p. 38].

5. *Positive Theory*, p. 237.

6. *Ibid.*, p. 260. The other reasons given are: (1) differences in want and provision in present and future (*Positive Theory*, p. 249); and (2) underestimate of the future (*Positive Theory*, p. 253).

7. *Positive Theory*, p. 22.

8. *Ibid.*, p. 264.

9. *Einige strittige Fragen der Capitalstheorie*, Wien u. Leipzig, 1900. Published first as three articles in the *Zeitschrift für Volkswirtschaft, Sozialpolitik, und Verwaltung*, in 1899. Reviewed by F. A. F. in the *Political Science Quarterly*, vol. xvii. pp. 169-173, March, 1902.

10. The first explanation Böhm-Bawerk offers is an appeal to practical examples. It can easily be shown that he wavers greatly in his thought and statement of the degree of validity in the proposition. See, e.g., *Positive Theory*, pp. 20, 22, 82, 84, 260; *Einige strittige Fragen*, pp. 39, 40. The second reason given to account for the greater productiveness of roundabout methods is that thereby natural forces are enlisted in the service of man. *Positive Theory*, pp. 12-33; *Einige strittige Fragen*, p. 10. This second reason is open to the criticism to be given in discussing the third (see below, p. 177); and the two will stand or fall together.

11. *Quarterly Journal of Economics*, vol. xv. pp. 1-45.

12. These words occur in *Einige strittige Fragen*, p. 11.

13. *Einige strittige Fragen*, p. 11: "Die Arbeit desto productiver ist, mit je mehr capitalistischen Hilfsmitteln sie ausgerüstet ist."

14. This modifying phrase is needed, as there are several different conceptions of capital used by Böhm-Bawerk. See "Recent Discussion of the Capital Concept," *Quarterly Journal of Economics*, vol. xv. pp. 8, 40.

15. *Einige strittige Fragen*, p. 11: "Was ist denn eigentlich das 'Capital'? Es ist, wie es mit einer zwar nicht ganz schulgerechten aber wenigstens im Groben recht zutreffenden Definition bezeichnet zu werden pflegt, 'vorgethane Arbeit.' " The note reads: "Genauer ist es zu sagen, aufgespeicherte, vorgeschossene Productivkraft, die nicht nur Arbeit, sondern auch wertvolle Naturkraft oder Bodennutzung sein kann."

16. *Einige strittige Fragen*, p. 12.

17. The "production period" with Böhm-Bawerk means not the entire time elapsing from the first labor applied to goods, but the average time from the embarking of labor in products until its emergence as enjoyable goods, the whole produced value being thought of as ultimately consumed. This is carefully restated by the

author in *Einige strittige Fragen*, pp. 4, 5. Misunderstanding on this point has led to most of the criticisms to which Böhm-Bawerk has replied. We must recognize also that Böhm-Bawerk uses the conception of the production period as that of the average for all industry.

18. *Einige strittige Fragen*, p. 11.

19. It may seem that this is not true of Böhm-Bawerk's concept of capital, as he has defined it in terms of concrete things and not according to its money expression. Yet as in this very passage he has employed the money expression, and as the discussion of "units" of capital is impossible without violating his definition, it is permissible to cite this against him.

20. *Einige strittige Fragen*, note, p. 12.

21. One can imagine the reply that the greater proportion of interest is the result, and expresses the lengthening of the period of production; but this fails to explain profits and monopoly gain. It is shifting entirely the test by which the length of a period is to be measured; for, if only one-sixth of the results of the year's labor is at any time bound up in the form of capital, evidently five-sixths of it are applied to current uses, are on an average consumed at once, and only two months elapse on an average from the moment a unit of labor is applied until it emerges as product. And, finally, it brings us back to the difficulty that the amount of capital must, if it includes an element of interest, vary according to the rate of interest: it must involve already the rate of interest which it is the problem to explain.

22. *Einige strittige Fragen*, p. 11 and note.

23. *Positive Theory*, pp. 262, 266, 267, 269.

24. See above, p. 189 note 17.

25. *Positive Theory*, p. 260.

26. *Ibid.*, p. 262.

27. *Ibid.*, p. 264.

28. *Positive Theory*, p. 268.

29. *Capital and Interest*, p. 428.

30. Given above, p. 189 note 6.

31. *Positive Theory*, p. 227, note.

32. The reader will recall the distinction between the action of the different causes, the first two being called cumulative, the second alternative. See *Positive Theory*, pp. 273-277.

33. See *Capital and Interest*, e.g., pp. 111-119, 180, 181, and 183, quoted below.

34. See *Capital and Interest*, e.g., pp. 116-118.

35. *Capital and Interest*, p. 138.

36. *Positive Theory*, p. 263.

37. *Ibid.*, p. 264.

38. After this article was in print the new edition of the *Positive Theory* came to hand. It proves, however, to be a *verbatim* reprint, not a revision of the first edition, the author's official duties having prevented his undertaking its rewriting at this time. This will be a source of much regret to economic students, although recent magazine articles by the author make it clear that he has in no essential way modified the concepts or theories presented in the first edition.

39. E.g., *Positive Theory*, pp. 352-357.

The Relations between Rent and Interest

PART I. NEGATIVE CRITICISM OF THE CONVENTIONAL RENT AND INTEREST CONCEPTS

1. Logical clearness and practical needs call for a reexamination and restatement of the economic concepts of rent and interest.

This proposition expresses the thought of many contemporary economic students. The thought is reflected in the recent remarkable revival of interest in this phase of economic theory. The truth of the proposition is, however, not recognized by all. Some look upon the Ricardian doctrine of rent as an eternal verity, and deem the agitators of new economic concepts to be the pernicious disturbers of theoretical calm. Some economists cling to the traditional views as some theologians cling to outgrown creeds, oppressed with the thought that if the ancient faith gives way nothing can take its place. With rock-ribbed conservatism argument is vain, but such an attitude has one considerable justification: the recent rent controversy has been almost entirely of a negative character. The period of destructive criticism has elapsed; but erroneous concepts will not be discarded until positive and practically applicable ones are put in their places.

Reprinted from American Economic Association, *Papers and Proceedings of the Sixteenth Annual Meeting* 5 (February 1904). The discussants of Fetter's paper included Thomas N. Carver, Jacob H. Hollander, Charles W. MacFarlane, Lindley M. Keasbey, W. G. Langworthy Taylor, Richard T. Ely, James Edward LeRossignol, Franklin H. Giddings, and Winthrop M. Daniels (see ibid., pp. 199-227). Fetter's reply to their criticisms is reprinted here.

2. The generally accepted definitions of rent and of interest are imperfect in that they mark only a small portion of the boundaries of the concepts actually employed.

Criticism of definitions should not be unreasonably exacting. It is sufficient that the definition state the essential characteristic of the concept, for it is impossible to include in a sentence all the logical and practical developments of the central thought. It is no vital fault that the statements that rent is income from natural agents, and that interest is the income from products used in production, do not tell everything about rent and interest. But the prevailing belief is that all of the essential contrasts of rent and interest so much dwelt upon for a century past, result from the one defined and simple difference as to the kind of goods yielding the income. In fact, however, the concepts of rent and interest are not developed along parallel lines, other most fundamental terms being unconsciously introduced into them. The prevailing concepts of rent and interest, therefore, have an exceedingly complex character, and what is worse for clear thinking, this complexity is concealed beneath a simple form.

The two propositions above state the negative portion of the thesis to be here maintained. Part I of this paper, given to negative criticism, is continued in propositions 3 a, b, 4, 5 a, b, c, and summarized in 6, these together forming a demonstration that the conventional rent concept contains several conflicting thoughts. Part II, consisting of propositions 7 a, b, and 8 is an examination of two possible but inexpedient ways of making the rent and interest concepts formally consistent, by developing propositions 3 and 4. Part III, the positive solution, points out in propositions 9 a, b, c, the logical and practical line of distinction to be found in propositions 5 a, b, c, when they are consistently developed, and concludes in 10 and 11 with the outline of a new theory of distribution.

3a. Since the beginning of modern economic theory, rent and interest have been defined by social marks; rent has been said to be the income of land owners, interest that of merchants, manufacturers and city men of wealth.

This distinction deserves mention, when the most recent and

one of the keenest critics in this field expresses himself as follows: "It is a commonplace of historical economics that land was first given the rank of a factor in production coördinate with labor and capital for the simple reason that in England, the home of classical political economy, the landlords formed a social class distinct from the capitalists and laborers."[1] Adolph Held, probably the first to suggest this origin, states quite dogmatically, without discussion, that "the social classification appeared so sharply in England that Adam Smith accepted it without question, and accordingly distinguished the kinds of incomes without inquiring how far property in land and capital belong together."[2] However it originated, this thought of rent as a personal income of the members of a social class, persists to-day, as may be seen in many representative definitions.[3] The conscious distinguishing of the conceptions of economic and contract incomes is a recent phase of thought, as yet but slightly reflected in the formal definitions. Ownership, though frequently thus included in the definition, has not played an essential part in economic discussion because, as used, the definition became a mere truism. Goods and incomes were not classified according as they belonged to members of different social classes, but, on the contrary, social classes were distinguished according as they were receiving incomes from particular kinds of goods. The income of the landlord as a person was made up of the yield from such varied agents that to the personal mark (membership in the land-holding class), necessarily was added at once an impersonal mark (the kinds of agents yielding the income). A man was considered to be a landlord if his most important income came from land. As the thought of rent as landlord's income and as income from land never have been very sharply distinguished, we may designate this second phase of the thought as 3b.

3b. Rent, in the conventional treatment, was therefore said to be the income derived from natural agents, and interest that from produced, or artificial agents.

When this is made, as it was, the central thought of rent, that part of the income of landlords that is derived from improvements is excluded and is declared to be interest. A minor fallacy then appears in that rent is either landlord's income or income from land, as is most convenient to the immediate purpose of the writer. The principal thought in rent remains, however, that of income from the use of natural agents. The grave difficulties in the application of this thought will be later criticized (in 7b). Other ideas now to be noted were, however, from the first, associated with the original thought.

4. The characterization of rent as that income from material agents which does not enter into cost of production, and of interest as the income which *does* so enter, was a shifting of the central thought of the concept; what was, at first, thought to be a merely incidental peculiarity of land rent, became its essential feature, and then the center of a more general concept of rent.

If this idea did not originate with Malthus and Ricardo, it was emphasized strongly in their criticisms of Smith as the main peculiarity of land rent. The supposed peculiarity of the relation of land rent to price rested on fallacious reasoning, due to the unconscious introduction of new conditions into the concept.[4] The gradual displacement of the earlier conception of rent as income from land, by the no-cost-of-production concept, is one of the interesting chapters in the history of economic theory. First, the no-cost camel thrust only its nose into the tent, then it crowded out entirely the former occupant. To-day the no-cost concept is in large degree dominant, although the old definitions, the old arguments, and many inconsistent conclusions of the older treatment remain. Marshall's treatment of rent and quasi-rents shows the orthodox order of distributive theory dissolved into chaos by illogically conserving the older thought while developing a newer one. The quasi-rent doctrine, however, takes a long step in the right direction, for it recognizes the likeness of the yield of land and of other concrete goods.

What is most pertinent to the present purpose is that this thought of rent, as usually developed, is in its nature a compromise. The old idea and the new are entertained, together. The same old formal definition is retained; the newer distinction, brought in to modify and explain, only complicates and confuses the rent concept. Certainly none of the contemporary supporters of this view have as yet framed a definition that is more than temporizing. But even if a choice were made between these two essentially different concepts of rent (and of interest) ambiguity would not be banished, for in all the older discussion of rent and interest another distinction has been assumed whose significance usually has been quite unsuspected, but which in fact contains the key to the problem.

5a. An essentially different distinction between rent and interest is tacitly introduced into the discussion when the amount of the bearer, or source, of rent is expressed in physical terms as to quantity and quality, while the bearer, or source, of interest is expressed in the general value unit as a principal sum.

That this distinction is made a part of the conventional concepts will be recognized by all students of economic theory. Equally evident is it when once attention is called to the fact, that this is done without recognizing the changed point of view thus taken toward the two kinds of goods. The Columbus of economic theory who stood this egg on end is Professor John B. Clark. All the standard texts declare, in discussing interest, that capital consists of concrete goods, and is neither mere money nor mere abstraction, yet at the same time they speak of capital as of uniform quality and as yielding a uniform rate of income. This is said to contrast capital strikingly with land, which is measured by the acre, and differs from unit to unit. Professor Clark, in his brilliant criticism of this confused thought, has vividly pictured the varying grades of "capital goods" as he calls them, and has shown that artificial agents can be viewed in concrete form and expressed in physical terms in the same way as natural agents usually are. Most students, therefore, are ready to recognize the truth of a statement that would have been startling some years ago: the contrasts supposed to reside in the objective differences between natural agents and capital are but subjective differences due to the points of view taken by the thinker when he chooses to express the quantity of goods in different modes.

These differing modes of expressing the bearers of the two incomes involve corresponding differences in the conceptions of their maintenance and of their income. As these conceptions are but phenomenal forms of the thought expressed in 5 a, the statement of them will be numbered 5 b and 5 c.

5b. In estimating its net income, the bearer of rent is thought of as materially unimpaired by use, being preserved in identical form or in kind; the bearer of interest is thought of as maintained of undiminished value, expressed in terms of some conventional standard.

This is a contrast in point of view that is entirely unrelated with the contrast presented in the formal definition, and confusion results. The taking of different points of view is allowable; indeed, it is necessary if all aspects of any subject are to be considered. The inconsistency is in unconsciously shifting the point of view and believing that the differing natures of the objects were the cause of the differences observed. Two similar houses viewed, the one from the front and the other from the rear, appear to be very differently planned. The one blind man who got his idea of the elephant by touching the tusk is said to have argued long with the other who had caught hold of the animal's tail. Debates as hopeless as this, result from the shifting of the concepts here under discussion.

A side light on the theoretical analysis above may be given by a brief suggestion of the historical conditions in which the distinction took its rise. The rent contract, almost universally employed in the Middle Ages in transferring the temporary control of wealth, involves a legal fiction. Land, houses, cattle, whose use is delegated to the tenant, must, according to the terms of the contract usual in such cases, be returned in the same condition as when borrowed. The performance of this contract is literally and physically impossible; but by means of agreements as to repairs and replacements, the agents can be restored in equally good condition. Every rent contract for the use of agricultural land is in its terms a disproof of the idea that rent is paid alone for the original and indestructible qualities of the soil; yet the fiction of a perpetual rent-bearer deceived Ricardo and has continued to deceive. The interest contract came into use much later, as a money economy arose; hence, its employment was confined, until the last century, almost entirely to money loans and to the transfer of city wealth. This chance historical parallelism between land, rent, country and landlord on the one hand, and machines, interest, city and merchant on the other, explains many of the fallacies that beset economic thought in the first conscious attempts to analyze value.[5] The rent contract and the interest contract are not in any essential way connected with land and produced agents respectively, and the chance use of them for transferring certain kinds of goods has within the last century become less and less common. The contrasting form of contract in rent and interest (and a corresponding contrast in the mode of estimating the income bearer in economic rent and interest) was introduced into the older concepts alongside of the formally recognized characters, making the concepts complex and contradictory.

5c. Contract rent (corresponding with the thoughts in 5a and 5b) is treated by all writers as an absolute amount, not as a percentage of the income bearer; contract interest is treated as a percentage of a principal sum. A similar distinction is made in the case of economic rent and economic interest at certain moments.

The conception of economic income being more subtle than that of contractual income, is less easily grasped. Contractual income is personal, economic income is impersonal. While it was contractual rent that drew the attention of the earlier economic students, it is economic rent (using the term in a broader sense than mere land rent) that constitutes the real problem in economic theory.

Here also a word of economic history throws light on the origin and occasion of this distinction as applied to the contractual incomes. The theorists of 125 years ago found contract rent in extensive practical use. While mainly used in reference to the income of land, the word rent was taken in a much more general sense both in English and in the continental languages. Houses and machines were then rented as pianos and automobiles are now. At first the income from land was specifically distinguished as "land rent," but Ricardo's authority specialized the term "rent" in English economic theory, and, ever since, economists have struggled in vain to establish their word usage in the place of that sanctioned by many centuries. A part of every conventional discussion of rent is given to explaining that "in the economic sense" it means only the income from land considered apart from improvements.

The renting contract doubtless was the exclusive mode by which the temporary use of wealth was given and acquired in primitive communities. It certainly continued throughout the feudal period to be all but universal in the rural economies. The interest contract was an impossibility until the rise of a money economy. Money came into use first in the cities, and there also was felt most strongly the inconvenience of the renting contract. The ventures of the merchant at home and abroad required goods so various in quantity and quality, so difficult to measure exactly except in terms of value, that the borrowing of them was hardly possible except in the form first of general purchasing power, that is, under the interest contract. And it is so to-day. The differing practice was due to business convenience, not to an essential difference in the economic nature of the goods, and while in fact machines can be and are "rented," land and other natural agents are often temporarily acquired nowadays under the interest contract. As contractual incomes both rent and interest are found alternating in practice, and just because the contracts are so different in outer form, the incomes appear to have in many ways essentially different characters.

6. There are thus included in the generally accepted concepts of rent, without formal recognition, three essentially different and often conflicting thoughts:

(a) It is the income of a special social class, marked by the ownership of a special class of physical agents (the characteristics being somewhat shifting).

(b) It is any income having a special relation to price, namely, that "it does not enter into the cost of production."

(c) It is an income that is yielded by wealth measured physically and that is expressed as an absolute sum.

In each case rent is in contrast with interest which is (a) received by a different social class, and from a different class of agents, or (b) has a supposedly different relation to the value of products, or (c) is estimated as a percentage of a principal sum or value of wealth.[6]

If the incomes from wealth are to be grouped logically and classified practically as rent and interest, the three foregoing tests must be applied to each income as it appears. It is assumed in the conventional treatment that these tests give consistent results. Unless, however, the three tests are logically related, it is incredible that the results of their application should coincide in more than a small number of cases. Indeed, every contradiction that is possible by combining these independent tests occurs at one time or another in the conventional treatment of rent. The entire collapse of the old rent doctrine has been prevented only by failure to apply the tests to all cases and in full measure. The thought is shifted as convenience suggests. Starting with the formal definition framed about the first thought, the treatment shifts to the second or third. Such a method cannot be defended as a legitimate employment of a continuity concept. Continuity does not justify the cross-logic of a three-fold or four-fold principle of classification. These is no continuity in the jump from natural agents to consumer's rent, or from landlord's income to the contract to restore in kind.

In concluding the merely negative part of this paper it should be reiterated that propositions 3, 4 and 5, summarized in 6, are to be interpreted collectively. In the foregoing argument it has not been maintained that any one of the three principal thoughts contained in these three propositions cannot be made formally logical if it is developed by itself consistently. It is, however, maintained here that when these several thoughts are employed together without a recognition of the resulting complexity, fallacious contrasts and conclusions result. Differences between rent and interest, that are assumed to arise out of the nature of the two classes of agents, are but the reflection of the changing subjective attitudes of the theorists.

In Part II is to be considered the logical character of the

concepts resulting from a consistent development of each of the first two thoughts here recognized.

PART II. EXCLUSION OF TWO POSSIBLE FORMAL SOLUTIONS OF THE INCONSISTENCIES

7a. Formal consistency might be gained if the distinction between rent and interest were made to turn on the difference in the social classes that receive the incomes; but this is almost purposeless in economic theory.

A merely formal concept of rent might be framed about the thought of a social class. Rent might be defined as the income of wealthy men or of those moving in the best society. English conditions naturally suggested to the thinkers of a century ago the contrast of agricultural land holders and city men of wealth. But it is safe to say that no such social classification ever has been or ever could be presented that is either exact or significant enough to serve in the analysis of value. The economic theory of value is essentially an attempt to explain impersonally the origin and degree of importance of goods. The social class concept of rent thus involves a distinction not primarily economic, and one that is incapable of even a moderate degree of exactness in practical application. When, moreover, membership in a social class is tested by ownership of a particular kind of agent, the social aspect of the concept almost disappears. The connection of the thought of land rent and landlords as a class could continue only in the peculiar social conditions of England, and then it corresponded only in a broad, not in an exact way, with realities.

7b. Formal consistency is possible if the distinction between rent and interest be made to turn *solely* on the difference in the classes of physical agents that yield them; but this distinction is quite incapable of practical application.

The only classification of wealth that ever has been suggested for this purpose is that into natural and artificial, or unproduced and produced agents, or land and "capital." Such a classification may be required to meet two tests. It is expedient only if the two classes of agents can be practically distinguished by marks or evidences that can be taken account of in the practical world; it is logical only if it is consistently applied.

Land in an unimproved state is rare if not unknown in modern societies. As nearly every concrete thing is a bit of natural material adapted artificially to some degree to man's use, everything according to this conception should have in it elements of capital and interest, and elements of land and rent. No practicable method of deciding whether a thing is land or capital ever has been suggested, much less applied.[7] When one considers the nature of the case, it appears impossible even to conceive of such a test.

Therefore economic theory, unable to make the division between land and capital along a concrete and objective line, has been led to make it along an abstract line. Rent was said to be the income from land "considered as unimproved," or "considered apart from improvements"; while interest was that part of the income of land that was to be considered as due to improvements or to produced agents. Ricardo put it that rent is paid to the landlord for the use "of the original and indestructible qualities of the soil." Few writers that have accepted the Ricardian definition, have failed to apologize for the evident error in the phrase. Ricardo apparently meant, not that all qualities were indestructible, but that they might be spoken of as undestroyed, if annually repaired. Indeed it would be difficult to find a writer that does not, both in theoretical and practical problems, give up the impossible task of distinguishing all the value due to improvements on land. It is so much easier to wave the difficulty aside by "incorporating" or "merging" the improvements into the land. It has not been recognized that the original thought has thus been departed from, that the practical difficulty has been slurred over, and that a metaphysical division has been substituted for a concrete classification. The designating of an improved field as land or natural agents, and of an improved piece of iron as capital, becomes a purely arbitrary matter. The test is not found in immobility. Are the Suez Canal, the Hoosac Tunnel, the ploughed field, land or capital? A touch of human labor is at one time believed to convert the entire material into capital, a larger amount of labor at another time is declared merely to incorporate itself with the land and become indistinguishable from it.[8] The notion that it is a simple matter to distinguish between the yield of natural agents and that of improvements is fanciful and confusing, is responsible for many errors, including the cruder part of the single tax doctrine. The distinction doubtless more nearly approaches business realities in the case of city building sites than in that of agricultural land. It must, however, be maintained that the objective classification of land and capital as natural and artificial agents is a task that always must transcend human power of discrimination.

The vagueness of the line between natural agents and capital is increased by the fact that money and artificial agents measured as "capital" can be and are so often invested in land. Where land becomes a commonly marketed form of wealth, the classification of rent and interest according to the social class of owners becomes meaningless, and the classification accorded to kind of agents grows quite out of harmony with business usage. An attempt to meet the difficulty is seen in the more recent contrast between capital from the individual and capital from the social point of view, which is an abandonment of the distinction according to the class of agents in most of its possible applications. This complicates instead of solving the difficulty, which must be logically met.[9]

8. Formal consistency may be gained if the distinction between rent and interest is made to turn on their supposed relation to cost of production.

It is always a scientific service to carry to its extreme possibilities any abstract distinction, for thus only can be made apparent its merits and defects. In the gradual enlargement of the no-cost-of-production notion of land rent (noted in proposition 4) until it becomes the essential thought in the rent concept, the view of Mr. John A. Hobson represents nearly this ultimate development.[10] Moved by the desire to find a basis in the theory of rent for a juster system of distribution and of taxation, he reexamines the problem and arrives at the conclusion that "the law of rent, in its extreme application, is valid for each factor." A fund is required as well to keep land and labor, as to keep capital in repair, above which sum, he thinks, the differential expenses of production "whether they be rent, interest, or wages, will not enter into the market price of the supply." While he thus narrows the conception of rent in some ways, he widens it greatly in others. He retains, though after modification, the notion of a no-cost-factor, and broadens it greatly. He stops just short of rejecting the whole distinction between land and capital as unproduced and produced agents. As a result of this and other recent criticisms, a doctrine of general rent, or of quasi-rent, is the dominant idea regarding rent to-day in many minds.[11] As a negative criticism Hobson's essay has the highest merits, demonstrating, as it does, how illusive are many of the supposed peculiarities of the various incomes in the older treatment of distribution. His idea of cost and "no-cost" factors is moreover closely in touch with realities, for cost in his discussion is a very concrete thing, representing the repair and replacement fund needed for each factor. Moreover, there is for the theory of social legislation much suggestiveness in the idea of the surplus feature in each income that is above "cost," and therefore amenable to taxation. For all this, Hobson's treatment does not yield a satisfactory solution of the problem of the rent concept, notably because rent is left quite unadjusted, and unrelated to, the interest concept. Though Hobson, in concluding, expresses the hope that he has laid the basis for a "sound theory of distribution," he recognizes the complexity of his concept and the difficulty of its application.[12]

The distributive system presented by Dr. C. W. Macfarlane[13] is, however, a further step into abstraction. That writer, believing that any given factor may, at a given moment, have various relations to price, reaches the somewhat bewildering conclusion that land (which "includes all natural forces except labor") and entrepreneur's service, each may yield both rent and profit; capital may yield rent, profit and interest; and labor may yield rent, profit and gain. Whether and how far any income is thus to be named depends on whether it is "price-determined" or "price-determining," a transcendental inquiry as difficult to apply as the small boy's method of catching birds by salting their tails. As the conception that some incomes bear a peculiar relation to price grows out of fallacious reasoning, no logically sound classification of incomes can be based upon it.[14] But if it were sound, it still would be the extreme of abstraction, confined to the most subtle and probably useless economic speculation. Even if such a no-cost-of-production concept of rent could be made formally logical it still would lack expediency for a theory of distribution.

PART III. POSITIVE SOLUTION OF THE THEORETICAL PROBLEM OF RENT AND INTEREST

9a. Consistency must be gained by substituting for the older futile distinctions, that between the wealth aspect and the capital aspect of material goods.

Neither the physical classification of agents, nor the metaphysical classification of abstract types of income, affords an answer to the theoretical and practical problem of rent and interest; but in the consistent development of the third important thought contained in the old and confused rent concept, the desired solution is found.[15] Rent and interest, until recently, have been looked upon as corresponding respectively to two different factors of production. In recent criticism the idea of correspondence or parallelism between each factor and its income has been abandoned, but the two material factors (natural and artificial) are still retained. A better positive theory must clear up the confusion as to the differing nature of these factors. Present in the thought of the older economists, along with the distinction between natural and artificial agents, and coloring their conclusions, has been the distinction here suggested. Durable goods were sometimes thought of as yielding uses (the wealth aspect), but land was the only important class of agents that was regularly so viewed. Durable goods were sometimes thought of as saleable at their present worth (the capital aspect), but only produced agents, the materials and instruments of manufacture, were usually so viewed. Both classes of agents can be looked at consistently from either point of view, can be considered either as bearer of rent, or as discounted sum of rents, either as wealth or as capital. It is in the confusion of these contrasts that most of the old opposition between income from land and income from artificially produced agents was found. This fog is lifted when the sources of rent and of interest cease to be considered as physically distinct and objectively differing kinds of goods, and are seen to be simply the same body of income yielders, differently viewed, calculated and expressed for theoretical and practical purposes.

9b. Corresponding with the distinction between the wealth aspect and the capital aspect of material goods, are the differing thoughts as to the maintenance of the factors.

In the earlier industrial stages when exchange is rare and money but little known, it is inevitable that the uses, or rents, of durable agents should be primarily thought of. In estimating the uses, allowance must first be made for keeping the agents in physical repair. This calculation is necessary not only in making the rent contract, but in conducting the individual economy, if net income is to recur. As was shown above, the supposed durability of land and of its qualities for which rent is paid, is largely an illusion due to ignoring its constant repair. The preserving of the rent-bearer in identical form or in kind is essential to the concept of a perpetual rent.

As the money economy displaces the barter economy, and the thought moves from the valuable present rent to the present saleable value of the rent-bearer, the capital sum of value is thought of as kept intact before a net income from it is estimated. This is a primary condition of the contractual money loan, requiring the repayment of a principal sum apart from interest and this becomes the leading type of modern business calculations.

The blunder of the older economics in connecting land and rent with the one mode of calculation, and artificial agents with the other mode, has been noted above in proposition 5. Not only is it possible to view both aspects of use-bearers consistently, but clear theory and sound business practice require that this be done.

9c. As a necessary result of the distinction between the wealth and the capital aspects of agents, and of the thoughts as to the maintenance of the factors, rent must be expressed as an absolute amount, and interest as a percentage of a principal sum.

This is stated mainly for formal completeness, but it emphasizes the retention of a feature of the older treatment whose significance was unsuspected. In fact the expression of interest as a percentage marks interest as the form of income most connected with mobile and saleable agents, it makes of interest a "marginal" factor in price, a fact so much emphasized in the older treatment, it connects interest peculiarly with the element of time, as so many writers have felt it should be. Yet the percentual form of expressing interest is impossible when the income bearer is measured by physical norms, it is practically inevitable when the income bearer is expressed as a capital sum.

10. The rent and interest concepts, when looked upon as successive steps in the analysis of value, instead of as coördinate shares dividing between them the income from material agents, are made consistent internally, mutually, and with the foregoing conceptions of wealth and of capital.[16]

It was suggested in proposition 5 that the treatment of land rent as an absolute amount, and of interest on produced goods as a percentage of their value, grew out of prevailing practice in the contracts for the use of wealth. Either mode of expressing income may be logical if consistently employed, and if divorced from the confusing prejudice that the difference is due to the different nature of the factors yielding the two incomes. This error recognized, economic theory must abandon the old distinction as to the differing factors. What is left in place of the old rent concept? All that was best in it, freed of error: rent is the usufruct attributable to any material agent. The uses of material agents considered apart from the using up of the agents, are in this view always and only rents. This is a logical thought, a useful one and one applicable to practical problems.

When to rent has thus been assigned all current incomes from material agents there is no place for the old concept of interest as the yield of produced agents. But rents accrue at different points of time and vary in value accordingly. Present uses and future uses differ. A more or less durable agent represents a series of rents. The capital value of a good is the sum of its prospective rents and uses, discounted at a rate that reflects the prevailing premium on the present. Capitalization, thus viewed, is logically a later stage of the problem of value than is rent; and interest first appears in connection with capitalization. As the market expression of the all-pervasive premium of present over future, interest may appear in connection with any gratifications, whether they be yielded by natural or by produced, by material or by human, by durable or by perishable agents. There is not a writer from Ricardo to the present time by whom this universal application of interest is not vaguely recognized; there probably is not one by whom its application is not more or less inconsistently restricted.[17]

11. The propositions above imply the need of a radical restatement of the theory of distribution, and suggest its essential outlines.

The prevailing theory of distribution rests upon the idea of three (more often lately, four) objectively differing factors, to which correspond three (or four) different kinds of income. Some later, more subtle, attempts to restate the theory have left it far from realities and quite unusable. Another solution may be found by combining into a logical system the three typical modes in which goods appeal to wants. First, goods appeal directly, as want-gratifiers immediately available. Here is required a theory of wants and enjoyable goods, and the technical analysis of marginal utility. The mental process here examined is chronologically the first stage of evaluation in the history both of the individual and of the race. Secondly, goods appear as more or less durable, and may be made comparable by being considered, through repairs, to be lasting use-bearers, yielding in a given short period a group of uses. Here is the place for the theory of rents. This is chronologically the second stage of evaluation, when durable goods are thought of and expressed in terms of their usufructs. Thirdly, whenever two non-synchronous gratifications, rents or series of rents, are exchanged, they must be discounted to their present worth to be made comparable. Here is required a theory of capitalization, that is of economic interest. This is historically as well as logically the latest stage of evaluation, characteristic of a developed money economy and of a "capitalistic" era. These three phases must be observed in every complete analysis of value. They are in some respects analogous to the three dimensions in geometry. The older economic theories were curiously crude caricatures of such an analysis. The cost-of-production theory of the exchange value of commodities, (assumed to be the whole theory of value) roughly corresponded only with the first. The old theory of land rent caught a fragmentary view of the second. The old theory of interest on a narrowly conceived class of "capital," was an ineffective attempt to express the third. The theory of value in the present conception proceeds from the simple to the complex, from the immediate to the distant gratification, from the goods directly in contact with the senses, to those whose utility is indirect and only in expectation. While the negative criticism of the past three decades has wrecked the old distributive theory, many admirable positive contributions, widely diverse in character, converge to the solution here presented.

DISCUSSION

All taking part in this discussion have shown their belief that economic theorizing is worth while, and that theories both good and bad are affected by, and in turn affect, practical life. In accordance with this view, the leading proposition of the opening paper that the conventional concepts of rent and interest are illogical and inconsistent, has a corollary that these concepts are unfitted to explain the problems of the business world, and that another conception must be adopted.

To the frank and friendly criticisms offered in this debate, I shall reply as brevity permits. Those taking part in the discussion may be arranged in a continuity classification (the validity of which I fully admit) from those who for regard of traditional theories would overlook a lack of logic, to those who for regard of logic are willing to adopt new theories. The conservatives are far from harmonious in their beliefs, and by mutual cancellation they have left for consideration only a residuum of argument.[18]

The prime contention of the first part of my opening paper is not, as it was assumed by Professor Hollander to be, "the historical relativity of the traditional theories."[19] That thought is a minor one, and the brief historical paragraphs were given merely as "side lights" on the origin of the errors.[20] It would be an easy task to defend and strengthen these historical references had any one of the speakers sought to controvert them at any specific point. Even the critic who first waived the whole opening paper aside as "conjectural history" gave to the historical suggestions "conditional assent."[21]

Prejudgment has, I fear, caused more than one of my critics to shut his eyes to the repeatedly avowed purpose of the paper, which was to show that the traditional concepts are internally inconsistent, illogical, containing several conflicting thoughts, and that they were thus defective even in the days of Ricardo. In recognizing that some practical issues in Ricardo's time served to obscure this lack of logic, the paper had, to be sure, a suggestion of historical relativity. It is admitted by all the speakers that of recent years the emphasis on the various thoughts of these concepts has been shifted; and some would believe that this shift has cured the infirmities in logic. On the contrary I maintain that it has aggravated them. Thus, changes in industry and changes of thought have combined to enhance the difficulties *inherent from the first* in the older concepts.

Professor Carver has dissented generally from the negative part of the opening paper, regretting the attempt "to show that there is no basis for the scientific distinction."[22] He would explain the confusion by declaring that there are two clearly distinguishable concepts, the popular and the scientific, which at times contradict and overlap each other. As none of my critics attempted a specific disproof of this portion of my opening argument I may limit myself here to a reassertion that the so-called "scientific concept" is *inconsistent in itself*, that no writer has employed it without shifting thought and untenable conclusions. It is for the reader to determine whether I have not shown that the so-called "practical concept" has been confused with the so-called "scientific concept" in economists' minds. If this is true it follows that some of the supposed contrasts between rent and interest are but the reflection of the unconscious shifting in the subjective attitude of the thinker.

A test is thus afforded for any revision of the concepts; no valid contrast can be drawn between the concepts of rent and interest where there is an unconscious change from one to another of the three conceptions that have been noted. A shifting eclecticism becomes impossible when these different thoughts are clearly recognized. My critics, however, avoid a clear-cut decision, and uphold conceptions uniting two or more discordant elements. It is not easy, therefore, to say on just what ground they take their stand. They defend in the main the attempt to distinguish between land and artificial agents objectively, but their reasons are largely drawn from supposed differences in the relation of the income to price, and yet according to their own statements this distinction is not co-extensive with that of the two objective classes of agents. Moreover, their arguments involve a use of the third distinction,[23] which they are endeavoring to overthrow.

This confusion may be seen in Professor Hollander's contention that the critics of the traditional distinction overlook "the composite character of the law of diminishing returns." He says that the characteristic that suffices to "differentiate land from capital as a productive good" is its diminishing efficiency in extensive cultivation; "while capital is available . . . . . in identical homogeneous quality with respect to extensive use." Observe the reasoning by which this conclusion is reached.[24] The assumption, however, that any particular enterpriser, in enlarging his business, is forced to take up poorer land, surely is not warranted. Except in the rare case that the particular enterpriser had been using the one best piece of land, he can hire more land as good as he has, or even better, if he cares to pay the prevailing rental, just as he can hire more and better machines. The thought evidently shifts to the old dynamic and social conception of the growing scarcity of land with increasing population, and from the particular entrepreneur to the personified total population.

There is another shift, for while the physical conception of land is retained, and it is thought of in terms of acres, the particular produced goods called capital, are thought of in terms of a value unit. This creates the illusion that the differential return is peculiar to land, and that the value units of capital are of homogeneous quality. The varying yields of land are looked at in a way that makes them necessarily appear as differentials, and the varying yields of other agents are by reason of the mode of their capital expression, converted from differential incomes into homogeneous capitalized sums. What is this capital but the incomes (or I should call them rents) of productive goods, capitalized at the prevailing rate of interest? A given rent thus corresponds to one unit of capital, a double rent to two units of homogeneous capital, and a free good, or rentless unit, to no capital at all. This capitalization of rents is possible in the case of land also, the price of land being the sum of the anticipated future rents, discounted to their present worth; and the enterpriser can purchase x dollars' worth of land as easily as x dollars' worth of machines, and the units are just as homogeneous in one case as in the other. In fact, both kinds of agents frequently are bought as value units. The word "amount" in the contrast between an amount of land and an amount of capital begs the whole question, for in one case it means units measured by area and differing in yield, in the other it means the homogeneous value expression of differing units. It is impossible to escape these errors if the analysis insisted upon in the opening paper is overlooked.

Professor Carver has maintained[25] that there are abundant reasons for distinguishing between the income from land and the income from produced goods, in that interest as a personal income is a necessity to insure waiting, and thus is a condition of efficient production. This is retaining the traditional conception of the distinction between the objective classes of goods, while repudiating the traditional reasoning, and while broadening the conception of rent to any surplus or unearned income. The idea of surplus is generally very vague, but under the application of any suggested surplus-test the concept of rent would extend to numberless incomes and fractions of incomes not derived from land, and would fail to include numberless incomes and fractions of incomes that are derived from land in any usable sense of that term. Replies that, to my mind, are conclusive on the principle here involved were given in the course of the discussion.[26] It follows from this surplus conception that any portion of the income derived from produced goods that would have been saved if the rate of interest had been lower, is rent, not interest; and that any natural element of fertility in land that would have been used up except for the factor of waiting, would thereafter yield interest, not rent. Adopting for the moment the terminology of the critic, his challenge may be accepted; the proposition that "men must receive interest as a personal income to induce them [*i.e.*, the marginal abstainers] to wait" and that "interest as a personal income is necessary to secure efficient production," not only can be but must be paralleled by like propositions concerning rent. Men must receive land rent as a personal income to induce them to bring the marginal land into cultivation and to maintain undiminished the supply of productive qualities. Thus land rent is necessary to secure efficient production continuously from land. The margin in question is not a hair line, it is in practice a zone of wide extent. This fact is the basis of private property in land as broadly and surely as the other fact is the justification of interest. We are not concerned here with the ethical question, but in each of the two cases a social policy is based on the need of maintaining the marginal units of supply, a policy which always appears unjustified when attention is directed only to the surplus cases.[27] It is in conflict with all experience to assume that the actual supply of land would be kept up to its efficiency if rent did not go to some personal agent who made himself responsible for the repairs, the restoration of fertility, and the waiting for the future involved in refraining from "Raubbau," the immediate exploitation of the land. (In some cases, it is true, this agent may be a group of men acting collectively through government, as in the case of any form of public ownership.)

As Marshall says: "The greater part of the soil in old countries . . . . has in it a large element of capital. Man can turn a barren into a very fertile soil."[28] To deny first that the supply of land either as extension or fertility has any marginal relation to sacrifice, or is within man's control, and then when this is shown to be an error, to assert that such land is not land, but capital, and that the income from it is not rent, but interest—this is the approved mode of showing the exceptional character of rent. Are the terms land and rent thus to be refined away from any relation to the real things about which the economist begins to reason, and of which the practical world thinks whenever those terms are used?[29]

Professor Taylor admits that my thesis is valid when confined to static conditions, but he adheres to "the relation-to-cost" concept in discussing dynamic conditions.[30] In his very suggestive remarks he has not revealed his thought fully enough to make clear the ground of his reasoning, but it would appear to be essentially the one just examined. While Taylor and Carver differ in some points, they agree in others, both alike rejecting the static reasoning on which Hollander bases his conclusion.

Dr. MacFarlane also holds a relation-to-cost concept of rent, but most of his discussion is given to a negative criticism of my position. His own views, though known to many readers, were not developed in this symposium. Some points will be noted below.

The attacks on my positive proposals refer in part to their supposed implications and consequences, in part to the advisability of the terms suggested.

1. Professor Taylor objects[31] that the first of the three stages in the analysis of value is not fundamental and precedent to the others, but is co-extensive with them. This criticism probably

proceeds from a misunderstanding of the briefly expressed proposition. Not all goods, but only *immediately enjoyable* goods were said to present the first problem in the analysis of value. The second problem, that of the value of usufructs, and the third, that of the value of future uses, are, as my critic suggests, but developed phases of the general problem of value.

2. Professor Taylor believes that in criticizing Marshall's attempt to trace a continuity between rent and interest, I have denied the validity of reasoning by continuities.[32] It is not to a true continuity concept that I object, but to a pseudo-continuity concept. As the thought passes along the series from rent as an income yielded by one kind of concrete goods, to interest as the income yielded by another kind, there is unconsciously introduced a new contrast. The value expression of capital and the percentage expression of interest are equally applicable to the rent end of the series, and it is an error to assume that they are applicable only at the other end. My suggestion is to apply consistently each distinction in turn.

3. Dr. MacFarlane declares[33] that the outcome of my proposal is the obliteration of all distinctions between rent, interest, profit and wages. This conclusion, drawn from my statement that "interest may appear in connection with any gratification," is due to the failure to apprehend how and how far the proposed conception differs from the one apparently taken in this discussion[34] by the critic himself, that each kind of income corresponds to a particular kind of income bearer. The proposal is to look upon interest in all cases (as it is now in many cases) as being that particular phase of value connected with differences in the time of accrual of incomes. Recognizing that a day's work to-day is worth more than one next year, does not identify interest and wages. Wages payable at different points of time vary in value as do rents at different points of time, and the comparison of each series is expressed by the interest rate.

4. Dr. MacFarlane objects[35] further that the proposed view of capital identifies the capitalized value of monopoly surplus with capital in general. True it does; there is no other logical way.[36] It is not quite clear what monopoly means as the critic uses the

term, but any source of income that is continuing and foreseeable can be capitalized and sold, and thus becomes homogeneous with the value of the continued control of other sources of income. When from any cause income ceases, the capitalization collapses, monopoly or no monopoly. The puzzle as to whether the $5,000 or the $12,000 are to be called interest, is merely a confusion of the problems of economic income and contract interest.

5. Dr. MacFarlane says[37] that I have tried to identify land and capital by a mere arithmetic device that does not touch the substantial differences. I would reply that because an arithmetic device has been inconsistently applied in the traditional theory, illusive contrasts not existing objectively, have been created. I dissent from Professor Carver's opinion that it is merely a question of terminology in dispute,[38] and I agree with Dr. MacFarlane that there is involved more than a question of definition.[39] The arithmetic device is significant at least in a negative criticism of the supposed contrast between rent as a differential and interest as a homogeneous income; it serves to show the fallacy in the old view as to the special relation of rent to entrepreneur's cost of production; and it sets in a clear light the error in the traditional contrast between the value expression of "capital" and the concrete expression of land. This proof of the substantial unity and continuity of the body of income yielding wealth has been suggestively styled by Professor Taylor[40] in a phrase drawn from chemistry, "allotropism." One group of elements has been mistaken under differing conditions for two elements, (the condition in this case being the subjective attitude of the thinker). Take away the fallacious contrast, apply the arithmetic device consistently, and the objective classes of "natural agents" and "capital goods" are seen to be merged into one body of wealth, presenting three value aspects: gratifications, usufructs, expectations. But identifying the substance does not identify the allotropic states; coal is not diamond, though both are allotropic states of carbon; and no more is rent the same as interest. Like most analogies, however, this one is not perfect, and may become misleading. But this has brought us to

another question deserving special answer.

6. It is taken for granted that my proposition is to treat rent and interest as identical. Several of the speakers have assumed that the idea of the paper was that of John B. Clark, and thereupon they have criticized his views, not mine. My indebtedness (shared in common with all contemporary students) to the inspiration of this ablest of theoretical economists, should not impose on him any responsibility for the theory of distribution here presented. The prepossessions of some of the speakers make it difficult for them to see the full import of a denial of the parallelism between the two incomes, rent and interest on the one hand, and the two objective classes of goods, land and capital on the other. They therefore attribute to me conclusions deduced from premises of their own supplying. This is seen in the assumption that a denial of the conventional contrasts between valuable natural agents and (conventional) capital is a denial of the difference between rent and interest. It is consistent with my views to speak, as Professor Daniels does, of the identification (or merging), of the classes of wealth composing "land and capital" (in the conventional sense); but this is not an identification, as others consider it to be, of rent and interest. Having made this point as clear as I could in the limited space allotted, I can merely re-assert that this lack of parallelism is of the very essence of the contention in the opening paper.

7. Finally, it is said[41] that if the old concepts are to be rejected, it is better to devise new terms than to adapt old ones having misleading associations. To this view must be conceded a large measure of validity. Regarding the term rent there is less difficulty, as the broad meaning here suggested not only has strong historical support, but in many languages, including our own, is grounded so deeply in popular usage that no economic authority has been able to uproot it. There is needed only an elimination of inconsistent thoughts from the concept and the retention of one of the ideas that always has been present in it. Regarding interest the decision is more difficult. Only yesterday economists talked of "the theory of profits" when they meant what is now called "the theory of interest." The term interest, until recently, was

used almost if not quite exclusively, as meaning the income from a money loan. This is a contractual, not an economic income, and as such is not a genus coördinate with economic rent, rather it is species of the genus contractual rent. Is it not significant that even in the classical treatment interest as an accruing or realized income expressed as a percentage never appears except as the result of a contract?

The essence of the so-called problem of interest, according to the view in the opening paper is not fundamentally contractual interest, but capitalization. The problem logically following that of rent is not that of analyzing a coördinate income, for rent absorbs all the incomes accruing from material agents at any moment of time; but it is that of the value-calculation on future incomes. The title of the opening paper might perhaps better be: "The relations between rent and capitalization." That, however, would have misled the reader approaching it with the older conceptions in mind. Either "the theory of discount" or "the theory of capitalization" would be a more appropriate term for this part of the problem than is the theory of interest, and possibly some still better term can be found. The final use of terms is a matter of social convention; but when the real nature of the problem is understood, and then the fitting terms are suggested, they will not long fail of acceptance, as the example of the rapid change in the usage of the word profits gives reason to hope.

Whatever other impression may be left by this discussion I trust it will be that I have contended for a merely verbal change. On the contrary I have outlined, whatever be its defects, a radically new conception of the whole theoretical analysis of distribution. Doubtless this session has been most profitably spent in considering the more negative phases of the subject; but the scant attention that has been given to the yet more important positive outcome of the study may leave an impression of negation and verbal criticism that is misleading.

I welcome the able, forcible and somewhat unexpected support that has been given to my thesis in this discussion by the advocates of a realistic theory.[42] Opinion on this subject is unquestionably in process of change. Even the more conservative speakers in this session have made concessions that would have been startling a few years ago. The immediate result of such a friendly interchange of views as this has been, may be to strengthen each in his own opinion; but in the end the result must be to help us all towards the right solution of these difficult and important problems in the realm of abstract economic theory.

NOTES

The argument in this paper, forced into excessive brevity at many points, should be interpreted in conection with other essays by the writer, published from time to time in the past three years. Arranged, as nearly as their special nature permits, in a logical series, they are as follows:

1. The next decade of economic theory, Publ. of Amer. Econ. Asso., 3d ser., vol. 2, no. I, p. 236-246 (read Dec. 29, 1900). Points out the relative and temporary nature of the old concepts of rent and of capital, and suggests the general direction that may be taken in their restatement [see above, pp. 74-83].

2. The passing of the old rent concept, *Quar. Jour. Econ.*, vol. 15, pp. 416-455 (May, 1901). A detailed criticism, purely negative, of Marshall's doctrine of quasi-rent, as typical of the prevailing unsettled condition of thought on this subject [see pp. 318-354].

3. Recent discussion of the capital concept, *Quar. Jour. Econ.*, vol. 15, pp. 1-45 (Nov., 1900). A review of the contributions of Clark, Irving Fisher and Böhm-Bawerk to this subject, criticizing especially the last named in his distinction between social and individual capital, between consumption and production goods, between natural and produced agents; concluding with a positive statement of a concept of capital, as distinguished from wealth [see above, pp. 33-73].

4. The "roundabout process" in the interest theory, *Quar. Jour. Econ.*, vol. 17, pp. 163-180 (Nov. 1902). A criticism of Böhm-Bawerk's "Positive theory," showing that his retention of a defective capital concept is the cause of his retaining (inconsistently) a productivity theory of interest; concluding with a suggestion of the true relation of productivity to a theory of interest. The present paper unites, and develops somewhat, the various arguments in this series of articles [see above, pp. 172-191].

1. A. S. Johnson, Rent in modern economic theory, p. 19, Publ. Amer. Econ. Asso., 3d ser., vol. 3, no. 4. Probably most students would not consider this explanation a commonplace and would even deny

that it truly states the principal cause of the distinction in question. The author quoted makes it the main thesis of his book that the difference between land rent and interest, though thus originally observed as a merely transitory historical fact, remains of permanent significance.

2. Zwei Bucher zur socialan Geschichte England's, p. 160.

3. Note for example, Ricardo, 1817: "that portion of the produce of the earth, which is paid to the landlord," etc.; F. A. Walker, 1887: "the remuneration received by the landowning class," etc.; Marshall, 1890: "the income derived from the ownership of land," etc.; Bullock, 1897: "the return that is secured by the owner," etc.

4. This question is dealt with more fully in "The passing of the old rent concept," especially pp. 333-350.

5. This thought was stated with a somewhat different emphasis in "The next decade of economic theory," pp. 80-81.

6. Still other distinctions find partial recognition in current economics. See "The passing of the old rent concept," 325-332, for a discussion of space extension and of time in this connection.

7. The ablest attempt to face this difficulty formally, that of Böhm-Bawerk, in his "Positive theory," pp. 55-56, is quite unsuccessful. A criticism of his argument is given in "Recent discussion of the capital concept," pp. 57-65.

8. This idea as held by Böhm-Bawerk is more fully criticized in "Recent discussion of the capital concept," p. 63.

9. The "land concept of rent" in the somewhat complex form as held by Marshall, is criticized in "The passing of the old rent concept," pp. 320-325.

10. "The law of the three rents," article in *Quarterly Journal of Economics,* vol. 5, p. 263; restated in his "Economics of distribution," 1900. Likewise in vol. 5, p. 289, appeared John B. Clark's remarkable paper on "Distribution as determined by a law of rent."

11. The change in the rent concept is reviewed in "The next decade of economic theory," pp. 78-79.

12. "The law of the three rents," pp. 287-8.

13. Value and distribution, 1899.

14. The mistaken origin of the no-cost concept is shown in "The passing of the old rent concept," especially pp. 345-350.

15. This solution was implied in the capital concept presented in "Recent discussion of the capital concept," pp. 65-70.

16. This conception was briefly suggested in concluding the criticism of Böhm-Bawerk: "The 'roundabout process' in the interest theory," pp. 185-188.

17. The broader conception of interest was presented in "Recent discussion of the capital concept," pp. 33-73, especially pp. 49-57.

18. Brevity compels me to confide these closing comments to the

criticisms adverse to the opening paper.

19. Hollander, "Discussion, A.E.A." *Proceedings* 5 (February 1904): 204.

20. See above, pp. 197-198.

21. See Hollander, pp. 204, 205.

22. See Carver "Discussion, A.E.A." *Proceedings* 5 (February 1904): 205.

23. See above, p. 205.

24. See Hollander, passage beginning "No entrepreneur" and ending "only in inferior efficiency," p. 208.

25. See Carver, pp. 200-201.

26. See Daniels, p. 226. Dr. Whitaker's remarks to the same effect unfortunately were not obtainable for this report.

27. This applies also in answer to the remarks of Professor Ely.

28. Marshall, Principles of economics, 4th edition, p. 224. He does not draw the conclusion, however, that is here suggested as necessary.

29. The interesting facts cited by Professor LeRossignol, p. 224, seem to me to illustrate, not to disprove, the view I have taken, which is far from a denial of the "surplus return" to the investor in land, or in other wealth, in a new country.

30. See Taylor, "Discussion, A.E.A." *Proceedings* 5 (February 1904): 221.

31. See Taylor, p. 218

32. See Taylor, p. 220.

33. MacFarlane, "Discussion, A.E.A." *Proceedings* 5 (February 1904): 215.

34. As is well known to students of economic theory Dr. MacFarlane has in his work "Value and distribution," obliterated the distinctions between the objective classes of agents yielding rents, and other incomes, more fully than has any other writer.

35. See MacFarlane, pp. 213-14.

36. See Professor Gidding's reply, "Discussion, A.E.A." *Proceedings* 5 (February 1904): 226.

37. See MacFarlane, p. 212.

38. See Carver, pp. 203-4.

39. See MacFarlane, p. 214.

40. See Taylor, p. 219.

41. Hollander, p. 209.

42. Daniels, Giddings, Marburg, Whitaker. Unfortunately no report was secured of Mr. Marburg's brief and pointed remarks or of Dr. Whitaker's subtle discussion. Professor Keasbey's attitude toward the question is favorable to the opening paper as against its critics, but his point of view is original, and his treatment in several ways not consistent with the views I have expressed.

Review of Gustav Cassel, *The Nature and Necessity of Interest,* and Eugen von Böhm-Bawerk, *Recent Literature on Interest*

These two books, published almost simultaneously last year, testify to the attention which the theoretical problem of interest still commands. The first is a well-executed translation of the new material embodied in the second German edition (1900) of Böhm-Bawerk's *Geschichte und Kritik der Capitalzinstheorien.* The translators well say in their preface:

Whatever may be the final verdict of science regarding the agio theory, no one can doubt that the splendid example of criticism and analysis which is contained in Böhm-Bawerk's work has raised theoretical discussion to a higher level and has been a constant and powerful stimulus to investigation in this field.

The preface is largely taken up with the translators' epitome of the criticism of John Rae, to whose ideas the author's attention had been called after the first edition of his work appeared. The

---

Reprinted from *Political Science Quarterly* 20 (March 1905). The reviewed works are: Eugen von Böhm-Bawerk, *Recent Literature on Interest: A Supplement to Capital and Interest,* trans. William A. Scott and Sigmund Feilbogen (New York: Macmillan Co., 1903); and Gustav Cassel, *The Nature and Necessity of Interest* (London: Macmillan & Co., 1903).

translation is made up mostly of somewhat detailed replies to Marshall (a modified abstinence theorist), Carver (an abstinence theorist), and Wieser (a productivity theorist), and to various advocates of labor-cost and exploitation theories.

The book has, on the whole, a negative rather than a positive character. To borrow a phrase from recent politics, the author "stands pat" on what he had written fifteen years before. More clearly than before he realizes and frankly confesses that he is an eclectic. He admits (p. 137) that something may be said against eclecticism of every kind, but the objection seems to him least when "incoherent elements of different theories are combined into an external unity." He repeats his familiar condemnation of the productivity theory, declaring (p. 121) that "the solution of the problem of interest can never be found in the process of thought peculiar to that theory." But he here means complete solution, and again and again he repeats his belief that two elements coöperate in the explanation (p. xxxii), that psychological and technical points of view must be harmonized (p.8), that interest has several sources, including the roundabout process (pp. 45, 46, 143, 145 *et passim*). He contrasts (p. 142) his own partial productivity theory with "the genuine, outspoken productivity theories," which leave out "a full half of the actual causes of the phenomenon of interest." So far from seeking to evade the appearance of eclecticism, he takes pride (p. 146) in the two-fold nature of his explanation, and declares it to be "a recognized truth" that a correct solution must be an eclectic one. We must express an emphatic dissent from this lame and impotent conclusion which, however, completely verifies the opinion of the reviewer as expressed in the *Quarterly Journal of Economics* (vol. xvii, p. 177) that Böhm-Bawerk's theory, "so far as it rests on the productiveness of the roundabout process, is a productivity theory." An eclectic conclusion disappoints the high purposes with which Böhm-Bawerk began his study of the subject, and the high hopes he inspired. His whole discussion goes astray for lack of a consistent conception of capital. He seems at times near to a broader and truer conception of the problem of time-discount, but fails at such points to develop his thought.

The author is entirely untouched by those currents of thought which, beginning with J.B. Clark and Irving Fisher, have developed an entirely new literature of the subject of the capital concept. For lack of such a point of view, most of the subtle controversy of the present volume must appear to many readers to be the echoes of ancient opinions. The argument does not move forward, but merely marks time. The familiar ideas, when reiterated, may still engage the attention of a small group of special students of abstract theory, but they have lost their power to stimulate and inspire.

Dr. Cassel attempts first to develop a new theory of interest and secondly to examine the causes why interest is and always will be necessary. He presents a theory of interest as the pay for "waiting," and differs with Böhm-Bawerk, to whom he refers slightingly (p. 22), whose review of the history of the subject he criticizes as one-sided, and to whose roundabout process he presents essentially the same objections that had been pointed out a year before by the reviewer (in the *Quarterly Journal of Economics*, vol. xvii, pp. 163-180). But Dr. Cassel meets some of the same difficulties that befell Böhm-Bawerk, for he also fails to get a consistent capital concept. He connects the payment for "waiting" with the definite factor capital (p.67), and then after some delay limits capital to "produced goods except such consumable goods as are already in the hands of the consumer" (p. 88; see also p. 133). He does not see that waiting may be present both in the case of consumable goods in the hands of the consumer and in the case of land (which, in the old-fashioned way, he usually thinks of as not being an object of waiting). He wavers somewhat when (p. 167) he declares that interest is paid not for "the use of a piece of concrete capital . . . but for 'goods in general,' " for land must here also be included. But it is needless to adduce other examples to show that such a limitation of the capital concept makes impossible a complete theory of time-discount.

In the part dealing with the necessity of interest, the book is more original. It discusses at length and suggestively the changes that would be worked in the motives of men if the rate of interest fell from three per cent to two per cent or lower. The shifting of the margin of application of agents is described, and "the main argument of the book" (p. 157), which is to show "the necessity of interest," is strikingly brought out. The argument is strong as directed against the notions of the over-production of capital and the fallacy of saving. By this, its most interesting and valuable feature, the book should be judged as a contribution to economic theory.

Interest Theories,
Old and New

Abstract theory, always of fundamental importance, has, as truly as practical policy, its "topics of the day," and just now discussion of the interest problem is especially active. Notable among recent articles are those by Professors H. R. Seager, Irving Fisher, and H. G. Brown.[1] Mere individual differences of opinion concern us little; but certain impersonal equities which other students of economics have in the interest problem, are involved; for in recent discussion is fairly presented the issue between the old and the new conception of the interest problem.[2] And yet the case for the newer view might seem to be on the point of being lost before the bar of economic opinion. It is a duty, therefore, to attempt a more adequate statement of the neglected truths.

The rival views may be characterized as the technological[3] and the psychological interest theories. For more than a decade, the psychological theory has been gaining adherents in America. There has not been lacking adverse criticism in scattered book reviews and in occasional footnotes; but in the main, the opposition has been of a merely negative sort, in that most economists have failed to reckon with it and have adhered to the older theory.

1. PROFESSOR IRVING FISHER AS A PRODUCTIVITY THEORIST

Seager's paper, just cited, is the first systematic attempt that has been made to disprove any version of the newer theory (for

Reprinted from *American Economic Review* 4 (March 1914).

Fisher's "impatience theory," which Seager attacks, has been generally supposed to be a psychological theory). The discussion started by Seager necessarily follows in large part the lines determined by Fisher's treatment. Let us first, therefore, try to get our bearings as to that. My own position on the general question involved in this discussion has in the past been with Fisher so far and so long as he adhered to a psychological explanation. And yet, I must recognize the merit of Seager's argument in several respects, and, as a psychological theorist, I find myself more disquieted by Fisher's reply than by Seager's direct attack. Particularly regrettable is the impression of confession and avoidance which Fisher gives. He seems to capitulate on the main issue. To the charge that he failed "to take account of the elements of productivity or the technique of production," Fisher enters a denial[4] in terms which seem to imply that he is a good productivity theorist. This reply comes as a surprise even to those who were aware of certain ambiguous expressions on this point in Fisher's writings. For if he has not meant to deny, in his previous writings, the validity of productivity theories, one knows not what to believe. Here are some significant passages:

There are many who, consciously or unconsciously, ascribe the phenomena of interest to the productivity of capital in general. . . . Yet a very slight examination will suffice to show the inadequacy of this explanation.[5]

To raise the rate of interest by raising the productivity of capital is, therefore, like trying to raise oneself by one's boot-straps.[6]

Absence of interest is quite compatible with the presence of physical-productivity, and . . . therefore whatever element is responsible for the existence of interest in the actual world, that element cannot be physical-productivity.[7]

The conclusion, therefore, from our study of the various forms of the productivity theory is that physical-productivity, of itself, has no such direct relation to the rate of interest as is usually ascribed to it; and in the theories which we have examined, the rate of interest is always surreptitiously introduced.[8]

"Interest is due to the productivity of capital" . . . This proposition looks attractive, but it is superficial . . . the superior productiveness of roundabout processes of production . . . has no power whatever to create interest.[9]

Now, however, instead of meeting the question directly, and re-affirming his disbelief in the productivity theory, he seems to surrender his position as the easiest way of ridding himself of criticism. He says that he pleads "not guilty to the charge of neglecting the 'productivity' or 'technique' element." He speaks of "the true way in which the 'technique of production' enters into the determination of the rate of interest;"[10] he says, " 'the productivity' or 'technique' element, so far from being lacking in my theory, is one of its cardinal features;"[11] and, again, "Productivity has not been neglected in my treatment of interest."

Now it is true that these somewhat general expressions alone merely raise the reader's doubts. For to say that he does not neglect "productivity" or that it is not lacking in his theory does not positively commit Fisher to belief in a productivity explanation of interest as distinct from an essentially psychological explanation. But other expressions deepen the reader's doubts, and suggest strongly that Fisher objects only to certain formulations of a productivity theory, not to productivity theories on principle.

He admits[12] that in his book he has criticized "*the ordinary*[13] productivity theories*," but says that he then "explained to the reader that later in the book *I would rebuild the 'technical' feature* which, in the theories of others, I sought to destroy." Again[14] he speaks of his strictures on "*the ordinary* productivity theories," implying that some productivity theory or theories may be tenable. Again he reproaches Professor Seager with being "open to the charge of regarding all productivity theories as alike sound in principle" (implying that some *are* sound?). And he expresses the belief that "every one who has read Böhm-Bawerk should believe that *the ordinary*, or as Böhm-Bawerk calls them, *the 'naïve'* productivity theories are snares and delusions."[15]

These passages taken by themselves give the impression that the author is at heart as good a productivity theorist as any one; indeed, he collates them himself, seemingly, for the purpose of producing just this impression. This clearly is out of accord with the spirit and letter of much else that Fisher has said in denying productivity as a causal explanation of interest. The most lenient interpretation is that Fisher is here speaking in the spirit of an earlier statement:[16]

If after all has been said and understood, any one still prefers to call such a loan "productive,"no objection is offered, provided always that it is made wholly clear what is meant by the term "productive."

Here it seems clear that Fisher did not think the term productive, which he carefully enclosed in quotation marks each time, was a fitting adjective for such loans, made by borrowers for the purpose of gaining a profit. In his reply to Seager, however, Fisher's mood is all for so emphasizing any earlier statement of the tolerant sort as to make it appear that he does not deny the productivity theory of interest. He cites several passages in his earlier writings in which he has used such expressions as "the elements of truth contained in the claims of the productivity theories."[17] He says: "It was through mathematics that I saw the nature and importance of productivity in relation to interest," giving the impression that he at one time disbelieved in productivity as a causal explanation but had come to see his mistake. He says that his book "was written expressly for that purpose" (rendering of the technique element).[18] Despite his ability to adduce these evidences of his innocence of the charge of disbelief in the productivity interest theory, Fisher is penitent for not having made his position clearer. He declares that he has himself "to blame" "for the mistakes he (Seager) has made." He concludes this recantation:[19]

I ought, I doubt not, to have put forward the productivity element more prominently and with less avoidance of the term "productivity." I remember consciously avoiding this term so far as possible lest the reader should associate my theory too much with *the many false theories of productivity.*[20]

The most clear-cut evidence that he cites from his writings to prove that he never intended to deny the validity of the productivity theory *per se* is this:[21] "Again I specifically stated (*The*

Rate of Interest, p. 186): 'But while the slowness of Nature is a sufficient cause for interest, her productivity is an additional cause.' " A phrase which might have been deemed an oversight when taken in connection with other earlier statements, is here deliberately reaffirmed, and casts doubt upon the meaning of much of Fisher's previous writings. Just what is his position on the productivity theory? His recent apology, appearing at the same time that his colleague, Dr. H. G. Brown, publishes an elaborate defense of an eclectic productivity theory, is most disappointing to the group of true psychological interest theorists in America who a few years ago welcomed Professor Fisher as an accession to their ranks, and who still cherish the hope that, after he has fed for a time on the husks of the productivity theory, they may greet him again as a returning prodigal.

2. ORIGIN OF THE CAPITALIZATION THEORY

As a basis for further discussion, a brief review must be given of the origin and main features of "the capitalization theory" of interest as I had developed it several years before the publication of Professor Fisher's theory of interest in 1907. My attention was drawn to the subject repeatedly between the years 1895 and 1900 while I was studying the theory of distribution; and in an article on the capital concept, in 1900, I said:

> I would not exaggerate the significance of the change here proposed in the capital concept, yet it would be folly to ignore the consequences its acceptance would involve for economic theory . . . The current theories of land value, of rent, of interest, to a greater or less extent rest on the unsound ideas which have been criticized throughout this paper. On another occasion the writer will attempt to state the outlines of an economic system of thought in harmony with the capital concept here presented.[22]

Again, in a paper presented the same year at a meeting of the American Economic Association, it was said among other statements pointing in the same direction:

With this change [of the capital concept] must go a change in the whole conception of interest, which likewise is connected in the still current treatment with a factor that has been produced by labor. The multitudinous and naïve inconsistencies of the older treatment became apparent when viewed in the light of the later value theory.

The doctrines of rent and interest as currently taught are hopelessly entangled in these old and illogical distinctions. The two forms of return for material goods must be considered as differing in modes of calculation, not as to kinds of agents and as kinds of return. The object of this paper may now be restated ... to show the necessity of rewriting the theory of distribution along radically new lines ... and the acceptance of doctrines, the readjustment of which is shown to be inevitable.[23]

More than a year later, in reviewing some essays by Böhm-Bawerk,[24] I said:

Great as have been the services of our author in stimulating to clearer and deeper thinking in economic theory, his presentation of a *Capitalstheorie* evidently is not destined to be a finality. Some development it is sure to undergo, and is undergoing. And that development lies along the lines of a value concept as opposed to a cost-of-production concept.

Again in the same year, at the conclusion of a critical article on Böhm-Bawerk's theory:[25]

Let us venture an opinion as to the nature of the difficulty and the direction that must be taken to reach a correct solution. . . . Let us suggest the view that rent and interest are very dissimilar aspects of the value of goods. Rent[26] has to do with "production" of scarce and desirable uses of things. To the interest theorist this is in the nature, one might almost say, of an ultimate fact. The interest theory begins with the valuation of these different rents or incomes, distributed through different periods of time. The 'productiveness' of a material agent is merely its quality of giving a scarce and desirable service to men. To explain this service of goods is the essence of the theory of rent. Given this and a prospective series of future services, however, the problem of interest arises, which is essentially that of explaining the valuation set on the future uses contained in goods. Interest thus expressing the exchange ratio of present and future services or uses is not and cannot be confined to any class of goods; it exists wherever there is a future service. It is not dependent on the roundaboutness of the process; for it exists where there is no process whatever, if there be merely a postponement of the use for the briefest period. A good interest theory must develop the fertile suggestion of Böhm-Bawerk that the interest problem is not one of product, but of the exchange of product,—a suggestion he has not himself heeded. It must give a simple and unified explanation of time value, wherever it is manifest. It must set in their true relation the theory of rent as the income from the use of goods in any given period, and interest as the agio or discount on goods of whatever sort, when compared throughout successive periods.

A year later, in 1903, I outlined the same conception of a thoroughgoing psychological analysis, and for the first time gave the name of "a theory of capitalization" to the proposed treatment of what usually is called "economic interest."[27]

Another solution may be found by combining into a logical system the three typical modes in which goods appeal to wants. First, goods appeal directly as want-gratifiers immediately available. Here is required a theory of wants and enjoyable goods, and the technical analysis of marginal utility. The mental process here examined is chronologically the first stage of evaluation, in the history both of the individual and of the race. Secondly, goods appear as more or less durable, and may be made comparable by being considered, through repairs, to be lasting use-bearers, yielding in a given short period a group of uses. Here is the place for the theory of rents. This is chronologically the second stage of evaluation, when durable goods are thought of and expressed in terms of their usufructs. Thirdly, whenever two non-synchronous gratifications, rents or series of rents, are exchanged, they must be discounted to their present worth to be made comparable. Here is required a theory of capitalization, that is, of economic interest. This is historically as well as logically the latest stage of evaluation, characteristic of a developed money economy and of a "capitalistic" era. These three phases must be observed in every complete analysis of value.

In an elementary textbook published in 1904 (*The Principles of Economics*) this conception of the interest theory was embodied, not as a thing apart from, but as an integral part of, a general theory of value. This mode of treatment, though new,[28] was not labeled with a distinctive name, and, being presented in an elementary text, has doubtless remained unread by many economists, and its true import unrecognized by some who have read it.

As is shown in the passages cited above, my conception long has been that in the analysis of the value problem the value of enjoyable goods must be first considered; that this should be followed by the valuation connected with the *physical productivity* of agents; and that only after full consideration of income expressed in psychic terms, in physical terms, and in monetary terms, is it in order to take up the theory of time value, which is then to be developed as the basis of capitalization of incomes and of a resulting rate of contract interest.

3. POSITIVE STATEMENT OF THE CAPITALIZATION THEORY

Accordingly, in my text, the first forty pages are devoted to psychic income and to the process of valuation which results in a price of things considered as directly enjoyable objects of choice. In the next division, comprising nearly sixty pages, is taken up the physical productivity of wealth, the uses of goods, and the valuation of those uses. Contract rent is here based upon the valuation, to individuals, of the productive uses of durable agents, just as contract-price is based upon the valuation of enjoyable goods. A hundred pages were thus given to explaining as well as I was able to do it in a first sketch of the theory of distribution for elementary students, what income is, and how income arises, so that it may be the object of choice and of exchange. In the next division (Capitalization and Time-value) I discussed, in seventy pages, the various problems of value that arise from a comparison of goods in point of time. I treated capitalization as the problem of valuation of durable agents, and developed a theory of the rate of interest on contract loans based on this conception of capitalization.

For the reader unacquainted with the capitalization theory, its essential features may be here outlined. At the outset let us seek to avoid the confusion caused by the use of the word interest in

two senses, first, of a payment for contract loans made in terms
of money, and, secondly, of the difference in value between like
goods available at different times. Economists have of late
generally recognized these two meanings, and have sought to
distinguish them by the terms contract and economic interest.[29]
Though such a terminology is an improvement upon the old, it
leaves an ambiguity that continually reappears in the discussion.
I therefore used the word interest solely in its original and still
almost universal commercial sense of contract-interest, and I
used the term time-value to designate the other problem of
"economic" or "implicit" interest.[30]

Seeing the two problems as in large measure distinguishable,
and seeking for the logical starting point in the study, I asked:
Which of these two questions was prior in history and which is
primary in logic? In both cases the answer was time-value. The
canon of priority in economic reasoning applied here:
whichever of two interrelated problems or mutually acting
forces can be thought of as existing without the other, must be
primary in the explanation. A rate of interest on money loans
would be unthinkable if there were no differences relative to
time in the estimates men placed on some goods available at
different points of time. On the other hand, the use of money
and the practice of borrowing and lending in terms of money are
of comparatively recent origin; and the estimate of time-value
today is thinkable, and is actually made, apart from the use of
money or from any act of borrowing or exchange between
persons. It must always have been found, as it now is in countless
cases, in an impersonal relation between man and objects.
Further, I applied the same test to determine the priority of
capitalization and the rate of interest on loans (taking capitalization to mean simply putting a valuation, a present worth, upon
a more or less durable group or source of incomes). The usual
view has been that capitalization is subsequent to a rate of interest. But capitalization, as the process of putting a present
worth upon any durable source of wealth and thus discounting
its future uses by the act of exchanging it for other things, must
have occurred many times before a rate of contract interest

existed. This process surely occurs now in many cases without previous reference to such a rate. If, however, the less crude view be taken, that the interest problem studied is economic interest (time-discount) rather than contract interest, it is clear that this also is an aspect of the capitalization rather than antecedent to it. This rate of discount ("implicit" or "economic interest") is in itself nothing but an arithmetic reflection, in no sense causal, of the preference implied in the valuation of goods. Robinson Crusoe, in his individual economy, must, by his choice of goods which embody uses maturing at different periods, wrap up a scale of time-values which only later, if ever, except in a very vague form, appear as an arithmetic rate. The primitive economy in its choice of enjoyable goods of different epochs of maturity, in its wars for the possession of hunting grounds and pastures, in its slow accumulation of a store of valuable durable tools, weapons, houses, boats, ornaments, flocks and herds, first appropriated from nature, and then carefully guarded and added to by patient effort—in all this and in much else the primitive economy, even though it were quite patriarchal and communistic, without money, without formal trade, without definite arithmetic calculations, was nevertheless *capitalizing*, and therefore embodying in its economic environment a rate of premium and discount as between present and future.

This, then, is the essence of the capitalization theory of interest as nearly as we can put it in a proposition: The rate of interest (contractual) is the reflection, in a market price on money loans, of a rate of capitalization involved in the prices of the goods in the community. The price of durable agents is a capitalization which involves a discount of their future uses, and this is logically prior to the rate of contract interest. The logical order of explanation is from numberless separate acts of choice of goods *with reference to time*, to the value (and prices) of durable goods embodying future incomes, and finally to the market rate of interest.[31] This interest theory was new in its *order of development* from elementary choice; in the *priority it assigned to capitalization* above contract interest; in its *unified psychological explanation* of all the phenomena of the surplus that emerges when undervalued expected incomes approach maturity, the surplus all being derived from the value of enjoyable (direct) goods, not by two separate theories, for consumption and production goods respectively; in the *integration* of the interest theory *with the whole theory of distribution;* and in a number of details necessarily related to these features.

A just opinion of the newer theory is possible only to those who are willing to re-think the fundamental economic concepts. The change in the interest theory is only a part of the general reformulation of distributive theory which has been under way for a third of a century. It is to be understood only in that light.

4. SOME DIFFICULTIES IN FISHER'S IMPATIENCE THEORY

From the standpoint of the capitalization theory, the various questions raised in the discussion between Seager and Fisher and in Professor Brown's paper, appear from a new angle. It seems to be a different standpoint from that of Fisher, although at times he may appear to hold it. It is true that in his work *The Rate of Interest* (1907), in which his theory was first presented, he introduced his "first approximation" with a chapter on time-preference, which he declares to be "the central fact in the theory of interest," giving in a footnote without comment at this point[32] a page reference to my text. He says that "the income concept plays the central role."[33] But he treats capitalization as subsequent to a rate of interest, saying:[34]

When any other goods than enjoyment incomes are considered their values already imply a rate of interest. When we say that interest is the premium on the value of a present house over that of a future house we are apt to forget that the value of each is itself based on a rate of interest. We have seen that the price of a house is a discounted value of its future income. In the process of discounting there lurks a rate of interest. The value of houses will rise or fall as the rate of interest falls or rises. Hence, when we compare the values of present and future houses, both terms of the comparison involve the rate of interest. If, therefore, we undertake to make the rate of interest depend on the relative preference for present over future houses, we are making it to depend on two elements in each of which it already enters.

And again he says:[35] "The value of the capital is found by taking the income which it yields and capitalizing it by means of the rate of interest." Still later he writes:[36] "Capital value is merely the present or discounted value of income. But whenever we discount income we have to assume a rate of interest."

From the moment Fisher begins his first approximation[37] he takes his standpoint in the money market and supposes an existing rate of interest to which rates of time-preference of individuals are later brought into conformity. His treatment throughout is of the actuarial, mathematical type, concerned with the explaining and equalizing of incomes which are assumed to be present. I feel as strongly as does Professor Seager the neglect, in this treatment, of the element of productivity in accounting for the existence of the incomes.[38] From my point of view the difficulty appears to inhere in Fisher's general conception of the problem.[39] I differ from the productivity theorist, however, in looking upon the interest problem as that of explaining not the existence nor yet the magnitude of those incomes, but the rate of their valuation to the valuation of the capital sum (principal) to which the contract rate (percentage) refers.

I share with Seager the opinion that there is no "sovereign virtue in mathematical modes of thought" which safeguards the mathematical economist from error. Indeed, there seem to be characteristic mathematical illusions.

I share Seager's doubt of the aptness of the proposition that impatience is "a fundamental attribute of human nature" or is "the essence of interest," though my doubts are for a different reason.[40] It is interesting to notice that Fisher himself did not seem to hold this view when he wrote *The Rate of Interest,* in 1907. He said:[41]

It shows also that the preference for present over future goods of like kind and number is not, as some writers seem to assume, a necessary attribute of human nature, but that it depends always on the relative provisioning of the present and future.

In an article in 1911,[42] he for the first time used the term impatience in this connection, which he confesses is but a "catchword" in place of time-preference. With this change of name has gone a change in the conception of the thing designated.

In my own book, *The Rate of Interest,* for instance, this term was unused because unthought of, and the clumsier and less explanatory term "time-preference" was employed instead. The proposal to employ the term "impatience" is here made for the first time. . . . Impatience is a fundamental attribute of human nature.

In 1912,[43] he restates the same view: "It [impatience] is a fundamental attribute of human nature. . . . Interest is, as it were, human impatience crystallized into a market rate."

My objection to this change of terms is that if the new word is more "catchy" it is less fitting than the word it displaces. Impatience is freighted with suggestions of "eagerness for change, restlessness, chafing of spirit, fretfulness, passion" (Webster). Time-valuation or time-preference better expresses the complex of motives which at one time impels men to get goods earlier, and again leads them to postpone use by storing goods and by working for the future in many ways. A prevailing rate of interest is the resultant of all kinds and degrees of time-preference in a community, *preference for goods in the future* in some cases as well as preference for goods in the present, and it seems a great straining of words to attribute the resulting rate of interest to impatience alone. Patience, self-denial, the quality expressed in the old term abstinence, have a no less important part in the explanation.

Let us pass with brief mention the question which takes up a goodly space in Seager's criticism and Fisher's reply—whether individuals are able to, and actually do, bring their "rate of impatience" (time-preference) into exact accord with that implied in the market rate of interest. Seager did well to question the statement, and Fisher's concessions on this point do not leave very much in dispute. The individual brings his rate of time-preference into accord with the market rate, so long as that adjustment yields him an advantage, and so far as he has something to exchange, can furnish security, or is not hindered by friction in other ways. Within the larger national economy, there are many imperfectly connected, provincial, class and family groups living in diverse economic conditions, and having diverse capitalization rates. In the central credit-market, as in the simplest typical price problem of the sale of commodities, we may always conceive of some excluded would-be buyers, and likewise sellers, who remain outside the limits of actual trading because valuing their purchasing power and the sale-goods in a ratio which gives no margin of advantage at the market price.

5. PHYSICAL- AND VALUE-PRODUCTIVITY DISTINGUISHED

The more serious theoretical issue involved here is the ground of Seager's objection, which Fisher does not touch in his reply. It is that the technical productivity of agents is the cause of the impatience. Seager says:[44]

So far as I can see, with the technical superiority of present over future goods, or the productivity of capital, absent, the question as to whether interest would continue or not is an entirely open one. . . Is it [time-preference] not rather a result of the present industrial organization of society arising chiefly from the fact that capital plays such a tremendously important role in production and that, under the system of private property in the instruments of production and free competition, capitalists can secure a return corresponding, at least roughly, to the part of the value-product that is economically imputable to the assistance which their capital renders? That is the view of the productivity theorists.

Whereupon Seager enters into a defense of the productivity theory, *via* a direct denial of Böhm-Bawerk's criticism of it as adopted by Fisher.[45]

Seager's argument at this point seems, indeed, to imply, as

Fisher says,[46] that Seager regards "all productivity theories as alike sound in principle." Seager's opinion has, however, an element of progressiveness in it, for he says that nothing has shaken his "confidence in the essential soundness of the productivity-theory explanation of interest, when presented not as the complete explanation but as the necessary supplement to the discount theory."[47] He suggests in his explanation (also eclectic) of the way in which expenses of production and prices are related, that it is "nearer the truth to say that prices . . . determine the expense of production than the reverse." Yet he concludes,[48] "the chain of causation is not straight, but it turns upon itself in a circle." He seems about to avow the same doctrine of coördinate rank and mutual influence as between technical productivity and time-preference, but he turns to the view that the part of productivity is in a fuller sense causal and primary, and that time-discount is the resultant of this.[49] He declares that it is borrowers' "demand for capital growing out of" the productivity which is "the positive, active influence determining interest."

The capitalization theorist is compelled regretfully to reject the compromise involved in this enlightened eclecticism. For this is the way Seager begins his indication of what his theory "does and what it does not involve:"[50]

It starts out with the proposition that entrepreneurs desirous of making profits by supplying goods at current prices compete against one another for control of the factors necessary to production. This competition tends to keep their own profits down to a large or small "wages-of-management" and to force them to pass along as the remuneration of the factors which they hire, subject to this deduction and to a deduction for the replacement fund, the total price which they receive for the things which they sell. It is, therefore, contended that it is the part these factors play in production as compared and measured by the entrepreneurs that determines the shares of this total price that are assigned to them. The part that capital plays presents two aspects: that of capital goods available at a given instant of time, and that of the purchasing power tied-up in these capital goods during the period that they are performing their productive function. In relation to the first aspect, entrepreneurs appear as buyers. Normally, under conditions of free competition, the prices which they must pay for capital goods conform to their expenses of production. In relation to the second aspect, entrepreneurs appear as users of capital. How much interest they can afford to pay for such use, entrepreneurs estimate through comparing the productive services of capital goods at current prices with the productive services of workers, who at some points are interchangeable with capital goods, at current rates of wages. Through these comparisons the general rate of interest, so far as it depends upon the demand for capital for use in production, is determined.

Space does not permit of detailed comment to show that almost every sentence of this argument clashes with the physical productivity theory.

The productivity of which use is made when the explanation is really begun is not technical or physical productivity at all, but is the capacity which goods bought with judgment *at current prices* have in the hands of enterprisers, of yielding a net surplus, sufficient not only to remunerate them, but to pay contract interest to lenders. The amount of interest which "enterprisers estimate" they can afford to pay (*i.e.,* the maximum amount) is the difference between the discounted, or present, worth of products imputable to these agents and their worth at the time they are expected to mature. The prices of the agents, which are the costs, involve (not presuppose) a rate of discount. As was said in my text:[51]

When the agent is bought outright, the very concluding of the bargain fixes a relation between the expected value of the income and the value of the capital invested. In other words, the exchange of durable agents virtually wraps up in them a net income which it is expected will unfold year by year when rents mature and are secured.

Undoubtedly, at this point is the crucial test of the competing theories. Is it productivity of agents that makes business men willing to borrow and pay interest? Could they afford to pay interest varying with the time element, if the value of the productivity, however large or small, were not discounted in the price of the agents they borrow (or buy with borrowed money)? I think not. Seager says:[52]

It is their [the business men's] demand for the savings of others for use in business enterprises that causes the balance always to be on the side of a positive rate of interest.

But this demand cannot reasonably begin unless there is already a balance on the side of a discount of values of the future uses of agents. Viewed from the standpoint of the capitalization theory, the causal order is the reverse of that of the productivity theory. Of course, there must be future expected uses (incomes), that is, productivity, as there must be men, if there is to be a valuation process, and as there must be some social organization if there are to be markets and prices. But if the future value of the products were not discounted, there could be no rate of interest. It varies with the magnitude of the time-discount at which borrowers, on the whole, are able to buy the title to the future products; and time-discount varies with changes in the whole complex economic situation, of which technical productivity is but one element, others being forethought, provision for needs in accordance with a prevailing standard (itself a complex thing), social and moral ideals, political conditions, etc., etc. It is the opportunity which the possession of ready money gives to the enterpriser to buy goods at a price involving a discount proportional to the futurity of the expected returns, that makes him willing to contract to pay interest. When these expected returns (the products) do appear in the course of time, their value-magnitude is, or should be, greater than was their investment magnitude, and it is out of this value-surplus, directly *conditioned on an antecedent discount of the value-productivity,* that contract interest is paid.

Before leaving this phase of our subject, let us look at it from one more angle, in the hope that some reader may find this a more helpful point of view. My contention throughout has been that the productivity theory in any of the versions known to me, and, specifically, in the entrepreneur version, defended by Seager, involves a confusion between physical-productivity and value-productivity; that in the course of the reasoning there is a shift from the one idea to the other. Seager admits that this confusion "has sometimes occurred,"[53] but he believes that there is a "necessary or logical connection between physical-productivity *as a general phenomenon of capitalistic production* and value-productivity." To bridge this logical gap seems to him, however, to be so simple a task that express proof of it may be assumed "to be superfluous," for he thinks it is merely "an obvious deduction from the accepted principles in regard to the determination of exchange values and prices." His proposition, therefore, is substantially this: [54] The capital (agents) by virtue of its technical productivity here and now, produces more goods, and these goods have (when commodities generally are considered, and not some exceptional commodity) a greater value than the goods which would have been obtained without the capital. Hence, Seager concludes:

Admitting the physical-productivity of capital . . . the value-productivity . . . or more accurately an increase in the total value-product as a consequence of the assistance which capital renders to production seems to me to follow as a logically necessary consequence.

Here, where Seager would expect dissent, I readily agree; but hasten to add that *this* value-productivity is not at all *that* of which the productivity theorist speaks in his interest theory. Here we are saying merely: If agents used at this moment produce more, the products (speaking of the general and usual result) have more value here and now than the products that could have been obtained without the help of the productive agents. But the value-productivity which furnishes the motive to the enterpriser to borrow and gives him the power, regularly, to pay contract interest, is due, not to the fact that these products will have value when they come into existence, but to the fact that their expected value is discounted in the price of the agents bought at an earlier point of time. The two relations are in different planes. It is a problem of two dimensions which may be represented as follows:

                                    A (Physical-productivity)

                                    │ synchronous
                                    │ relation
                     Time   │
C (Capitalization) .... B (Value-productivity)
                     relation

Present   *Future*

The modern productivity theorist assumes as quite obvious
the value-productivity B, as derived synchronously from the
physical productivity A, but he ignores the problem of the
discount relation in time between B and C. The pseudo-value-
productivity assumed in the productivity theory of interest is all,
however, involved in the unexplained discount relation between
B and C, not in the identity relation between A and B. This is the
petitio principii of the theory.

The value-surplus referred to is that part, imputable to, and
varying with, the time element, and not that due to the peculiar
commercial skill, or to the luck, of the enterpriser, in finding
unusually low valued agents in one place, or unusually high
valued products in another. If one did not bear in mind the
complex character of the gross income "profits," one might be
tempted to exclaim: If the enterpriser must pay as interest the
whole amount involved in time-discount, he never would have a
motive to borrow. It is just here that appears so plainly the
middleman's character of the productive borrower. The rate of
interest is a market price at which (security, etc., equalized) the
individual borrows; but those with superior knowledge and
superior foresight are able to buy in one economic group and to
sell their products in another, to buy "underestimated" goods
and to find a favorable market for highly esteemed products.
They are merchants, buying when they can in a cheaper and
selling in a dearer capitalization market,[55] acting as the equalizers of rates and prices. It is the mercantile function everywhere
to do this. So we must dissent again when Seager says:[56]

And it is this demand for capital growing out of the important role capital plays as a factor in production, that is the positive, active influence determining interest, in the same sense that utility may be said to be the positive, active influence determining value.

Rather, this demand for capital determines interest in the same sense that the merchant's demand determines the wholesale price of merchandise, he merely judging and transmitting to the wholesaler and manufacturer the ultimate consumer's demand for various goods. In this case, the middleman's demand for capital (that is, for loans) is a reflection of the time-valuation of consumers as embodied in the prices prevailing in the markets for goods.

Professor Seager seems so near at times to abandoning the cost-of-production theory of prices with which the productivity theory of interest is related, and has contributed such valuable and needed criticism to the present discussion, that it is to be hoped that he may yet bring his powerful aid to the capitalization camp.

6. THE CAPITAL CONCEPT IN THE INTEREST THEORY

The difficulty of seeing the capitalization problem in a broad way, as something touching all sources and groups of income, is, however, insurmountable so long as one adheres to the old concept of capital. Seager uses capital[57] "in the sense of the produced means of further production," and distinguishes land and capital as two groups of concrete objects, one of which owes its value to nature, and the other to labor. It is, of course, futile to attempt here a restatement of the reasons, negative and positive, against this view. They have been pretty fully stated elsewhere. Seager seems still to conceive of the interest problem as connected only with produced means of production, as did the older English economists, and as all productivity theorists incline to do. This inclination is found along with a treatment limited mainly, if not entirely, to contract interest.

But how can the "economic interest" aspect of the problem be limited to the income yielded by tools and machines? Why is not this problem presented in the case of incomes from land (or from an orchard, to which example Seager objects as not being typical of all forms of capital)? How account for the capitalization of this land and of this orchard? By applying a rate of interest derived from the money market as Fisher would seem to do, or a rate taken from the market for the loan of purely "produced" capital goods (whatever that may mean)? Cannot unproduced agents be capitalized unless the rate of discount is first discovered by making produced goods? Is not a capitalization rate conceivable in a community where land is the only form of wealth that is bought and sold? If so, then the thought is not avoidable that a rate of interest on contract loans to purchase land may prevail, reflecting this implied rate of capitalization—the chance for profit operating as a motive for the loan just as it does in manufacturing and commerce. Is interest not connected with a loan of money to buy "natural" agents as fully as with that to buy "artificial" agents? An answer to these questions inevitably carries one into the atmosphere of the capitalization theory, where the arbitrary limitation of the interest problem to loans made to buy "produced" agents becomes unthinkable.

But there is still the old question, how account for the tendency of profits (in the old broad sense of the term, including interest) toward equality; how explain the fact that on the average, though with many exceptions and fluctuations, the rates of profit to be had by productive borrowers in the various industries do not get so very far apart? There is the old explanation of cost-of-production of capital, upon which the latest productivity theorists still rely, and there is the capitalization theory. Both of these concede a place to the enterpriser. In the older view, the place is worthy to be called causal, in that, when any agent yields an abnormal return, he produces more agents, by incurring "costs" (which are either assumed to be fixed or are left quite unexplained), putting the price of more labor and materials into them and thus bringing their price into conformity with other agents of the same cost. The citadel where the productivity theorist feels his position to be impregnable is just here, in the thought that the amount and the value of "capital" (produced agents) is "brought into conformity with the expense of producing them," thus regulating the interest rate. Seager is on familiar ground when he says:

Since there is nothing in the assumption that the productivity of all instruments is doubled that involves any serious change in the expense of producing the instruments.[58]

We must dissent. The doubling of the productivity of all agents alike would have very diverse effects upon the prices of the various enjoyable goods, and these prices would be reflected in the valuation process to the prices of the different natural sources and of all other agents, thus altering greatly the whole scale of costs in "producing" more agents.

But is this not a recognition that technical productivity has *some* influence upon the comparison of present and future gratifications, and hence upon the rate of interest? Surely, some influence it has, but the causal order of explanation is very different from that of the productivity theory. Technical productivity is one of the facts, physical, moral, intellectual, which go to make up the whole economic situation in which time-preference is exercised. That this, however, is not going over to the productivity theory of interest is shown by the fact that it points to an opposite conclusion as regards the resulting rate. The greater provision for present desires thus made possible leads us to expect a reduction of the preference for present goods and a lowering of their valuation in terms of future goods. This (other things being equal) would be reflected in a lower rate of time discount and a lower, not a higher, rate of interest, as the productivity theorist believes.[59]

May we not then conclude that the cost-of-production-of-capital explanation of interest is a partial glimpse of an intermediate and subordinate process of the adjustment of prices, in part a mistaking of effect for cause? It assumes a dual theory of investment prices; some prices are explained as due to demand and others as due to cost. The prices of the factors (materials, tools, labor) are taken as a basis from which to calculate the rate of interest, a sort of turtle's-back (as in the ancient theory of the universe) on which the giant, Entrepreneur, stands while carrying on his back the burden of interest.

The capitalization theory views the causal order very differently. First, time-valuation being embodied in durable agents with incomes extending over a period of time, becomes the capitalization of agents containing future uses, this involving a rate of time-discount. This, in a market with exchange, becomes price, which is cost to the enterpriser seeking a profit by buying these factors, combining them more or less with his own services, and selling them. This process is constantly levelling down inequalities in capitalization as between different commodities and markets. All men together are helping to evaluate all of the economic goods in the community. Within this larger circle of explanation, the part of the enterpriser is secondary and intermediate. He does not represent any additional "technical productivity" cause, coming in alongside of the psychological explanation of interest. The chance of income for himself exists before he makes a move, partly because the future incomes have already been discounted (the pure capital-income aspect), and partly because all agents are not discounted at any moment at exactly the same, or exactly the right, rate (the commercial profit aspect). It is because of the chance of private profit already inherent in the situation that the producer is led to act in his intermediary capacity.

7. THE SAME DIFFICULTIES AGAIN

The article by Professor H. G. Brown,[60] a former pupil and present colleague of Fisher, appeared almost simultaneously with Fisher's concessions to the productivity theory. Professor Brown, agreeing almost completely with Seager, formulates an eclectic theory.

The position taken by the present writer is, that productivity and impatience are coördinate determinants, *i.e.*, that productivity is as direct a determinant of interest as is impatience, and that productivity may be, in a modern community, the more important determinant.[61]

At every point where Professor Fisher is at his best, and rejects productivity "as a direct acting cause," Professor Brown disagrees with him, and accepts productivity. Yet the article is marked by a number of just observations and seems at one point to touch upon the truth of the capitalization theory:[62]

We may say that a person's valuation of capital, along with the valuations of other persons in like situation, is less the direct result of the previously existing market rate of interest, than it is, by affecting his and their attitude towards the market, a determinant of the rate of interest.

But the argument on the whole is on the plane of that conception of productivity criticized above. Every feature of the old argument is reproduced. The explanation is hardly begun until the productivity is assumed to be a five per cent, a ten per cent, or a twenty per cent productivity. Per cent of what? Of the capital valuation, or the prices at which the borrower can buy the agents. Productivity in what way? In that the present prices, being the discounted value of the incomes that are expected, emerge at their maturing value as time elapses. The discount-rate involved in the capitalization is the "rate of productivity" which appears again and again in the argument. The borrower pays contract interest of five per cent only when he thinks he sees the opportunity to get this increment and something more for his trouble. Simple and true as an explanation of why men borrow at a rate of contract interest related to the prevailing rate of time-discount, but no proof whatever that the rate of interest is due to technical productivity.

Here, as always, the productivity theorist looks at the proximate influence, not at that one step removed; examines the middleman's motive, and ignores the ultimate consumer. The productive borrower is but the intermediary, transmitting to the market of consumers through the agency of prices, the effects of time-preference. Forgetting the motives and influences of the really determining group of minds, Professor Brown looks only at the "productive" borrower and says: "In what possible sense can it be said that he borrows only because he is impatient?"[63] "All question of impatience aside";[64] "For even those [productive borrowers] who are not by nature impatient" etc.[65] Professor Brown shows well[66] the inaptness of the word "impatience," but his argument is futile as a refutation of a true psychological theory, for he is quite overlooking the substance, while he chases the shadow, of time-preference.

This motive to borrow exists as well when the agent to be bought with borrowed money is land, as when it is another agent. But just here[67] Professor Brown withdraws to the citadel, the cost-of-production of capital, as that which tends "to fix the rate of interest and of discount." He reaffirms the

importance of the distinction which Professor Seager has recently emphasized, between land and made capital, between original natural resources and "the produced means to further production." Land is already present. For the most part, there is no balancing of choice as to whether or not we shall produce it.

What is the force of "already present"? Does "for the most part there is no balancing of choice" etc., mean that the way we use land has not affected its quantity in the past, and does not affect it for the future, either as acres or as productive power? In this day of the conservation and reclamation movements, are we to forget the part of repairs and depreciation, and assume the immutability of acres, arable and other kinds? Is there not involved in any standard of husbandry where soil-fertility is maintained, an adjustment of the cost-of-production and of the capitalization of each arable acre to its price based on its expected return quite as this is done in the case of factories?[68]

It is not for us here to discuss further the older conception of capital here involved. We had supposed that it had become unthinkable in the atmosphere of Columbia and of Yale, under the influences of J. B. Clark and of Irving Fisher.

8. SUMMARY

Surely we are making some progress in formulating more clearly the issues involved in the interest problem. The opinions we have reviewed face in at least three different directions, not squarely opposing each other.[69] Seager and Brown stand together on one side of the circle of opinion, glancing now and then with one eye at a psychological explanation (for consumption loans) and with the other eye fixed most of the time on the enterpriser-productivity explanation. They are not far away from Böhm-Bawerk, who is likewise eclectic; but their conception of productivity goes little farther than the personal enterpriser, whereas Böhm-Bawerk seeks, though vainly, in his roundabout theory, to extend his explanation formally to the impersonal productive powers in the agents. Nearly opposite them stands Fisher, directing his attention mainly upon the market for money loans, but giving many glances before and after to the psychological causes, in accord with the capitalization theory. The capitalization theorist at another point in the circle is faced directly toward the psychological explanation of interest, and sees the other features of the picture in due perspective to this central fact.

Seen from any of these standpoints, the interest paid on *consumption* loans is and must be explained in purely psychological terms. The capitalization theory, alone, is not eclectic, and explains interest on consumption and on production loans, in the same psychological terms. It alone sees the enterpriser's part embraced within the larger circle of time-preference, and explains interest on productive loans as but the reflection of the time-preference in the minds of the great body of buyers in the community, whose representatives and intermediaries the enterprisers are.

NOTES

1. *American Economic Review,* Dec., 1912, H. R. Seager, (critique of) "The Impatience Theory of Interest"; Sept., 1913, Irving Fisher (reply), and H. R. Seager (comment) "The Impatience Theory of Interest."

Quarterly Journal of Economics, Aug., 1913, Harry G. Brown, "The Marginal Productivity versus the Impatience Theory of Interest."

2. To prevent misunderstanding, let us say that Böhm-Bawerk is here classed among those holding to the old theory, for his "roundabout process" explanation is technological, though united with strong psychological features in the explanation of consumption loans.

3. This somewhat unusual word is here employed in the sense of physically productive, a technological interest theory being one which finds the explanation of the rate of interest in the actual, practical performances, or uses, of agents in producing other goods.

4. *American Economic Review,* Sept., 1913, p. 610.

5. *The Rate of Interest,* 1907, p. 12.

6. *Ibid.,* p. 15.

7. *Ibid.,* p. 22.

8. *Ibid.,* p. 28.

9. The Impatience Theory of Interest," *Scientia,* vol. IX, 1911, pp. 383, 384, 386.

10. *American Economic Review,* Sept., 1913, p. 610.

11. *Ibid.,* p. 610.

12. *Ibid.,* p. 611.

13. My italics throughout.

14. *Ibid.,* p. 611.

15. *Ibid.,* p. 617.

16. *The Rate of Interest,* p. 251.

17. *American Economic Review,* Sept., 1913, p. 612.

18. *Ibid.,* 613.

19. *Ibid.,* p. 617.

20. My italics.

21. *Ibid.,* p. 612.

22. "Recent Discussion of the Capital Concept," *Quarterly Journal of Economics,* vol. XV (Nov., 1900), p. 45.

23. Proceedings of the Thirteenth Annual Meeting, Dec., 1900, "The Next Decade of Economic Theory," *Publications of the American Economic Association,* 3d series, vol. 2, pp. 240, 246.

24. "Einige Strittige Fragen der Capitalstheorie," *Political Science Quarterly,* vol. 17 (Mar., 1902), p. 173.

25. *Quarterly Journal of Economics,* vol. 17 (Nov., 1902), p. 179.

26. The reader will observe that the term rent was there used in the more general sense of the income from the use, or the usance, of agents, not merely in the sense of contractual rent. This particular terminology which was due to the influence of J. B. Clark, has since been modified, not to weaken but to strengthen, the conception involved.

27. *Publications of the American Economic Association,* 3d series, vol. V, in a paper on "The Relations between Rent and Interest," p. 197.

28. Believing this conception to be logically involved in much of Böhm-Bawerk's argument in his critical volume, "Capital and Interest," I credited him with "the fertile suggestion" (see above, p. 231, quotation from the article, "The Roundabout Process"). But he has not accepted this interpretation; indeed, this would invalidate the greater part of what is distinctive in his positive theory of the roundabout process, to which he adheres without change in the latest edition, 1912.

29. Fisher prefers to call the one explicit and the other implicit interest. However, throughout his book he uses the phrase "the rate of interest" almost if not exclusively for contract interest, and other terms, such as rate of preference, time-preference, etc., when implicit interest is meant.

30. Other expressions, to designate various aspects of the same problem, used in my *Principles of Economics* (1904), were "choice between different values," p. 104; "difference in want-gratifying power," p. 144; "time-difference"; "time-discount"; "the rate of time-discount," p. 145; "estimate of time value," p. 145; "a choice between present enjoyment and future provision," p. 146; " a premium rate on present goods," p. 146; "the exchange in time-valuation," p. 146; "preference of the future over the present," p. 158; "the preference of present over future," p. 159.

31. When, however, attention is given to the details in the modern loan market following the action of this man or that, or studying a temporary situation such as a sudden demand for loans on the occasion of a war or in a financial panic, we break into the explanation at a different point. The change in the immediate status of the loan market is reflected in widening circles and for a time affects the capitalization of much of the wealth in the economy (of the nation or of the world). This and many other needed interpretations are briefly indicated in my elementary text. It is fundamental to the conception of the capitalization theory, however, that these impulses from the money market are not, as they superficially appear, primary or causal in a theory of interest, in the same sense as is the preference in time for enjoyable goods and the resulting level of capitalization. See especially chs. 17-19, in my *Principles of Economics,* 1904.

32. *The Rate of Interest,* p. 88.

33. *Ibid.,* p. 88.

34. *Ibid.,* p. 91.

35. *Elementary Principles,* 1912, p. 229.

36. *Ibid.,* p. 336.

37. *The Rate of Interest,* p. 117.

38. *American Economic Review,* Dec., 1912, pp. 836-837.

39. My purpose, in large part, in calling attention to my mode of approach to the interest problem as outlined above, is to show that the psychological theory, in its original form, is not open to the criticism which Seager forcibly directs against Fisher, "that he dissociates his discussion completely from any account of the production of wealth." To be sure, Fisher's reply begins with a categorical denial, "I did not dissociate" (*American Economic Review,* Sept. 1913), but he immediately admits that in his "first approximation" the income streams were "temporarily assumed." And while in his larger theoretical book, he believes that "this assumption gives place to the more complicated conditions of the actual world," when he comes to the second and third approximations, he confesses that those complications were, "for the most part, omitted (as too difficult and controversial)" from the elementary book. Seager's comment (*American Economic Review,* Sept., 1913, p. 618) is pertinent: "A methodology that causes an author to drop out an essential link when he tries to restate his theory in elementary form seems to me to be almost self-condemned." At this point may be recalled my own criticism of Fisher's treatment of capital in his *Capital and Income.* Reviewing this in the *Journal of Political Economy,* March, 1907, vol. 15, p. 147, I spoke of a "certain isolation in Fisher's capital theory. He began the analysis and reconstruction of the capital concept as if it were a task apart from the theory of distribution as a whole. . . . The capital theory presented has therefore a certain character of intellectual aloofness that leaves it out of touch with the larger theory of distribution, of which it should be but one part." The same criticism applies in general to *The Rate of Interest,* published a year later.

40. Seager, *American Economic Review,* Dec., 1912, p. 835.

41. *The Rate of Interest,* p. 184.

42. "The Impatience Theory of Interest," *Scientia,* vol. IX, p. 387.

43. *Elementary Principles,* p. 371.

44. *American Economic Review,* Dec. 1912, pp. 841-842.

45. Fisher has followed Böhm-Bawerk in presenting objections to the productivity theory in terms that logically invalidate every productivity theory and, apparently, is again following his example in withdrawing the objections insofar as they apply to any but the naïve theories. (See above, pp. 227-228.)

46. *American Economic Review,* Sept., 1913, p. 617.

47. *Ibid.,* Dec., 1912, p. 849.

48. *Ibid.,* p. 845.

49. *Ibid.,* p. 848.

50. *Ibid.,* pp. 847-848.

51. *The Principles of Economics,* 1904, p. 127.

52. *American Economic Review,* Dec, 1912.

53. *American Economic Review,* p. 842.

54. *Ibid.,* pp. 842-843.

55. See above, pp. 235-236, 240-241.

56. *American Economic Review,* Dec., 1912, p. 848.

57. *Ibid.,* p. 844.

58. *American Economic Review,* Dec., 1912, p. 847.

59. On this Fisher has taken a position in accordance with the capitalization theory. See *American Economic Review,* Sept., 1913, p. 614.

60. Cited above, p. 252, n. 1.

61. *Quarterly Journal of Economics,* Aug., 1913, p. 634. Here impatience and productivity are said to be coordinate determinants, though productivity may be the more important; and again, page 645, impatience is said "to enter into the chain of cause and effect" in a certain connection "as effect rather than cause"; and, finally, page 650, impatience "is also, to some extent, a joint consequence, with interest, of the other cause, the superiority of indirect production."

62. *Quarterly Journal of Economics,* Aug., 1913, p. 644.

63. *Ibid.,* p. 638.

64. *Quarterly Journal of Economics,* Aug., 1913, p. 639.

65. *Ibid.,* p. 640.

66. *Ibid.,* p. 637.

67. *Ibid.,* p. 644.

68. Professor V. G. Simkhovitch's illuminating article on "Hay and History," in the *Political Science Quarterly,* Sept., 1913, gives new evidence of the effect upon agricultural industry of enlarging man's power over the production of fertile and arable qualities in land.

69. A different conception, apparently a unique variation of the enterpriser- productivity theory, is the dynamic theory of Professor Schumpeter, as presented in his *Theorie der Wirtschaftlichen Entwicklung,* 1912, and reviewed at length by Böhm-Bawerk in the *Zeitschrift für Volkswirtschaft,* 1913.

Capitalization versus Productivity: Rejoinder

Dr. Brown's restatement of the productivity theory of interest has one distinctive merit. It abandons the attempt to make a fallacious enterprise-profit rate of productivity an element in the explanation. Every previous formulation, not excepting Dr. Brown's own, has been open to this charge. The recent discussion has yielded a substantial result in this admission that the productivity theorist is bound to show the existence of a definite rate of physical productivity to which the rate of interest conforms, quite apart from any borrowing producers' rate of profit. Dr. Brown courageously undertakes this task, and his results must be judged by this criterion.

At the same time, however, he prudently limits his defense to the very narrowest scope that ever has been claimed for the theory. He makes a virtue of eclecticism (p. 349), and claims for productivity only a little part, an irreducible minimum. In the manner much in vogue since Böhm-Bawerk led the way, he concedes much of the field to the purely psychological explanation. Interest admittedly would exist in a world of desires and mere scarcity, without physical productivity, either direct or indirect for that matter. The capitalization theory alone could apply in such cases. It is admitted further that time-preference exists in every case, as well where there is as where there is not physical production of indirect agents. The claim Dr. Brown

Reprinted from *American Economic Review* 4 (December 1914). This is a critique of an article by Harry Gunnison Brown entitled, "The Discount Versus the Cost-of-Production Theory of Capital Valuation," *American Economic Review* 4 (June 1914): 340-49. Brown's article was written in reply to Fetter's "Interest Theories, Old and New," see chapter 15.

makes now is merely that when a physically productive process is employed to create an indirect agent, *then* the rate of productivity which he believes is involved *may* assume the dominant role and determine the rate of time-preference. I say "*may* assume," not necessarily assumes, for here the claim is narrowed astonishingly as compared with previous versions of the productivity theory. In previous versions the supposed regulative rate has been believed to dominate wherever there was an indirect (roundabout) process. In Dr. Brown's version this claim is limited to situations where fruits are being produced *at the same time,* in the same economy, by labor used in two different technical processes, one direct and the other indirect, one productive of more, the other of fewer physical fruits. Of this, more later. I note it here only to show how large a field has been conceded to the capitalization theory in productivity's masterly retreat. Dr. Brown has here probably tricked himself quite as much as his readers. He is defending a mere shadow of the old doctrine.

In still another respect Dr. Brown attempts (as he says on page 340 was his purpose in his former article) to limit the productivity theory, namely by treating it not as a part of the value-theory, but as dealing "with quantities of goods instead of with values." It is no minor matter to which I am here directing the reader's attention. It concerns the whole conception of the problem. The proposition speaks a different language from that of an interest-theory, and concerns a different question. So long as Dr. Brown limits his attention to amounts of income as absolute quantities, he is in the realm of the rent-, or more broadly, of the income-problem. This is arguing at cross purposes with the capitalization theory, and is not within range of the interest problem. A theory of interest must be *essentially* a value-theory. The thing to be explained is the ratio between the value of the income and the value of the income-bearer. There is a courageous logic, to a certain point, in Dr. Brown's attempt. The only way the productivity theory could be saved from the vicious circle would be to find a rate inherent in the physical process, in the relation between *quantities* of future goods and *quantities* of indirect agents, independent of the value-expression. But this attempt is vain. Fruits can be expressed for economic purposes as a percentage of trees not as physical quantities, but only as value-relations in terms of some standard. Usually the money-standard is chosen: Dr. Brown chooses a present-fruit value standard and does not see that he is doing it. To say that 1,000 present fruit *equals* 1,100 future fruit is to express a value relation. Equal how? Evidently not in quantity, for they are unequal, but in value. It is a psychological not a physical ratio. If, now, the productivity part of the problem be considered, 10 present trees equal 1,100 future fruit. Again we ask, equal in what way? Evidently not in quantity, but only in value? Where then is the ten per cent ratio? The answer comes that 10 present trees equal 1,100 future fruit and *at the same time* equal 1,000 present fruit; herein lies a ten per cent rate of productivity. A certain value of labor invested in trees yields a ten per cent value surplus at the end of a year. Enter the value relation disguised as a rate of physical productivity.

One who for years has trailed the elusive cost-of-production fallacy, can not fail to see in Dr. Brown's novelty the old illusion in a very thin new disguise. It is a very versatile and persistent fallacy. Böhm-Bawerk effectively exposed the old form of the doctrine, and then, as every student now knows, fell into the same pit when he formulated his own positive theory. Whoever lays claim to the discovery of some slightly different device for squaring this circle, opens up anew for himself, if not for others, all the old puzzling questions. To answer all the doubts reawakened in his mind it would be necessary to resurvey the whole wide field of the interest-controversy. Space will be taken for only one other brief criticism (among many possible), but that one alone destructive of Dr. Brown's central conception of a regulative rate of physical productivity. With this I will be content to rest, for the present, the case for the capitalization theory.

The semblance of a rate of physical productivity which Dr. Brown discovers, appears only when, side by side, two methods of production are in use, one new and the other old. As long as the two methods so continue, a unit of labor has equal value whether applied to present fruit or to trees; but how long can this continue? Only so long as the rate of time-preference happens to coincide with this so-called rate of productivity. Time-preference existed before the new method was discovered; it continues to exist afterward. If when the new technical method is discovered in the assumed case, time-preference happens to be over ten percent, the new method is uneconomic and can not be adopted; if it happens to be under ten per cent then the old method is uneconomic and must be abandoned as fast as the shift can be made. Time-preference dominates the choice among technical methods. When *all* the fruit comes to be obtained by the roundabout method, and the supply of present fruit is 1,100 a year, where is the supposed regulative ten per cent ratio of physical productivity? It does not exist. Abandoned methods of production simply do not function in fixing either the present price of goods (either trees or fruits) or the rate of time-preference. The abandoned method becomes ancient history. Time-preference must be adjusted in the new conditions—a more bountiful environment. (In my former article I touched upon the probability as to the rate of time-preference in such a case.) There is greater productivity than before but no "*rate* of productivity" whatever, is the sense of Dr. Brown's theory. The capitalization theory is alone left to explain the rate of interest in this situation, and time-preference never ceases to function.

Now and then in a maladjusted economy the interest rate might be found to coincide with this curious phenomenon which Dr. Brown believes to be a rate of physical productivity. It is only the semblance of such a rate, being but the reflection of a rate of time-preference when an indifferent choice is possible between a direct and an indirect method of production. This is always but a limited aspect of a dynamic situation (where I have always recognized that it has a place), which in the theory before us is hopelessly confused with the static problem of interest.

Interest Theory and
Price Movements

*PART I. HISTORICAL STAGES IN THE CONCEPTION OF THE
INTEREST PROBLEM*

1. *Purpose of this essay.*—What is now usually known as "interest theory" will perhaps be conceded by all to be the subtlest and most difficult problem in the broad field of economic theory. Various opinions upon it and its solution have in turn been dominant, and probably every one of these still survives and is today held in some quarter, scientific or popular. Even in the narrower circle of experts and special students, the differences of conception are perhaps more fundamental and far-reaching than in any other subject of theory.

This problem being intimately related to many others having theoretical and practical bearings, the center of discussion has shifted greatly throughout the centuries. In ancient and medieval times, it was viewed as little more than a phase of *just price,* and attempts to explain the phenomenon of interest rates were merely incidental to arguments on the ethics of usury. Even the more recent discussions of the subject from Senior's abstinence theory to the work of J. B. Clark, of Böhm-Bawerk, of Wieser, and of others, reveal clearly this motive. The income taking the form of "interest" has borne and still has to bear the main shock of communistic attack upon the institution of private property, although Henry George's brilliant sally diverted a considerable part of the reforming zeal to the attack upon land

Reprinted from *American Economic Review,* suppl. 17 (March 1927). The discussants of this paper included Irving Fisher, Wesley C. Mitchell, Melchior Palyi, and Waldo F. Mitchell (ibid., pp. 106-113).

rent. However, the notable development of a more truly detached scientific spirit in theory which has occurred, at least in a small esoteric circle, has shown itself in part by the ardent pursuit of a "theory of interest" as matter of pure reason, regardless of its bearings on any particular practical questions. This sort of "mere theory" has been not only ignored but deprecated by some of those economists, who, armed with new statistical weapons of correlation, are in pursuit of quantitative measurements. They for their part have been doing notable work in collecting, analysing, and charting the growing mass of banking and commercial data regarding price changes and rates of interest, as aspects of the business cycle.

There ought to be at this time no such mutual suspicion, but rather closer co-operation between the students of quantitative measurements and those dealing with the more philosophic phases of economic inquiry. Each method and each point of view is in turn needed—now to present working hypotheses, then to test them; now to relate newly discovered facts to the existing body of knowledge, again to reappraise older accepted views in the light of new evidence.

Especially in this phase of the study of the business cycle, to wit, the relation of interest rates and interest theory to general price movements, the interchange of thought between students with different methods has been lacking. Apparently most of those especially devoted to the study of the business cycle have remained indifferent to, and negligent of, the more recent novel studies and radical conceptions in this field of theory. There is, to be sure, still lacking agreement among economists both as to the theory and as to the terminology of interest. But it seems possible that a resurvey of interest history and theory, and a statement of some of the newer speculative aspects may result in some fruitful cross-fertilization of thought in this important subject.

2. *Amount-of-money conception of the interest problem.*— David Hume, writing around 1752, combatted prevailing opinion when he declared: "Lowness of interest is generally ascribed to plenty of money." This seems to be a fair statement of the notion

implied at least, if not always clearly formulated, in the moral condemnation of interest on money loans from Aristotle through the era of the church canonists. Interest was thought of as paid for the use of money, as land rent was paid for the use of land. But money "cannot breed money," as land can breed crops and feed flocks; money is the "barren breed of metal." Even to scholars, as well as to the populace, the price paid for the use of money (quite like that of other things) seemed to depend on the plenty or scarcity of the precious metals. Certainly this notion still is the natural, naive, popular view, coming to the surface again and again, as in the Greenback program of the 70's and 80's, in the Populist movement of the 90's, in many contemporary pamphlets sent for the enlightenment of academic economists by amateur reformers, and even promulgated by distinguished inventors and manufacturers, who are novices in economic theory.

This erroneous notion Hume rejected, declaring at once: "But money, however plentiful, has no other effect, if fixed, than to raise the price of labor" ("and," he added a little later, "commodities"). After appealing to certain economic facts since the discovery of the Indies, he concludes: "The rate of interest, therefore, is not derived from the quantity of the precious metals." Before examining Hume's more positive thesis, let us observe that his negative thesis relates to static conditions as to the money stock, the quantity of monetary metals, in a country. He touches elsewhere only briefly on certain historical dynamic conditions, long-time rather than short-time in nature, in which he thinks that increase in a nation's money and a sinking interest (rate) go together. But, he says, it is a mistake to consider the greater quantity of money the cause of the lowness of interest. This is to mistake "a collateral effect for a cause."

3. *Amount-of-riches conception; Hume's psychological germ.*—What was Hume's positive thesis; what explanation of the rate of interest did he propose in place of the one he rejected? The real cause of lowness of interest, he says, is growth of industry in the state, etc., which same cause both attracts "great abundance of the precious metals" and lowers interest. "The most industrious

nations always abound most with precious metals; so that low interest and plenty of money are in fact almost inseparable." The generally accepted interpetation of Hume's view was expressed more than a century later by Böhm-Bawerk in these words: "The height of the interest rate in a country does not depend on the amount of currency that the country possesses, but on the amount of its riches or stocks."[1]

Since Hume's time until very recently that proposition, with various explanations and elaborations, has been the center of nearly all the theories of interest having a considerable following among liberal economists. It is the core of all the productivity and use theories. But Böhm-Bawerk's generally accepted summation of Hume's thought is far too simple to do justice to it, and Böhm-Bawerk's notion of "riches or stocks" is much narrower than is necessarily implied in Hume's words. One must, to be sure, beware of the temptation to read into Hume's language an attitude toward modern issues of which he was quite unaware. But Böhm-Bawerk himself has not escaped that error. His interpretation of Hume's essay is that of one holding firmly, as the Austrian economist did, to the tripartite division of the factors, and to the notion of capital as a distinct group of artificial agents—as he did after elaborate studies despite some inconsistences.[2]

But there is required no undue stretching of Hume's words to find in them room for a broader thought of a psychological explanation of interest, though the dim outlines of this are only imperfectly sketched. Hume says: "High interest arises from *three* circumstances [and italicizes *three*]: A great demand for borrowing, little riches to supply that demand, and great profits arising from commerce. . . . Low interest, on the other hand, proceeds from the three opposite circumstances: a small demand for borrowing, great riches to supply that demand, and small profits arising from commerce." It is true that this merely states the problem rather than gives a full explanation, recognizing which, Hume says: "We shall endeavor to prove these points; and shall begin with the causes and the effects of a great demand or small demand for borrowing."

Our limits forbid following here his detailed argument. We would point out only that it abounds with references to psychological factors as causal and antecedent to the quantity of riches and to the rate of profits: different tempers, prodigals, misers, desire to consume, pursuit of pleasure, differences in habits and manners, and in customs; and along with these goes a penetrating discussion of the comparative influence of large landholding and commerce upon the motives of industry and frugality, determining whether or not money gathers into large stock into the hands of those who are *willing* to lend it at a low interest. The discussion of the third circumstance requisite to produce lowness of interest is, however, very superficial, dissolving into the agnostic proposition that the two things, low interest and low profits, "both arise from an extensive commerce, and mutually forward each other" but it is "needless to inquire which is the cause and which the effect."

Indeed, Hume's discussion, as a whole, never gets very far beneath the surface; it merely makes a beginning along lines in which little progress was made (excepting only in the abstinence concept) for nearly a century and a half. In one respect, however, Hume's essay indeed marks an epoch in the history of the interest theory; thereafter (except as a popular fallacy) the abundance-of-money-conception was definitely displaced by the abundance-of-goods-conception. The orthodox liberal doctrine (despite other differences) became Hume's proposition that we really and in effect borrow labor and commodities when we take money upon interest.

4. *Turgot's limited capitalization theory.*—Turgot's brilliant little essay in 1770 displayed in several respects an insight into the essential nature of economic problems, hardly to be equalled again for more than a century. Though he begins his discussion of interest with a narrow conception of "capitals" as consisting of "the accumulation of annual produce not consumed," otherwise called "moveable riches," he at once speaks of these riches as "advances" (not just when loaned—that is, "advanced" to a person— that comes later—but "advanced" when used on land, in industry or in commerce). He then gives throughout his

treatment unusual prominence to the notion of time, using repeatedly the term "waiting" to describe what the advances enable workers of all kinds to do. He then turns his thought at once to the various "employments of capitals" among which a person may choose who has "accumulated value"; that is, funds available for investment. It is remarkable that he speaks first not of manufacturing, agriculture (i.e., capitalist farming), and commerce, and the loan of money at interest (these follow in order), but of "the purchase of an estate of land." Here he sketches, in scanty lines, to be sure, but clearly, a capitalization theory of land value, "what is called the penny of the price of lands," resulting from "the varying proportion between people who wish to sell or buy lands." Böhm-Bawerk in his critique dismissed this disparagingly as "a fructification theory of interest," "an explanation in a circle" because he believed Turgot was trying to explain "all forms of interest as the necessary result of the circumstance that any one who has a capital may exchange it for a piece of land bearing a rent."

But this seems to me to miss in Turgot's discussion its most significant and unique feature. Turgot is seeking to explain, as he says, the valuation of lands in accordance with the proportion which the revenue bears to the value for which they are exchanged, and he does this first without once referring to the current rate of interest on loans or to the current rate of profits in other business (or without taking a rate found in financial markets to use as a capitalization rate in explaining the price of lands). Turgot pretty clearly conceived of an investment rate in land (that is, a discount, or capitalization rate) as discoverable and usable by the simple adjustment of supply and demand of buyers and sellers of land. It is true that Turgot, as he proceeds, shows that the various employments of capital are mutually related in their rates of return by the possibility of shifting investments. But this is valid and does not conflict with his thought of the capitalization of land as occurring primarily through the working of forces independent of the market for monetary loans. Such a view of the possibility of the land capitalization process being prior to the contractual interest rate is not found again until after the beginning of the twentieth century. It is still quite rare. Turgot's view of capitalization, it should be observed, though clear, is limited to explaining the valuation of land. He does not go on to develop a general capitalization theory that would explain in an analogous way the valuation of other "capitals" such as houses, machinery, etc., as built upon and derived from the revenue (or series of future uses) contained in them. Such a conception seems never to have entered his mind. His discussion abounds, however, with references to the influence of waiting, and of time.

One other remark before leaving this question. It may be retorted to Böhm-Bawerk's characterization of Turgot's interest theory as one of "fructification," that more truly Böhm-Bawerk himself (and every other productivity theorist holding the conventional artificial goods capital concept) may be said to uphold a partial fructification theory, the very counterpart of that which he accuses Turgot of presenting. To wit: having explained the contractual interest rates superficially as arising in the market for monetary loans, and then having sought to carry the explanation deeper by tracing this contractual interest rate to the "productive services" of "artificial" man-made capital goods, the productivity theorist then has no other way of explaining the capitilization of land and natural agents, but to borrow the interest rate determined in the field of "artificial capital" with which to discount the rents and other expected incomes of "natural" agents.[3] This is done without the slightest misgiving or thought that in the individual valuation and the purchase or sale of natural durable agents there can reside an independent source of discount and capitalization rates.

5. *Time and Senior's abstinence concept.*—Many passages glimpsing the relation of time to the employment of capital could undoubtedly be collected from the economic literature of the nineteenth century, but they were nearly all ultimately fruitless of effects upon the development of interest theory. The outstanding exception is Senior's notion of abstinence (1836) which was a theoretical seed of a different, more psychological conception of the interest problem. It did, indeed, fall by the

wayside, but it germinated and lived on there the sole sprig of psychological capital-theory until the new era of thought at the end of the century. It is a curious jumble of ideas as set forth by its author. Senior called abstinence variously a third agent, an instrument of production, a principle, a productive power, alongside of, but distinct from, "labour and the agency of nature, the concurrence of which is necessary to the existence of capital." He called abstinence "the conduct of a person," and "an additional sacrifice made when labour is undergone for a distant object"; he described it as "providence" united with "self-denial." But again he said the name was a substitute for "capital," defined as "an article of wealth," and he spoke repeatedly of labor, natural agents, and abstinence as the three instruments of production. This was very confused thinking, but at least it brought into the foreground of the problem the much neglected motives involved (in Senior's words) in "the production of remote rather than of immediate results" in undergoing labor "for a distant object," in abstaining "from the unproductive use" of what one commands, or, "from the enjoyment which is in our power." Incidentally, also, Senior discussed rather more than was usual "the average period of advance of capital," and recognized that before the capitalist can retain a profit he must see to "keeping the value of his capital unimpaired." But these ideas underwent no systematic or satisfactory development at his hands.

6. *Influence of the artificial goods capital concept.*—The history of interest theory among liberal economists for more than a century, from Adam Smith to Böhm-Bawerk, runs narrowly within the limits of the amount-of-goods ("riches or stocks") conception of Hume. But it was profoundly affected by the chance that the term "riches or stocks" came to be identified with the artificial goods concept of capital in the tripartite division of the factors of production, land, capital, and labor. A false symmetry was thus given to the structure of the theory of distribution, rent as a *form* of income being limited and bound to the *natural* factor land as its source, and interest as a *form* of income being viewed as coextensive with the "artificial" man-made fac-

tor capital. There was nothing in the inherent nature of the case to prevent the term "riches or stocks" from being taken in a broader sense, including in amount of goods everything to buy which borrowed funds might be used, such as lands for arable and other agricultural uses, and all natural agencies such as residence and business sites, mineral deposits, etc. But already with Adam Smith this linking of interest (and profits) with artificial stocks was apparent, and Ricardo's development of the labor-theory of value and its application to the capital concept (capital merely embodied labor) crystallized this notion that interest was a phenomenon and a form of return linked solely with "produced means of production," not with goods in general.

This conception of the economic factors and their related yields remained almost unquestioned until near the last decade of the nineteenth century. I uphold the opinion that both on theoretical and on practical grounds the attempt to classify material goods as artificial and natural according to the assumed source of their value is unsound. Enough that it involves the fallacy of the labor theory of value. But even those who still accept this classification must concede that it led to a very unreal and illogical restriction of the broader problem of interest. It quite obscured the significance of time as a general factor in the use of goods of every kind, though always in a vague way time was felt to have somewhat more to do with interest and artificial capital than with rent and land. The linking of abstinence exclusively with the origin of artificial goods dwarfed the development of that conception and prevented the recognition of "conservative"[4] abstinence as an essential form of conduct in the use, maintenance of and investment in, material resources and agents, no matter what their physical origin or the cause of their value. Such a narrow conception of the "riches or stocks" whose amount determined the rate of interest blocked the way to any general theory of capitalization applicable alike to "natural" land and to "produced" capital. All problems of capitalization of lands, i. e., natural resources in general, have by this conception to be treated as outside the realm of interest-fixing facts.

Capitalization in all such cases can only be explained by the naive device of applying to land rents, mining royalties, and other future incomes from various sources, a rate of interest (or discount) that is supposed to be determined solely in the realm of artificial agents (in essence a "fructification" theory of the sort condemned, yet used, by Böhm-Bawerk.)[5]

7. *Böhm-Bawerk's promise and disappointment.*—These notions were deeply imbedded in the "classical" economics and still continue to have a phenomenal influence on thought. A most striking example is seen in the case of Böhm-Bawerk. Though at one point in his studies he had the conviction that the interest problem was really the broad one of the "agio," or difference in value, of labor and of uses of goods of all kinds in relation to time, he finally relapsed into the old simple conception of interest as arising only in connection with "produced" capital. (But note his incidental and inconsistent treatment of land rent as a case of interest from durable agents.) Böhm-Bawerk in his great critical first volume saw, as the essential lack in all foregoing theories, the failure to explain adequately the *rate* of interest as a valuation relationship between the capital sum and the interest (income or yield). He condemned in principle all productivity and use theories. Likewise his elaborate preparatory work on the theory of prices in his second volume, "Positive Theory," seems to have been directed toward the end of explaining the valuation of capital as the sum of the expected values, the summation of the *future* uses and rents contained in stocks of economic agents. But he had closed the door to any solution in that direction by adopting the old Ricardian capital concept, "produced means of production," thus seeking to explain the origin of this group of durable artificial indirect goods *and their valuation* by means of a thinly disguised labor theory of value—in their *past*, not in their future uses. That is, he developed no theory of capitalization, though several times he seems on the point of doing so.[6] He relapsed into a productivity theory of interest, and he failed, just as he had shown so many others to have failed, in explaining the *rate* of interest as a percentage of a principal sum, as a surplus of price over and above the initial capital price of the series of

future uses.

8. *Clark's "pure capital" and timeless production.*—J. B. Clark, like Böhm-Bawerk, became convinced of the inadequacy of past interest theory. But the beginning of his contribution lay at a very different point, namely, in exposing the ambiguity of the current capital concept, especially in his recognition of its neglected value aspect alongside of the conventional artificial concrete goods aspect.[7] Hardly second to this in significance and intimately connected with it, is Clark's broadening of the conception of the things comprising capital, making it inclusive of land and natural agents, indeed, logically, of every intangible right to income in which "a fund of pure capital" (as he calls it) may be invested. Pure capital as a private, business concept, became essentially an investment fund, though Clark gave it less practical expression. It cannot be said, though, that Clark succeeded any better than Böhm-Bawerk in explaining the genesis of capital valuations. He too seeks the answer in the past of goods rather than in the anticipation of future uses, and develops an abstinence theory to account for the technical, physical beginnings of "capital goods" in a manner inconsistent with his own inclusion of land together with artificial agents in the capital goods concept. He too accounts for the valuation of the pure capital by sacrifice incurred at the origin of artificial goods—a psychic cost concept. Clark too is wanting in any capitalization or recapitalization theory that relates capital value to anticipated incomes in general. He too concludes with a productivity theory of interest, in which the "interest" sum is looked upon as the specific product of the capital and is related to the capital-goods as a rent rather than as a rate per cent upon a capital-sum.

In one important feature Clark's treatment of this problem is reactionary just where the Austrian advanced the discussion most; that is, in the importance of the role assigned to time. Böhm-Bawerk, it is my belief, started on the right road toward an understanding of the time-factor, though he ultimately went astray on other paths without ever clearly recognizing how he had lost the road. But Clark never was on the right road and arrived at an explicit denial of any significance for time in the explanation of interest. It is the function of (pure) capital, he declared, to synchronize the outlay of labor and its fruits, and he attempted to prove this by an argument palpably fallacious.

It is one of the misfortunes of economic theory that Böhm-Bawerk and Clark, who had many theoretical virtues in common, could not have got together on their main differences. Böhm-Bawerk's initial conception of time needed to be combined with Clark's value concept of capital, and both freed from a labor theory of value influence. The results surely would have been much nearer a true solution than is either of the old-fashioned productivity theories of interest dressed up in new-fangled terminology with which these two pioneer thinkers terminated their arduous labors. Each was destined to give a new impulse to thought, and each disagreed with the main conclusions of the other; yet both came to results that seem singularly alike in certain respects. Böhm-Bawerk's interest theory after some early attacks upon it by the older school of economics, English and American, was adopted by them very generally with little modification, and is now the theory most widely accepted, in type, if not in all details; while Clark's notion of capital value has likewise gained wide vogue. Thus, views which their authors had expected to be revolutionary could be accepted and incorporated into the conventional system of thought of the orthodox school just because the original ideas had not been consistently developed. The doctrines at first novel were at last accepted not as strangers but as old, familiar friends.

9. *Productivity interest theory.*—The negative and critical work of Böhm-Bawerk and Clark raised issues which their positive theories did not suffice to settle. It is true that two dynamic decades of widespread discussion of this and related topics in economic theory were followed after about 1900 by an equal period of reaction, or at least a prevailing lassitude, in theory. The majority of economists were inclined to take the various more or less novel and conflicting notions that had appeared, and to merge them into an eclectic body of doctrine, which it was believed, or hoped, might be generally accepted and initiate an

era of theoretical harmony. To a remarkable degree this policy seemed to succeed. Alfred Marshall, the leader of this eclectic movement as well as its most typical representative, took from the first this attitude toward the work of Böhm-Bawerk.[8] Marshall's eclectic formula of the two qualities in capital of prospectiveness and productiveness became the mode among English and American economists. To the influence of J. B. Clark, and perhaps in part to Wieser's general imputation theory, is traceable a related but more systematic formulation of a general theory of the specific productivity (or productive contribution) of each of the factors, a conception almost, if not quite, as widely favored in the text books as that of Marshall. In all these cases the "productivity" of capital (as a certain limited group of material artificial agents) is viewed as the cause and source of the yield or income called interest (implicit as well as explicit). It is assumed that this "productivity" (vaguely assumed to be a technological fact, but always shifting its character to value-productivity, a fact of private profit in the broader sense) serves to explain not merely the amount or price sum yielded by a group of "capital goods" but also the *rate* per cent of yield computed on the valuation of the principal, or capital value. It ought to be evident without argument to any one acquainted with Edwin Cannan's work[9] that when this shift is made the interest rate per cent of "productivity" of capital value becomes something quite unco-ordinated with the per acre amount or per man amount of productivity of the other factors. A rate per cent yield from the investment of borrowed "capital" is a fact of general bearing, not related solely to the "productivity" of artificial agents contrasted with that of land per acre and of labor per man, but related equally to the profit productivity of labor hired and of land and natural agents either hired or bought by the use of any investment fund (owned or borrowed).

All this relates solely to the explanation of interest on "productive" capital, used in business, but what of the case of interest on enjoyable goods ("consumption goods" so called)? When this problem is recognized at all (frequently it is not) in no case is the claim made that interest can be explained by "productivity."

Another, supplemental, explanation is here conceded by the productivity theorist to be necessary, which is essentially that of time-preference. Thus every productivity interest theorist who has faced the whole question holds a dual theory, or, rather, two quite distinct theories, of interest, one to cover the case of indirect goods (sometimes limited to those employed in commercial ways) and another to cover that of direct (i. e., enjoyable) goods. Numerous further difficulties of the productivity theory have been discussed by the writer elsewhere, and need not be repeated here.[10]

10. *Sources of a general time-valuation theory.*—Böhm-Bawerk and Clark, united, were more potent to arouse discussion of the interest problem than, divided, they had been to give it a satisfactory solution. This at least was the verdict of a small group of students who were not satisfied with the eclectic results just indicated. Though the subject claimed the attention of a much smaller proportion of economists after 1900, it continued to be studied with undiminished zeal by a few. They felt profound discontent with the outcome and they had hope of something better, of winning, so to speak, some purer metal from the rich nuggets of truth that had been unearthed by the newer criticism. Negative criticism of unprecedented keenness and quality had revealed the ambiguity or untenableness in logic of various of the older conceptions and thus had made deep breaches in the old structure of distributive theory, calling for some fundamental reconstruction. Yet with superficial repairs the old structure had been restored and reoccupied. The most brilliant flashes of insight by the pioneers in the interest discussion had faded into darkness and had not lighted the way to any constructive results.

Suggestions have been given above of some of these ideas that were glimpsed by Böhm-Bawerk and by Clark, especially those of a pervasive premium (agio) for time, of the true nature of the capitalization process in the case of any series of uses, of the capital value concept, etc. No one of these was consistently developed, and they were left as mere passing suggestions off the main line of economic thought. Besides these squandered or misprized resources of theory, there were many others waiting to be utilized. There was the abstinence concept, still, after nearly three-quarters of a century, in as crude a form as that in which Senior had left it, confused between technological and value or investment relationship, and tied to a narrow notion of artificial capital. There was the thought, given wide currency in the text by F. A. Walker (borrowed by him from some earlier source), that time change is a cause of value co-ordinate with stuff, place, and form. This thought, to be sure, was not developed by Walker, and he did not see in it the revolutionary possibilities of a general theory of time-valuation in relation to all kinds of goods. There was the new academic subject of accountancy beginning to attract attention to the exacter mathematical expression of time relations in investments, and especially to the process of recapitalization according to changes in earnings. There were certain elementary notions of actuarial science and practice that began to filter into the class rooms of theory, as insurance, forestry, corporation finance, valuation of utilities, and other related subjects were taking their place in the university curriculum. There was the increasing attention to the human and psychological aspects of economic problems, begun by "the marginalists" Jevons, Clark, and the Austrians. However faulty their technical psychology (ranking thus probably in the order just named) and however faultily applied, they had in this matter initiated a new era, whose broadening application of psychology to economics and sociology we are still witnessing.[11] And finally (for we can here touch only a few of the high points), there was the influence of the newer economic history in which, at least a few avid students of theory began to find rich suggestions for destructive critique of the conventional, orthodox, commercial system of economics (especially distributive theory). No eclectic can hope to begin to understand the continued discussion of the interest theory after 1900 unless he gives due consideration at least to these elements in the situation. Otherwise he catches only fragmentary glimpses of the movement and fails to see its broader implications. Many minds contributed some elements to this process of thought though the participation of some was either meagre or of short duration. Besides those whose names have repeatedly appeared above, noteworthy contributions were made by Ashley, Cunningham, Toynbee, Edwin Cannan, Carver, Veblen, Davenport, Turner, and others.

The positive outline of the time-valuation theory has been most fully presented in two versions—that of Professor Irving Fisher and that of the writer. These differ in the mode of approach and in emphasis, and in a number of details, some of them unquestionably of considerable importance.[12] But in regard to the larger issue, the two versions are in substantial agreement. Fisher's treatment is that of the mathematician and accountant, conceiving of the whole process as one of buying and selling future incomes. My approach and treatment has always been rather historical and genetic, with a greater stress on the psychological and human factors. Though begun and largely developed before the term "institutional economics" was coined, it might even be deemed to be in some respects an essay of that type. Especially, it treats the interest rate not as a thing apart from the general price system, but rather finds its explanation interwoven with the whole process of price formation, from its earliest beginnings to the complex price system of the modern world. Such a view of the interest problem is much more closely bound up with the business cycle than any productivity theory limited to artificial capital goods or to industrial profits could possibly be. We will therefore seek to restate the time-valuation theory with more definite regard to its use in this connection, in the hope that by the cross-fertilization of ideas ways may be found to make the statistical analysis of the business cycle yield larger fruits.

PART II. TIME-VALUATION AND THE CAPITALIZATION THEORY

1. *Individual time valuation without trade.*—Contractual interest (as a rate per cent) is a relatively superficial phenomenon. It is also in economic history a very recent phenomenon on any considerable scale. It appeared subsequent to the use of money

and to a regime of monetary prices. If, therefore, any causal relation is historically traceable, interest appears as an effect rather than as a cause of prices. It is impossible to conceive of a general rate of interest, expressed as a percentage of the principal sum, antedating any system of prices; whereas it is possible to picture, as antedating both interest and monetary prices, a system of non-monetary, barter prices, involving ratios of exchange between commodities. Indeed early economic history shows us such systems on quite extended scales, interwoven more or less on the one hand with caste, status, feudal and manorial relations, and on the other with the embryonic forms of monetary trading. The ancient and medieval conception of *justum pretium* was deeply rooted in this notion of the fair and normal ratios of goods. However, after monetary prices do appear, they may become mutually related to barter prices, and somewhat modify them through causing changes in modes of trade and of production.

But we must go deeper still in tracing back historically and analysing logically into its simplest elements the modern complex relations of the time element to prices. Even the exchange ratios of goods in the simplest barter and in primitive barter markets appear subsequent in time, and must be logically subsequent to, long-prevailing schemes and systems of valuations of goods in terms of each other, in tribal, village, family, and individual life. In all the modern textbook expositions of price, it is assumed that the individual trader approaches a trade with some scheme of choice, or state of mutual valuations of goods, and the careful use of this notion will hardly be denied validity. But this must not be taken to imply that once the individual has access to barter and markets, his scale of valuation is unaffected by trading opportunities, by past experiences, and by habits formed, in the market.

In the very earliest pre-barter, pre-market choices of primitive man, time-valuation must have entered into the scheme of choice, as it must today in the most simple, isolated acts of men apart from markets and the developed apparatus of price adjustment. Except for a due recognition of the mutual influence of folks on each other's social standards, etc., it would be putting the cart before the horse to find the cause of the individual's time-preferences in the state of preference discovered by him and borrowed by him from other persons in the market. Rather we must seek an explanation outside of this circular, endless chain of causation, to wit, in the nature of man's desire for goods and in the particular circumstances of plenty, scarcity, and provision for need, as modified by intelligence, customs, training, habit, and social relations.

The fact that time differences in the availability of concrete goods (and also of their separate uses) do cause choice-differences cannot be disputed. Generally viewed, it appears that the more animal-like the stage and the more primitive the people, the greater the preferences for immediate appropriation and use over postponement. However, some curious exceptions are found in primitive communities, supported usually by religious tabus or sanctions. It is only slowly that this difference in choice is diminished, with the growth of social institutions, customs and habits. We cannot imagine, therefore, any individual, family, or larger group economy, either the most simple or the most complex, where there would not be involved in the system of valuations reflected by and implied in the relative valuations themselves, differences in choice due to *time;* that is, due to the differences in the desires for goods at certain time locations and not due to physical differences either in quality or quantity of the goods when they are ripe for use. It is a case where quality and kind are the "other things equal," and time preference reflects the unequal conditions of choice, such as appetite, mood, fatigue, companionship, etiquette, and many other things that affect merely the time of greater impulse, drive, or desire.

Experience and observation teach that in the vast majority of cases the preference is very marked for present goods over future goods (and vice versa as to present and future ills) with children, savages, and the masses of mankind. But the growth of the spirit of providence and frugality means the growth of power and readiness to inhibit this choice of present in relation to future goods. It is not doing violence to the facts to say that individuals and families have, involved in their schemes of valuations, more or less definite rates of time-preference. This changing nature and force of time-choice cannot fail to modify the actions of men, determining what, when, and how they do things, what material things they use and how they use them, determining in large part what are the kinds and amounts of durable agents with which men surround themselves. Observe that this is all conceivable and actually occurs in countless cases, before or without the expression of these valuations in terms of monetary price, or even without the simplest barter. It is a system of individual choices of goods with implicit ratios of time-preference.

2. *Time-valuations under barter.*—The beginnings of barter arise out of such a system of time-valuations operating in individual, family, and group economies. The essential motive for the simplest trade can be found only in the fact that the trading parties have at a given moment unequal valuation ratios between specific goods (at least implicit in their drives and desires), and by trading bring these ratios more nearly into accord. Time-value is not a quality separate and apart from the total value of a concrete object (wealth) or of a specific act (labor); it is merely that part of the total value which in the particular circumstances is due to time relations, just as other parts of the value may be logically attributable to conditions of place, stuff, form, proprietorship, and manifold subjective factors in men. The time-value may be negative or nothing or little or much or all of the value of a certain good in a particular situation. It requires no stretch of imagination to picture trader A having no present use whatever for commodity m which he possesses, but an intense desire for immediate use of commodity z; while trader B has no present use whatever for commodity z which he possesses, but an intense desire for commodity m. Yet at a later time the attitude of these two traders in respect to these two commodities might be reversed. Barter in such a case is simply the exercise of choice, in social circumstances, as to time-relations of goods and uses. Even when the contrast in the traders' intensities of desire is less

extreme than in the example, there must be usually some limit at which one or the other trader would cease to have a motive for trade, due to time-relations. These same differences in time-value explain likewise the simplest process of deferring payments, borrowing and lending, where the borrowed goods are returned later in kind, often because of tribal *mores* without bonus, but with usury exacted from a stranger. There appears no reason to doubt that time-differences are just as real and just as clearly the explanation of particular economic choices of wealth and of actions in the simple states of status and of barter, as are any other differences in the conditions of choice. When this time-valuation is not consciously expressed as to amount in a separate unit (as money) or as to rate per unit of time (discount or premium per annum), it may be very effectually embedded in a person's general system of contemporary valuations in the ratios of certain goods with others.

3. *Time-valuation in a monetary price regime without loans.*— Böhm-Bawerk, to whom we owe much for his emphasis of the psychological factor and for awakened thought on the interest problem, declared that "the kernel and center" of his own theory was the proposition: "as a rule, present goods have a higher subjective value than future goods of like kind and number."[13] He recognizes that this rule is subject to some exceptions but he considers these to be very rare.[14] In reality, many present goods may be worth less to any and every individual than a like kind and number of future goods, notably seasonal goods, as ice in winter, fruit in summer, etc., as well as in many other specific situations where present individual desire is small compared with anticipated need for particular goods at some later point of time.

Now, suppose that one finds that his relative valuations of present and future goods of a certain like kind and quantity expressed in the price unit are out of accord with his own relative valuation of the time element in certain other kinds of goods. Or, again, suppose that one finds that his own time-valuations of particular goods are out of accord with the market rate which reflects the time-valuations of others, their estimates of the ratios of the present and future prices of the specific goods. In either case the person (except as deterred by the trouble of choosing and trading) would buy some and sell other specific goods, giving up the money that he has left or acquiring the money that he will either spend at once or keep as a "storehouse of value." By this use of money evidently a person may often get some one else to supply him with more present goods or with a greater total of present and future goods of specific sorts than he could otherwise have, and at the same time the other person may gain by distributing his possessions better throughout time periods. In such cases money serves as a "storehouse of value" better than the other sorts of specific goods. And such a process of buying and selling (without lending or the use of credit) must tend to weave into the whole price fabric a certain general, average rate of premium of present dollars over future dollars which has resulted from leveling out and rounding off a great part of the individual differences, though considerable may remain. So, then, each unit of money would evidently buy durable goods which (barring mistakes and accidents) would rise in price throughout a given period in the ratio of the prevailing time-price embodied in the price of goods; and vice versa, the seller of durable goods to be used in the future would have to sell them for less than the price that would emerge in course of time. In other words discounts on future goods and uses, and premiums on present goods and uses, must interpenetrate into every corner of a price system and enter into almost every price quite apart from the use of credit in any form, to say nothing of lending money at interest.

4. *Time-prices and time-shifts of goods.*—In this process of price adjustment of goods in relation to time-periods many intricate practical problems must arise because of the different degrees of durability and preservability of goods, and because of the differences in the trouble and expense of keeping certain goods or of hastening the ripening of others. From the primitive eras of human industry, the shifting of goods in point of time was the purpose of many kinds of economic activities such as drying foods, smoking, cooking, salting, burying in the ground, storing,

building caves and warehouses, oiling, painting or otherwise protecting many kinds of tools, agents, and supplies; and again the purpose is to ripen or otherwise hasten the time at which specific goods can be had for use. Some goods lend themselves readily to this process and others with difficulty. It is little trouble to keep some things, and they deteriorate little or none (e. g., the precious metals) while at the other extreme are things which defy all attempts to delay their use (or vice versa, to hasten it). Now almost every process of keeping things involves the giving up of labor and other goods which have value (or price) for alternative purposes; and besides there may be a loss in quality or in quantity, as in the rotting of fruit, the spoiling of meat, etc. All these subtractions from the physical quantity and quality of the goods to be kept, plus all the subtractions from other goods needed in the process, taken together, are charges upon the transfer of goods from one time-period to another quite analogous to freight charges for physical place change. (Conversely, there may be gains in physical quantity or quality.) This must give rise to many and complex adjustments in the relative prices of goods both contemporaneously and over periods of time. To take a comparatively simple case: suppose that apples may be kept in an ordinary cellar from September until March, but that one-half of those thus stored rot in the six months. A price per bushel in March twice as much as in September, plus the price (actual or alternative) of labor and storage space, might easily be three times as high as a September price. But at the ratio of three to one, March and September prices might not contain that prevailing premium on present dollar purchasing power needed to induce its investment for keeping these particular goods six months. The investment does not promise the prevailing increment of a higher net price in March while all around in the existing price system are alternative investments which do contain it. By choice the line is drawn between that time-shifting of goods which is warranted by time-price relations and that which is not. These differences may be reduced by shifting goods, but not to zero, any more than local differences in prices of goods can be reduced to nothing by transporting goods from the place of lower to place of higher valuations. Local prices of two exchanging markets still differ by the amount of the freights. The price system in any period of time viewed statically, contemporaneously, is linked up by countless acts of choice with the price system in succeeding periods of time, into a time-embracing price system. This is an unescapable conclusion from the phenomenon of individual time-valuations.

5. *Capitalization in the pricing of durable agents.*—We have spoken thus far of the price of concrete goods as wholes, having in mind, typically, goods that afford single uses (even though the goods may be preserved over a period of time). We now come to the price problem found in another more complex class of objects, which the older speculations on interest almost ignored. These are durable agents giving off a series of uses over a period of time. Such agents, as Böhm-Bawerk showed (without fully developing the thought in his interest theory) may be looked upon as containing separable uses arranged in time series which, like particular goods, often may be shifted forward and back in time in accord with differences in time-valuations. Around these durable goods, too, is built up a structure of time prices. The explanation of this process is the theory of capitalization that may fairly be said to be a product of twentieth century thought, so meager were the traces of it before.

It was one of the triumphs of the psychological marginal theorists, and pre-eminently the work of the Austrian school, to overthrow the old cost-of-production theory of prices and to replace it with an explanation beginning in the value of ultimate uses, and traced backward from them to agents. Every indirect agent derives its value (and its monetary price) from its products; it has not and cannot have ultimately any basis for its price except the price of its products, actual or expected; its price is simply the present price of the sum of all its future products (or of its separable uses). But in every existing price system the prices of like uses and of like ripe products differ according to time location; therefore the price (capitalization) of durable agents containing series of products equal in number and maturing price, must differ according to the maturing dates. For example, let one agent contain ten units of product yielded within a year (the agent being then used up) and another agent contain those same ten units yielded once a year for ten years, or once every two years for twenty years; clearly these various durable agents though they may contain equal sums of products (taken at their par, maturing valuations) would have unequal present (capital) values, if and whenever the present claims to the future products are taken as the sums they represent in the actual system of prices.

This way of looking at the origin and nature of the capitalization process is revolutionary of traditional and still widely current conceptions. The counting house and banking habit of mind has largely dominated economic thinking since the eighteenth century, and "interest theory" has been a phase of commercial economics with its disposition to regard as normal and permanent things just as they are. The economic man (still with us) is pictured as a merchant in a modern market, equipped with interest tables, aided by accountants, resorting every day to banks and the loan market, and consciously and mathematically estimating the present worth of durable agents and all other time series of products or incomes, by reference to the interest rate prevailing in his circles. So economists, even since they have begun to give attention to the capitalization process, continued to explain it by taking a mathematically expressed interest rate determined antecedently in the loan market and applying it as a discount rate to rents and future incomes to arrive at their present worth. The illusion persists even among some who in large measure accept time-valuation doctrines, that in no other way could capital values be arrived at by investors.

But our view of the capitalization process is utterly different. It is genetic and sees capitalization as a part of the earliest system of prices. It does not conceive of private property as "given in its finished scope and force" (as Veblen asserts is erroneously done in most current economic thinking). Rather it looks upon the price system of today and the habits of mind that go with it as comparatively recent developments, though having their origin before our banking and credit systems. The capitalization theory here outlined has been far more shaped by anthropology, economic history, and genetic psychology, than by continuing deductive, dogmatic, speculative studies.

Our thought is not that the earlier type of the capitalization process (which still persists in large measure today) involved the conscious recognition or explicit expression of a capitalization rate either derived from outside or inherent. But some rate becomes automatically involved in every price of durable goods (or series of incomes and of products) where time-location in any degree affects the valuation of the constituent elements making up the whole price of the thing. This phenomenon of discount of uses contained in any agent or source of incomes is correlated not with artificiality but with durability of the income bearer, because durability means continuance through time, and more or less extended periods between the present valuation and the maturity of the future use, product, or income, that is taken to be one of the constituent parts of the present agent. Thus the prices of ephemeral goods of present use contain little or no time-discount, and durable goods (notably land and natural agents) contain more and more in proportion to the distance and time distribution of their uses.

The process of time-valuation is in large part one of trial and error, affected by imitation, habit, custom, social training, etc., and constantly adjusted in the light of experience within both the individual and the group economies. When, and to the extent that, competition operates, the persons who succeed, more or less gropingly or intuitively, in bringing their time-estimates into some semblance of a true system of time-prices, are more successful buyers, holders, and users of wealth. Certainly after the use of money became common in medieval towns and markets, it was inevitable that time-discounts and premiums should permeate everywhere into the enlarging system of prices that was created. And these time-valuations (discounts) on future uses and products within the larger system of prices must themselves be built into a system reflecting a general rate, though varying just as prices do, in the various economies outside the larger central markets. Such a price system as this is logically conceivable in a creditless, loanless, interestless community, and is indeed the kind of situation disclosed by economic history as existing before the rise of modern financial institutions and methods.

6. *Capitalization and "the normal rate" of profits.*—Such a price system embodying time discounts is not, however, conceivable without the accompaniment and result of a usual, normal rate of profit accruing to the buyers and owners of the durable agents. Since at least the days of Hume, a close connection has been seen to exist between the rate of profits secured by active enterprisers in their own businesses, and the prevailing rate of interest on commercial monetary loans.

However, from the first, it was seen that a distinction must be drawn between the usual, average or (as it came to be called) "natural" or "normal" rate of profits (which must be in the long run if the business is to attract enterprisers, and above which active competition will not for long periods permit it to remain) and the higher or lower rates which may prevail temporarily perhaps in particular places or branches of trade, and which may be attributed to accidental and unforeseeable causes, or to the presence or lack of special skill and of efforts by individual enterprisers.

It is therefore true that the close connection between the profit rate and the interest rate exists only at the moment of investment, as anticipated probable chance of profit (or income), and any additional profit (or loss) is either attributed to human effort or is absorbed in a recapitalization of the principal, the price of the enduring agents or property rights that give control of the income. The significance of this was, before recent capitalization theory, quite missed in the futile attempt to explain capital-values by cost of production. The long remarked "tendency of profits to equality" in various employments is rather more the result of the constant re-evaluation of existing durable agents and the tendency of their valuations to accord with revised estimates of their products than it is the effect of the cost of production of new agents of like kind, as held in orthodox doctrine.

At the moment of investment, however, the individual investor sees the two "normal" rates (of profits and of loan-interest) as mutually reacting and affecting each other, without having to think of their causal relations. Each offers to him a chance of gain and a choice for investment, and even economists' thinking has often seemed to rest at that point. But if the question is raised, there are three possible types of answer. The interest rate might be the cause of the "normal" profit rate; or the reverse might be the case; or both rates might be the results of a common cause. The last of these is implied in the capitalization theory; but heretofore only one or the other of the first two theories seems to have found adherents.

7. *The general interest rate and the profits rate.*—Here, at length, we have arrived at the interest problem in the strict sense. What is the cause of, what makes possible, the prevailing interest rates on monetary loans? If the questions have been put, is interest the cause of profits or are profits the cause of interest, the answer, yes, has generally been given to the latter. For the "productivity theory" of interest, which in its various versions and degrees has held an overwhelming predominance in this field of thought, is really, when examined, found to mean this if it means anything. The vague and ambiguous term "productivity" is at first assumed to mean some kind of physical creation of product; but this conception being utterly unusable in an explanation of an interest *rate* (ratio of the *value* of product to the *value* of the agent or source), it is always quietly abandoned in favor of the value conception. Productivity is taken to mean an increment of value (price). But what kind of *value* and where found? Even in the most elaborate recent attempts to apply the marginal analysis to this question, the outcome of the reasoning is simply this: capital (as an investment sum) is "productive" in the sense that one having capital has normally a chance of making profits at the average prevailing *rate*, by investing it. So-called "productivity" means profit yielding, and "product" means merely investors' profit. And what is the source and essential condition of this profit emerging at a rate on an investment? It is explained neither by physical productivity of agents nor by the value of

products (or uses) taken at the time of their realization and maturity. It is explainable only by reference to the existing price system wherein goods containing postponed or future uses have been and are, when the loan is made, so priced (summed up, capitalized) in relation to time that as those uses mature and ripen they rise toward the parity of realized valuable uses. This normal profit-making "productivity of capital" is thus nothing but the reversal of the former discount-valuation applied to distant incomes. It is a psychological, valuation process, not a physical, technological process. Thus profits no more explain interest than interest explains profits. They offer alternative investment opportunities but neither is the cause of the other. Both opportunities result from discounts and premiums permeating the existing system of prices, and these are traceable to the fundamental factor of time-preference exercised by men individually and collectively in the complex environment of modern markets and prices.

8. *Separate markets for time-prices.*—A considerable usefulness cannot be denied to the notion of a general interest rate. But this notion, like that of a "normal rate of profits" is abstract; actually interest rates appear in great variety, and differ at any particular time among individual transactions, groups of traders, kinds of business, and types of loans. But, as in the case of profits, so of interest, the notion of a general, or normal, or prevailing rate is the result of analysing the various gross rates, attributing a large part of the differences to other causes (various kinds of chance, luck, individual skill, various service charges, and costs of making the loans, etc.), and looking upon the remainder as true or pure interest. Parts are thus imputed to costs, other parts to enterprise, and other parts perhaps for a time to rents (more or less permanent) which sums, in fact, enter into the recapitalized principal of the investment.

But if the safest, simplest and most marketable kind of loans, such as government bonds, give the index approximately to "pure interest," quite persistent differences are seen to prevail among the rates in various loan markets, for commerce, for urban real estate, for agriculture, etc. Many such differences can be readily explained as due to the special factors of cost. The gross, or apparent, rates of interest do differ far more than the true, net interest, both to the lenders and to the borrowers.

It is impossible by this analysis to reduce all the apparently different rates in a country to a single true rate, either to lenders or to borrowers. The problem is analogous to that of differences between the commodity prices of two localities; these to be sure, differ by costs of transportation and tend toward a net equality to actual shippers, i. e., marginally; but that does not change the fact that local sellers get and local buyers pay higher prices in the one market than do sellers and buyers respectively in the other market. The differences persist, on the whole, through long periods as our own economic history abundantly shows. So likewise it is evident that in many neighborhoods and among various economic groups, larger or smaller, real differences in the prevailing interest rates may and do persist indefinitely. This may be despite extensive loans and the constant import and export of merchandise. Evidently, too, in such cases, the whole structure of prices must be both reflected in, and reflect, these differences. Capitalizations, the relative prices of present goods and of durable agents, and normal rates of profit in active business investments, as well as rates of interest, must, through the operation of competition and substitution, be brought into some measure of consistency, as respects the time-discounts in various goods and employments. Crude tools, ephemeral structures, high business profit rates, low present prices (large discounts) on future uses, and high rates of interest go together. Even within countries, provinces, neighborhoods, and in particular employments, real differences in all these facts can arise and persist, moderated but not destroyed by borrowing or by trade in goods. A limit to the equalizing of the time-rates in different markets is set by the lack of purchasing power to buy goods, and by inability of borrowers to give security enough to lenders in other communities to induce them to keep on lending. But not infrequently lenders in regions of lower time-valuation lend up to the limit of the wealth that backward communities can pledge, and even beyond, until a collapse of credit teaches its lesson. In the same country within the markets for commercial, agricultural, and urban real estate loans, within loan markets affected by different tax laws, and among groups of borrowers and lenders affected by tax-free features, there must be differences in rates that persist and that are reflected in the whole set of economic choices and the whole system of prices in each market and group.

Whatever be the relative prices of particular classes of goods, these prices would all be interpenetrated more or less consistently by the time-discount rate peculiar to each market or group. Any such system of prices having become fairly stable at any time and in any country, may be disturbed and altered by changes originating (1) in the medium-of-exchange mechanism, affecting more or less alike all prices, i. e., the general level of prices as expressed in index numbers; or (2) in conditions of time-valuations, acting upon time-prices and capitalization; or (3) in special conditions of demand and supply determining relative prices. The last of these is not negligible, but is of least importance to our present theme and must be passed over here. The first is for our purpose the most important and it will be considered on the assumption that a change occurs from the side of money without any change *originating* in the psychological factor of time-preference. Finally and more briefly, will be observed the case of individual time-preference changes (so widespread that they affect the prevailing market rates of time-discounts, etc.) without any change *originating* in the money supply or other exchange mechanism. We say "originating in" not "occurring in" to avoid any suggestion that such changes may not and do not occur as a result of the repercussions of the particular price adjustments in the new situations taken as wholes. Neither of these two problems (1 and 2 above) is simple, and it may be questioned whether the true nature and full bearing of either had been clearly recognized until within the last thirty years.

PART III. INTEREST RATES AND SOME PROBLEMS OF GENERAL PRICE CHANGES

1. *Long-time changes in the general price level, and compensatory interest rates.*—When, after 1873, the general price level had continued to fall for some years, the accompanying fall in interest rates on long-time loans attracted the attention of economists, notably that of J. B. Clark and of Irving Fisher, in the decade of the nineties. Alfred Marshall had briefly called attention, as early as 1886, and again in 1890,[15] to the phenomenon later designated by the title of Professor Irving Fisher's notable monograph, "Appreciation and Interest." Indeed it seems to have been glimpsed as early as 1802 by H. Thornton, and by Ricardo in his "Principles," 1817. The discussion of this problem has been in part deductive and in part inductive through the use of statistical data. Take a period of falling prices resulting, let it be assumed, from a decrease, absolute or relative, of gold production. Then it was shown that when this trend becomes fairly definite and generally expected, prospective borrowers become more wary and prospective lenders more eager; for each compares the purchasing power of dollars when the loan is made with that of dollars when payments of interest and of the principal, respectively, will fall due. The borrowers are warned by the outcry of the debtor class, and that group of capitalists that lives in the neutral zone between active and passive investment is tempted to shift over to passive money lending unless and until the interest rate falls to a degree that offsets the fortuitous advantage accruing to creditors from rising prices. (Of course, the converse of all this would be the case if prices were rising.) In principle this process is competitive adjustment, on both sides, of expected gains and losses from price changes, resulting in a compensatory rate of contractual interest. The "true" interest rate translated into terms of goods (the commodity interest rate) would be no higher or lower than under a regime of stable general prices, if this process operated without lag or friction. But of course it does not so operate. At the best, the uncertainties of price changes make this process,

though good as far as it goes, but little better than a gamble. Several independent statistical tests[16] have shown that in part the compensation takes place, but only tardily, imperfectly, inequitably, unequally in the various branches of trade and in countless transactions. So far as it does occur, it can affect only newly made loans or old loans at the moment of renewal, and leaves the vast outstanding bulk of contracts in terms of dollars to be settled on the level of the new and ever-changing prices. In historical fact, no sooner has the downward trend of prices seemed to be established, and interest rates on newly made loans become more or less roughly adjusted to it, than general prices changed to an upward trend, and for years even the ignorant and unskillful among the active capitalists reaped unexpected profits on new loans still made at low interest rates. Then the whole "money lending" class, including as it does the many little lenders who are the equitable owners and beneficiaries of vast trust and insurance funds, endowments, and savings accounts, are the innocent losers.

2. *Changing general prices in relation to particular prices and to industrial equipment.*—Most of this doctrine is so generally accepted now that repetition is scarcely necessary. But there is another somewhat deeper-lying problem that calls for further attention from future students of prices. For is it not evident that during such a process of price change the whole scheme of relative prices would be disarranged, compared with what it would have been, or would be, under a regime of stable general prices? Where interest rates were compensated fully (or excessively) in relation to falling prices, there long-time investment in durable equipment would be "normally" large; while if interest rates are as yet compensated little or none, investment for the future must lag and even in renewing old loans many debtors would face ruin. Such things might raise some kinds of prices in the future by causing physical depreciation of existing wealth (lands, machinery, equipment) but reduce present prices in those industries by causing producers to continue to turn out goods under the pressure of need for ready funds.

The same uncertainty and chance that hangs over the whole

process of borrowing from others to invest in particular ways, hangs over the process of employing one's own capital in active business. (We are concerned here only with the time-value and time-price aspects of these price relations.) There must be overinvestment at one place in durable goods, and underinvestment in others, compared with what would have been the case in a state of economy where general prices, as determined by the relation between the exchange mechanisms and the volume of exchanges, remained stable. While the contractual interest rate is out of accord with the profit rate, more or less, in different employments, both must be more or less out of accord with the "true" commodity interest rate, and at the same time the capitalizations of agents in various uses as well as the supplies and prices of various "ripe" goods must be greatly dislocated. A market rate of time-discount would in such periods cease to "prevail" with any precision, throughout any one of the structures of prices. The existing uncertainty as to price trends special and general, the inequality, the accidental gains and losses of enterprisers and investors, the resulting discouragements and prodigalities of individuals and large classes, extend even to the more fundamental psychological fact of time-preference. On the whole it would seem to have the effect of reducing abstinence and investment, though the factors must be varied and often conflicting.

3. *Short-time general price changes, bank credits and discount rates.*—In an historical chart of price index numbers, the long-time fluctuating curves, representing the greater tidal waves of general prices, may be as much as forty or fifty years from peak to peak; and they are broken up into a succession of uneven, shorter waves formerly thought to extend over eight to ten years but which some more recent studies indicate to run now nearer three or four years. In any case these briefer curves mark what are now called business cycles. Naturally the peaks and hollows of the long-time curves coincide with the high and low points respectively of certain of the shorter cycles, whereas between the greater peaks and hollows the shorter cycles may be pictured as superinscribed upon the long-time curves. At the few coincident

points there might be a common cause, but the intervening divergences of the business cycle from the general trends certainly suggest the working of two somewhat independent causes.

Without committing ourselves to an inflexible theory, it seems now a good working hypothesis, in view of the known facts, to connect the long-time curves mainly with changes in the fundamental monetary conditions. Chiefly these relate to gold (and silver) production, together with the accompanying conditions as to the use of gold as the "standard" money and unit of prices in the world (if one likes, "the supply of and demand for" gold for use as the standard price unit in the monetary system). Since 1914 irredeemable paper money, crowding gold entirely out of circulation and becoming the sole fluctuating "standard," has a part even more important than gold in the explanation of the price levels of particular countries, and has a very significant part in the explanation of the value of gold throughout the world. Similarly we may find the larger part of the cause of those briefer fluctuations that diverge from the long-time trends, in the changes occurring in that part of the exchange-mechanism consisting of credit agencies (in relation, of course, to the accompanying psychological conditions of hope, fear, confidence, expectations, whether based on calculation or resting merely in emotion, in the business community).

Now it is well recognized that modern developed banking and credit systems, by the use both of bank notes and of discount deposits, permit of large and rapid expansion of the dollar-expressed purchasing power, without substantial changes or any increase whatever at once and at the same time in the amount of standard money in the particular community. Any bank or group of banks starting at the close of a period of depression with a good percentage margin of reserves above the legal (or popularly reputed safe) minimum, can rapidly increase its earning assets and earned income by expanding credits on the basis of the same (or even less) standard (or legal) money in its vaults. This additional purchasing power in the hands of bank customers and borrowers may be assumed to have somewhat, if not just, the same immediate effect on prices as would a per capita increase of money in the community. As soon as any considerable number of enterprisers begin to share the confidence and belief that prosperous times are in prospect, the number of borrowers increases. The earlier an individual acts, the greater, probably, will be his eventual profit from the transaction, as funds borrowed at the lowest rate of interest are used to buy goods and equipment (and labor) at the lowest levels of prices, to be held and used while they are advancing to higher levels. There follows, therefore, on a smaller scale, and over a shorter period, the same kind of compensation between prices and interest rates as when prices advance because of the relative increase of standard money throughout the world. Wages rise at first more slowly and then more rapidly than prices of most products, until the wide profit margins shrink. Discount rates then rise with the growing demands of customers. The relation of various particular prices in the general system of prices undergoes rapidly various modifications, notably the relation between capital-valuations of durable and indirect goods with near-finished direct goods. Then every miscalculation, especially the overestimate of capital values (based on the combination of low discount rates on borrowed funds and high expected product-prices) reveals itself, the margin of security shrinks or vanishes, and many bank credits are "frozen."

4. *Public aspects of bank-credits in relation to stable prices.*—As to the banks' part in the movement of the business cycle, public and economic opinion in the past has thought it should be guided only by individual (or corporate) self-interest and the motives of private competitive profit, limited only by the minimum legal percentage of reserves. The banks have accordingly acted independently and indeed had to do so or lose the chance of profits for their stockholders. Midway in the upward price movement, long before its culmination, other banks (and the country as a whole) would benefit if some of the banks would cease expanding their credits. But as a private competitor the individual bank could not afford to do this. Only by acting in combination, and therefore monopolistically, could the banks together share the gains and losses of early restriction of credit

while yet having an ample reserve percentage margin and legal lending power. And in this matter, as for long years in respect to transportation, the public could see nothing but good in competition, and has been very reluctant to admit the good in any measure of monopoly, even with governmental control. Popular fear of combination of moneyed institutions is still great.

In the Federal Reserve System, two monopolistic features were incorporated (doubtless without recognition of all their bearings): virtually centralized rediscount, and centralized note issues, both under control of the Federal Reserve Board. Very fortunately also (in contrast with the plan proposed by the National [Aldrich] Monetary Commission and almost unanimously preferred by the bankers of the country), the Federal Reserve System was given a far more public character and control, notably in not granting to the member banks all the profits as the Aldrich plan proposed. As a result of limiting to 6 per cent the dividends from the Federal Reserve Banks going to member banks the attitude of the whole banking community toward the sacrifice of earning assets (and therefore profits) of the Federal Reserve Bank since 1921 has been very different from what it otherwise would have been. It would be difficult to exaggerate the contrast. If only in the period between 1918 and 1920 the Federal Reserve policy had not become entangled and confused, through the mistaken zeal of the treasury department, with the policy of low interest rates on bonds, the country might have been spared a large part of the loss of that period of ridiculous price inflation.

There has been revealed of late the possibility of stabilizing in considerable measure the minor swings of prices (business cycles), by increasing the percentage and even the amount of reserves of standard money (impounding gold), at the sacrifice of possible bank profits, instead of passively letting the speculative demands of business precipitate a period of inflation. It is at last seen by a few, though not as yet generally by the public (nor confessed by the Federal Reserve Board), that the paramount use for public welfare that can be made of surplus assets is not to inflate credit and raise prices, but to keep prices as nearly level as possible. The index number, not the reserve percentage, might better be the compass by which to guide the discount policy of the great central, noncompetitive bank. But such action has pretty definite limits which are frequently ignored. It cannot long control or defy the larger swings correlated with standard money production and use, but only or mainly the minor savings caused by bank credit expansion. Ultimately the balance between gold and production costs in marginal mines must determine the valuation of the standard unit and the level of prices on the gold standard throughout the world.

5. *Various types of loans and divergent interest rates.*—We have spoken[17] of the differences in interest rates existing side by side in different markets for loans. Such are seen in the higher interest rates long prevailing in the newer compared with the older states; in agricultural compared with urban districts; in the rates on bonds of long successful compared with doubtful enterprises; and in the varying rates for bank and mercantile credit, granted on poor, fair, or prime security. Such contemporaneous differences may be largely explained as due to risk (of losing principal and interest), to trouble of placing and collecting loans, etc., as seen from the standpoint of marginal lenders that are in a position to choose between the two forms of investment (vice versa as to borrowers). But evidently the true market net interest rate to non-marginal lenders within each territorial or other class of credit market must be genuinely different because of the prevailing competitive conditions (reflected in the particular system of prices in which they live and work). We are not now concerned primarily with these contemporaneous differences, connected either with geography or risk, but merely with time differences, the fluctuations over periods of time which occur in each of these kinds of loans, and more or less parallel with those in the other kinds of loans.

It has been a common observation that interest rates vary (in frequency and degree of change) somewhat directly with the shortness of the term of the loans.[18] This means, of course, the more frequent necessity of renewals, and the greater proportion of all the loans of that type becoming subject of bargaining for renewal at any one time or state of the loan market. Thus something like 75 per cent of all outstanding loans now are in corporation and government bonds and real estate, rural and urban, aggregating perhaps ninety to one hundred billion dollars.[19] On these the current rates for new loans and renewals are the most stable, following on the whole, most closely the general trend of long-time contractual (or nominal) and adjusted (commodity) interest rates. At the other extreme is the much smaller, quite elastic volume of fluid funds, consisting of call loans, commercial paper, bankers' acceptances and Federal Reserve rediscounts, on the average perhaps five billion dollars (say 4 per cent of all loans). The current rates on these are most fluctuating (extremest on call loans); for these are the marginal loans, on the frontier, so to speak, of speculative investment, and made with reference to the more ephemeral changes of prices and opportunities for profit.

Midway between these two classes of loans stands the very considerable class of the more ordinary bank loans to commercial borrowers, together with the casual business credit by manufacturers and merchants to customers, totaling perhaps something less than thirty billion dollars, or something more than 20 per cent of all existing credits. The nominal rates on these change little, but the actual effective rate is very considerably modified by altering terms of collateral, of customers' balances, refusal to renew, etc.

6. *Underlying relationship of these various loan markets.*—No doubt these three (and correspondingly their various subdivisions) are imperfectly connected markets, between which, because of legal restrictions, commitments, habits, lack of financial machinery, etc., there is a tardy transfer of funds by either borrowers or lenders. Moreover persistent average differentials in rates reflect risks and costs and trouble of placing and collecting loans. These markets to a large extent go their separate ways, and their time fluctuations of interest rates, be they large or small, manifest a considerable degree of independence. Long time real estate loans, continue to be made at about the same rates throughout periods when short time commercial loans are

undergoing wide fluctuations. Likewise a large degree of independence must subsist at times in the several minor price systems, but fundamentally they are all connected and related to each other by the slow, though imperfect, transfer of marginally located funds until what may be called the "normal" differential is re-established. We might picture these various time-discount rates as the cars of a train hitched together by elastic couplings, all drawn along by the same engine. On a perfectly level track, moving at a perfectly even speed, they would keep the same relative positions and distances apart. But they would lag or catch up as the engine changed its speed and as, with varying grades of the track, gravity now retarded, now accelerated, their motion.

This view seems true of moderate or ordinary fluctuation of business; but some evidence indicates that in times of critical credit changes, the readily marketable, staple, long-time bonds (on the larger exchanges) may undergo notable swings of price (and reciprocally, their long-time yields).[20] Viewed as mere dips in price, likely to be followed in a few years, at most, by recovery, the changes of capital value plus the regular interest make a total sacrifice by the seller (and gain to the buyer) possibly commensurate with, if they do not exceed, the larger fluctuations of the rates on call loans. Is not the explanation to be found in the fact that in the periods of financial catastrophe, a considerable number of even the best bonds become, so to speak, the last line of reserves to be thrown into the battle by speculators and bankers, the one asset convertible into ready funds? Therefore bonds are brought out of strong boxes by wealthy market operators and by financial institutions. The "supply" of funds available for their purchase is so small that the "marginal price" registered by sales is very low. But the actual sales represent a very small proportion of the outstanding amounts. These securities are mostly held by more passive investors whose valuation is much higher than that of the market, who would not think of selling at the momentary prices but who yet have little or no new funds by which to add to their holdings.

7. *Different kinds of inflation as affecting prices and interest rates.* —

In the foregoing comparison between long and short time changes in price levels, we may have a clue to the unraveling of an old puzzle (at least a trial may be worth while); that is, the contradictory effects upon interest rates that seem to follow changes in prices at different times. To survey the problem briefly: before Hume it seems to have been generally thought that if money increased (and prices rose) the interest rate would fall and stay there. Hume declared (he seems to have been considering only the effects after the adjustment to a new level was complete) that prices and interest rates were independent, and the rate the same after the price level had changed that it was before. Then the theory of appreciation and interest, though not contradictory to Hume's view of the problem he was examining, showed that just during the period of gradual general price change in one direction, interest rates are affected, but precisely opposite to the popular notion. Interest rates then fall while money and prices decrease and rise while they increase. Not only has the old notion persisted popularly, but it has from time to time appeared in the more professional economic circle. Certain facts as to foreign trade movements, rates of foreign exchanges, bank reserves, note issues, increase of bank credits, commercial prices and ease of commercial credit, refuse stubbornly to chime with the simple sweeping proposition that rising prices always cause (or at least accompany) rising interest and discount rates. At times the outstanding and anomalous fact is a rapid expansion of trade and rise of prices continuing for months (in rare cases even for years) with little or no increase, possibly some reduction, in discount and interest rates in commercial circles.

We are tempted to find the explanation in the contrast between long and short time price changes, and in the lag of the interest rate, as the effect, behind rising prices as the cause. There may be some truth here, but the larger part promises to be found in the contrast between the two main sorts of price inflation in respect to their origin or cause, the one resulting from an increase in standard money, the other from an increase of bank credits. Ordinarily the standard money is gold or silver which, following changes in physical conditions of mining output, comes into circulation and is paid out by mine owners and workers gradually to buy goods without having been at any time in the hands particularly of a lending class. Likewise (whether or not we designate it as standard money), the irredeemable, political paper money issued from the printing press by needy governments, comes into circulation day by day directly as means of payment of current expenses, not assuming even momentarily the form of a loan fund. The first and immediate effect of money coming into circulation directly thus as means of payment is to raise prices of commodities, whatever effects, if any, it may later have indirectly on interest rates (notably the compensatory adjustment of contractual rates, already discussed).

Quite otherwise is it in the case of price inflation by means of bank credit; it matters not immediately whether the particular form which the new purchasing power takes is deposit and discount or bank note issues (credit currency). Any surplus percentage of reserves above legal requirements is to banks potential lending power, (e. g., 80 per cent in a central bank when the minimum legal requirement is 35 per cent, or 25 per cent for member banks when the minimum legal requirement has just been reduced to 13 per cent). Viewed as private enterprises merely, the banks have at such times not only the power, but the profit motive, to expand their loans, to convert this useless, ornamental surplus reserve into earning assets as fast and as far as possible. If the central bank management has misgivings about letting this occur, these may be overridden by Federal fiscal influences because of a predetermined policy to float governmental loans at low rates of interest.

8. *Abnormal bank-loan expansion and commercial discount rates.*—Now what happens to prices and interest rates under these conditions? Note that if prices are to be affected, it is to be through putting into the hands of business men the purchasing power represented by this huge latent loan fund, and it cannot be until that is done. Let it be assumed that, dollar for dollar, purchasing power of that kind will at least for a while have the same effects as an increase of standard circulating money in

raising prices in commercial circles (immediately and directly, no matter how the later adjustments may differ).[21] The latent inflating medium-of-exchange has no effect on prices until it becomes actual. It is first a huge loan fund concentrated in the hands of bankers and only after being loaned to bank customers does it increase the ratio of dollar purchasing power to goods for sale. The moment that it begins to be loaned, it tends to shift the balance of buyers and sellers of loan funds in the market for commercial credit, in favor of the borrowers, and to lower discount rates, or keep them low despite large borrowing. If the shift is sudden, if the potential amount of this loan fund is large, and if the movement, therefore, can be long continued (as between 1915-1920), it is easily understandable how bank (and other related commercial) discount rates would behave abnormally, and remain low while prices were steadily, and at last rapidly, advancing. Customers are tempted and, so to speak, bribed by the low discount rates, to borrow this new purchasing power, than as commodity prices rise, customers borrow more, and thus the vicious circle of loans raising prices which in turn increase loans continues so long as the discount rates remain level, or rise little. Only the approaching exhaustion of the surplus reserve percentages calls a halt.

Meanwhile, of course, there would have been the constant tendency not only for the discount rate, but for the whole price system in this banking and commercial world to get out of accord with the underlying forces of time-valuation, and with the previous (and in a sense more "normal") scheme of capital-valuations and prices. Commercial loans pretty closely connected with banking are barely one-fourth of all loans, and for the other three-fourths (now around one hundred billion dollars) little of these banking funds would be available. Further, the capitalization of several hundred billion dollars of existing wealth would be only very imperfectly adjusted to this artificial and temporary cheapness of banking credit. The whole situation is such as to deceive the judgment and demoralize the business policies in every line of enterprise. Political pressure may prolong this movement even after the banks, if left to their own judgment and self-interest, would have curtailed credit and raised discount rates. It is probably the most outstanding case in which contractual interest and discount rates on commercial loans appear to find their cause and explanation for considerable periods outside of fundamental time-valuation factors, and out of accord with them, though in the end those factors govern. This situation has served to mislead some economists into the development of a general theory of interest based on bank credit.

9. *Bank loan elasticity and the needs of business.*—The foregoing presents the extreme case of the expansion and contraction of bank loans in relation to prices but in principle quite small changes in the loan policies of banks affecting the volume of commercial loans, discount rates, and percentages of reserves, are of the same nature.[22] They cause and constitute inflation and deflation of the exchange medium and of commercial purchasing power, not originating in changes in the amount of standard money but in the elasticity of banking loan funds. This word "elasticity" has long been used in discussion of banking policy to designate a quality assumed to be highly and wholly desirable in bank note issues and in customers' credits, but with only vague suggestions as to what is the need, standard, or means, with reference to which bank loans should expand and contract.

Rather, it may be more exact to say, the tacit assumption has been that the bank loan funds should be elastic in response to "the needs of business." But "the needs of business" appears to be nothing but another name for changes in customers' eagerness for loans; and this eagerness increases when prices are beginning or are expected to rise, and often continues to gather momentum while prices rise and until, because of vanishing reserve percentages (and other factors), the limit of this elasticity and also the limit of price increase, are in sight. In this situation, the most conservative business operations become intermixed with elements of investments speculation, motivated by the rise of prices and the hope of profit that will be made possible by a further rise. Throughout this process the much esteemed elasticity of bank funds is the very condition causing, or making possible, the rising prices which stimulate the so-called "needs of business." Truly a vicious circle, to be broken only by crisis and collapse when bank loans reach a limit and prices fall. Then business failures, depreciation and losses written off, and the readjustment of capital values, bring the system of prices again into some semblance of self-consistency, and particularly bring the scheme of prices in active commercial markets which are most influenced by bank discount rates, into better accord with the larger, more inert volume of long-time loans and with the greater mass of the capital-valuation in owned wealth more rarely bought and sold.

Quite different would be the course of events if "the needs of business" were to be judged with reference, not to the speculative desires of individual traders (however "natural" and excusable) to expand operations because of and in expectation of rising prices, but were to be judged rather with reference to the "need" (or desirability) of a stable level of prices for the whole community. Then an official index number of general prices might better than customers' clamor indicate the social-welfare need of expanding bank loans. Given a bank reserve-percentage rate in excess of legal requirements, bank inflation would truly fill a (public) need when prices were falling, but not when prices were rising. If this index were followed, that portion of the fluctuations of prices and of the business cycle due to the vicious circle of bank inflation to meet the so-called "needs of business," would be minimized instead of caused or accentuated.

No doubt there must be a limit to the possible operation of such measures at either end of any legally enacted scale of reserve-percentage rates, and in any long-time movement of prices either up or down. It would seem that in principle the influence of such a policy of bank credit control upon price changes must be confined in the main within the short-time fluctuations of the business cycle, and must eventually in any country whose standard money is a precious metal, yield place to the major influences determining the world production and supply of the standard metal which influence the long-time swings.

We are not concerned here with the difficulties in the way of practical application of such a plan because of habits of thought, old usages, and administrative details; we are only indicating the nature of the problem and the possible contrasting policies. The whole subject has been viewed in the past in the light of the acquisitive, private-profit conception applied to banking, which, at least in part, defeats its own ends, as well as the ends of general welfare.

10. *The Bank of England rediscount policy and the price level.*— The nearest approach to a policy of deliberately manipulating bank loans in relation to national, rather than to individual, "needs" is the practice, originating with the Bank of England, of varying its rediscount rates. An adequate treatment of this highly technical subject would transcend our theme and our powers, but some aspects we may venture to glimpse. The purpose of raising the rediscount rate is quite definitely to protect the country's central reservoir of gold when a turn of foreign exchange rates threatens to deplete it by causing exportation. However, the purpose only one step removed (indeed bound together with main purpose as means to end) is to reduce commercial borrowing at home, thus reducing commercial purchasing power and thus checking the rise of, or deflating, English prices in commercial circles. Two results follow almost simultaneously: one, English commodity prices cease rising, or are slightly reduced relative to foreign prices, and thus English exports are stimulated and imports to England are discouraged; and two, the higher discount rates tempt back English assets held abroad as well as induce foreign bankers to extend or to increase finance bills and other credits to England. Both of these changes reduce, and may remove entirely for the time, the adverse foreign exchange rates calling for the net export of gold from England. The artificial raising of the rediscount rate really effects a lowering of commodity prices in England (both absolutely and relatively to those of other countries) and if it does not increase absolutely the amount of standard money in the country, it has at least the negative effect of preventing the decrease that otherwise would occur.

The plan really works. It is well to inquire carefully, however, whether this process shows more than a restricted, temporary, and superficial power to determine the level of prices or the form of the price system by changes artificially initiated in interest rates. In our view, in accord with the general theory of time-valuation, this process is nothing more than an anticipation of the bank-fund deflation that would otherwise be forced by the continued export of gold. Raising the rediscount rate merely puts springs under commercial prices to prevent their dropping later with a jolt. Moreover it is essentially a process of readjustment of *relative price levels* and of the stock of international standard money, in different geographical areas of the world, prices and money stocks in different national markets having become more or less out of alignment with world conditions. Fundamentally it is almost entirely unrelated to the problem of the long-time level of general prices either in the particular country or in the world at large.

11. *Wicksell's startling doctrine of discount policy examined.*—Such a role (however useful) is more modest than seems to be attributed by a good many economists here and abroad to the rediscount policy. The extremest view, that taken by the late Professor Knut Wicksell, has gained a wide hearing and some following loyal enough to claim "Wicksell as the originator of the modern theory of discount policy, which constitutes the chief advance of monetary theory since Ricardo."[23] Wicksell's thesis is this: If, other things remaining the same, the banks from any cause whatever together fix their interest rates somewhat below the *normal* level (assumed to be fixed by "marginal productivity") all commodity prices will rise and continue to rise without any limit whatever; and vice versa. There is an incredible rigidity in the claim of lasting effects from a temporary change of bank discount rates: "When commodities have risen in price, a *new level of prices* has formed itself which in its turn will serve as basis for all calculations for the future and all contracts. Therefore, if the bank rate now goes up to its normal height, the level of prices will not go down . . . . there being no forces in action which could press it down"[24]

Criticism of this proposition is difficult because of the elusive order and ambiguous nature of Wicksell's discussion. For at times he implies that the thesis has an important and useful application to real conditions and again confesses that "it is only an abstract statement," and even that it is one of such nature that it can have no meaning or use in the financial world as it is. However, it can be shown that in either case the proposition is unsound—even taking it most "hypothetically." A gross fallacy is contained in the very first phrase, "other things remaining the same," for this does not have its legitimate meaning and purpose of limiting to one (a change of the bank rate) the new conditions or causal factors assumed to be different from the normal reality. The attentive reader soon discovers that Wicksell is assuming, or confessing, in order that the thesis shall hold at all, that before the bank rate could have the effect indicated, several other very important things must be quite different from what they are. First, all the banks of a country must act together, the individual bank, even a strong central one, would be powerless; then, this not being enough, all the banks of the world must act together, the single nation would be powerless; then, there must be *"no circulation whatever of coins or notes,"* or the attempt to maintain an artificially low discount rate would break down by the exhaustion of reserves; and it appears by this time that the thesis is meant to be defended only in the case of a complete regime of bank credit, with a zero reserve percentage.

Now in such a banking Utopia where bank credit were the only medium of exchange, if credit continued indefinitely to be extended to all applicants at an artificially (or arbitrarily) low rate of interest (not determined by the "normal" or usual forces), then there seems nothing to prevent constant bank credit inflation and a constant rise of prices, in turn creating a motive for more commercial loans, *ad infinitum,* just as in the case of Russian and German paper money inflation. Under such conditions the price of a shoe string or of a loaf of bread in terms of the nominal monetary unit may burst the mathematical tables. Either a regime of irredeemable paper money or a complete regime of bank credit without any money or any reserves, can be said to make possible a rise of general prices without assignable limits. But Wicksell's doctrine as a guide to practical banking policy is more to be shunned by stable money theorists than poisoned alcohol as a beverage. With the gold standard or some other definite standard of reserves, Wicksell's policy would be utterly unworkable, as he concedes quite casually. If he had presented his doctrine in a different order, introducing first the wildly unreal condition under which alone it could be imagined to operate, probably no one could have been deceived, not even its inventor, into thinking it could give any guidance in actual situations.

At times Wicksell's thought seems to be in a confused way that in the situation which he propounds prices rise indefinitely not because bank loans are continuously expanded, but because the discount is kept artificially low (while loans are restricted). But the superficiality of such a view is patent. It is simply unthinkable that all prices should rise continuously without continuous increase in the exchange mechanism either of standard money or of bank credit, or in the rapidity of turnover. If, however, discount rates were kept artificially low in Wicksell's imaginary banking regime, this would create a speculative "need" for loans (a demand for credit at a rate low compared with the time-discount rates pervading the general price system) and the amount of loans would steadily increase unless they were artificially restricted by rationing credit, or by favoritism, or by confining it to commercial purposes, or otherwise. Such a policy would affect unequally the prices and time-valuations involved in different kinds of goods. The notion that it would determine the time-discount rate embodied in the community's whole price system appears when viewed in the light of the capitalization theory, as foolish as "lifting one's self by one's bootstraps," or as "the tail wagging the dog." Bank loans are but a small proportion of all loans, and a much smaller proportion of the total wealth in private hands which is from time to time evaluated in terms of dollars. In all the durable sources of income are involved time-differences determining the shape in manifold ways of the whole system of relative contemporaneous prices. This system of prices itself rests upon, or grows out of, the totality of psychological time-valuation conditions. In the causal order of things the bank discount rates do not determine, they are in the long run determined by, these underlying conditions. With all their elements of artificiality, bank rates must, so far as competitive conditions prevail, tend to come into accord with the system of prices.[25]

12. *Fundamental conditions and government loans in war time.*— We have mainly assumed the general underlying conditions of time-valuation to remain stable in the larger community, and have directed our attention almost entirely to changes originating on the side of the mechanism of exchange (either standard money or credits, banking, or other). A symmetrical treatment would require an equally full examination of the problems originating in changes from the side of time-valuation, assuming no change originating on the side of money and credit. But a few suggestions must suffice us here. Recall that in all the phases of time-valuation, from the most subjective in the simplest individual economy to the most objective in developed commercial markets where a general price prevails for time (interest rate, capitalization rate, etc.) differences may co-exist as between individual groups and different fields of investment. There are more or less distinct fields of time-valuation and time prices, only imperfectly connected. It must happen also, that changes even in relative prices in particular markets (e. g., through a sudden demand for certain kinds of ripe, direct goods, compared with others) may react on time-valuations of durable wealth, often profoundly. Some indirect durable agents that make up the larger part of the wealth in one branch of industry (e. g., agriculture) may suddenly become much more or much less in demand relative to other indirect durable agents (e. g., mines or railroads or some kinds of machines). Now this, because of friction and imperfect substitution, may for a while throw the time-discount rates of different trading groups even more out of accord with each other than they were before. The individuals within these groups are readjusted (and readjust themselves) marginally to the need situation, and even those of greatest

frugality and thrift now buy and sell goods at the prevailing prices in their group. Whether or not the implicit rate of time-discount will be changed depends alike on transfers from outside as well as on the latter strength and prevalence of individual frugality and providence within the group. Conversely, changes in time-preference originating within smaller groups must slowly change their respective marginal (market) rates of capitalization, etc., up or down, and these rates in turn, by substitution of investments, would gradually modify the time-valuation levels everywhere else.

The occasion or cause of change may be of such a general nature as to affect in large measure the real and actual time-valuations of all individuals and groups within a country, as notably on the outbreak of war. Then the immediate need of the equipment and munitions of war, not present in adequate quantities, must be met with an almost utter disregard of the future and of premium rate, and a large and costly equipment of indirect agents must be rapidly created which will be of little or no use when the war is ended. The effect is to raise quickly the whole general level of time-discounts and time-premiums. Countries with large saleable or pledgeable assets may for a while retard such a rise by selling claims, securities, credits, against others or against themselves, to wealthy neutral nations, as Great Britain and France sold securities to and borrowed from the United States between 1914 and 1919. But this at the same time raises the marginal time-discount rates in the lending countries. Or it may happen (as in the period of the Napoleonic wars and in 1917 on our entry into the world war) that most of the capitalistic world becomes involved, and the fundamental marginal time-valuations are everywhere raised. At such times there is an inevitable competitive bidding and rivalry between the borrowing needs of the government for war purposes and those of private business (both in nonessential industries and in those directly and indirectly producing war supplies). Because of the pressure of business opinion and its political bearings, the administration always is betrayed into the illogical and self-defeating policy of trying to borrow at low rates and at the same time trying (one aspect of a price-fixing policy) to keep commercial interest rates artificially low by encouraging bank inflation. The enforcing of artificially lower bank discount rates to buyers of national bonds by giving them preference as collateral (as in the case of Liberty and Victory bonds) combined with patriotic pressure and quota bond selling, leads to bond purchases largely or purely by bank loans rather than from thrift and saving, and to the extensive pledging by business borrowers of whatever equities in national bonds they have.

Here is a place where, as to the general commercial discount rate, the consistent and practical policy would be laissez faire, as a high interest rate would be one effective means of cutting off the demand for loans by the "nonessential" industries, and thereby would prevent diverting labor and materials from the war industries. Higher interest rates as costs in "essential" industries could be directly and frankly compensated by higher prices of those particular products, rather than by a course which inevitably raises the prices of all commodities. Another policy always used more or less in connection with price fixing (both of commodity prices and of loans) is that of rationing and, by the high hand of a governmental agency, apportioning credits only to "war-essential" industries. Despite the danger of mistaken judgment and the occurrence of abuses, this is potentially both more logical and more effective than price fixing in securing the real end in view, viz., to use for war purposes, not for private enjoyment, the all too inadequate stocks of goods and human labor at hand. There are deductive grounds, never yet shown to be unsound, for condemning as fallacious and self-defeating the ever-repeated attempts of governments to float loans at less than those warranted by the general state of the price system. The attempt always involves tinkering with the exchange mechanism (either currency or bank credits and notes, usually both), with the result of price inflation. This ultimately imposes upon the nation as a whole burdens and losses incomparably greater than the petty saving in interest charges on the public debt for a few years. To depress interest rates on public loans artificially and by governmental pressure to manipulate bank discount rates is to treat superficial symptoms while ignoring underlying conditions. Just so far as present purchasing power in greater amounts and at artificially depressed interest rates is, in wartime, put into the hands of those who clamor for "business as usual," so far is reduced and retarded the most needed shift of goods from present private use to capital equipment and to present goods for war purposes, paid for by public loans. Prices become inflated, war costs are increased, and the people really pay usuriously both as taxpayers and as the victims of the inevitable financial crisis.

13. *Interest theory and after-war recovery.*—Conditions in which time-valuations change in an opposite direction from that taken in wartime, occur at the close of a great war. These cannot be adequately discussed within the limits of this paper; but certainly recent events (1918-1926) as well as a broader theory of time-valuation, unite to discredit the belief of J. S. Mill, that a country devastated in time of war and from which "nearly all the movable wealth existing in it" has been carried away, will "by the mere continuance of that ordinary amount of exertion which they are accustomed to employ in their occupations . . . . in a few years" acquire "collectively as great wealth" as before.[26] The root of Mill's error (in fact and in theory) more clearly appears in his affiliated discussion of "government loans for war purposes." The amount borrowed (and spent for goods destroyed in war uses) "was abstracted by the lender from a productive employment" concedes Mill, and "the capital, therefore, of the country, is this year diminished by so much." But (here begins the error) he declares: "The loan *cannot*[27] have been taken from that portion of the capital (concrete goods) of the country which consists of tools, machinery, and buildings. It *must have been* wholly drawn from the portion employed in paying laborers . . . . But . . . . there is *no reason* that their labor should produce less in the next year than in the year before." This is all wrong; there is no such "cannot have been," no such "must," and there is abundant "reason" to the contrary. The whole thought is tainted with the labor theory of value. For in truth, from the moment that war begins to raise time-discounts, and progressively until

peace returns, physical depreciation proceeds, the normal peace time repairs, replacements, and improvements of many durable agents are curtailed, especially those in the non-essential industries, normal building operations and additions to industrial equipment are suspended, while current production is applied not only to procuring the materials to be immediately consumed in the war, but even more to building the elaborate equipment of indirect agents which are to become nearly worthless the moment the war is ended. This would be true even in a victorious uninvaded country. In a conquered land, from which "nearly all the movable wealth" had been carried away, the case would be far worse. Returning to the arts of peace, the population even with herioc self-denial and efforts, may for years be unable to obtain again the pre-war stream of commodity income. The peasant is lacking in beasts of burden and agricultural equipment; the artisan is forced to return to simpler tools and machinery; both are lacking in stocks of raw material; while highways, bridges, and other means of transport are in ruins. The mass of the population, even to exist, is forced to adjust itself to a lower standard of living, a condition which makes peculiarly burdensome any effective "abstinence" to create loanable funds and additions to the durable wealth directed toward future needs. These evils, it need hardly be said, are usually greatly aggravated by political disorders and by the monetary demoralization resulting from both paper money and bank credit inflation. In this situation no doubt large loan funds (to be used mainly to buy imported industrial equipment) could in many cases, if wisely chosen, be "profitably" borrowed from more prosperous nations. That is to say, the price system is such in the devastated country, that all sorts of goods with future uses are so priced that investors can "profit" (individually) by contracting to pay abroad high interest rates to buy, build, and increase the number of such long-time, durable bearers of future uses. The greatest difficulty is that borrowers lack good enough security and the moral factor of credit to obtain, even at high interest rates, the loans needed either for public or private uses.

14. *Conclusion.*—The foregoing are but illustrations of the

practical questions, the answers to which presuppose and imply some general theory of interest. They vary widely in scope and nature as do also the answers that have been offered. There is but little evidence in the large volume of recent discussion of price movement and the business cycle that the implicit question of interest has been explicitly considered as an integral part of the price system. Interest theory receives attention only incidental to or aside from the price system. An interest theory is advanced which does not originally apply to all kinds of prices. Interest (so far as attributed to impersonal forces) is explained by an ambiguous technical "productivity" of a restricted group of "artificial" agents, the rate so determined being then thought to be applied in the capitalization of other agents; or it is explained as fixed in the realm of bank loan credit, and then somehow to permeate all other loans and prices. These are piecemeal interest theories which fail to find general cause for interest inherent in the relation of all kinds of goods to man's nature and needs. They are what Böhm-Bawerk called fructification theories, rightly condemned by him in principle,[28] as an attempt to stretch a partial explanation so as to make it appear to be a complete one. Such an attempt is an almost infallible sign that the explanation is not only incomplete but unsound. Not discovering the generally valid ground of explanation, it has chosen an invalid— not even partially valid—ground.

It may be too much to attribute to the lack of sound interest theory alone all the inharmonious and discordant ideas and policies regarding interest rates and prices that have lately stalked abroad. Human thought has a remarkable capacity to go wrong at many points and in many ways. But the thesis of this paper is that a unified time-valuation theory makes it clear that time-discounts and premiums enter into the formation of all prices both of direct and of indirect goods, and are an inseparable part of even the earliest price systems; that the price system is logically and chronologically antecedent to all forms of contractual interest, which is merely derivative from the capitalization process; that finally this view gives a clear, consistent criterion by which to test various notions with respect to price changes and policies with respect to the fixing of interest and discount rates by government or banks, and it shows the limits of their possible application. Our object will have been attained if theoretical discussion shall have been aroused, statistical inquiry stimulated, and in the end, practical efforts to stabilize prices helped to move along right lines.

NOTES

1. *Capital and Interest,* English translation, p. 47.
2. E.g., he speaks of political economy, "from Say's time to the present," as having been "captivated by the deceptive symmetry that exists between the three great factors of production—nature, labour, capital." *Positive Theory,* p. 1.
3. Many examples of this could be cited. Even Irving Fisher lapses into this thought at times; e.g., *The Rate of Interest,* p. 91; and *Elementary Principles,* pp. 229 and 336.
4. A term introduced by the writer in *Principles of Economics,* 1904.
5. See above, sec. 4.
6. *Positive Theory,* pp. 348-9.
7. *Capital and Its Earnings,* 1888.
8. Explicitly, first, it seems in his *Principles,* 3d ed., 1895, pp. 142 and 664, cited by Böhm-Bawerk in preface to his second edition of his *Geschichte,* etc.
9. *History of Theories of Production and Distribution,* 1894.
10. See "Interest Theories, Old and New," *American Economic Review,* vol. 4, March, 1914 [see above, pp. 226-255].
11. See the writer's paper on "Value and the Larger Economics," Journal of Pol. Econ., 1923, pp. 587, 790.
12. Some of these are indicated in "Interest Theories, Old and New," op. cit.
13. *Positive Theory,* p. 237. Of course this proposition is not itself a theory of interest, but merely the statement of a broad empirical fact whose explanation constitutes "the interest problem." The truth is that Böhm-Bawerk does not make and keep this "the kernel and center" of his "positive theory," for to do so would seem to require a consistent "agio" or time-preference theory such as he promised to give. But instead, as he went on, he made technical productivity of capital (in the roundabout process) more and more the kernel and center of his explanation, "the third reason why present goods are, as a rule, worth

more than future." *Positive Theory,* p. 260. This becomes in his view "the principal form assumed by the interest problem." Ibid., p. 299. It is the circumstance giving "the phenomenon of the higher valuations of present goods an almost universal validity" whereas on the other merely psychological grounds "an overwhelming majority (of men) would have no preference for present goods." Ibid., 277. This prevailing preference becomes in his explanation almost entirely the result of technical productivity, presented as the chief cause of this premium on present goods (and therefore of interest) independent of any of the two already mentioned. Ibid., p. 270.

14. Ibid.,e.g., pp. 250, 251, 297. The frequency of these exceptions seems to be greatly minimized in Böhm-Bawerk's view by his practice, in nearly every case where he seeks to test the matter by an example, of shifting from particular goods to a sum of money. E.g., ibid., pp. 250 ff., 255, 256, 276, *et passim.* It can happen much more rarely that a present dollar would be worth less than a future dollar, in a modern community with a developed financial system, with borrowing, saving accounts, etc.; in fact, it could occur only in periods of catastrophic changes in general prices, or because of some peculiar personal choice of particular goods that are undergoing great changes in their relative prices. This adjustment of particular prices to the general time-premium on money is in part touched on below.

15. *Principles,* 1st. ed., p. 627.

16. Prof. Waldo F. Mitchell alone, it seems, claims now to find in the statistical data no evidence of such a result.

17. Part II, Sec. 8.

18. See Mr. Carl Snyder's discussion and formulation in *American Economic Review,* December, 1925, pp. 684-699, esp. p. 690.

19. Approximately Snyder's estimates, op. cit.

20. See some data given by Waldo F. Mitchell, in *American Economic Review,* June, 1926, p. 216.

21. As shown by the statistical studies of Holbrook Working, *Review of Economic Statistics,* July, 1926, p. 120, "Bank Deposits as a Forecaster of the General Wholesale Price Level"; earlier article in *Quar. Jour. Econ.,* Feb., 1923.

22. See Holbrook Working, op. cit., for striking statistical confirmation of the principle.

23. See *Economic Journal,* vol. 36, p. 503 (and especially p. 507) Sept., 1926, obituary notice of Knut Wicksell by Prof. B. Ohlin; *Economic Journal,* vol. 17, p. 213, "The Influence of the Rate of Interest on Prices," paper read by Prof. Wicksell before the economic section of the British Association; *Jahrbucher,* 1897, p. 228, "Der Bankzins als Regulator der Warenpreise," by K. Wicksell.

24. *Econ. Jour.*, op. cit., p. 216.
25. As shown above in sections 5 and 6.
26. Book 1, Chapter V. Section VII.
27. Our italics.
28. See above, part I, sec. 4.

PART 3:
THE THEORY OF RENT

The Passing of the Old Rent Concept

Since the time of Ricardo the Rent Concept has been constantly under criticism, and many amendments of it have been suggested. Yet it holds its place in the texts and in discussion, and still determines to a large extent the outlines of our economic systems. No suggested amendment has succeeded in winning more than a meagre following until of late. Within the past decade, however, the attractive statement of new doctrines by Professor Alfred Marshall has contributed more than any other influence to bring about a remarkable change of opinion on this subject. He has met in a manner that has proved to be generally satisfactory the demand that had become imperative for a restatement of the old concept. In view of the wide and well-merited influence of his *Principles of Economics*, it may be allowable to take it as typifying the state of contemporary thought on the subject of the rent concept; and it is for this reason that frequent reference will be made to it.

The present paper is an attempt to determine what are the difficulties admitted to-day in the old concept of rent and what defects must be recognized in the newer and dominant form of the concept. Five central ideas may be distinguished in contemporary discussion of rent, giving thus five concepts,—the land, the extension or space relation, the time or long period, the exchanger's surplus, and the no-cost concepts. These will be taken up in order.

Reprinted from *Quarterly Journal of Economics* 15 (May 1901).

1. THE LAND CONCEPT.

The original form of the rent concept makes it an income arising from land, one of the three factors of production. The essential thing distinguishing it from other incomes is the kind of agents for whose use it is paid. This is the first concept defined by Professor Marshall: "The income derived from the ownership of land and other free gifts of nature is called rent."[1] The definition is given in connection with a statement of the kinds of incomes derived from wealth, the other kind mentioned being interest on capital (profits are analyzed into interest of capital and earnings of management). This view of rent is found so repeatedly expressed in the text-books that it may be called the conventional view. The chapter on the agents of production begins:—

"The agents of production are commonly classed as Land, Labour and Capital. By Land is meant the material and forces which Nature gives freely for man's aid, in land and water, in air and light and heat." The next chapter begins, "The requisites of production are commonly spoken of as land, labour and capital: those material things which owe their usefulness to human labour being classed under capital, and those which owe nothing to it being classed as land." A few lines further the explanation is added, "The term 'land' has been extended by economists so as to include the permanent sources of these utilities, whether they are found in land as the term is commonly used, or in seas and rivers, in sunshine and rain, in winds and waterfalls."[2]

The usual three shares are not distinctly enumerated when Book VI., on "Value or Distribution and Exchange," is reached; yet the thought appears and determines the order of treatment and the chapter headings. It is said that there has been "left on one side, as far as might be, all considerations turning on the special qualities and incidents of the agents of production"; but there is promised a "more detailed analysis in the following three groups of chapters on demand and supply in relation to labour, to capital and business power, and to land, respectively."[3] The treatment of distribution, accordingly, falls into these three main conventional divisions: "earnings of labour" (chapters 3-5); "interest of capital" (chapters 6-8); and "rent of land" (chapters

9, 10),—where each of the three shares is linked with a corresponding factor.

The land concept of rent, thus presented, involves many difficulties;[4] and a recognition of these leads to a modification of the concept. 1. It is shown that the distinction between land and the products of labor is a loose one, impossible to make in practice. 2. It is said that the distinction is of no importance to the practical business man. In these two statements the distinction seems to be abandoned or discredited. 3. But it is said to be valid, because land is a fixed stock for all time, while capital is not. These points will be considered in order.

1. In the following passages the difficulty of trying to distinguish between land and capital is recognized:—

Those material things which owe their usefulness to human labour [are] classed under capital, and those which owe nothing to it [are] classed as land. The distinction is obviously a loose one: for bricks are but pieces of earth slightly worked up; and the soil of old settled countries has for the greater part been worked over many times by man, and owes to him its present form.[5]

Further on is emphasized strongly the control that man has over many of the utilities connected with land:—

If the soil be well provided in other respects, and in good condition mechanically, but lack [only certain elements] then there is an opportunity for man to make a great change with but little labour. He can then turn a barren into a very fertile soil by adding a small quantity of just those things that are needed. . . . He can even permanently alter the nature of the soil by draining it, or by mixing with it other soil that will supplement its deficiencies.

All these changes are likely to be carried out more extensively and thoroughly in the future than in the past. But even now the greater part of the soil in old countries owes much of its character to human action; all that lies just below the surface has in it a large element of capital, the produce of man's past labour; the inherent or indestructible properties of the soil, the free gifts of nature, have been largely modified; partly robbed and partly added to by the work of many generations of men.[6]

Later is added: "In an old country it is seldom possible to discover what was the original state of the land before it was first cultivated. The results of some of man's work are for good and evil fixed in the land;

they can not be distinguished from the results of nature's work, but must be counted with them. The line of division between nature's work and man's work is blurred, and must be drawn more or less arbitrarily."[7]

In these passages the concept first stated seems to be given up; for, if only those things which owe nothing to labor are classed as land, and if it is then shown that there is no material thing in settled countries of which this can be said, it follows that everything must be classed as capital.

2. The distinction between land and capital is formally given up by thinkers of this school, so far as it concerns the individual owner, the investor, or business manager. It is said:—

The balance of usage and convenience is in favour of reckoning rights to land (*sic*) as part of individual capital.[8]

It is to be observed that land is but a particular form of capital from the point of view of the individual producer.[9]

A manufacturer or trader owning both land and buildings, regards the two as bearing similar relations to his business....When he comes to decide whether to obtain [more] space by taking in an extra piece of land, or by building his factory a floor higher, he weighs the net income to be derived from further investments in the one against that to be derived in the other....This argument says nothing as to whether the appliances were made by man, or part of a stock given by nature.[10]

It is true that land is but a particular form of capital from the point of view of the individual manufacturer or cultivator.[11]

There is likeness [between land and appliances made by man] in that, since some of the latter can not be produced quickly, they are practically a *fixed stock for short periods*, and for those periods the incomes derived from them stand in the same relation to the value of the produce raised by them, as do true rents.[12]

It may be well to refer once again to the relations between land, whether agricultural or urban, and other forms of wealth regarded from the point of view of the individual investor. Even from the point of view of normal value, the distinction, though a real one, is slighter than is often supposed; and even in an old country, the distinction between land and other forms of wealth has very little bearing on the detailed transactions of ordinary life.[13]

The impossibility in practice of distinguishing accurately

between things that are "natural" and things that are produced, the absence of any suggestion of a measure to aid in classifying the things that compose land and capital, require the usage approved in these quotations when practical questions are considered. Nearly all economic discussion is from the standpoint of the individual producer. We will note later some of the results of the adoption of this usage.

3. These changes in the concepts of land and capital are not treated as equivalent to an abandonment of the distinction entirely, for it is justified from a different standpoint.

When regarding capital from the social point of view it is best . . . . to separate the capital, which is the result of labour and saving, from those things which nature has given freely.[14]

The reason for this distinction is given as follows:—

[Although land and other wealth appear alike to the individual], there is this difference from the point of view of society. If one person has possession of another farm there is less land for others to have. His use of it is not in addition to, but in lieu of the use of a farm by other people. Whereas if he invests in improvements of land or in buildings on it, his investments will leave as good a field as before for an increasing population to improve other land or put buildings on it. . . .There is likeness amid unlikeness between land and appliances made by man. There is unlikeness because land is a *fixed stock for all time:* while appliances made by man, whether improvements in land, or in buildings or machinery, &c., are a flow capable of being increased or diminished according to variations in the effective demand for the products which they help in raising.[15]

The same argument is presented in replying to the suggestion that the farmer considers in just the same way whether he shall try to get more work out of his stock of ploughs or out of his land, and that, therefore, the income does not enter into price any more than does rent. It is answered:—

So far as the individual farmer is concerned the two cases are indeed, parallel. But if he decides to have another plough instead of getting more work out of his present stock of ploughs, that will not make a lasting scarcity of ploughs since more ploughs can be produced to meet the demand: while, if he takes more land, there will be less left for others; since the stock of land in an old country cannot be increased.[16]

The argument contained in these passages will be criticized in two particulars; and we shall seek to show that it involves in the first place a comparison of one factor viewed statically with another viewed dynamically, and in the second place a comparison of the total supply of one factor with that portion of another factor used in a single industry or by a single undertaker.

(*a*) The argument assumes that the land is in an old settled country, and that therefore its quantity is fixed. Later, however, it is shown that inventions that will turn the soil deeper, discoveries and new means of transportation that will bring into competition great areas of new land, and improvements that make available the resources before unused are constantly changing the limits of the supply of natural resources, in the economic sense of the word "supply." The view that land is a fixed stock for all time is contradicted when it said:—

The supply of fertile land cannot be adapted quickly to the demand for it, and therefore the income derived from it may diverge permanently much from normal profits on the cost of preparing it for cultivation.[17]

Despite this it is assumed that the economic supply of land is necessarily and always fixed; and it is then contrasted with the stock or supply of other things, which is supposed to be increasing and capable of indefinite increase. Whether a static or dynamic view be taken, it is logically necessary to take it alike of both factors: either land must be recognized as an increasing and increasable factor, as well as capital, in which case the question becomes the somewhat speculative one as to their probable future rate of increase compared with the urgency of the demand, or both must be treated as fixed for the moment. In either case, when they are looked at from the same standpoint, the appearance of an essential difference in the two kinds of wealth disappears.

Again, objection must be made to the view of the increase of capital. Capital, as the term is here employed, can be increased; but it does not increase because it is employed in one industry rather than in another. It is sure to be employed in some industry or it is not capital. Why should its use in a particular industry increase the total supply? The additional ploughs can be produced to meet the demand only by the use of the available appliances, which are limited in amount, and which, if used for the ploughs, cannot be used for other things. There will be less productive power to put into other industries unless the general stock of wealth is increased. It is hard to see how the use of the existing stock of capital in one industry rather than another can be assumed to be the cause of this.[18]

If the historical or dynamic view is taken, the supply of utilities connected with land cannot be treated as fixed in amount. If the static view is taken, it cannot rightly be assumed that capital increases instead of being a limited supply which must be economized. It is from inharmonious assumptions that the conclusion is drawn that an essential difference exists between these things in the real world.

(b) It is argued in the passages under consideration that land and other wealth are different from the point of view of society. This can only mean when both are viewed from that standpoint; but in the argument stated the land only is thus viewed, the capital is still considered only from the individual standpoint. In the case of land the total supply is clearly borne in mind, and the use of land in one industry is seen to take it away from another. But in the case of capital there appears to be a shift to the individual view and the supply used by one undertaker; and, because he can increase or decrease the capital employed in his industry "according to the effective demand" (which means in that one industry), it is concluded that the total supply of capital is thus altered. The objections that have been given in the preceding paragraphs apply here also. The line of reasoning here criticized is interwoven with the idea of the static and dynamic supplies of the various factors; but here and there it can be plainly distinguished.

2.
EXTENSION AS THE FUNDAMENTAL ATTRIBUTE OF LAND AND THE BASIS OF RENT.

Many of the difficulties just considered are generally recognized in current discussion of the rent concept. The old classification of the material things composing wealth, into land and capital, is admitted to be impossible for some purposes, and only justifiable for others by reasoning that is foreign to the Ricardian treatment. In current discussion of the rent concept the view appears that, although the reasons usually given for contrasting land and capital may not hold, yet there is a sound ground for the distinction. One suggestion has just been considered. Another closely related to it is that,

underlying [the distinction between] those material things which owe their usefulness to human labour . . . classed as capital, and those which owe nothing to it . . . classed as land, there is a scientific principle. . . . When we have inquired what it is that marks off land from those material things which we regard as the products of land, we shall find that the fundamental attribute of land is its extension. The right to use a piece of land gives command over a certain space—a certain part of the earth's surface. The area of the earth is fixed. The geometic relations in which any particular part of it stands to other parts are fixed. Man has no control over them.[19]

It is stated that this principle has important bearings on economic theory.

We shall find that it is this property of "land" which, though as yet insufficient prominence has been given to it, is the ultimate cause of the distinction which all writers of economics are compelled to make between land and other things. It is the foundation of much that is most interesting and most difficult in economic science.[20]

Then, after some statements as to the way in which the soil can be enriched by man's action, it is said:—

> We may then continue to use the ordinary distinction between the original or inherent properties, which the land derives from nature, and the artificial properties which it owes to human action: provided that we remember that the first include the space-relations of the plot in question, and the annuity that nature has given it of sunlight and air and rain; and that in many cases these are the chief of the inherent properties of the soil. It is chiefly from them that the ownership of agricultural land derives its peculiar significance, and the Theory of Rent its special character.[21]

(*a*) In these statements an initial difficulty results from a lack of positiveness in their expression. In the last paragraph it is stated that the distinction in question may be retained because it rests on the property of extension in land; but, instead of concluding that the only inherent or original properties to be considered in the land concept are the space relations, it is said that they "include" the space relations. This leaves the statement still undefined, for it implies that other things also are included. The intention to include other things appears further in the phrases "in many cases," "the chief of the inherent properties," "chiefly from the ownership." Such phrases give vagueness at the outset to the "fundamental attribute," "the scientific principle," that is being stated.

(*b*) There are some difficulties in the reasoning of the passages quoted. This attribute of land is singled out as the essential one in the distinction between land and other kinds of wealth, for the reason that it is thought to be the one property which man is incapable of influencing. It is thus stated:—

> There are other utilities over the supply of which [man] has no control: they are given as a fixed quantity by nature. . . . The area of the earth is fixed: the geometric relations in which any particular part of this stands to other parts are fixed and man has no control over them.[22]

Here is a jump in thought from the "supply" of utilities furnished by the extension of land, the accompanying natural forces of rain, sunshine, and the like, to the physical area of the earth. One could dispute the truth of the statement that the physical extent even of arable land is fixed; but, neglecting the small area of made land, the supply of natural utilities and the existing area of land are widely different things. Part of the earth's surface undiscovered or inaccessible does not exist for economic purposes: it is not a part of the supply, although it may become such in the future. The utilities of new areas become available to man, become a part of the "supply," when, as is constantly happening on a large scale, they are brought into relation with industrial communities. The geometric relations, physically considered, are as nothing in economic discussion, compared with the time relations and what might be called the sacrifice relations of two parts of the earth's surface. New transportation routes and new motive agents are constantly changing the time and toil relations of two areas. When districts which were a month's journey apart are brought within a day's journey of each other, when continents are brought into economic relations with markets and with wants, does not the statement that "geometric relations remain unaltered" become a play on words? In cutting tunnels, levelling hills, building railroads, bridging rivers, connecting oceans by new waterways, man exercises as great a control over space relations, it would seem safe to say, as he does over any other material conditions. In the work which has been quoted is discussed the development of new countries, and the effects on prices of products, and on the values of lands in the older countries with which the new countries are brought into competition; and it does not seem possible to consider these facts other than a negation of the idea of a fixed supply of the utilities connected with land.[23]

(c) The statements under consideration raise hopes of a contribution to economic theory that are unfulfilled. The thought of extension as the essential attribute of land and the foundation of rent has never been developed and applied to "elucidate the interesting and difficult" parts of economic science. "Extension" is not again mentioned in the succeeding six hundred pages of the work quoted, nor is there anything essential in the argument which can be traced to its influence. The concept is distinctly repudiated in the supposed case of meteoric stones which fell in a shower and proved to be of great value in industry. The income from their use, it is said, "would be a true economic rent, whether [the owners] used the stones themselves or loaned them out to manufacturers."[24] The illustration is introduced to show "that the immovability of land, though a most important attribute of land for many purposes, is not essential to the eminent claim which the income derived from land in an old country has to be regarded as a true rent."[25]

The illustration, it is said, shows "a perfect form of true rent yielded by a movable commodity." Here what is called the attribute of extension is apparently implied in immovability, but it is not considered fundamental, it is not essential: it is merely "important for many purposes," though what those purposes are is not stated. Here is a case of "true rent," though it was said that the theory of rent derives its special character from space relations. The theory of rent is presented in a number of ways quite independent of space relations. It appears that the old concept of rent as a payment for the bounty of nature is not displaced in this treatment by the concept of extension.

Closely allied to the thought just noted is the one that in the rent of land there is an element due to environment, or to situation, which is spearable from the elements due to the "value of the soil as it was made by nature," and that due "to improvements made in it by man." It is said that in "the full rent of a farm in an old country" the third element, "which is often the most important of all, [is due] to the growth and rich population, and to facilities by communication by public roads, railroads, etc."[26]

This idea is not further developed until we reach the chapter on "Influence of Environment on the Income from an Appliance for Production. Situation Rent. Composite Rent." Reference is made to the two preceding chapters as dealing with "the income dervied from the ownership of the 'original powers' of land and other free gifts of nature, and that which is directly due to the investment of private capital."[27] The purpose of the chapter is then stated:—

But there is a third class, holding an intermediate position between these two. It consists of those incomes, or rather those parts of incomes which are the indirect result of the progress of society, rather than the direct result of the investment of capital and labour by individuals for the sake of gain. This class has to be studied now.

Then follows a discussion of "situation rent." The distinction heretofore considered is that between the first and second elements, land and capital: the distinction now suggested is one between the part of land value due to the free gifts of nature and the part due to environment or situation. This appears to be open also to serious objection. No matter what are the "original powers" of land, they have no fixed or predetermined value: they have value only with reference to the social situation, to the needs of men. The value of a piece of land is apparently thought of as a given amount due to nature in one given set of circumstances; and then, changes such as those mentioned being supposed to take place, the increased value and income of the land is attributed to a new element, the situation. But it may be objected that the situation of the "gifts of nature" near human wants was essential to their value in the first case, just as the presence of certain qualities in the gifts is essential to their value in the second place. In considering time, place, form, and elemental value, it may be assumed for logical and practical purposes that any three of the four features of value are given, and then the change in the value may be attributed to the fourth feature. A ton of ice on a July day in a city may be said to owe its value to its situation, if you contrast it with another ton a thousand miles to the north; but you may also contrast it with a ton of ice six months earlier, or with a ton of water then and there, and then its value appears to be due to other things than situation. The value is equally dependent on the substance, form and time, place, and the presence of wants that can be satisfied. In the case of land the social environment is not a new element which imparts a value separable from that due to nature. The social environment is always one of the conditions which make it possible for the gifts of nature to have any value whatever. While, therefore, it may be permissible, in looking at the subject

historically, to speak of a change in the value of natural resources
as due to a change in the advantages of the situation, it does not
seem allowable, in viewing the subjects statically, to speak of two
classes of income from natural resources, one due to the free
gifts of nature and the other to the increase in value of those gifts
with social progress.

3.
TIME AS THE GROUND OF THE DISTINCTION
BETWEEN RENT AND INTEREST.

It is said that the distinction between rent and interest may be
made to turn on a difference of time. It is probably true that
nowhere in current discussion will the statement be found that
this is the *whole* difference, but it is put thus:—

The greater part, though not the whole, of the distinction between
rent and interest on capital turns on the length of the period which we
have in view.[28] [And again:] For the time they [the net incomes derived
from appliances for production already made] hold nearly the same
relation to the price of the things which they take part in producing, as
is held by land or any other free gift of nature.[29]

The idea recurs frequently that "for the time" the supply of
any agent may be regarded as fixed, and, therefore, as not
conforming to its cost of production; and in such case the income
yielded by it is "of the nature of rent."[30] The reservation in the
phrase, "though not the whole of the distinction," leaves in doubt
the value of the statement for exact theory. But the trend of the
thought is evident. It is a departure from the land concept,
wherein rent is always a return for the gifts of nature, and from
the extension concept, where rent is paid for one property of
land. It is a continuity concept of a peculiar sort, the difference
between rent and interest appearing gradually as the time is
lengthened within which the productive agents are considered.
"In passing from the gifts of nature through the more permanent improvements in the soil to less permanent improvements

. . . we find a continuous series."[31]

In this conception, as the period under consideration is lengthened, the rent bearer, if it is a perishable thing, gradually becomes an interest bearer, rent gradually merges into interest, and there is no sharp dividing line between them. In the static view of industry, the income from material agents is rent, and interest is nonexistent. If there is any thought here of the bounty of nature or of the attribute of extension, it comes in the dynamic view of industry in considering long periods. The income derived from the durable sources is always rent (in this conception), and never becomes interest; while the income from appliances which must be renewed, is sometimes rent (in short periods), but becomes interest if a period of some length be considered.

In this brief restatement and explanation is implied no adverse criticism. That this concept has a much different content from the others may make an inconsistency in an economic treatise, but not necessarily within the concept itself, which may be an improvement on those found defective. That it is a continuity concept, and that only the two extremes are in logical opposition, is not necessarily a fault. The question is, What sort of continuity is shown? The difficulty is that this concept is never thought of by business men in the conduct of practical affairs. Such a usage of terms cannot be maintained except on the most abstract plane. A terminology which does not reflect distinctions present, though perhaps but vaguely, in the minds of practical men, does not meet the requirements even of the abstracter economic theory.

Further criticism may be reserved, for the time concept is nowhere in contemporary discussion fully worked out; and it may perhaps be looked upon as an undeveloped thought suggested by the recent mode of treating costs and rent. Those goods which are worn out and renewed more or less frequently tend, in the long run, to conform (it is thought) to the cost rule, while the durable goods are independent of the cost rule. In the latter case the income is a true rent; but all the other appliances yield what appears to be a rent, if they be studied for short periods, within which their value cannot be adjusted

to their cost. This supposed relation between cost and rent
—the no-cost concept of rent—will later be given a fuller
consideration.

4.

RENT AS A GENERAL SURPLUS.

The word "rent" is frequently used of late in reference to
almost any surplus gain. For example, the term "consumer's
rent" is applied to "the excess of price which [a buyer] would be
willing to pay rather than go without [a thing], over that which he
actually does pay."[32] Rent is here not connected with any particular kind of agents, nor is it any regular form of income; but it
is merely a margin of advantage in an exchange. It must be noted
that the term is used cautiously: "It has some analogies to a rent;
but is perhaps best called simply consumer's surplus."[33]

The word is used also in connection with the "extra incomes
which are earned by extraordinary natural abilities."[34] It is said
that there is strong "cause for regarding them as of the nature of
a rent, or producer's surplus, resulting from the possession of a
differential advantage for production, freely given by nature."
Several cases are cited where the term might be misleading; and
it is said that "the greatest caution is required in the application
of the term rent to the earnings of natural ability."[35] Yet the use
is sanctioned under some circumstances.

The term "producer's surplus or rent" is used still more
broadly of the earnings of the most ordinary ability, as indicating
a surplus of pleasure to the workers above the sacrifice involved
in their work. As they are paid for the earlier hours "at a rate
sufficient to compensate them for the last and most distressing
hour," they are said to be "reaping a producer's surplus, or
rent,"[36] on the earlier hours.

Still another variation is given to the term when it is said that "a
negative rent" is "reaped" by the man who would prefer to stop
work an hour earlier, but cannot.[37] In all these cases the thought
is that an income, or share, of the product should be called a rent

whenever it represents a value greater than that which is attributable to the sacrifice that is or must be made to secure it. The rent concept has become one of surpluses found throughout the whole range of industry.

5.

EXAMINATION OF THE DOCTRINE THAT RENT DOES NOT ENTER INTO MONEY COST OF PRODUCTION, PRELIMINARY TO THE STUDY OF QUASI-RENTS.

Pervading the current treatment of rent is the thought that it is a share of the product (or an income, or the yield of a factor) which "does not enter into the cost of production." This comes to be the very essence of the rent concept. The criticism of this concept naturally divides itself into two parts, corresponding to the generally recognized double meaning of cost of production.

The term cost of production [is used] in two senses, sometimes to signify the difficulty of producing a thing, and sometimes to express the outlay of money that has to be incurred in order to induce people to overcome this difficulty and produce it.[38]

The "efforts and sacrifices" required to make the commodity are called "the real cost of production," while "the sums of money that have to be paid for these efforts and sacrifices" are called "the money cost of production, or, for shortness, the expenses of production," "or, in other words, they are the supply price."

There is no question that it is with cost in the money sense that rent is linked in the proposition above quoted.

The price of the whole produce is *determined by* the expenses, or money cost, of production on the margin of cultivation; and rent does not *enter into* cost of production.[39]

It is this doctrine which will now be examined with the view of determining what basis it affords for a concept of rent. First, let it be noted that, in viewing the money costs of production as regulating value, one is taking the individual standpoint. The costs are thought of as incurred by the undertaker when he pays out money. We are told that in studying this feature of rent "the easiest as well as the most practical course is to go straight to production for sale in a market."[40] There is no question as to how much sacrifice is involved to the laborer, to the capitalist, or to the landlord, in giving services or the use of the wealth which they control to the undertaker who pays for them. Cost of production is said to regulate or determine the value of products because, if the price is not high enough to meet these money costs, some undertakers will reduce their output, others will go out of business. *Vice versa*, if prices rise, other undertakers will be tempted into the business by the more than ordinary balance over and above expenses. In this view, everything that an undertaker pays out in order to produce a commodity would seem to be a necessary part of his costs, and, it being supposed that he is not a land-owner, rent is a part of these as much as is any other payment. The typical undertaker is supposed to rent his land, to hire his labor, and to borrow his capital. To the undertaker, be he farmer, manufacturer, or merchant, these various costs stand in just the same relation to his production. No one of them is to him a surplus, for he is paying their full value as fixed by competition in the market. The only surplus to him is a surplus of the price over and above the sum of costs entering into the product.

A consideration of these facts gives an appearance of self-evident error to the doctrine in question. It seems to be a denial of the good sense of the undertaker. It suggests the thought that those who state the doctrine have overlooked the fact that the undertaker pays rent. Indeed, it will be shown later that the idea of rent as a surplus starts with the thought of the owner who has especially good land and thus gets a surplus product;[41] but, in the argument at the stage we are now considering it, the facts above stated are fully conceded. It is said:—

The doctrines do not mean that a tenant farmer need not take his rent into account when making up his year's balance sheet. When he is doing that, he must count his rent just in the same way as he does any other expenses.[42]

This argument does not imply that a manufacturer when making up the profit and loss account of his business would not count his rent among his expenses.[43]

In making up the profit and loss account of the cultivation of land, the farmer's rent must be reckoned among his expenses.[44]

These imply also that rent must be taken into account just as any other expense in any increase of the business which involves the use of more land. The doctrine would thus seem to be given up; but it is justified by this reasoning:—

What they do mean is that, when the farmer is doubting whether it is worth his while to apply more capital and labour to the land, *then* he need not think of his rent; for he will have to pay this same rent whether he applies this extra capital and labour, or not. Therefore if the marginal produce due to this additional outlay seems likely to give him normal profits, he applies it: and his rent does not *then* enter into his calculations.[45]

It has before been assumed that it is possible to estimate the expenses of production while omitting rent; that is, "on the margin of cultivation."

That is, they are estimated for a part of the produce which either is raised on land that pays no rent because it is poor or badly situated; or, is raised on land that does pay rent, but by applications of capital and labour which only just pay their way, and therefore can contribute nothing towards the rent. It is these expenses which the demand must just cover: for if it does not, the supply will fall off, and the price will be raised till it does cover them. Those parts of the produce which yield a surplus will generally be produced even if that price is not maintained; their surplus therefore does not govern the price: while there is no surplus yielded by that portion of the produce the expenses of production of which do take direct part in governing the price. No surplus then enters into *that* (money) cost of production which gives the level at which the price of the whole supply is fixed.[46]

The last unit of product which the undertaker attempts to secure, it is said, contains no element of rent, whether it be produced on rich rent-bearing land (on the intensive margin) or on the poorest piece of land (on the extensive margin). Most stress is placed, however, on the argument as to the intensive margin; for that is present in every industry.

A number of reasons may be adduced for rejecting the doctrine that has been stated.

1. The statement that rent does not enter into the cost of production, when interpreted as has been shown, is a violation of the plain and usual meaning of the words, and one that is confessed. Nearly all the attention that has been attracted to the phrase has been due to its evident contradiction of the facts as understood by the practical man.[47] It is here justified by giving it a most unpractical meaning. It is said that, while rent is practically a part of the expenses of production at every moment of time, exactly as every other outlay is, yet in a certain logical sense it may be looked upon as not being a part. Even if the logic of this were sound, it comes very near being a quibble on words.

2. The logic by which it is shown that the undertaker need not consider as part of his expenses the rent of the last or marginal unit of product proves too much to be sound. In exactly the same way one can seem to show that interest, wages, and profits do not "enter into" the cost of production,—a *reductio ad absurdum* which has not failed to appear under the light of recent criticism.[48] Nor does this possibility escape the ingenious thinkers who hold the doctrine under criticism. Speaking of the farmer, it is said:—

The question whether he has carried his cultivation of a particular piece of land as far as he profitably can, and whether he should try to force more from it, or to take in another piece of land, is of the same kind as the question whether he should buy a new plough, or try to get a little more work out of the present stock of ploughs. . . . That part of his produce which he is in doubt whether to raise by extra use of his existing ploughs, or by introducing a new plough, may be said to be derived from a marginal use of the plough. It pays nothing *net* (*i.e.*, nothing beyond a charge for actual wear-and-tear) toward the net income earned by the plough.[49]

Again, it is said more generally of the manufacturer or trader:—

That part of this production which he just forces out of his existing appliances, being in doubt whether it would not be better worth his while to increase those appliances than to work so intensively those which he has, contributes nothing of the income which those appliances yield him. This argument says nothing as to whether the appliances were made by man, or part of a stock given by nature.[50]

When it is noted that these statements are made in connection with the thought that all material agents are capital from the standpoint of the undertaker, the conclusion seems necessary that all claims of any exceptional relation of rent to money costs, and hence to value, must be given up. But such consequences do not appear to be recognized.

To restate our argument: If it can be shown that each of the productive factors employed by an undertaker, in a certain logical sense, costs him nothing in the marginal product, it follows that no one of these factors and no one of the items of expenses is on this account in an exceptional relation to the value of the product. Either one must say that none of the undertaker's outlay "enters into" the cost of the product, which to the business man would appear to be a very Pickwickian statement, or one must say that all of them enter in just the same way, hence this can be no peculiarity of rent.

The same argument may be made to apply to each and every item of expense entering into costs. If seed, ploughs, horses, reapers, fences, barns, are used by a farmer in producing a certain crop, the amount of every item but one can be increased, and another unit or product procured, without any addition to the cost of that one item. Thus each item may be shown, with equal fallaciousness, to be no part of the cost of production of that unit of product supposed to be price-determining.

It must be borne in mind that the supposed peculiarity of rent is not made dependent on the element of time, the length of the period under consideration, but is based on reasoning applicable at any given moment, as appears above, to each and every item entering into production. By a mere logical device the actual expenses of production may be conjured away, while the burden of their payment rests with undiminished force on the shoulders of the undertaker.

3. The doctrine contradicts the conditions which it postulates. A fundamental assumption of the whole argument is that there is free competition among intelligent renters. It is assumed that the tenant who rents the land knows what the land would be worth when used in connection with the best possible proportions of other agents, and bids that amount for rent. Of course, the best proportions are relative to the general state of knowledge at the time. Under the justifiable assumption of diminishing returns with increasing applications of labor and capital, there is an ideal point at which the maximum economic result would be secured from the land, and beyond which the application of the slightest additional capital would involve a loss. It is this ideal point which every practical undertaker is striving to attain. In theoretical discussion the additional doses of capital are supposed to be infinitesimally small, as are the additional units of product. The argument under criticism assumes that a blunder has been made by the undertaker, and that it would pay to add more capital than he had counted on. But, if the rent has been really a competitive one, and the doses be considered as infinitesimally small, there must be some product secured for rent for each added unit of capital and labor up to the very last, in order that the tenant may pay the competitive rent. The last unit of product of any finite amount would contain this element of advantage, and under competition would have to pay its corresponding rent. The only product obtained, in the strict theory of the case, without paying rent, would be one unit infinitesimally small,—in plain Anglo-Saxon, would be nothing at all. No finite unit of product can be shown to be a no-rent unit in the theory of the intensive application of labor and capital with regularly diminishing returns. The concrete units are produced at varying costs for labor and interest on capital, and every one contains an element of rent. This rent is a part of the undertaker's costs, and equalizes the total costs of the various units of product; for under perfect competition he is compelled to pay it,

if he is to retain control of that quantity of land which is economically most favorable for the output he is producing.[51]

4. The marginal costs in one industry may contribute to rents in another. If it were logical in the case of any business that is paying rent to look upon certain marginal units as contributing nothing to money rent in that business, and if these units, because just paying, were considered as regulating the price of the whole supply, still is it not a begging of the question to say that a payment to rent is not a part of the money costs of the marginal unit? For the marginal units of money cost are not ultimate factors of value. They are a complex of many payments for various elements, and there is no proof that these do not contain an element of rent which must be paid if the supply of materials is to be obtained and the supply of the product is to be maintained. Some of these elements may be secured from natural resources having a high rental value: some of them, in fact, may be bought from landlords who have received them as rents in kind. So when the theorist, seeking to show that rent is not a necessary part of money costs, has eliminated the rent of the immediate product, a final answer has not been reached: the difficulty has only begun. He must again take each portion of the costs and eliminate the rent found in it, seeking, if he may, the marginal units of these marginal units, in which no troublesome element of rent is found. These complex units of cost, which are admitted to enter into the price and determine it, are thus seen to be in many cases made up in part of payments to rents, to "price-determined" things of value. They are not the homogeneous, rentless units they were assumed to be.[52]

5. Such rentless marginal units could not be considered as regulating and determining the value of the product in any causal or exceptional sense. The four preceding reasons all are in support of the view that rent is a necessary part of the expenses of any product in the same sense that any other outlay of the undertaker is. If those reasons are sound, the supposed peculiarity of rent in relation to costs is sufficiently disproved. But it may be made clearer that rent bears just the same relation to the money costs that every other outlay of the undertaker

does, if the analysis is carried one step farther to show that, if some units could justly be looked upon as rentless, they could not, except by chance, be the ones that fix the limits of supply and hence govern price, even in an abstractly logical view.[53] The marginal units of supply which it just pays the undertaker to produce may be those containing a large element of rent.

Start with the existing market price. It is determined by the market conditions at the moment. If price falls, there is a readjustment or reduction of supply because costs are not met on some units. If price rises, there is an increase of supply because other agents seek that industry. The only sense in which it is claimed that these marginal costs determine price is by their effect on supply. The marginal units produced with the poorest land (or other agents) or with the poorest powers of agents used, are assumed to be the regulative units. But neither is there practical proof of this nor is it logically evident. Any unit that is added to supply or taken from supply, because not paying at any moment, may be just as logically considered the marginal unit in determining supply. Suppose that a large fertile source of supply for wheat is newly discovered or made available. Coming into the market in large quantities, these units of product increase supply, depress price, and drive large areas of land either out of cultivation or into other industries.[54] There is a readjustment of the old sources of supply, a loss of the weaker units on the margin; but it is no causal matter, it is the effect of a change at another point. The employment in the industry and the very costs (that is, value) of these supposedly determining units are seen to be determined by other units of supply. Constantly some of the better agents are being tempted into other uses or agents yielding a high rental are brought back into the industry. Those sources of supply and units of product which have large elements of rent in them are just as effective in determining the final equilibrium of supply as any rentless units can be. The work of preserving the supply just where it will cause the price on the market to cover these costs is not left to a few rentless units along the margin. In the case of any important product it is performed by thousands of units of supply of the better agents, any one of which is ready, at the slightest change of price, to shift into or out of the industry, if thereby it can earn a greater rental. If these marginal units of supply, which it just pays the undertaker to secure, thus usually contribute to rent, rent must be said to contribute to the marginal money cost of production.

The facts above noted are admitted in the current defenses of the doctrine under discussion. It is said:—

"Each crop strives against others for the possession of the land. If any one crop shows signs of being more remunerative than before, relatively to others, the cultivators will devote more of their land and resources to it." As a result, any one crop, as oats, must pay even for the poorest land on which it is grown enough rent to hold the land from a competing use. There thus results "a modification of the classical doctrine of rent and value." "The margin of cultivation has now to be described as the margin of the profitable application of capital and labour to all land which the competition of other crops yields to oats." And this means, as it is further explained, that "the expenses of production of those oats which only just pay their way, are increased by the diversion to other crops of land which would return large crops of oats; land which would yield a good rent under them, but which yields a better rent under other crops."[55]

Let us note what effect these facts are admitted to have on the doctrine under discussion. It is admitted that marginal units in one crop, which it just pays to produce, do contain an element of money cost sufficient to pay the rent that would be earned by a competing crop, and that the demand for land in other uses raises the marginal expenses and the price. It is distinctly stated that the argument is valid for urban as well as rural land. This would seem to cover the great majority of products, and nearly all the rent that is paid for any purpose. If the rents of all competing crops *mutually* enter into each other's prices, the door has been opened quite as effectually for the entrance of rent into price as if the relation had been made more direct. It is implied, further, that, in considering this competition for the use of fertile soils, "the classical economists" are not followed. It is admitted that "it requires a modification of the amended doctrines as to rent and value," that the statement that the normal value of a single crop is determined by cost of production under the most unfavorable circumstances (that is, on land paying no rent) was incomplete in the way above noted; and, finally, it is admitted that the phrase "rent does not enter into the cost of production," when applied to a particular crop or to any particular product, "is liable to misinterpretation," should be avoided, "and its use is inexpedient."[56] The phrase, when meaning the money cost of production, never is applied except to a particular product. So the doctrine appears to be effectually discredited by its defenders. But this conclusion is rejected, and the claim is made that "it is still true that rent is not an element in those expenses of production of marginal oats to which the price of the whole conforms." It does not seem to us possible to harmonize this with the facts above admitted. The only reason given, one considered sufficient to justify the doctrine, is the one fully considered in another connection,—the logical device of a rentless unit of product.

The suggestion may be ventured that, when considering the money costs of production as regulating the supply of various goods, the marginal unit is logically the no-profit unit for the undertaker. A no-profit unit of product, moreover, is, in an abstract view of the case (that is, assuming that there has been neither blunder nor miscalculation), the last unit that can be made to earn enough in the business to pay its burden of rent, wages, and interest. The no-profit unit results from just that ideal right combination of instruments which yields the highest net product in the whole industry. No change in the proportion of the various factors could make any one of them contribute a particle more to the net result of the undertaker's profits. When money costs of production are looked at concretely, as they are by the business men, all kinds alike are essential, and all enter into the cost. If the yield of the various factors be studied by the methods of marginal product and mathematical increments, each can be considered as reaching at last a point of no-yield to the undertaker. It is this which in an empirical way the business man is striving to locate. The marginal or no-profit unit, to any undertaker, is the unit where *every factor* may be logically looked upon as having reached this point.

6. The doctrine is by logical necessity given up when land is classed as a particular form of capital from the point of view of the individual undertaker.[57] Passages have been cited in another connection[58] to show that contemporary defenders of the rent doctrine give up the attempt to distinguish between land and capital, and justify it only because of differences which are said to appear from a social standpoint. But, as has several times been pointed out in this paper, the undertaker views the payment of "rent" and "interest" in precisely the same way, as the purchase of so much productive power. All of these expenditures are, by means of the money expression, reduced to comparable and homogeneous units of money cost. All costs represent capital expended by the undertaker.

The giving up of the distinction between land and capital, when taking the business man's standpoint, involves as a consequence the giving up of the old distinction between rent and interest, when considering the money costs of production. The maintenance of the distinction and the founding upon it of an important doctrine (that of quasi-rents) can hardly be explained except as due to the survival of economic traditions, and to a failure to adjust the older and the newer thought.

The conclusion of this long series of arguments is not only that the time-honored doctrine is unsound, but that this is by logical implication repeatedly admitted by those who still formally assert its validity.

6.
THE NO-COST CONCEPT OF RENT.

The doctrine just stated, far from being rejected, is made the basis of the concept of rent which may be considered the dominant one at present among the economists of England and America. On the assumption that the doctrine has been proved, this peculiar relation to value is made the essence of the rent concept; and all the incomes which are thought to share this peculiarity are classed as rent. It is explained that the "incomes derived from appliances for production made by man" are called quasi-rents, "partly because (in short periods) the stock of them has to be regarded as *temporarily* fixed," but essentially, as is stated in the next sentence, because "for the time they hold nearly the same relation to the price of the things which they take part in producing, as is held by land or any other free gift of nature, of which the stock is *permanently* fixed; and whose net income is a true rent."[59]

In such cases the incomes from improvements on land "do not take direct part in determining the price of the produce, but rather depend on them" *(sic)*.[60] Hence these incomes are called quasi-rents; that is, of the nature of rent. The point repeatedly insisted upon is that the mark of rent or of quasi-rent is that it does not "enter directly into the marginal cost of production."[61] In this concept rent is an income that is "a result and not a cause of selling price."[62] Rent is a share, or an income, that does not correspond to a cost which must be met if the supply of the product is to be maintained. The expression "a cause of selling price" means the same as "enters into the cost of production." Instead of a sharp classification of *sources* of income, as was involved in the original concept of rent, there is here presented a continuity classification of the incomes themselves, ranging from those at the one extreme, which never enter into the cost of production, in a continuous series to those which do not enter when very short periods are considered, but do enter at any other time. At the head of the series are the free gifts of nature, whose supply is said to be fixed, and likewise must be logically the incomes flowing from the possession of strictly unreproducible articles, as masterpieces of art, autographs, though these are not mentioned: all such are true rents. At various points along the scale come the incomes from appliances made by man, the supply of which can be renewed or increased in varying periods of time.

The attempt will now be made to show that this concept of rent as the no-cost income, and the doctrine of quasi-rents connected with it, involve a number of fallacies; that they are radically out of harmony with the principles just criticized, on which they are supposed to rest; and that they grow out of a confusion between the two sets of ideas enumerated in parallel columns, as follows:—

1. Between the undertaker   and the owner.
2.   "   undertaker's cost   "   owner's income.
3.   "   production of the good   "   production of the appliance.
4.   "   money cost   "   real cost.
5.   "   the individual   "   the social standpoint.

1. The undertaker's *vs.* the owner's standpoint.

As we have seen, the consideration of money costs of production and their relation to the value of goods compels the adoption of the undertaker's standpoint. The costs of goods act on their value, so far as they do it at all, through the medium of the undertakers, who adjust supply according to the price. We have maintained that in so doing they must count the rent of land precisely as they do any other item; while the doctrine here criticized seems to be that, just as the undertakers need not count their rent, so they need not count any other items of expense, for not one of them enters into the cost of production in short periods. Such a *reductio ad absurdum* must cause the no-cost doctrine to be renounced; but the conclusion is escaped because the thought has passed on from the undertaker and his burden of costs, and his constant endeavor to adjust supply to the price, and has gone over to the owner of the appliances of production.

2. Undertaker's cost *vs.* owner's income.

This shift of thought is evident in the first paragraph of the chapter on quasi-rents. It is said that

The farmer pays "rent" to his landlord [this is rent as undertaker's cost] without troubling himself to distinguish how much of the annual net value of his land is due to the free gifts of nature and how much ... to improvement.

In the next sentence the shift to rent as the owner's income is made:—

Now the income derived from . . . appliances of production made by man have really something analogous to true rents. . . . For the time they hold nearly the same relation to the price of things which they take part in producing, as is held by land.[63]

Every item of outlay by the undertaker may be viewed from two sides: to the undertaker it is always a money cost, and never an income; to the one who receives it[64] in payment for labor or the use of appliances it is always a part of income, and never a money cost. Now, in the chapter[65] on quasi-rents, after the first sentence, the discussion is all of incomes: "the incomes from buildings," "the net incomes from appliances for production already made may be called their quasi-rents," "the extra income derived from improvements that have been made in the land by its individual owner,"—these are a few of a large number of expressions showing that the payment is not looked upon as a money cost, but as an owner's income. This helps us to understand how it is possible to say that none of the shares are money costs: it is an unannounced and doubtless unconscious shift to a quite different conception.

In this connection it may be suggested that the idea that rent is not a part of undertaker's costs originated in just this fallacy. Here *no* share of the produce is a cost, because all are viewed as owner's income: there rent is not a cost, because for the moment it is assumed that the undertaker is an owner and has no rent to pay. The thought appears at the beginning of the chapter on Rent in these words:—

When a person is in an advantageous position for any branch of production, he is likely to obtain a "producer's surplus,"—that is, a benefit in excess of what is required to remunerate him for his immediate outlay. This surplus is likely to exist when he produces for his own consumption, as much as when he produces for sale.[66]

It requires no argument to prove that this is a surplus only to the owner, and that competition keeps it from being a surplus to the undertaker and makes it a cost. So that, if the standpoint of money costs be held consistently, almost the exact opposite of the usual statement must be made. Instead of rent being to the undertaker a "surplus above costs," it is essentially that payment which, as a part of costs, prevents the undertaker from getting any surplus which can be attributed to the rented agents.

3. Production of the commodity *vs.* production of the appliance.

The changes just noted involve a change of thought also from the production of the commodity in question to that of the production of the appliances. The things these appliances take part in producing are still spoken of, but the interest is indirect. In the case of the production of the commodity, the undertaker pays what he is forced to in each case for the agents of production "without troubling himself" about their origin. The period within which the supply affects price is that within which appliances can be diverted from one use to another. Here, however, the price of commodities is supposed to remain unchanged until new appliances can be brought into existence, tempted by the higher income: the period considered important is that within which the supply of "improvements" or of "means of production" can be increased. Their (real) cost is thought of as reflected on in the price of the goods; but let it be noted in passing that this can never raise, it can only lower the price, through increased supply. Only occasionally is it impossible to divert some of the existing appliances almost immediately to other uses with greater or less ease, so that the period sufficient to increase the supply of the commodity rarely is the same as that needed for creating new appliances. When the relation of money costs to the price of commodities was talked of, it was with reference to their influence in increasing or decreasing the supply of the various commodities: when the relation of owner's income to prices is talked of, it is with reference to the effect they will have in increasing or decreasing the supply of available appliances. The undertaker reaps his unexpected profit when the price of his product suddenly rises, and he has either a large stock of it or has contracts out for the materials, so that he can get a large margin between costs and price by producing quickly and more cheaply than his new competitors. The owner reaps an unexpected income when his appliances are suddenly in greater demand. The case to test what the effect is of a relatively fixed supply of appliances on the undertaker's costs is that where he has no standing contract for materials when the increased demand for the product arises; and here can be seen most clearly that money costs do enter into price. The value of the appliance for the time limited would rise, its owner would get an increased income, and the undertaker must meet increased costs if he is to continue to produce the article.

4. Money cost *vs.* real cost.

All of these shifts of thought seem to be traceable to the perennial source of error,—the confusion of money costs and real costs. In speaking of the cost of the undertaker, it is usually money cost; in speaking of cost to the one whom the undertaker pays, whether he be a laborer, capitalist, or land-owner, it is real cost that is meant. In the quasi-rent discussion this error is palpable. It is said that

for periods that are long in comparison with the time needed to make improvements of any kind, and bring them into full operation, the net incomes derived from them are but the price required to be paid for the efforts and sacrifices of those who make them. . . . But in short periods . . . these incomes may be regarded as quasi-rents which do not take direct part in determining the price of the produce, but rather depend on them.[67]

Here all the points are combined. It is the owner's income, the supply of improvements, and the cost in the form of effort and sacrifice which must be met. There is no hint of the thought that even in the shortest periods the payment that is income to the owner must be a cost to the undertaker. So throughout "the free gift of nature" is said to yield an income that is not a cost. The "made appliances" have cost "effort and sacrifice," which is no more than enough to remunerate the owner. This is the very heart of the quasi-rent doctrine,—the thought that there is a difference in the cost which must be undergone to bring into existence different productive agents. Some are free gifts, and involve no cost (sacrifice): others are made by man, and cost

effort. It is not clearly seen and borne in mind that money costs
have no correspondence with these, but are merely the market
value of the agents of which a producer makes use.

Here mention may be made of a troublesome fallacy in the
very definition of land as "the free gifts of nature." If it is defined
in this way, man cannot increase land by his efforts; for it is then
not land, not being a free gift. Everything to which man has
given the slightest effort becomes capital. But, if land be taken in
the usual practical sense, as the earth and the materials it affords, whether difficult to get at or not, it is evident that most
kinds of land can be secured with varying degrees of difficulty.
All economists drop into this conception sooner or later.[68] In this
sense, land has a supply price, just as any other good has. The
supply is increased when the price is sufficient to meet the
money costs in the same practical sense in which this is said of
other things. This is plainly admitted when it is said that

the supply of fertile land cannot be adapted quickly to the demand for
it, and therefore the income derived from it may diverge permanently
much from normal profits on the cost of preparing it for cultivation.[69]

5. The individual *vs.* the social standpoint.

The distinction between the individual and the social views of
land, on which much stress is laid by contemporary economists,
rests on the recognition of the two points of view indicated. By
individual point of view is meant that of the undertaker who
considers money costs. By the point of view of society is meant
apparently that of owners in general, who are considered as
expending effort, making sacrifices, incurring real costs, in the
increase of productive appliances. This distinction is made
repeatedly,[70] and it must be noted that it is fatal to anything but a
"real cost" conception of rent. If land is but a particular form of
capital to the undertaker, then there is no difference between
rent and interest as money costs to the undertaker. It is only
when real costs are considered that there is any difference to
note. Now real costs are very little considered in practical business under a money economy. As they are not capable of

mathematical expression, they are dismissed pretty effectually from any discussion of practical business problems, of rent in its relation to market values, and from the economist's analysis of industry. It is difficult to see how the conclusion can be evaded that the distinction still insisted on in current discussion between rent and other shares of industry as they affect value, and the quasi-rent doctrine itself, [rests] on a confusion of these two essentially different conceptions.

7.
REVIEW AND CONCLUSION.

This paper has been mainly critical and negative, yet some positive results may appear in glancing over the ground that has been traversed.

(1) The land concept, the first of the rent concepts, was one that rested on a classification of material things. When anything had been classified as land, it followed that the income from its use was rent.

(2) The extension, or space relation, concept is an attempt to escape some of the difficulties of this classification by narrowing the concept of land to those properties only which were assumed to be neither increasable nor destructible. The fertile qualities of soil, the many destructible and removable material elements, would thus be classified as capital, even though they had not been produced by man. This concept is hardly more than suggested. It is not fully developed by any author.[71]

(3) Next in logical order is the one we reserved for the last and fullest treatment, the no-cost concept. It originates unquestionably from the land concept, in the thought that free gifts have no "real" cost, and, therefore, the material services rendered by them do not involve a cost. The application of this notion to rents has two phases, separately considered above. First, by an error of reasoning, the idea that rent is a surplus and not a "real" cost to the owner of land is carried over to the undertaker; and rent is assumed not to be a money cost to him.

So strongly does this notion take root that, when reasons are sought, a very evident fallacy is taken as convincing. It is then assumed that the reason why rent does not enter into the cost of goods is that land cannot be increased in quantity (though this was not the reason that had been given),[72] and the same relation to cost must be found in anything else that is fixed in supply. Here the land concept is subordinated; and land is thought to yield a rent only because it has no cost of production, and does not enter into the cost of production of commodities.

(4) The time concept is but a variation of this. It takes time to increase the stock of productive agents, and an income from any agent is to be considered rent when brief periods are considered; for within that period, it is assumed, rent does not enter into the money costs of the commodities.

(5) The exchanger's surplus concept is merely a loose extension of the thought that any surplus may be looked upon as rent, any gain which does not involve a real sacrifice. It abandons the idea that rent is a regularly accruing income. It is carelessly thought out, and nevertheless has found its way into wide and reckless use during this period of psychological economics.

One feature marks all these concepts: it is the inclusion of land, the "free gift of nature." In the land concept it is the very essence. The extension concept is narrowed to those of these gifts which are deemed to be fixed in supply: in the other three, land becomes only one of many things which yield at one time or another a rent, yet it remains the typical rent, the "true rent," the "rent proper," because it is the one thing that is looked upon as unvarying in supply and incapable of increase. Yet this common feature does not bind these various concepts together into a consistent series: it does not make them mere variations of one another. In the land concept and in the no-cost concept, for example, there are essentially different central thoughts. Within the later concept, land is included merely because it is one of many things which are found to have the rent character.

The golden rule of the critic of art, never to judge a picture by its defects, may perhaps be adapted to the criticism of economic theory. The errors, if they be such, in the work of the distin-

guished economist from whom we have quoted, are inherited
from the past. There is not one of them without a history. They
merely become evident in their statement along with the newer
ideas. In that which is most characteristic, original, and positive
in his work, Professor Marshall has left the old concept of rent
far behind. The logical consequence of his treatment is that all
the division fences between the different sorts of material wealth
have been levelled; and rent is the income of any material agent,
when static problems, practical business rent, and the money
aspects of production are under discussion. And this is a service
of high order to economic thought.

The main conclusions of this paper may be summed up in
these statements:—

The old concept of rent is passing; it is not being undermined
by attacks of the old sort, by those who do not seek to understand
it; but it is now abandoned in all but form by those who represent
the most conservative wing of economic thought.

The various new concepts considered are imperfect and
unsuccessful efforts to escape the difficulties of the older view.

The use of the term "rent" for any surplus above "real" cost is
out of harmony with the conception of rent as a regularly accruing income, and with the practical needs of a money economy in
which the concept must be employed.

The doctrine of quasi-rents, involving the idea that no income,
or share, enters into market prices in short periods, cannot
stand. On the other hand, the recognition that there is no difference in short periods between land and other wealth in relation to market values is a great advance.

The relation which rare and not easily producible appliances
have to market price over long periods of time is of just the
opposite character from that asserted. The less capable of increase particular appliances are, the greater income they yield,
the more therefore it "enters into price" as the demand for their
products increases.

The need for a new concept of rent which will evade the
difficulties of the old is evident.[73] The way is prepared for it by
the break-down of the old and the patent difficulties of the

substitutes that have been presented.

NOTES

1. P. 150. References are to the fourth edition, 1898.
2. Pp. 213, 220.
3. P. 628.
4. A number of these are noted in the article on "Recent Discussion of the Capital Concept" in this journal for November, 1900 [cf. 33-73].
5. P. 220. He adds, however, that "there is a scientific principle underlying the distinction, which is the fixity of the supply of utilities connected with land." This is discussed below, p. 322.
6. Pp. 223, 224. The indestructible properties are said to be robbed!
7. P. 233.
8. P. 144.
9. P. 492.
10. P. 493.
11. Pp. 607-8.
12. P. 494.
13. P. 717.
14. P. 144.
15. P. 493.
16. P. 478, note.
17. P. 494. See other examples, pp. 714, 760, 765. Note also the point discussed below, p. 327.
18. *E.g.*, p. 608, where this view is taken.
19. P. 220.
20. P. 221.
21. Pp. 224, 225.
22. Pp. 220-1.
23. See above, pp. 319, 322.
24. P. 501.
25. *Ibid.*
26. P. 233.
27. P. 504.
28. Preface, p. x.
29. P. 489.
30. Especially pp. 489-499.
31. P. 496.
32. P. 199.

33. *Ibid.* See also the diagram of producer's and consumer's rent, p. 521.

34. P. 661.

35. P. 663.

36. P. 598.

37. P. 599, notes.

38. P. 418, note.

39. P. 477. This is shown by many other passages; *e.g.,* pp. 418, 423, 426, 428, 430, 431, 433, 473, 477, 561, 608.

40. P. 476.

41. See below, pp. 345-346.

42. P. 478.

43. P. 486.

44. P. 487.

45. P. 478.

46. P. 477.

47. See recognition of this, p. 482, note.

48. This point has been noted, doubtless quite independently, by Mr. H. M. Thompson, in *The Theory of Wages* (1892), pp. 49-80; by Mr. J. A. Hobson, *The Economics of Distribution* (1900), pp. 113-159; and by Professor J. B. Clark, *The Distribution of Wealth* (1899), pp. 354-365.

49. P. 492.

50. P. 493.

51. It is not intended to call in question the worth of the mathematical method of increments in economic studies, but only the correctness of this particular application of it.

52. This argument, if sound, invalidates the theory of distribution and the terminology presented by Dr. C. W. Macfarlane in *Value and Distribution* (1899).

53. P. 477.

54. Adam Smith, noting such facts, stated a doctrine opposed to that under criticism, saying that the most fertile coal and silver mines regulate the price of the whole supply. *Wealth of Nations*, Book I., chap. xi., Part II. This is equally unwarranted.

55. Pp. 481, 482. The thought is further illustrated, p. 487.

56. See pp. 481-483, *passim.*

57. P. 492.

58. P. 419.

59. P. 489. The italics are Professor Marshall's.

60. P. 491.

61. Pp. 419, 498.

62. P. 495.

63. P. 489.

64. If he be not merely another undertaker through whose hands the thing has passed and who must pass on to others a part of the price as part of his costs.

65. P. 489, Book V., chap. ix.

66. P. 476.

67. P. 491.

68. *E.g.*, p. 220.

69. P. 494.

70. See above, pp. 319-321.

71. Besides Professor Marshall, already cited, see Professor J. R. Commons's interesting and ingenious presentation of this idea in *The Distribution of Wealth* (1893), pp. 27-41.

72. See above, pp. 321-326.

73. It need hardly be said that a notable essay in the direction here indicated is the concept presented by Professor J. B. Clark.

Landed Property as an Economic Concept and as a Field for Research— Discussion

With the larger purpose of Professor Ely's valuable paper, I am in entire agreement. I would reserve judgment on a few of the minor statements, and I would express dissent on only one perhaps not very important point. The title appears to be somewhat of a misnomer. Landed property is not an economic concept, but a juristic one. The various classes of land mentioned in the paper are partly physical, partly technological, partly juristic, and only in small part economic. Of course the geological, topographical, and chemical qualities of soil, all have economic bearings, but primarily such classifications are not economic. It would, of course, be possible to correct or adjust this terminology without affecting the main purposes of the leading paper.

The two main aspects of the paper are the theoretical concept of land and the social policy of land tenure. The latter is perhaps more interesting but I will leave that to be discussed by the agricultural economists who are to follow me, and shall limit my discussion to the theoretical aspect of the question.

The largest theoretical proposition presented, the great truth, is that land as an economic category is not simple or unified. It

Reprinted from *American Economic Review,* Supp. 7 (March 1917). The paper to which Fetter refers is by Richard T. Ely and is entitled "Landed Property as an Economic Concept and as a Field of Research" (ibid., pp. 18-33). Other discussants included E. Dana Durand, B. H. Hibbard, Roy G. Blakey, R. R. Bowker, and John A. Ryan (ibid., 36-47).

never has been, is not now, and cannot be, a truly scientific concept. Science only in its cruder stages has to do with the classification of concrete objects. As the truly scientific stage is reached, the concern of the thinker is with the qualities and aspects of things, rather than with the concrete objects themselves.

Consider the different things that are called land. The concept land includes nearly all of our material environment. What common character have a tract of desert sand, an Iowa farm, a forest, an iron mine, a coal mine, a mountain side, attractive for residence because of the beautiful scenery, a waterfall, or a shore line suitable for docks and terminal facilities for railways? For what possible purpose could these different kinds of material things be grouped together into one logical economic category and contrasted with the economic agents? Ricardo from the first failed in his attempt to do so; his doctrine was limited to the use of soil for agriculture. He did not know what to do with the other kinds of land under his rent law. He took Adam Smith to task for using the expression "the rent of mines"; then he used that phrase as the heading of his own next chapter. He said never a word about urban sites. We must recall that at that time the reason for the rent of land was assured to be the peculiar chemical qualities of the soil used for the production of food. The modern conception of a general principle of proportionality in the use of economic agents seems not to have been glimpsed. Professor Ely's discussion ably shows that there is no final resting point in the analysis of the land concept until we come to the concept of the separable uses of material things.

But it may be said that the distinction between land and capital by the older economists was not made with respect to the *purposes* for which agents of production were used, but with respect to their *origin*, their naturalness, or artificiality. Observe that the older grouping of concrete goods into land and capital was not a continuity classification of goods which have more or less of artificiality. Land and capital were sharply defined and contrasted. Those goods which were called natural were treated (or were supposed to be treated) under the land and rent concept, and those that were artificial were treated under the capital concept. The material of everything in the world was once "natural." When did it become "artificial?" At what moment did the bit of iron ore, the piece of coal, the piece of wood, the piece of "land," miraculously become capital? Was it at the first touch of man's hand? Then is every cultivated bit of land artificial, and by that token is capital? This difficulty was recognized by J. S. Mill and troubled him greatly. But at this point the answer is given that the iron ore becomes capital when it is removed from the land while the land surface remains. Here the reason assigned for distinguishing capital from land is changed from artificiality to transportability. We have not time to discuss this further as a theoretical question. It has been already sufficiently threshed out,[1] and there can be no doubt as to the verdict to be rendered.

No wonder then, that many economists have lost their faith in the old Ricardian theory of rent and the land concept. This accounts in large measure for the great dissatisfaction among many teachers with the status of economic theory. The Ricardian theory of distribution having broken down, the economists of the older school are left without any unifying philosophy of economics such as is given by a general theory of distribution.

The theoretical aspect and the social-policy aspect of the land question are closely connected in thought. At whichever end we begin to study land we find ourselves necessarily approaching, after a time, the other aspect. Professor Ely was primarily interested in the social reform aspects of the land question. He has done a service in pointing out that the crudity and lack of logic of the old land concept is one of the great obstacles in the way of a better understanding of the practical problems involved in legislation in respect to the subject of property in land.

NOTE

1. See the discussion on "The Relations between Rent and Interest," still significant, though now appearing in some respects undeveloped, at the New Orleans meeting, 1903, *Publications*, Third Series, Vol. V.

Comment on Rent under Increasing Returns

A reawakening interest in problems of theory has been evidenced in recent years by an increasing number of thoughtful essays in the leading economic journals. Several articles and communications in the last number of the REVIEW present a good American example; but the tendency since the war is probably world-wide. Even in Germany, so long under the domination of a historical school most inhospitable to the logical, formative type of theory, may be seen renewed efforts to attain more generalized, logical statements of economic truths. Professor Adolph Weber of the University of Munich in the preface to his systematic text has recently expressed his full agreement with H. Herkner in the belief that the understanding of economic relationships is best to be attained by a timely rebirth of the methods and doctrines of the classical economists. Weber adds that "Herkner makes this confession at the end of his self-biography (in 1924), which he himself calls 'the life of a socialist of the chair,' and therefore it comes out of a camp in which for decades many of our best minds have felt compelled to combat the classicists with passionate zeal." Interpreted in the light of well-known circumstances in Germany, this is not a plea for the revival in its details of an antique Ricardianism, but rather is evidence of the growing influence of the Austrian psychological school which the German historical economists long embraced in one sweeping condemnation of every attempt to utilize deductive, logical and formative methods of study.

Reprinted from *American Economic Review* 20 (March 1930). The comments refer to a paper by Albert Benedict Wolfe entitled "Rent under Increasing Returns," *American Economic Review* 19 (December 1929): 580-604.

The article in the December REVIEW on "Rent under Increasing Returns" serves a useful purpose at this time in stimulating interest in the older rent doctrine. That grim ghost still is "doomed to stalk the night till the foul deeds done in its days of nature are burned and purged away." But, despite the earnest and laudable purpose of the article in question, it may contribute to further misunderstanding if it is accepted uncritically and without amendment.

Its thesis is perhaps best expressed in its final sentence: "It may be questioned whether theory has not assumed a more invariable and certain relation between rent and diminishing returns than the facts entirely justify" (p. 604). More specifically, the article denies what "most textbooks state that rent does not emerge until the point of diminishing returns . . . . is reached, and thereby imply that rent does emerge immediately that point is passed" (p. 581).

The results arrived at in this article are presented modestly as "of doubtful applicability to actual conditions in a settled and mature country," but as probably having a "practical bearing" under the conditions that will be necessitated by an "indefinitely continued growth of world population."

However, a careful reading of the article raises doubts as to even these very qualified claims, inasmuch as the results seem to be deduced from mutually contradictory assumptions, and from a mistaken interpretation of some of the very essentials of the doctrine that the author is seeking merely to revise in minor details. Let us consider the treatment in the article: first, of cost on the marginal no-rent land, and secondly, of the concept of increasing returns. The one question relates to the interpretation of the most valid feature of the Ricardian doctrine, the other to certain points of more modern theory.

(1) In the classical rent doctrine, cost (which Professor Wolfe not inaptly prefers to call input) is always held to equal, or to absorb, the *whole* product on the no-rent land. The Ricardian rent doctrine was really a study in the valuation of complementary agents by the residual method; the costs on the rent land

being reckoned from those on the no-rent land where there was no surplus above costs—on the marginal land, as it has been called recently. But in the article before us it is at once (see Figure 3) assumed as a fixed condition that the B land is and remains free, or no-rent, land and at the same time that no matter how intensive the cultivation or how large the surplus product, each dose of "input" (cost) continues to absorb (or equal in value) less than the product on the free land. When cultivation extends to and stops at 5 doses on the B land, as is assumed, total return, according to the illustrative table (p. 584), is 50 units of product, costs are only 25 units (5 doses each equal to 5 units of product), and there is a surplus over input of 25 units of product. The author repeatedly indicates such a situation as a possible and conceivable static equilibrium. But is this true? If B is free land, there can be no surplus product (physical or value) above input except on the extreme condition that the product itself is a free good, and in that case evidently there would be no rent on the A land or on any other. If B land is free when cultivated with 5 doses of input, then, in a static equilibrium, the input would have a value of 10 units of product per dose and absorb all the product of 50 units on B, and similar agents would "cost" 10 units a dose if bought for use on A (and a similar "opportunity" cost).

The erroneous method yields equally bad results as applied to the A land in its interrelation with the B land. A fleeting glimpse of the truth is given in the following words (p. 584): "If there were no free land productive enough to yield a surplus over expense of input, tract A would be given 16 doses of input." That is in accord with a feature of the old Ricardian rent doctrine frequently misunderstood in the old days, *viz.*, it is not necessary to have an *extensive* margin of no-rent land from which to measure the rent on good land; an intensive margin of no profit on additional doses of input is an equally effective no-rent margin. Professor Hollander away back in 1895 (*Quarterly Journal of Economics*, vol. ix, p. 175) corrected this then current misunderstanding. But immediately after the recognition above that cultivation on the A land (logically) stops at the point where additional costs produce no surplus above the added costs (and not until then), the argument turns to the assumption that "since land B is free, cultivation of A" stops at 13 doses, although the accompanying table shows that the total net surplus above costs on A can be maximized by going on to the fifteenth (or sixteenth) dose.

The error just noted is magnified in elaborate tables, calculations and diagrams (pp. 585-596), by which it is made to appear that under certain conditions, when the individual cultivator employs the equivalent of 13 doses, he will apply eight of them on the A land yielding a rent, and five on B, free land (p. 596). Observe that this all relates to what an individual will do in adapting himself to a general rent level and situation determined by broad, general forces beyond his control. This leaves the cultivation stopping (see Table III) where an additional dose of input (claiming 5 units of product) would yield 11.5 units of product on A and 12 units of product on B. The absurdity lies not in the slight inequality between the two surpluses— that is probably a mere accident of the arbitrarily chosen figures—but in the lack of correspondence at the margins in both cases between the inputs (costs) and the products.

At this point (p. 596), the true limiting factor being lost to sight, the curious suggestion is made that the rent on A is determined by the difference between the gross product which could be secured by first, distributing between A and B the 13 doses of input, and secondly, applying all 13 doses of input upon B (to wit, 164 minus 107, leaving 57). But this assumes a most irrational procedure and two errors. First, if B is really free land, then the 5 doses of input applied to it must have a value of, or be rewarded by, the whole physical product, that is, each dose by 10 units of product. Call this, if you will, the marginal valuation of input doses. If, then, 8 doses of input (costing 80 units of product) are used on A to secure a total return of 114, the remainder, 34, is the surplus on the better land and indicates the maximum possible rent under these conditions. It is still another error in this connection to assume, as is done, that if all the 13 doses were used on B land they would be applied intensively on one piece and give a gross product of only 107 units; whereas

Table I, containing the assumed data, shows that by spreading the 13 doses of input over two pieces of free land (6½ doses on each or 6 and 7 respectively) an average return of 10.3 units per dose or a total of 134 units of products could be secured.

(2) The second great source of difficulty in the argument is that elusive term "increasing returns." In the history of economic thought increasing returns (also its converse, decreasing returns) has been conceived of chiefly in connection with long-time dynamic changes in the whole national economy, accompanying changes in the state of the arts, etc., and in the pressure of population— long thus intimately related with the Malthusian doctrine. But sometimes ambiguously it has been used in connection also with the smaller problem of a single enterprise and the static situation in which the user of agents (tenant of land) seeks individually to adjust the proportion of the factors which he controls to the larger situation and equilibrium of which he is an almost negligible part. The former, a social welfare concept, is on historical and logical grounds, the better—indeed the only defensible usage in the study of rent levels. The other pertains only to the problem of individual profit. Professor Wolfe, if he is aware of this alternative, prefers and follows the second meaning and (as above indicated) is concerned throughout his discussion with this smaller problem of the individual enterpriser who is trying to adjust his own operations as best he can to a prevailing norm, or to improve upon it, and who, when he succeeds, gets the maximum profit from his agents. In this epoch of still divided and ambiguous usage of terms, an author is of course within his rights and still has respectable company when he thus chooses; but his choice entails certain illogical consequences now pretty generally recognized.

Some of these results appear in connection with the treatment of incremental and average returns in the article before us. It is said (p. 580) that "most writers mean by the phrase 'diminishing returns' diminishing average returns," though, as is added critically, "some do not take the trouble to say what they mean." This statement, in which "returns" pretty evidently refers to individual profit-returns, is doubtless right. The sufficient explanation of the preference for average rather than incremental lies in this simple fact, that in any comparison between two average returns resulting from the use of one dose more or less of input, there is contained and expressed all that is significant of an incremental nature. The question which the individual cultivator has to decide is not whether another dose of input will give a gross result greater or less than did a preceding dose, but whether it will increase the gross result by more than the amount (or value) of the added dose of input. If it thus gives any net gain, it is economically justified. Most of the comparisons in the article between the gross results of successive increments of input are thus beside the mark. As Ricardianism they are unorthodox, and as marginalism they are misconceived.

A crucial difficulty in the article is thus in the way of thinking of the alternative choices of levels of returns as giving increasing returns. The author professes to be using the terms "successive," etc., in a logical and not a time sense (p. 581). He declares that in his analysis he is assuming "static conditions." But the various average and incremental returns in all the invented tables and in the figures could not possibly exist contemporaneously. The moment that a new general rent level is reached (in imagination or in reality) as a result of technological changes causing a different proportion of input to be generally the more economic, the other points and levels become impossible choices for the individual. To think otherwise is an error of interpretation of marginal valuation curves once almost universal, and still common. It is involved in the notion of consumers' and producers' surpluses. Here it is erroneous to think of each dose of input beyond the first as having a separable amount of returns. When, say, 8 doses are used in combination, no single dose has the separate or distinctive return that it had when used separately, but only its *pro rata* now of the new total return. Moreover, in the problem treated in this article, the most profitable mode of use by an individual of a valuable (rent bearing) agent, the rent—either as contractual or as an alternative valuation—is a part of the "costs" of the cultivator, as is now conceded by neo-Ricardian enlightened economists such as Marshall and Taussig. Truly competitive rent implies the use of land by methods and to the degree of intensiveness abreast of current technology and practice. That being so, the attempt of the individual to use only 7 or 6 or fewer doses when 8 was the proper or best dosage, would simply mean loss or utter bankruptcy. These options do not exist in fact or in sound theory. The answer that Professor F. M. Taylor would give, which appears to be fairly stated (p. 596), is conceded by Professor Wolfe to be "in pure static theory . . . . unassailable." In seeking to weaken its force, he patently shifts to dynamic conditions which are not those of the problem he has been discussing. In sum, the static increasing returns, the effects of which upon rent it is the purpose of the article to elucidate, have no existence excepting in the whimsical sense of the correction by an enterpriser of successive costly blunders. This has been accepted doctrine in the newer theory for well-nigh a third of a century.

In the preceding comments Professor Wolfe's use of the word "rent" as the yield or income merely from agricultural land has been followed, although I cannot but look upon such a conception as passé in the light of a past generation of constructive criticism in this field. Can it now be doubted that the idea of a most profitable proportion of complementary inputs is equally applicable to all kinds of agents, or that the most useful aspect of the old rent concept is applicable as well to the durative separable uses of any kind of goods? I trust therefore that no reader will infer from certain expressions above, regarding the consistent interpretation of Ricardian doctrine, that I mean to signify my own adherence to it. *Gott bewahre!*

Rent

RENT. The word *rente* occurred in old French of the twelfth century, derived from the vulgar Latin *rendita*, from *reddita*, meaning return or yield. In the same century it occurred in English in the sense of an item of revenue or income (Oxford Dictionary). With varied spellings and shades of meaning it has been used in all the modern European languages ever since. Still today in the law "the word . . . may be generally defined as a compensation or return" (*Corpus juris*). In popular speech it is now, and possibly always has been, used generally as the sum paid for the hire of anything to be returned in the same physical form, as tools, machinery, houses and so forth. Both in economics and in law, however, the word has been most frequently associated with the payment for the use of land, especially of agricultural land; and Alfred Marshall's basic definition is representative of widespread economic usage: "the income derived from the ownership of land and other free gifts of nature is called rent." It is true that Marshall adds: "the economist must stretch it much further," leaving the reader in doubt as to his exact meaning. In law the technical sense of the word is said to be "the compensation received by a landlord for the use of land leased" (*Corpus juris*).

This association, both in economics and in law, of rent with income derived from land resulted from the shifting of a more generic meaning to a specific use which happened to be most frequent in practise. Throughout the Middle Ages the cases of fixed contractual income which most often came before the courts in such matters as settlement of estates, and in modern times those which have attracted the attention of economic students were derived from landed property. A similar result of

Reprinted from *Encyclopedia of the Social Sciences*, s.v. "Rent."

habit seems to account for the more recent peculiar use of *rentes* in French in the sense of incomes from investments in the consolidated governmental debt, *rentier* thus denoting a person who lives from the proceeds of coupons on public bonds. The use of rent in the special sense of an income derived from land while the more general meaning has persisted still contributes, no doubt, to the confusion of the whole concept.

English writers from the sixteenth to the eighteenth century used the word rent as meaning "interest" on a loan which is "only Rent for Stock," as Sir Dudley North said (*Discourses upon Trade*, London 1691), and also in the more special sense of an income from land. Repeatedly too they touched upon the relationship between commerce and land values and the rents of agricultural land. The history of the modern rent doctrine, however, as essentially connected with land may be said to begin midway in the eighteenth century. Although the French physiocrats centered their whole system of the *ordre naturel* about land and its peculiar powers, they preferred to call the yield, or the income, from land not rent but the *produit net*, the "disposable revenue" or "the current price of leases." But the physiocratic conceptions of the three main classes in the nation, of the supposed exclusive power of land to yield a surplus above labor costs and of the assumed non-shifting quality of taxes on cultivated land doubtless influenced English economic thought in the period of Ricardo and subsequently.

Adam Smith's views on rent were far less affected by his physiocratic contemporaries than were those of English economists a generation later, for Smith saw in the magic power of division of labor rather than in the powers of land the bountiful source of the wealth of nations. His preliminary analysis of the price of commodities into its "component parts" of wages of labor, profits of stock and rent of land was much in the spirit of the psychological school of a century later. His further treatment of rent nevertheless was the most confused and unsatisfactory part of his imperfect scheme of value and distribution. He groped for a "natural rate" of rent as well as of wages and of profits but got no further than the suggestion that it is the "ordinary or average rate of rent, which is regulated . . . partly by the general circumstances of the society or neighborhood in which the land is situated, and partly by the natural or the improved fertility of the land"—a solution satisfying to the most eclectic mind. He then attempted to find a line of distinction between one class of "produce of land (food) which always affords and necessarily affords some rent to the landlord," and other sorts of produce which sometimes may and sometimes may not, according to circumstances (mentioning as examples fur, wool, stone, coal, wood and a variety of other natural materials). He glimpsed the modern conception of marginality in the latter case but ignored it in the former. The easy disproof of this hazy doctrine of the two classes of products helped to convince the Ricardians of their superiority over Smith and to confirm their belief in their own false views of land rent.

Adam Smith's inexact ideas of a bare subsistence as the natural wage and of the power of land ordinarily to "produce a greater quantity of food than what is sufficient to maintain all the labour necessary for bringing it to market" bloomed into the Malthusian principle of population near the close of the century (1798). The peculiar circumstances of the next two decades, with continued war, excessive taxation, curtailment of food imports, unprecedented prices for wheat in England and inflated agricultural rents, served to magnify to abnormal importance the subjects of population growth and land rents. The so-called Ricardian doctrine of rent was independently formulated by several other writers—West, Malthus, Torrens and others between 1813 and 1815—when wheat prices were at their peak. It was destined to play a dominant role in economic theory until after the middle of the nineteenth century and thereafter gradually to lose its prestige.

It is not possible accurately to compress into a single proposition the whole Ricardian rent doctrine for in it several criteria of rent were combined and confused. Even the following analysis does not exhaust the minor details and differences. In the first place, the source of rent was deemed to be distinctly and peculiarly land, used as a mere geographic or geological term. Along with labor and capital land was one of the three factors of production, paralleled by the three incomes—rent, profits (including interest) and wages—and by the three classes of income receivers—landlords, capitalists and laborers. This tripartite arrangement corresponded fairly well with the main divisions in politics and in English society at that time. Secondly, land was regarded as unproduced, it being conceived as essentially a natural not an artificial agent, having therefore originally no psychic cost, in contrast with the psychic sacrifice involved in making, improving and modifying other things, which were thought to be ruled by the labor theory of value. Again land, even agricultural land, was considered as durable by its very nature, and its useful and fertile qualities were taken to be permanent. As a corollary the rent income was assumed to continue without limit and without impairment of its source, in contrast with physical capital. Land was looked upon as peculiar in that it alone among economic agents was subject to the law of diminishing returns, a doctrine which confused the idea of proportionality between two or more complementary agents with the idea of a historical trend toward less productive land and land uses. Further, land rent was assumed to be of a peculiar residual, or differential, nature, in contrast to wages, profits and interest, in which no differential quality was seen at that time. Closely related was the idea that land rent was peculiarly a surplus above cost (practical business cost), and moreover the one income that "formed no part of price." This was a mere play on words and was not meant to deny that the actual prices of all products where scarce land was used contained rents as well as wages and profits, or that rent formed part of the necessary competitive expenses of the enterpriser. The phrase involved a garbled marginality theory, which amended the words "formed no part of price" by the addition: of that portion of the supply which fixes (or determines) the price of the whole. Recent criticism has pretty effectually disposed of the fallacious idea of a certain marginal unit fixing the price of the whole or of the other units in the marketing of any sort of goods or uses.

Land rent in the Ricardian doctrine was further regarded as peculiar in that taxes on land, agricultural as well as other, were not shiftable. Land being deemed to be not only unproducible but indestructible, it was concluded that the quantity of usable land and the mode of its use could not and would not be altered in any degree through the taxpayers' choice as a result of changes in land taxes. Finally, all land values and all rents were held to be of a monopolistic nature, no matter how widely distributed landownership might be; this was palpably a confusion of the idea of "natural" scarcity and that of monopoly in its proper sense as control and artificial manipulation of supply and of prices through unified ownership or by agreement.

The subsequent history of the rent doctrine is largely a record of hostile criticism of these inconsistencies in the Ricardian theory and of the attempts of Ricardian apologists, such as J. S. Mill, J. E. Cairnes and others of the neoclassical school, to qualify, reconcile and evade its logical consequences. Most ingenious and elusive of the attempts of this sort were those of Alfred Marshall. He conceded that the distinction between land (natural) and other wealth must be abandoned from the point of view of the individual investor (the original problem) but suggested retaining it from the point of view of society. He then hopefully set forth still another property of land as "the ultimate cause of the distinction ... between land and other things"; that is, the attribute of extension, or its geometric relations. Not satisfied with this, he further suggested making the distinction between rent and interest (and between land and capital) turn "on the length of the period which we have in view."

Since the word rent etymologically means any income or yield from an economic agent, its limitation to a more special sense involves something of the arbitrary. This can be justified ultimately only by a general consensus of opinion and usage. Modern theoretical criticism has not only quite effectually invalidated the crude tripartite division of the economic factors (based on the labor theory of value) which linked rent with land but has also in varying degrees exploded all of the other supposed peculiarities of land and of land rent. Proportionality, for example, varying on either side of an optimum, is seen as a universal phenomenon in the use of all kinds of goods, whereas a historical law of diminishing returns finds no support in actual conditions or in statistical trends in any of the advanced countries.

To the writer it seems that the most useful and tenable definition of the word rent today must turn upon the one economico-legal criterion of the nature of the contract by which the uses of any more or less durable agent of production may be bought or sold. The content of such a concept would include nearly all of the cases which in practice have ever been included under rent, but the concept would be essentially different. Capital in the financial sense and its yield—profits and interest—are fully within the price system, both the principal sum and the amount of the income being expressed in monetary terms; rent is ordinarily only half way within the price system, that is, in respect to the periodic payment; whereas the borrowed agent is returnable in kind or as nearly as may be in identical form (i.e. the criterion is physical or technological rather than financial). Indeed some cases of rent contracts, as, for instance, renting on shares, retain the still more primitive form of contract in which both the borrowing and lending and the payment are "in kind"; that is, not expressed in monetary terms. Rent would thus be defined as: the amount paid by contract for the use of the durative (separable) uses of a more or less durable agent (use bearer), entrusted by an owner to a borrower for a limited period, to be returned in equally good condition except for ordinary wear and tear.

Consult: Johnson, Alvin S., "Rent in Modern Economic Theory" in American Economic Association, *Publications*, 3rd ser., vol. iii (1902) no. 4; Turner, J. R., *The Ricardian Rent Theory in Early American Economics* (New York 1921); Walker, F. A., *Land and Its Rent* (Boston 1883); Hobson, John A., "The Law of the Three Rents," Clark, John B., "Distribution as Determined by a Law of Rent," and Hollander, J. H., "The Concept of Marginal Rent" in *Quarterly Journal of Economics*, vol. v (1890-91) 263-88, 289-318,

and vol. ix (1894-95) 175-87; Fetter, F. A., "The Passing of the
Old Rent Concept" in *Quarterly Journal of Economics*, vol. xv
(1901-02) 416-55, and "The Relations between Rent and Interest" in American Economic Association, *Publications*, 3rd ser.,
vol. v (1904) 176-240; Carlton, Frank T., "The Rent Concept,
Narrowed and Broadened," and Orchard, John E., "The Rent of
Mineral Lands" in *Quarterly Journal of Economics*, vol. xxii (1907-
08) 48-61, and vol. xxxvi (1921-22) 290-318; Inama-Sternegg,
Karl T., "Theorie des Grundbesitzes und der Grundrente in der
deutschen Literatur des 19. Jahrhunderts" in *Die Entwicklung der
deutschen Volkswirtschaftslehre im neunzehnten Jahrhundert* (Leipsic
1908) vol. i, ch. v; Schumpeter, Joseph, "Das Rentenprinzip in
der Verteilungslehre" in *Schmollers Jahrbuch*, vol. xxxi (1907)
31-65, 591-634; Weiss, F. X., "Die Grundrente im System der
Nutzwertlehre," Weber, Adolf, "Die städtische Grundrente,"
and Ely, R. T., "Kosten und Einkommen bei der Bodenver-
wertung" in *Die Wirtschaftstheorie der Gegenwart*, ed. by Hans
Mayer, F. A. Fetter, and R. Reich, 4 vols. (Vienna 1927-28) vol.
iii, p. 210-58; Berens, E., *Versuch einer kritischen Dogmengeschichte
der Grundrente* (Leipsic 1868); Adler, A., *Ricardo und Carey in ihren
Ansichten über die Grundrente* (Leipsic 1873); Diehl, Karl, "Die
Grundrententheorie im ökonomischen System von Karl Marx"
in *Jahrbücher für Nationalökonomie und Statistik*, vol. lxxii (1899)
433-80; Bortkiewicz, L. von, "Die rodbertus'sche Grundren-
tentheorie und die marx'sche Lehre von der absoluten
Grundrente" in *Archiv für die Geschichte des Sozialismus und der
Arbeiterbewegung*, vol. i (1910-11) 1-40, 391-434; Spitz, Philipp,
"Das Problem der allgemeinen Grundrente bei Ricardo,
Rodbertus und Marx" in *Jahrbücher für Nationalökonomie und
Statistik*, vol. cvi (1916) 492-524, 593-629; Diehl, Karl, *Sozial-
wissenschaftliche Erläuterungen zu David Ricardos Grundgesetzen der
Volkswirtschaft und Besteuerung*, 2 vols. (3rd ed. Leipsic 1921-22)
vol. i, ch. ii; Oppenheimer, Franz, *David Ricardos Grundrenten-
theorie* (2nd ed. Jena 1927); Otte, Gerhard, *Das Differen-
tialeinkommen im Lichte der neueren Forschung*, Volks-
wirtschaftliche Studien, vol. xxviii (Berlin 1930); Samsonoff,
B., *Esquisse d'une théorie générale de la rente* (Lausanne 1912);

Lebreton, André, *Essai sur la théorie ricardienne de la rente* (Rennes 1926); Loria, Achille, *La rendita fondiaria e la sua elisione naturale* (Milan 1880); Sensini, Guido, *La teoria della "rendita"* (Rome 1912); Ferri, Carlo E., *La concezione energetica della rendita*, Collana di scienze politiche, ser. c, vol. iii (Pavia 1928).

BIBLIOGRAPHY OF FRANK ALBERT FETTER

BOOKS

Fetter, Frank A. *Versuch einer Bevolkerungslehre ausgehend von einer Kritik des Malthus'schen Bevolkerungsprincips.* Jena: Gustav Fischer, 1894.

————. *The Principles of Economics.* New York: The Century Co., 1904. (2d ed., 1910, 3d ed. revised, 1911.)

————. *Source Book in Economics.* New York: The Century Co., 1912.

————. *Economics.* Vol. 1: *Economic Principles.* New York: The Century Co., 1915.

————. Manual of References and Exercises in Economics for Use with Volume 1: *Economic Principles.* New York: The Century Co., 1916.

————. *Economics.* Vol. 2: *Modern Economic Problems.* New York: The Century Co., 1916. (2d ed. revised, 1922.)

————. Manual of References and Exercises in Economics for Use with Volume 2: *Modern Economic Problems.* New York: The Century Co., 1917.

————. *The Masquerade of Monopoly.* New York: Harcourt, Brace and Co., 1931.

Adapted from the bibliography of Fetter's works in Rev. John A. Coughlan, "The Contributions of Frank Albert Fetter, (1863-1949) to the Development of Economic Theory." Ph.D. dissertation, Catholic University, 1965, pp. 256-69.

TESTIMONY

——. "Testimony on basing-point pricing before the Federal Trade Commission on December 11, 1923."

United States of America before The Federal Trade Commission. *Docket 760: Federal Trade Commission vs. United States Steel Corporation et al,* Volume 2, pp 175-77; 191-217, 779-811.

——. "Testimony on monopolistic practices given before the Temporary National Economic Committee on February 28, March 7, and March 8, 1939."

U.S. Congress, [Joint] Temporary National Economic Committee, *Hearings on the Investigation of Concentration of Economic Power.* 76th Cong., 1st Sess., 1939.

Part 5, pp. 1657-80, 1903-46, 1952-82. *Verbatim Record of the Proceedings of the Temporary National Economic Committee.* Washington, D. C.: The Bureau of National Affairs, Inc., 1939.

Vol. 2, pp. 205-14, 325-35, and 353-64.

——. "The Fundamental Principle of Efficiency in Mass Production," *United States Temporary National Economic Committee Hearings,* Monograph no. 13 (1941), pp. 398-415.

ADDRESSES

——. "The Fundamental Conceptions and Methods of Economics," *International Congress of Arts and Sciences, Saint Louis, 1904.* Boston: Houghton, Mifflin and Co., 1906. Vol. 13, pp. 7-20.

——. "Population or Prosperity" (Annual Address of the President of the American Economic Association). *American Economic Review,* supplement, 3 (March, 1913), 5-19.

——. "The Land of Opportunity — Commencement Day Address," *Swarthmore College Bulletin,* June, 1913, pp. 11-23.

——. "The New Era of Social Work — President's Address," *New Jersey Conference of Charities and Correction Proceedings,* June, 1919, pp. 11-21.

————. "The Larger Vision of Social Welfare — President's Address," *New Jersey Conference for Social Welfare Proceedings,* November, 1919, pp. 109-15.

————. "A Word of Welcome — Address at Opening Exercises," *National Conference of Social Work Proceedings,* 1919, p. 779.

————. "The Economists and the Public" (Address delivered at the University of Wisconsin on the occasion of the unveiling of Dr. Richard T. Ely's portrait). *American Economic Review,* 15 (March, 1925), 13-26.

————. "Tribute to Professor John Bates Clark at Dinner in His Honor," *American Economic Review,* supplement, 17 (June, 1927), 11-13.

————. "Education as a Productive Process — Founders Day Address," *Occidental College Bulletin,* March, 1931, pp. 5-11.

————. "Drift or Mastery — Commencement Day Address, June 11, 1934," *Indiana University Alumni Quarterly,* 21 (July, 1934), 267-75.

————. "Democracy and Monopoly" (Lecture given on Stafford Little Lectureship at Princeton University, August 1, 1939). Princeton University Press, 1939.

————. "The Early History of Political Economy in the United States," *American Philosophical Society Proceedings,* 87 (July 14, 1943), 51-60.

REVIEW ARTICLES

————. Review of *The Nature of Capital and Income,* by Irving Fisher, *Journal of Political Economy,* 15 (March, 1907), 129-48.

————. Review of *The Economics of Enterprise,* by Herbert J. Davenport, *Journal of Political Economy,* 22 (June, 1914), 550-65.

————. Review of *Decline of Competition,* by Arthur Robert Burns, *Journal of Political Economy,* 45 (February, 1937), 95-110.

————. Review of *The Iron and Steel Industry in South Africa,* by C. S.

Richards, *South African Journal of Economics,* 9 (September, 1941), 235-50.

ARTICLES

————. "History of the City of Peru," *History of Miami County* (Indiana). Chicago: Brent and Fuller, 1887, pp. 362-92.

————. "Our University — Prize Essay," *Indiana Student,* June, 1890.

————. "Theories of Value in Their Application to the Question of the Standard of Deferred Payments," *American Economic Association Publications,* supplement, 10 (March, 1895), 101-103.

————. "The Exploitation of Theories of Value in the Discussion of the Standard of Deferred Payments," *Annals of the American Academy of Political and Social Science,* 5 (May, 1895), 882-96.

————. "Do We Want an Elastic Currency? — Discussion," *Economic Studies,* supplement, 1 (April, 1896), 105-106.

————. "The Gold Reserve: Its Function and Its Maintenance," *Political Science Quarterly,* 11 (June, 1896), 237-47.

————. "The Improvement of Our System of Township Poor Relief" (Report of the committee on public relief of the poor in Indiana, Frank A. Fetter, Chairman). *Indiana State Board of Charities Bulletin,* June, 1898, pp. 67-74.

————. "The Essay on Malthus: A Centennial Review," *Yale Review,* 7 (August, 1898), 153-67.

————. "Social Progress and Race Degeneration," *The Forum,* 28 (October, 1899), 228-38.

————. "Politics in Charitable and Correctional Institutions on the Pacific Coast," *National Conference of Charities and Corrections Proceedings,* 1899, pp. 242-54.

————. "Recent Discussion of the Capital Concept," *Quarterly Journal of Economics,* 15 (November, 1900), 1-45.

————. "The Next Decade of Economic Theory," *American Economic*

Association Publications, 3d series, 2 (February, 1901), 236-46.

———. "The Passing of the Old Rent Concept," *Quarterly Journal of Economics,* 15 (May, 1901), 416-55.

———. "The Subsidizing of Private Charities," *American Journal of Sociology,* 7 (November, 1901), 359-85.

———. "Subsidies — by the Committee on the Division of Work between Public and Private Charities, Frank A. Fetter, Chairman," *National Conference of Charities and Corrections Proceedings,* 1901, pp. 118-31.

———. Maps, diagrams, data, and statistical tables on housing conditions in Chicago, *Tenement Conditions in Chicago* (Report by the investigating committee of the City Homes Association). Chicago, 1901.

———. "The 'Roundabout Process' in the Interest Theory," *Quarterly Journal of Economics,* 17 (November, 1902), 163-80.

———. "Review of Legislation on Taxation in 1902," *Legislation Bulletin,* no. 19, New York State Library, Albany (May, 1903), pp. 785-94.

———. "The Relations between Rent and Interest," *American Economic Association Publications,* 3d series, 5 (February, 1904), 176-98, 227-40.

———. "Review of Legislation on Taxation in 1903," *Legislation Bulletin,* no. 22, New York State Library, Albany (October, 1904), pp. h12-h26.

———. "Report of the Committee on Politics in Penal and Charitable Institutions, Frank A. Fetter, Chairman," *New York State Conference on Charities and Correction Proceedings,* 1904, pp. 212-19.

———. "Review of Legislation on Taxation in 1904," *Legislation Bulletin,* no. 25, New York Library Association, Albany (October, 1905), pp. h1-h5.

———. "Changes in the Tax Laws of New York State in 1905," *Quarterly Journal of Economics,* 20 (November, 1905), 151-56.

———. "Thoughts on Cornell Democracy," *Cornell Era*, 38 (December, 1905), 74-79.

———. "Present State of the Theory of Distribution — Discussion," *American Economic Association Publications*, 3d series, 7 (February, 1906), 52-57.

———. "Change in Mortgage Taxation in New York in 1906," *Quarterly Journal of Economics*, 20 (August, 1906), 613-16.

———. "Review of Legislation on Taxation in 1905," *Legislation Bulletin*, no. 29, New York State Library, Albany (October, 1906), pp. 176-87.

———. "Review of State Finance in 1905," *Legislation Bulletin*, no. 29, New York State Library, Albany (October, 1906), pp. 171-75.

———. "The Need of Industrial Insurance," *National Conference of Charities and Correction Proceedings*, 1906, pp. 464-70.

———. "The German Imperial Inheritance Tax," *Quarterly Journal of Economics*, 21 (February, 1907), 332-34.

———. "Western Civilization and Birth Rate — Discussion," *American Economic Association Publications*, 3d series, 8 (February, 1907), 90-93.
American Journal of Sociology, 12 (March, 1907), 617-19.

———. "Review of Legislation on Taxation in 1906," *Legislation Bulletin*, no. 33, New York State Library, Albany (August, 1907), pp. 143-48.

———. "Review of State Finance in 1906," *Legislation Bulletin*, no. 33, New York State Library, Albany (August, 1907), pp. 151-52.

———. "Bibliography of Economic Science," *Bibliographical Society of America Papers and Proceedings*, 1 (1906-1907), 205-206.

———. "Imperialism and Cosmopolitanism," *Cornell Cosmopolitan Club Annual*, 1 (1906-1907), 27-29.

———. "Are Savings Income? — Discussion," *American Economic Association Publications*, 3d series, 9 (April, 1908), 51-55.

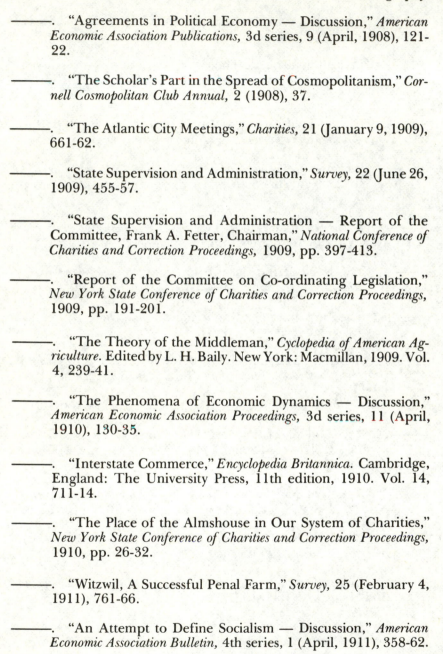

———. "Agreements in Political Economy — Discussion," *American Economic Association Publications,* 3d series, 9 (April, 1908), 121-22.

———. "The Scholar's Part in the Spread of Cosmopolitanism," *Cornell Cosmopolitan Club Annual,* 2 (1908), 37.

———. "The Atlantic City Meetings," *Charities,* 21 (January 9, 1909), 661-62.

———. "State Supervision and Administration," *Survey,* 22 (June 26, 1909), 455-57.

———. "State Supervision and Administration — Report of the Committee, Frank A. Fetter, Chairman," *National Conference of Charities and Correction Proceedings,* 1909, pp. 397-413.

———. "Report of the Committee on Co-ordinating Legislation," *New York State Conference of Charities and Correction Proceedings,* 1909, pp. 191-201.

———. "The Theory of the Middleman," *Cyclopedia of American Agriculture.* Edited by L. H. Baily. New York: Macmillan, 1909. Vol. 4, 239-41.

———. "The Phenomena of Economic Dynamics — Discussion," *American Economic Association Proceedings,* 3d series, 11 (April, 1910), 130-35.

———. "Interstate Commerce," *Encyclopedia Britannica.* Cambridge, England: The University Press, 11th edition, 1910. Vol. 14, 711-14.

———. "The Place of the Almshouse in Our System of Charities," *New York State Conference of Charities and Correction Proceedings,* 1910, pp. 26-32.

———. "Witzwil, A Successful Penal Farm," *Survey,* 25 (February 4, 1911), 761-66.

———. "An Attempt to Define Socialism — Discussion," *American Economic Association Bulletin,* 4th series, 1 (April, 1911), 358-62.

———. "Some Social Aspects of the Anti-tuberculosis Movement," *The South Atlantic Quarterly*, 10 (April, 1911), 129-33.

———. "Aspects of Economics of Importance in Household Science," *Journal of Home Economics*, 3 (June, 1911), 257-61.

———. "Summary and Analysis of Statistics of Charities," Albany, 1911.

———. "The Price Concept in Relation to Value — Round Table Meeting, F. A. Fetter, Chairman," *American Economic Review*, supplement, 2 (March, 1912), 89-91.

———. "The Definition of Price," *American Economic Review*, 2 (December, 1912), 783-813.

———. "People Enough to Feed," *Business America*, 14 (December, 1913), 540-544.

———. "Interest Theories, Old and New," *American Economic Review*, 4 (March, 1914), 68-92.

———. "Capitalization versus Productivity: Rejoinder," *American Economic Review*, 4 (December, 1914), 856-59.

———. "An Appeal to 'The Sober Reader,'" *Journal of Political Economy*, 24 (June, 1916), 596-605.

———. "Landed Property as an Economic Concept and as a Field for Research — Discussion," *American Economic Review*, 7, supplement (March, 1917), 34-36.

———. "The Choice (for Pacifists): Letter to the Editor," *Survey*, 39 (November 10, 1917), 151.

———. "Control of Wealth and Economic Life — Discussion," *American Economic Review*, supplement, 8 (March, 1918), 232-35.

———. "The Psychological Basis for the Economic Interpretation of History — Discussion," *American Economic Review*, supplement, 9 (March, 1919), 306-308.

———. "War Camp Community Service Policy During Demobilization," *Playground,* 13 (May, 1919), 66-67.

———. "Price Economics versus Welfare Economics," *American Economic Review,* 10 (September, 1920), 467-87.

———. "The Teaching of Economics," *College Teaching.* Edited by Paul Klapper, Yonkers-on-Hudson, New York: World Book Co., 1920, pp. 217-40.

———. "Introduction," *The Ricardian Rent Theory in Early American Economics,* by John Roscoe Turner. New York: The New York University Press, 1921. Pp. vii-xiv.

———. " 'The Course in Elementary Economics': Comment," *American Economic Review,* 13 (June, 1923), 245-49.

———. "Value and the Larger Economics. I. Rise of the Marginal Doctrine," *Journal of Political Economy,* 31 (October, 1923), 587-605.

———. "Value and the Larger Economics. II. Value Giving Way to Welfare," *Journal of Political Economy,* 31 (December, 1923), pp. 790-803.

———. "The Economic Law of Market Areas," *Quarterly Journal of Economics,* 38 (May, 1924), 520-29.

———. "Economics and Portland Cement Prices," "Reply to Letter of G. S. Brown," *American Economic Review,* 14 (December, 1924), pp. 649-57; 15 (March, 1925), p. 80.

———. "Teaching of Economics — Round Table Conference," *American Economic Review,* supplement, 16 (March, 1926), 76-78.

———. "Interest Theory and Price Movements," *American Economic Review,* supplement, 17 (March, 1927), 62-105.

———. "Clark's Reformulation of The Capital Concept," *Economic Essays Contributed in Honor of John Bates Clark.* Edited by Jacob H. Hollander. New York: Macmillan, 1927, pp. 136-56.

———. "Amerika," *Die Wirtschaftstheorie der Gegenwart, Friedrich Wieser in Memoriam.* Vol. 1: *Gestembild der Forschung in den einsel-*

nen Landern. Vienna: Julius Springer, 1928, pp. 31-60. "Present State of Economic Theory in the United States of America." 1926. (Mimeographed translation.)

————. "Comment on Rent under Increasing Returns," *American Economic Review,* 20 (March, 1930), 72-76.

————. "The New Conceptual Basis of Economics," *Economia politica contemporanea,* saggi di economia e finanza in onore del Prof. Camillo Supino. Padova: A. Milani, 1930, Vol. 1, pp. 93-102.

————. "John Elliot Cairnes," *Encyclopedia of the Social Sciences.* New York: Macmillan, 1930-1935. Vol. 3, 140.

————. "Capital," *Encyclopedia of the Social Sciences.* New York: Macmillan, 1930-1935. Vol. 3, 187-90.

————. "Rent," "Rent Charge," *Encyclopedia of the Social Sciences.* New York: Macmillan, 1930-1935. Vol. 13, 289-92.

————. "Population and Culture — Discussion," *Annals of the American Academy of Political and Social Science,* 162 (July, 1932), 196-97.

————. "The Economist's Committee on Anti-trust Law Policy," *American Economic Review,* 22 (September, 1932), 465-67.

————. "Anti-trust Laws and the Social Control of Business," *The Federal Anti-trust Laws.* (A Symposium Conducted at Columbia University.) Edited by Milton Handler. New York: Commerce Clearing House, Inc., 1932, pp. 14-19.

————. "By Way of Introduction," *Facing the Facts: An Economic Diagnosis.* Edited by J. G. Smith. New York: G. P. Putnam's Sons, 1932, pp. 11-16.

————. "Big Business and the Nation," *Facing the Facts: An Economic Diagnosis.* Edited by J. G. Smith. New York: G. P. Putnam's Sons, 1932, pp. 186-213.

————. "The Truth about Competition," *Annals of the American Academy of Political and Social Science,* 165 (January, 1933), 93-100.

Reprinted in the *Congressional Record,* 77 (June 8, 1933), 5315-5317.

———. "Basing Point Prices and the Purchaser," *Purchasing,* 23 (January, 1933), 6-11.

———. "Stabilization of the Oil Industry — Discussion," *American Economic Review,* supplement, 23 (March, 1933), 81-84.

———. "Forgotten Consumers," *Survey Graphic,* 22 (November, 1933), 546-48.

———. "Report of the Dinner Meeting in Celebration of the Fiftieth Anniversary of the American Economic Association, Frank A. Fetter, Chairman and Toastmaster," *American Economic Review,* 26 (March, 1936), 317-40.

———. "Business Price Practices and Social Price Policies," *Economic Principles and Problems.* Edited by Walter E. Spahr. New York: Farrar and Rinehart, Inc., 1936, pp. 522-44.

———. "Cost-prices, Product-prices, and Profits," *Economic Principles and Problems.* Edited by Walter E. Spahr. New York: Farrar and Rinehart, Inc., 1936, pp. 503-21.

———. "Desires, Choice and Value," *Economic Principles and Problems.* Edited by Walter E. Spahr. New York: Farrar and Rinehart, Inc., 1936, pp. 459-77.

———. "Markets and Prices," *Economic Principles and Problems.* Edited by Walter E. Spahr. New York: Farrar and Rinehart, Inc., 1936, pp. 478-502.

———. "Reformulation of the Concepts of Capital and Income in Economics and Accounting," *Accounting Review,* 12 (March, 1937), 3-12.

———. "The New Plea for Basing-point Monopoly," "Rejoinder to Professor De Chazeau's Reply," *Journal of Political Economy,* 45 (October, 1937), 557-605; 46 (August, 1938), 567-70.

———. "Competition or Monopoly," *Academy of Political Science Proceedings,* 18 (1938), 100-107.

————. "Foreign Commerce," *Government and Economic Life.* Washington, D.C.: The Brookings Institution, 1939-1940. Vol. 2, 527-615.

————. "The Passing of the Old Economist," *The Princeton University Library Chronicle,* 4 (February-April, 1943), 65-67.

————. "Lauderdale's Oversaving Theory," *American Economic Review,* 35 (June, 1945), 263-83.

————. "Edwin Walter Kemmerer, 1875-1945," *American Economic Review,* 36 (March, 1946), 219-21.

————. "Too Much Money," *Saturday Evening Post,* 219 (July 13, 1946), p. 124.

————. "Exit Basing Point Pricing," *American Economic Review,* 38 (December, 1948), 815-27.

————. "The Effectiveness of Anti-trust Laws: A Symposium," *American Economic Review,* 39 (June, 1949), 695-96.

BOOK REVIEWS

————. Review of *Produktion und Konsumption in der Volkswirtschaft,* by Julius Lehr, *Political Science Quarterly,* 11 (June, 1896), 336-338.

————. Review of *Wages and Capital: An Examination of the Wages Fund Doctrine,* by F. W. Taussig, *Political Science Quarterly,* 12 (March, 1897), 146-51.

————. Review of *Neue Beitrage zur Frage der Arbeitslosenversicherung,* by Georg Schanz, *Journal of Political Economy,* 6 (March, 1898), 277-79.

————. Review of *The Bargain Theory of Wages,* by John Davidson, *Political Science Quarterly,* 13 (September, 1898), 566-69.

————. Review of *Capital und Capitalzins,* by Eugen von Böhm-Bawerk, *Journal of Political Economy,* 9 (March, 1901), 286-88.

————. Review of *A Dividend to Labor — A Study of Employer's Welfare*

Institutions, by Nicholas Paine Gilman, *Journal of Political Economy,* 8 (June, 1900), 430-32.

————. Review of *The Early History of English Poor Relief,* by E. M. Leonard, *Journal of Political Economy,* 9 (March, 1901), 308-11.

————. Review of *A History of the English Poor Law, Vol. 3,* by Thomas Mackay, *Journal of Political Economy,* 9 (March, 1901), 308-11.

————. Review of *La protection ouvriere au Japon,* by Kashiro Saito, *Journal of Political Economy,* 9 (March, 1901), 307-308.

————. Review of *Le travail aux points de vue scientifique industriel et social,* by Andre Liesse, *Political Science Quarterly,* 16 (March, 1901), 170-71.

————. Review of *Distribution of Wealth,* by John Bates Clark, *The International Monthly,* 4 (July, 1901), 127-33.

————. Review of *Einige strittige Fragen der Capitalstheorie (Drei Abhandlungen),* by Eugen von Böhm-Bawerk, *Political Science Quarterly,* 17 (March, 1902), 169-73.

————. Review of *Natural Economy: An Introduction to Political Economy,* by Arthur H. Gibson, *Journal of Political Economy,* 10 (March, 1902), 289-91.

————. Review of *Social Control,* by Edward Alsworth Ross, *Charities,* 8 (March, 1902), 212-13.

————. Review of *The Last Days of the Ruskin Co-operative Association,* by Isaac Broome, *Journal of Political Economy,* 11 (December, 1902), 175-77.

————. Review of *The New Harmony Communities,* by George Browning Lockwood, *Journal of Political Economy,* 11 (December, 1902), 175-77.

————. Review of *Positive Theorie des Capitals (Zweite Auflage),* by Eugen von Böhm-Bawerk, *Journal of Political Economy,* 11 (December, 1902), 145.

————. Review of Principles of Economics, Vol. I, by N. G. Pierson,

Journal of Political Economy, 11 (September, 1903), 659-61.

————. Review of *The Nature and Necessity of Interest,* by Gustav Cassel, *Political Science Quarterly,* 20 (March, 1905), 149-51.

————. Review of *Recent Literature on Interest: A Supplement to Capital and Interest,* by Eugen von Böhm-Bawerk, *Political Science Quarterly,* 20 (March, 1905), 149-51.

————. Review of *Economic Methods and Economic Fallacies,* by William Warrand Carlile, *Journal of Political Economy,* 13 (June, 1905), 477-79.

————. *Review of Interest and Saving,* by E. C. K. Gonner, *Political Science Quarterly,* 12 (March, 1907), 160-62.

————. Review of *New Worlds for Old,* by H. G. Wells, *Economic Bulletin,* 1 (April, 1908), 53-55.

————. Review of *English Socialism of Today: Its Teaching and Its Aims Examined,* by H. O. Arnold-Forster, *Economic Bulletin,* 1 (June, 1908), 147-48.

————. Review of *The Iron Heel,* by Jack London, *Economic Bulletin,* 1 (December, 1908), 328-29.

————. Review of *The Case Against Socialism,* by G. E. Raine, *Economic Bulletin,* 3 (March, 1910), 177-78.

————. Review of *Present-day Socialism and the Problem of the Unemployed,* by G. E. Raine, *Economic Bulletin,* 3 (March, 1910), 178-79.

————. Review of *Problems and Perils of Socialism: Letters to a Workingman,* by J. St. Loe Strachey, *Economic Bulletin,* 3 (March, 1910), 179.

————. Review of *Socialism in Local Government,* by W. G. Towler, *Economic Bulletin,* 3 (March, 1910), 179.

————. Review of *The Triumph of Socialism and How It Succeeded,* by John D. Mayne, *Economic Bulletin,* 3 (March, 1910), 180.

————. Review of *Ertrag und Einkommen auf der Grundlage einer rein subjectiven Wertlehre,* by Robert Liefmann, *Political Science Quarterly,* 25 (June, 1910), 340-42.

―――. Review of *Karl Marx: His Life and Work,* by John Spargo, *American Economic Review,* 1 (March, 1911), 150-51.

―――. Review of *Correction and Prevention,* edited by Charles Richmond Henderson, *American Economic Review,* 1 (June, 1911), 394-96.

―――. Review of *Sociology and Modern Social Problems,* by Charles A. Ellwood, *International Journal of Ethics,* 21 (July, 1911), 500-501.

―――. Review of *The Theory of Distribution and Consumption,* by T. Lloyd, *Political Science Quarterly,* 27 (December, 1912), 706-707.

―――. Review of *Die gegenwartige Krisis in der deutschen Volkswirtschaftslehre,* by Ludwig Pohle, *American Economic Review,* 3 (September, 1913), 625-27.

―――. Review of *Die Volkswirtschaft der Gegenwart und Zukunft,* by Julius Wolf, *American Economic Review,* 3 (September, 1913), 625-27.

―――. Review of *Vorlesungen über Nationalökonomie, by Knut Wicksell, Political Science Quarterly,* 24 (March, 1914), 151-52.

―――. Review of *Readings in Current Economic Problems,* by Walton H. Hamilton, *American Economic Review,* 4 (September, 1914), 608.

―――. Review of *Economic Development of Modern Europe,* by F. A. Ogg, *Indiana University Alumni Quarterly,* 4 (October, 1917), 562-64.

―――. Review of *Learning to Earn,* by J. A. Lapp and C. H. Mote, *American Economic Review,* 7 (December, 1917), 902-903.

―――. Review of *Economics of Bridge Work: A Sequel to "Bridge Engineering,"* by J. A. L. Waddell, *American Economic Review,* 12 (December, 1922), 643-45.

―――. Review of *The Background of Economics,* by M. H. Hunter and

G. S. Watkins, *American Economic Review,* 14 (December, 1924), 722.

————. Review of *Economic Liberalism,* by J. H. Hollander, *American Economic Review,* 16 (June, 1926), 283-84.

————. Review of *Theory of the Location of Industries,* by Alfred Weber, *Journal of Political Economy,* 38 (April, 1930), 232-34.

————. Review of *Die Bedeutung des Einkaufs und Verkaufs auf Fractgrundlage bei bergbaulichen und industriellen Erzeugnissen,* by Emil Geisler, *American Economic Review,* 21 (September, 1931), 531-34.

————. Review of *Public Administration and the Public Interest,* by E. Pendleton Herring, *American Economic Review,* 27 (June, 1937), 415-17.

————. Review of *New Deal. Il nuovo ordine economico di F. D. Roosevelt,* by Eraldo Fossati, *Weltwirtschaftliches archiv Schrifttum,* 49 (1939), 24-26.

————. Review of *Ground under Our Feet: An Autobiography,* by Richard T. Ely, *American Historical Review,* 45 (January, 1940), 430-31.

————. Review of *The Bottlenecks of Business,* by Thurman W. Arnold, *American Economic Review,* 31 (March, 1941), 160-62.

————. Review of *The Economic Thought of Woodrow Wilson,* by William Diamond, *American Economic Review,* 34 (December, 1944), 888-890.

————. Review of *Origins of Academic Economics in the United States,* by Michael J. L. O'Connor, *Journal of Economic History,* 5 (May, 1945), 88-90.

————. Review of *Bureaucracy,* by Ludwig von Mises, *American Economic Review,* 35 (June, 1945), 445-46.

INDEX